CLASS, PARTY, REVOLUTION

Published in 2018 by
Haymarket Books
P.O. Box 180165
Chicago, IL 60618
773-583-7884
www.haymarketbooks.org
info@haymarketbooks.org

ISBN: 978-1-60846-919-2

Trade distribution:
In the US, Consortium Book Sales and Distribution, www.cbsd.com
In Canada, Publishers Group Canada, www.pgcbooks.ca
In the UK, Turnaround Publisher Services, www.turnaround-uk.com
All other countries, Ingram Publisher Services International,
ips_intlsales@ingramcontent.com

This book was published with the generous support of Lannan Foundation
and Wallace Action Fund.

Cover design by Eric Kerl.

Printed in Canada by union labor.

Library of Congress Cataloging-in-Publication data is available.

10 9 8 7 6 5 4 3 2 1

CLASS, PARTY, REVOLUTION

A SOCIALIST REGISTER READER

EDITED BY
GREG ALBO, LEO PANITCH, AND ALAN ZUEGE

SOCIALIST REGISTER CLASSICS
VOLUME 1

Haymarket Books
Chicago, Illinois

CONTENTS

CLASS, PARTY, REVOLUTION:
AN INTRODUCTION

When Haymarket Books first raised the idea a number of years ago of publishing the "classic" essays that have appeared in the *Socialist Register* over the past five decades, we were obviously both flattered and enthusiastic. Other pressing commitments initially delayed bringing this to fruition, not least the work involved in planning, commissioning, editing, and publishing each new annual volume of the *Register*. But as interest in socialist ideas and politics surged in the current political conjuncture and as leading figures in this renewal—from *Jacobin* in the US to Momentum in the UK and Syriza in Greece—told us how they were influenced by the *Register*, we realized we could delay no longer in making available to a new generation some of its key contributions over the years.

The *Socialist Register*'s emergence in 1964 was itself a significant moment in the emergence of the New Left at the time. As the *Register*'s founding editors, Ralph Miliband and John Saville, put it in their preface introducing the first *Register* as an annual volume of "socialist analysis and discussion," they believed that the possibility for this proving "fruitful" was "now greater than for a long time past." This indeed proved to be the case. Even before the mass radical political explosions of 1968, prominent essays in the *Register* sought to think through a way forward for socialists beyond the ideological bankruptcy and institutional sclerosis of both the social democratic and Communist parties. This was especially the case with the essay we have chosen to open this collection, one of the most famous and intellectually influential the *Register* ever published, André Gorz's "Reform and Revolution," first published in the 1968 volume. It reads today as an epitaph to what happened with the Syriza government in Greece—and as a clarion call for what strategic preparations should already be in train to avoid a Corbyn-led Labour government in the UK experiencing the same fate.

Beginning from the insight, far ahead of its time, that it was already then the case that the Keynesian welfare state's expanding social and collective services were no longer compatible with the pursuit of dynamic capitalist accumulation, Gorz posed—perhaps more clearly than anyone since—the stark choices facing any government with even reformist ambitions. New kinds of structural reforms were required, as Gorz understood so clearly, involving,

> a more rapid development of social services and public intervention than in the past, demanding a much more extensive socialization of the economy, including nationalizations, collectivization of saving and the investment function, global (i.e., planned) public direction of the economy, and priority of collective consumption and services.

Since all of this is "destined to make a political impact on the modes of development, consumption, and civilization, and on the style of life," the strategic preparation for this, which actually entails "uncovering its *possibility*," needs to be seen as educational, ideological and cultural as much as, or more than, technical in the policy and administrative sense. Ensuring that a socialist strategy for structural reform would "never be institutionalized" (in ways that would blunt the advancement of "popular and working class powers") requires the creation of "centres of social control and direct democracy" alongside "the conquest of positions of strength in representative assemblies." Even though such a strategy carries with it "the inevitable consequence of an intensification and deepening of the antagonism between the logic of social production . . . and the logic of capitalist accumulation and the power of management," it involves a new sort of gradualism, oriented to creating "the objective and subjective conditions to prepare the social and political positions of strength."

Written on the eve of May 1968, Gorz's essay may have struck many of its first readers as counseling undue strategic patience as opposed to looking for new insurrectionary possibilities. But by the time the 1969 *Register* appeared, Lucio Magri's renowned reflection on "The May Events and Revolution in the West" helped to clarify that while "reformist optimism, whether liberal or socialist, has come to an end," so did "the May events teach us that the question of revolution 'in its highest form' cannot just be taken up again at the point where it was interrupted in 1923." Insofar as the spontaneous movement was unable to do more "than express an extraordinarily radical spirit of revolt," what this proved was that there had to be already an alternative social force active within the social body, with the capacity to "illuminate the socialist perspectives within the present society." To be sure, Magri identified the leading role played by "two types of workers who had never previously been outstanding in trade union struggles"—on the one hand, young unskilled workers "condemned to the most repetitive and underpaid jobs" and, on the other, young technicians "skilled enough to perform delicate tasks" but faced with "the downgrading of the university degree" and no managerial possibilities—which showed that a socialist strategy still needed to be seeded in this transformed working class.

What May 1968 also revealed was the "profound gap [that] existed between the social movement that burst out in such a novel way and the strategy of the traditional revolutionary forces (the Communist Party and the left-wing 'groupuscules')." Yet it was also the "libertarian polemic against the party as such" that disarmed the May movement—"crucifying it on its own spontaneity." While recognizing that "the very concept of the revolutionary party seen in terms of an organized vanguard with a well-defined ideology and a centralized leadership" deserved to be fundamentally challenged, this called for a no less fundamental reappraisal of "the relationship between the party and the movement." Since "revolutionary praxis is many-sided," the party needed to be seen as "a point of synthesis, of fermentation, where the universal is extracted from the particular." This means that it is "not the movement that serves the party, but the party that serves the movement . . . it is not the party that will hold state power, but the masses that use the party to prevent political power from ossifying."

For Magri, all this involved finally saying "goodbye" to the Jacobinism which characterized so much of twentieth-century revolutionary politics, and going "back to the Marxian concept of the socialist revolution." This is in fact what the *Socialist Register* was already doing even before 1968, as exemplified by Monty Johnstone's comprehensive "Marx and Engels and the Concept of the Party" in the 1967 volume. As noted at the outset of Hal Draper's "The Principle of Self-Emancipation in Marx and Engels" from the 1971 *Register*, Johnstone's "admirable study" had "proved to the hilt" that it was utterly baseless to counter-pose Marx and Engels's notion of "self-emancipation" to their concept of the party's role in "class organization and political leadership." That said, Draper readily admitted that the principle of self-emancipation was quite incompatible with "a number of well-known party concepts held by self-styled 'Marxist' parties."

In the 1970 *Register*, Ralph Miliband himself had traced this prob-lem to "one of the sacred texts of Marxist thought," Lenin's *The State and Revolution* (1917). The "critical appraisal" Miliband offered high-lighted the strange anomaly that the concept of the party hardly ap-pears at all in that work, which is instead inflected toward redefining the already problematic concept of the "dictatorship of the proletariat" in terms of "*unmediated* class rule', a notion much more closely associ-ated with anarchism than with Marxism." The only one really relevant reference to the party in *State and Revolution*, Miliband pointed out, left entirely unaddressed the crucial question: "What is the relationship between the *proletariat* whose dictatorship the revolution is deemed to establish, and the *party* which educates, leads, organizes, etc.?" It was the "assumption of a symbiotic, organic relationship between the two" that was to prove so problematic: "an assumption that this kind of rela-tionship can ever be taken as an automatic and permanent fact belongs to the rhetoric of power, not to its reality."

Harold Wolpe's essay in the same volume similarly problematizes Lenin's treatment of the party's role in the creation of "revolution-ary consciousness," even while systematically critiquing all those approaches that merely assume that this consciousness "emerges spon-taneously from certain objective conditions." As Lenin confronted the dilemma "that 'left to itself'" the working class is able to develop only a trade union consciousness," and recognized that revolutionary propaganda and political education alone would not be sufficient to overcome this, he stressed "agitational activities by the party." This, Wolpe argued, still "assigned a determining role to ideology by means of, or through, political action of the party. But in so doing, [Lenin] . . . made the objective conditions irrelevant altogether and, therefore, necessarily had to treat ideological factors in isolation from them."

It was for these kinds of reasons that so many socialists had turned to reading Gramsci. The *Register* played its own role in introducing Gramsci before the *Prison Notebooks* were available in English translation, with John Merrington's seminal essay on "Theory and Practice in Gramsci's Marxism" in the 1968 volume. Reading Gramsci as a means of getting to "the root cause of the debility of strategic options on the Left" was especially useful for confronting "the problem of agency in the making of a revolution." From his earliest writings, Gramsci had emphasized the educative aspect of socialism, achieving through the mass transformation of consciousness "the 'creation of a new civilization,' a universal and integrated culture." This continued to inform his subsequent theory of the party, which "follows closely his ideas on intellectuals, hegemony, and the specificity of the superstructure."

Indeed, "the dialectical relation between the 'intellectuals' and the 'masses'" forms the core of Gramsci's conception of "the party and the active participation of its social base." This is understood, as Merrington quotes Gramsci, in terms of "a 'reciprocal relationship' in which 'every teacher is always a pupil and every pupil a teacher.'" It was precisely this that constituted the essential difference between Gramsci and Lenin, as Alastair Davidson explained in his important essay in the 1974 *Socialist Register*, which follows Merrington's in this collection.

> Unlike Lenin, Gramsci never organized to split the party even when it needed to be renewed, because he did not consider the fundamental problem of the 'conscious' revolution to be one of leadership, but one of the relationship between the leaders and the masses . . . This displacement of the problem of revolution in the West from the party (theory) and the masses (practice) to the relations and links between them is what constitutes Gramsci's novelty.

Yet it was the very estrangement of the Communist parties in the West from the radical temper of the 1960s mass confrontations amidst the crisis of social democracy that starkly revealed their "incapacity to oppose to social democracy a non-Leninist model" of the party. This was the conclusion Rossana Rossanda, at the time engaged with Lucio Magri in the *Il Manifesto* project to renew the Italian Communist Party, drew in her essay on "Class and Party" in the 1970 volume. Arguing that Lenin, "far from filling in Marx's outlines, [had] oriented himself in a different direction," she called for a return to Marx's conception of the party as a "flexible and changing instrument" in advancing actual class struggles. Rossanda argued that really "only Gramsci and Rosa Luxemburg made the attempt" to adhere to the "the process of struggle-consciousness which Marx had sketched out." Yet even Gramsci's own party, despite its powerful posture in Italy as the bearer of Marx's ideals, had proved "foreign to the process" and thus "rendered impossible a practical adherence to Marx's model."

Jean-Paul Sartre's central point in his masterful "Masses, Spontaneity, Party" (translated in the 1970 volume, drawn from *Il Manifesto*'s interview with him) was that the problem was actually a deeper one, which Marx had never resolved. The very role of the party in fusing the working class political subject beyond particular struggles in "this or that factory"—let alone those mass of workers who, not even united at this level of struggle, "are therefore incapable of spontaneity"—requires it to develop as a "structured group," "an ensemble of institutions" with "a tendency to sclerosis" in an "institutionalized mode of thought." To the extent that "the revolt of May was a failure and was followed by a victory of reaction," it was "because it lacked political direction"; yet the deeper dilemma was "how could an institutionalized structure, as in the case of the Communist parties, place itself in the service of something that took it by surprise?" Ironically, Sartre's own gesture at a resolution of this conundrum led straight back to Lenin, even though he was more forthright than the latter about the "duality of power." The relationship between "the *unitary* moment, which falls to the political organization of the class, and the moments of self-government, the councils," necessarily entails an "irreducible and permanent tension" between the party and the movements in all their "living partiality." But insofar as Sartre ends by defining social revolution in terms of "a progressive dissolution of the political element of society," "together with the state," this only rhetorically wishes away the "irreducible and permanent tension" between party and class—which was precisely the problem Miliband identified in Lenin's *The State and Revolution*.

We are convinced there is much to be gleaned today from the outstanding essays collected here from the *Register*'s first decade, especially in light of the emergence of new parties like Podemos and Syriza and the new remarkable support for the intraparty insurgencies, from Corbyn to Sanders, within some of the older parties. Of course, there is much to be taken into account in terms of what has happened since these classic essays were first published, and the class–party relationship remained a major theme, as could be seen from the extent to which the changing relationship between class and party was a major theme of the *Register* over the following decades. But the quick passage after 2011 on the radical left from the Occupy moment (with all its resemblances to the protests of 1960s) to a new wave of socialist mobilization in the party political arena has, more than ever, refocused the party debate and reopened the questions raised in the 1960s and 1970s. It is with this in mind that we conclude this collection with the two essays from *Socialist Register 2017: Rethinking Revolution,* which explicitly drew on the earlier classics, inspired by their central concern to forge a genuinely creative relationship between class and party to the ends of revolutionary transformation.

Rossana Rossanda's observation that new discussions on the theory of the party have "sought a solution in a 'return to sources'" has been once again confirmed by August Nimtz's essay for the 2017 volume, which pays homage to the "invaluable service" Monty Johnstone performed with his 1967 essay "in synthesizing for the first time— certainly in English—Marx and Engels's views on the revolutionary party." Taking into account all the materials that have become available over the fifty years since, Nimtz's essay decisively confirms Johnstone's argument that Marx and Engels not only "saw the fullest possible internal democracy as an essential feature of a proletarian party," but were passionate believers in democracy and pluralism outside the party. Nimtz's essay demonstrates more clearly than ever that Marx and Engels had a dynamic conception of the party, attuned to changing national, historical, and political circumstances, and always flexible in its adaptations as the terrain of class struggle altered. This was of course also the remit of Rossanda's call in the concluding line to her essay: "From Marx, we are now returning to Marx."

The final essay here, by Leo Panitch and Sam Gindin, also drawn from the 2017 *Register,* begins not by going back to the theoretical sources but instead by probing the distinct limits in the actual practice of Socialist and Communist parties in order to develop strategic orientations that could transcend those limits in the contemporary conjuncture. It contends that the most pressing question facing socialists today is how to reconstitute a dynamic relationship between class and party so as to finally meet the challenge of actually transforming the capitalist state into a socialist one. The essay explicitly builds on Gorz's understanding in his "pathbreaking essay" that this does not mean trying to install "islands of socialism in a capitalist ocean," but rather discovering and implementing the structural reforms necessary to sustain further shifts in the balance of class power and ruptures with the logic of capitalism. But the essay also goes beyond Gorz, to put on the agenda of the Left specific changes in the state structures themselves. These are needed to avoid the social democratization of radical left governments, and to promote the development of the political and administrative capacities capable of bringing to fruition a transformative strategy.

The essays in this collection, both classic and contemporary, speak to the profound challenges facing the Left today. The lingering crisis of neoliberal globalized capitalism and the delegitimization of so many of its political institutions—including the parties of the center-left that sponsored it—has been accompanied by a palpable fading of the near overwhelming skepticism that for so long characterized discussions of party renewal. This was underwritten by so many theoretical and political waves of postmodernism, horizontalism, and anarchism, the retreading of superficial and misleading warning-lessons from previous revolutions, and the academic political science fetish with the collapse of parties. But as all this wanes, there is already visible a certain naive enthusiasm about how much can be quickly accomplished by way of party renewal and state transformation, let alone the complete overturning of capitalism, which can only lead to debilitating disillusionments.

The strategic goal, in this respect, must be to escape from the view of the party as an instrument either of insurrection against the state or of parliamentary advantage within the state, and instead embrace the task of developing parties capable of being the facilitators of renewed working-class formation that is transformative of both capitalist social relations *and* the capitalist state. The "return to Marx" re-poses this problem but the question remains how to do it. This is the central challenge involved in the remaking of socialist politics today.

REFORM AND REVOLUTION

André Gorz

I. TOWARDS A SOCIALIST STRATEGY OF REFORMS

The working class will neither unite politically, nor man the barricades, for a 10 percent rise in wages or 50,000 more council flats. In the foreseeable future there will be no crisis of European capitalism so dramatic as to drive the mass of workers to revolutionary general strikes or armed insurrection in defense of their vital interests.

But the bourgeoisie will never surrender its power without struggle, without being forced to do so by the revolutionary action of the masses.

It follows that the principal problem of a socialist strategy is to *create* the objective and subjective *conditions* which will make mass revolutionary action and engagement in a successful trial of strength with the bourgeoisie possible.

There may be disagreement with the terms in which I have posed the problem; some may think socialism unnecessary for the liberation and fulfillment of men. But vast numbers of those working with hands or brains think or feel in some confused way that capitalism is no more acceptable today than it was yesterday as a type of economic and social development; as a mode of life; as a system of relations of men with each other, with their work, with nature, and with the peoples of the rest of the world; in the use it makes—or does not make—of its technical and scientific resources, of the potential or actual creative capacities of each individual. If this feeling or decision leads one to opt for socialism, these are the terms in which the problem of its realization must be posed.

This realization can never be the result of a gradual reform of the capitalist system, designed to rationalize its operation and to institution-

9

alize class antagonisms; nor of its crises and irrationalities: capitalism can eliminate neither their causes nor their consequences, but it has now learned how to prevent their becoming explosively acute. Nor will socialism be achieved as a result of a spontaneous rising of the discontented or by the annihilation of social traitors and revisionists by means of anathema and quotations. Socialism can only come about through *long-term and conscious* action, which *starts* with the gradual application of a coherent program of reforms, but which can only proceed by way of a succession of more or less violent, sometimes successful, sometimes unsuccessful, trials of strength; and which will as a whole contribute to the formation and organization of the socialist will and consciousness of the working classes. In this way, the struggle will advance, on condition that within the capitalist system each battle reinforces the positions of strength, the weapons, and also *the reasons* that workers have for repelling the attacks of the conservative forces, and for preventing capitalism from regaining lost positions.

There is not and cannot be an imperceptible "gradual transition" from capitalism to socialism. The economic and political power of the bourgeoisie will not be whittled away by a slow process of erosion, nor destroyed by a succession of partial reforms, each one apparently innocuous and acceptable to capitalism, but which cumulatively would amount to a discreet siege of the enemy by a secret and masked socialist army, advancing soundlessly, under cover of night, until one fine morning it would find itself in power.

This cannot be the real issue. What can and must be gradual and cumulative in a socialist strategy is the preparatory phase that sets in motion a process leading to the edge of the crisis and the final trial of strength.[1] The choice of this road, incorrectly called "the peaceful road to socialism," is not the consequence of an *a priori* option for gradualism; nor of an *a priori* refusal of violent revolution or armed insurrection. It is a consequence of the latter's actual impossibility in the European context. It is a consequence of the necessity to create the objective and subjective conditions, to prepare the social and political positions of strength, on the basis of which a working-class conquest of political power will become possible.

It may perhaps be objected that there can be no reforms of a socialist character as long as power remains in fact in the hands of the bourgeoisie, as long as the capitalist state continues to exist. This is true. A socialist strategy of progressive reforms does not mean the installation of islands of socialism in a capitalist ocean. But it does mean the conquest of popular and working-class powers; the creation of centers of social control and direct democracy (notably in great industrial enterprises and production cooperatives); the conquest of positions of strength in representative assemblies; and the abstraction from the domination of the market of goods and services answering to collective needs, with the inevitable consequence of an intensification and deepening of the antagonism between the logic of social production according to the needs and aspirations of men, and the logic of capitalist accumulation and the power of management.

It is essential that this antagonism should never be institutionalized, as it usually is in neocapitalist and social-democratic regimes, by the integration of working-class organizations in the state and their subordination to it, by compulsory negotiation and arbitration. The autonomy of trade union and political organizations must bring the antagonisms into the open and allow them to develop freely, and then bring the existing organization of power into question and into crisis, and upset the balance of social forces and of the capitalist economy—a balance which tends to reconstitute itself at a higher level after every initiation of partial reforms, a point which will be taken up presently.

A socialist strategy of gradual reforms can neither be conceived as a simple electoral conquest of a majority, nor as the promulgation of a series of reforms by a chance coalition of social democrats and socialists.[2] The electoral struggle, even when it is ultimately victorious, has never enabled the working classes to forge a collective will or real political power. As Marx and Engels wrote, suffrage gives the right, not the power to govern.[3] It makes possible an assessment of a multiplicity of individual wishes, expressed in the secrecy of the polling booth, of men and women whose convergence of demands does not yet make at all possible their organization and unification for the purpose of common action.

This is one of the mystifications of bourgeois democracy. Its institutions are so conceived as to perpetuate the separation of individuals and their molecular dispersion, to deny them all *collective* power over the organization of society, leaving them merely with the possibility, as a substitute for popular power, of a *permanent delegation of power* every four or five years to representatives with no direct relations with the masses, to parties which are only considered "acceptable partners" on condition that they represent vis-à-vis their electors the superior interests of the capitalist state, rather than the interests of their electors vis-à-vis the capitalist state.

In short, electoral victory does not give power: electoral victory acquired on the basis of a program of reforms, however timid, does not give the power to initiate these reforms. This is one of the profound reasons for the persistence of conservative majorities except in periods of grave crisis and conflict, and for the regular reelection of the government in office, whatever its policies. For in their general tendency, if not in detail, these policies reflect the existing relation of forces in the given situation.

However eloquently it may be advocated by the opposition, a different policy will neither convince nor appear possible *unless there has already been a virtual demonstration of the power of promulgating it*, unless the relation of social forces has been modified by direct mass action which, organized and led by the working class parties, has created a crisis for the policies of the government in office.[4] In other words, the power to initiate a policy of reforms is not conquered in Parliament, but by the previous demonstration of a capacity to mobilize the working classes against current policies; and this capacity of mobilization can itself only be durable and fruitful if the forces of opposition can not only effectively challenge current policies, but also resolve the ensuing crisis; not only attack these policies, but also define other policies that correspond to the new balance of forces, or rather—since a relation of forces is never a static thing—to the new dynamic of struggle that this new relation of forces makes possible.

Without a change in the balance of forces between classes, without a shift in the economic and social balance of the system through the struggle of the masses for their demands, there is a fatal tendency for electoral logic to play into the hands of those political leaders for whom the role of the "left" is reduced to carrying out "better than the right" *the same policies as the right*; and for whom interparty competition reduces itself, in Lelio Basso's words, "to the competition between cliques of political leaders who present their credentials for a more efficient administration of power within the framework of a common political choice."[5] If, on the other hand, mass struggles succeed in upsetting the balance of the system and in precipitating a crisis without being accompanied at the party level by the definition of a really new economic policy capable of resolving the crisis to the political and material advantage of the working classes (as has happened in the recent past in most of the countries of Western Europe), then the situation rapidly decays and, despite their victories, the working classes are soon thrown back by the bourgeoisie to their starting point. Famous precedents for this are France (1937, 1947, and 1957), Belgium (1961), Italy (1962–1964), etc.

At the present time there is a danger that this same process of decay of a situation favorable to the working class will be reproduced every time a coalition coming to power on a program of reforms is a heterogeneous alliance of neocapitalist reformists and socialists. This touches on the strictly political conditions of a socialist strategy of reforms.

Such a strategy, it is worth repeating, cannot, in present-day Europe, aim at the immediate installation of socialism. Neither can it aim at the immediate realization of anticapitalist reforms that are *directly* incompatible with the survival of the system, such as the nationalization of *all* important industrial enterprises or of all sectors with monopolistic or oligopolistic structures. Such reforms, included within a short-term program, would not constitute the *setting in motion* of a revolutionary *process* during which class antagonisms would steadily intensify to the point of a decisive trial of strength. They would constitute directly the destruction of capitalist structures and would *already* demand sufficient maturity of the working class for the immediate revolutionary conquest of political power. If the socialist revolution is not immediately possible, neither is the realization of reforms immediately destructive of capitalism. Those who reject any other kind of reforms in fact reject the very possibility of a *strategy of transition* and a process of transition to socialism.

We should not conclude from the impossibility, failing a prerevolutionary situation, of passing directly to reforms destructive of the system, that a socialist strategy of reforms can or must be limited to isolated or partial reforms, called "democratic" because they have not only no socialist content, but no socialist perspective or revolutionary dynamic. In practice, what distinguishes a socialist strategy of reforms from a neocapitalist reformism of a social-democratic type is less *each* of the reforms proposed and *each* programmatic objective than: 1) the presence or absence of *organic ties* between the various reforms; 2) the rhythm and modalities of their initiation; 3) the presence or absence of a will to profit by the collapse in the balance provoked by the first reforming actions for new disruptive action.[6]

The fact that social-democratic leaders and socialist forces may find themselves in agreement on the necessity of *certain* reforms must never be allowed to confuse the basic difference between their respective goals and perspectives. If a socialist strategy of reforms is to be possible, this basic difference must not be masked, nor dismissed to a lower level by tactical agreements at the summit. On the contrary, it must be placed at the center of political debate. If not, the socialist movement, by seeming to give a totally unmerited "socialist" warrant to the social-democratic leaders through tactical agreements at the summit, will have prepared the rout in ideological and political confusion of the whole of the working class movement and particularly of its avant-garde.

These remarks are particularly applicable to the present European situation, in which the precarious economic balance no longer allows, as it did in other periods, the financing by inflation of social programs and public intervention. It follows from this situation that a program with a "social" character—concerning the raising of low wages; the development of social construction and backward regions; the improvement of education and public services, etc.—must *either* use a coherent set of reforms to attack the logic and the core of capitalist accumulation, *or* retreat precipitately before the lightning response of capitalist forces whose interests are threatened or adversely affected.

If it is proposed that a popular front coalition should be brought to power on the basis of an agreement as to a minimum common program, entailing several partial reforms, and excluding by the very terms of the alliance reforming actions going beyond the limits of the program, then the fate of the coalition and its government is virtually sealed in advance.

In fact, the very essence of a minimum program is that, unlike a program of transition or a strategy of reforms, it debars the socialist forces, on pain of breaking the pact, from profiting by the dynamic of the process set in motion by the initial measures, and even from responding by counter-offensive to the offensive of the capitalist forces.

The nature of this offensive is now well known, as it always follows the pattern of France in 1936. The bourgeoisie reacts to the actions that threaten its prerogatives and powers by a flight of capital, an investment strike, and selective dismissals, aimed first of all at trade union militants; in short, by unleashing an economic crisis whose effects penalize the working classes. This crisis—which is not merely the result of a deliberate and concerted action by the bourgeoisie, but also of the objective impossibility of making capitalism work while attacking its internal resources—finally allows the bourgeoisie to negotiate from a position of strength the revision of the government program and the postponement in time (i.e., in practice, indefinitely) of its objectives. The bourgeoisie is the more insistent the more negotiation brings out the internal division of the coalition between partisans of intransigence and partisans of compromise. As the weeks pass and the economic and monetary crisis deepens, the former inevitably lose ground to the latter. For from this moment on the situation has already changed. The original minimum program has already become inapplicable. To apply it would now demand draconian measures which did not figure in the original common minimum program—e.g. exchange, controls, price ceilings, import quotas, nationalization of financial or industrial monopolies—and which could only be attempted by a government "striking while the iron is hot," at the moment of maximum popular support and mobilization.

But the weeks that have passed in sterile bargaining, the economic crisis, and the dissensions within the coalition produce a reflux of combativity in the working classes. The partisans of intransigence are already fighting a rearguard action. Confusion ensues, and the capitalist forces, conscious that time is on their side, harden their stand. The history of the coalition thus becomes that of a long retreating struggle. To regain the confidence of capital it multiplies concessions. When finally it is succeeded by a moderate government, better suited to appease the bourgeoisie and "cure" the economy, the popular front coalition has to its credit only the measures and partial reforms carried out in its first weeks of power, and which have been distorted, deprived of all real significance and even put to the service of the capitalist system.

The repetition of a similar process—which occurred in France after 1936 and 1945, in Great Britain after 1945 and 1964, in Italy after 1947 and 1963—can only be prevented if the coalition is sufficiently homogeneous and conscious of the trials awaiting it to respond to the offensive of the capitalist forces by a lightning reaction in the country of the working masses, and by governmental measures prepared preventively in advance, well before the victory.[7]

But an effective reaction from the working class movement presupposes that the reforming action is not conceived as an action centralized in the state, in support of which the coalition demands of the masses a permanent and disciplined delegation of powers; rather it presupposes that the promulgation of the economic program goes hand in hand from the beginning with democratic reforms allowing the development in factories, cooperatives, regions and local councils of centers of popular power and initiatives adapted to local circumstances.

On the other hand, preventative measures against the offensive of the capitalist forces presupposes that from the start the coalition had no illusions about the possibility of appeasing the bourgeoisie and reconciling it with a loyal collaboration with the new state.[8] But social-democratic leaders are supporters of a popular front. According to them, initially there should be a sincere attempt at a policy resting on indirect controls and freely accepted managerial prerogatives. It would be incorrect to reject this method of approach *a priori* if its supporters were conscious from the start that it *cannot constitute a lasting policy,* but must inevitably lead to an acute conflict *which must be prepared for.* In other words, a policy of indirect public control of the mechanisms of accumulation and circulation of capital should not necessarily be rejected, on condition that it must only be conceived as a *transition* towards the policy of direct control, which it will inevitably demand as its logical continuation under pain of a blockage in the system and retaliations on the part of the economic forces.

To believe that the state can *in the long term* contain, orient and regulate the activity of the economic forces without encroaching on the regime of private property is in fact to abstract from the political and psychological dynamic of capitalism. No doubt it is technically true that a selective policy in fiscal, price, and credit matters can imprint qualitative social and geographical orientations on production, differentiating the growth of its sectors, services, and regions according to social criteria and a global economic rationality. But what is technically possible is not for long politically possible.[9]

The public desire to reduce the cost of growth; to eliminate waste (in the form of artificially expanded costs of marketing, management, advertizing, display and so on); to prevent the use of the resources of enterprises for private purposes; to prevent investment in new installations and new models that contribute neither to technical progress

nor to the improvement of products, but are rather aimed primarily
at justifying the rates of amortization allowed by the Inland Revenue, all this is rigorously technically possible through the tightening
of controls and the establishment of strict administrative rules: e.g.,
the limitation of advertizing costs accepted by the Inland Revenue;
the determination by sectors, or single cases (where monopolies are
concerned), of an acceptable rate of profit, of the use which may be
made of profit, of the direction and nature of investments which can
be made, etc., under pain of stiff tax penalties.

But the promulgation of such public directives quickly comes up
against the logic of capitalist activity and destroys its dynamic.[10] In fact,
it amounts to the destruction of managerial authority, to the factual
socialization of the activity of the entrepreneur, and to indirect public direction of firms. It would include as a sanction the confiscation
(or very severe taxation) of supranormal profits. It would thus remove
any reason why a private company should seek a rationalization or
innovation which would increase its profits beyond the rate reckoned
as normal, thereby destroying one of the major incentives to technical progress. In short, by controlling management, by weighing it
down at the top with bureaucracy, by attacking the profit motive, the
state would be attacking the very dynamic of the capitalist system, and
would encourage its paralysis or sclerosis.

There is no sense in attacking the mechanisms and dynamic of the
capitalist system *unless one intends to abolish it, not conserve it.* To attack
the consequences of the system's logic is necessarily to attack this logic
itself and to threaten the system. If this crisis is not to turn against those
who provoked it, it must be resolved by the transfer of centers of accumulation under public control. In default of more extreme measures
of socialization following initial reforms and tending to remove those
very obstacles raised by the promulgation of the program, the reforming coalition will be the victim of a war of attrition and of the process
of decay we have just described.

If intermediate reforms (in the sense that they do not reveal their anticapitalist logic *directly)* must certainly not be rejected in the perspective of a socialist strategy, this is only on the basic condition that they
must be conceived as means, not as ends, as dynamic phases in a process
of struggle, not as resting stages. Their function is to educate and unite
the actually or potentially anticapitalist social forces by the struggle

for undeniable social and economic objectives—above all, for a new direction for social and economic development—by initially adopting the method of peaceful and democratic reforms. But this method must be adopted *not because it is viable or intrinsically preferable, but on the contrary because the resistance, the limits, and the impossibilities that it will inevitably come up against after a short while are suitable simply for the demonstration of the necessity of socialist transformation to social forces not yet ready for it.*[11]

II. SOCIALISTS AND REFORMISTS: THE PROBLEM OF A PROGRAM

Obviously, such a strategy cannot be realized in the framework of a summit-alliance with neocapitalist formations, i.e., social democrats and centrists, who would immediately set out to limit reforming action to measures acceptable to the bourgeoisie and demand strict program-matic adherence to this principle from their partners. It presupposes that there is a clear consciousness of the nature of the process of transi-tion to socialism at the level of the political leaders: a consciousness of its mechanisms, its dynamic, of the aspirations of the working masses who support it, and of *the relatively short respite* in which the success or failure of the undertaking is determined.

To summarize, a socialist strategy of reforms must aim at disturbing the balance of the system, and profit by this disturbance to prepare the (revolutionary) process of the transition to socialism, which, as we have seen, can only be done at white heat. A strategy of this type is only practicable in periods of movement, on the basis of open conflicts and large-scale political and social movements. It cannot be conceived as a battle of attrition in a war of position. For once the social front is sta-bilized, once a balance of forces is set up, the battle of rupture—which it is precisely the function of a socialist strategy to prepare for—is post-poned. Of course, the new balance of forces may be more favorable to the working classes than the old one, the contradictions and elements antagonistic to capitalist logic more marked. But these contradictions, once the struggle for reforms has reached a new level—i.e., in practice, once its dynamism has been arrested—are muffled in the form of con-stant attempts by one side and the other to whittle away the opposing position. These essentially *tactical* skirmishes no longer allow the inter-vention of a *strategy*. For however precarious the balance of forces, it rests on the recognized impossibility for either side to force a decision.

It is thus unrealistic to assimilate these muffled tactical conflicts, which may be spread over a long period, to a "revolutionary process" that ripens over one or more decades.[12] However precarious the balance set up when the struggle for reforms reaches a level may objectively be, it is a balance; for the socialist and workers' movement it is a lean period. The contradictions introduced into the system by the reforms imposed previously no longer gnaw at its substance, and do not weaken it like a chronic malady. They do not retain their original disruptive potential. On the contrary, they lose it. There are no anticapitalist institutions or conquests that cannot in the long run be whittled down, denatured, absorbed, and emptied of all or part of their content if the imbalance created by their initiation is not exploited by new offensives as soon as it manifests itself. Constrained to coexist with institutions that originally opposed its logic and limited its sphere of authority, capitalism learns to subordinate them to itself without a frontal attack; insofar as it dominates the crucial sectors of capitalist accumulation and development and particularly those new activities imposed by technical progress and growth, it can regain all or part of the lost territory.[13]

This means that it is impossible to conceive the period of transition, or even the period preparing the transition, as a long period, of the order of a decade. If the transition is not begun after the disruption of the balance that provokes the struggle for reforms, then it will not take place in that period. The reforms will be disjointed, checked and digested by the system, and a balance reestablished at a higher level. A new period of preparatory struggles, comprising in their objectives new contradictions, will be necessary to create the conditions for a new offensive. The discontinuity of socialist strategy is that of history itself.

We should not conclude from this that the democratic reforms of the past were vain, which would amount to asserting the sterility of a century of working-class struggles. Even emptied of all or part of their content, the conquests of the past enable working-class and socialist forces in a new phase of their offensive to reach out for more advanced objectives. In this sense, Lenin considered state monopoly capitalism, the most advanced phase of the capitalist socialization of the productive forces, which has already set up certain levers that the socialist state will be able to use, as the "antechamber to socialism."

Given this, it must still be stressed that if past conquests make the domination of the capitalist class more precarious, and the balance of the system more fragile, *for this very reason* they make new partial reforms and new displacements of the balance *politically more difficult*. Precisely when new anticapitalist reforms risk compromising the survival of the system, the resistance of the bourgeoisie to any new reform becomes ferocious. *The shorter the step to the disruption of the system, or the closer it has been approached in the past, the more difficult it becomes to approach it again or to go beyond it.* For the bourgeoisie is now on guard; the working class movement runs the risk of political and economic failure in its undertaking; a higher degree of preparation, resolution and consciousness is now necessary to engage in a new battle.

The idea of "creeping socialism," gaining ground thanks to reforms achieved one by one until a "qualitative leap" is provoked, corresponds to nothing real except the very real vigilance of the bourgeoisie which this idea reflects. There can be no *cumulative effect* of reforms successively imposed over a long period, without a sharp trial of strength based on a strategy. Particularly in those societies where the mechanisms of capitalist accumulation are already objectively at the mercy of public intervention; where institutional reforms presenting no intrinsic difficulties would suffice to break the power of the bourgeoisie—even though the state does not use these instruments *against* the monopolies, quite the contrary—there above all do the capitalist forces use all their strength in every field (ideological, political, and social) to hinder the formation of a political will able to impose these reforms.

Several countries of Western Europe (France, the Scandinavian countries, and Italy, in particular) have today reached this threshold where, because of the structural vulnerability of the system, the bourgeoisie is defending its power positions tooth and nail, and posing an implacable opposition to the everyday claims of the workers' movement as much as to its struggle for partial reforms. This means that it is necessary to raise the struggle to the higher level of a global strategy, based on a general vision, and not to attack just the immediately intolerable effects of capitalism, but the very nature of the relations of production, social relations, and the civilization which has given birth to them.[14]

This elevation and "globalization" of the objects of struggle is imperative for the simple reason that the very survival of the system has now been objectively threatened even by the conquest of partial reforms, and the bourgeoisie knows it. It globally resists partial attacks. Winning a trial of strength is now inconceivable for the workers' movement unless it can achieve the subjective appreciation of the global character of what is at stake in the course of struggle; unless it succeeds in opposing its own global political will to the global resistance of its adversary. A battle in which *everything* is at stake for the enemy cannot be won unless the partial objectives that one is committed to imply a goal deserving *total* commitment.

Thus there is some truth and some error in the "maximalist" tendencies that are at present developing in the face of the degeneration of European social-democracy and the increasing difficulty of achieving partial victories and reforms. The error is to postulate that any struggle must now be entered into only with a clearly stated socialist intention and for aims that imply the destruction of the system. This amounts to claiming that the revolutionary intention *predates* the struggle that gives it strength. This undialectical position evades the problem by supposing it to have been solved. For in reality, the socialist intention of the masses never emerges *ex nihilo*, nor is it formed by political propaganda or scientific proof. A socialist intention is *constructed* in and through the struggle for plausible objectives corresponding to the experience, needs, and aspirations of the workers.

Further, it demands that the goals be articulated together in a strategic vision, and that as the struggle progresses, pressing on to the structural limits of the system, it gains not only in breadth, but also in depth. Such a dialectical development of the struggle presupposes a preexistent socialist intention among the masses. This intention is not manifested by polemic and revolutionary propaganda, but by the ability to order the goals, to raise the struggle to a higher level, to give it "intermediate" goals prefiguring workers' power, which must necessarily be transcended once they are obtained.

Nevertheless, there is some truth in the "maximalist" position, for the workers' movement will only advance toward socialism if the latter is the objective sense of its actions in pursuit of its aims, the sense that is destined to become conscious ("subjective"). Any protest or demand whatsoever, if it is presented in general, i.e., abstract terms (e.g., a general increase in wages and pensions, a growth in public housing, etc.) cannot have this objective sense; if only because the realization of the goal is not in the power of those who demand it and will not be achieved directly through their action, even when they succeed. Furthermore, this kind of demand has no internal anticapitalist logic necessitating the transcendence of its objectives once they have been obtained. These objectives are presented as new levels whose realization could be the result of government action based on technical (or technocratic) reforms. Their content exhausts them.

In present conditions, the workers' movement will only acquire the political maturity and strength necessary to destroy the accumulated resistance of the system if its demands are a living critique of the social relations and the relations of production, of capitalist rationality and civilization, in content, but also in the *way* they are pursued.

This critique, deepening the themes of the struggle, is particularly important in the neocapitalist context, where the workers' socialist movement has to measure up against the subaltern reformism of social democratic and centrist formations. In fact, these latter often advance *the same kind* of objectives as the forces of the Left (council housing, education, public amenities, "social justice", etc.)—but they subordinate their realization to the possibility of obtaining them without producing a "breakdown of the machine" of capitalism, i.e., without disturbing the economic balance or weakening the power positions of the bourgeoisie.

The great speciality of social democratic formations is to demonstrate that all problems can be resolved or made tolerable, all material needs satisfied within the framework of the system, given time and discipline. There is no call to "rock the boat" or engage in a trial of strength; be patient, realistic, and responsible and have confidence in the leadership. Let everyone keep to his place, and the neocapitalist state will act in the best interests of all.

It may well be useful for the socialist forces to show that the social democratic formations refuse to give themselves the means to carry out their program; that this program is either unrealizable, or requires such a long delay that its solution will be overtaken halfway by a change in the terms of the problem; or even that more and better can be expected and obtained if one is prepared to go further in transforming the structures. But however useful it may be, this kind of demonstration is insufficient. Essentially, it opposes promises of relative improvement by promises or more rapid or marked relative improvement. What it fails to say, and what the reformists are careful to shout at the top of their voices, is that these more rapid and more marked improvements would provoke a major crisis of the system: "You just want to break the machine, but we want to make it work better."

The socialist movement is ill-equipped to shake off this objection so long as it remains on the terrain of *relative*, general improvements. If it lets it be believed that there is only a *relative* difference, a difference *of degree* between its policy and that of the reformists; that basically it is seeking the same kind of objectives, but uncompromisingly and energetically, and is prepared if necessary to bring the matter to a trial of strength with capital, it is hardly likely to eat away the electoral support of social democracy and become the hegemonic force in the workers' movement. A relative difference or a difference of degree is not, in fact, enough to make the masses prefer the perilous and arduous road of confrontation with the forces of capital to the slow but "sure" road of subordinate reformism.

No one will take the risks of a political and monetary crisis or engage in a trial of strength with the bourgeoisie just to secure the building of 250,000 council houses a year rather than 200,000, an increase of 10 percent rather than 5 percent for lower paid workers, a forty-two-hour week rather than a forty-four-hour week, etc. The game is not worth the candle; if only because a more ambitious policy on the part of the socialist movement will initially provoke a brutal reaction on the part of the system, a major upheaval in the economy, and in all probability a deterioration in the material situation of the masses, at least for a short period.

Social democratic and centrist propaganda is thus very telling when it asks "What's the hurry? Why try to force the pace when a little patience and discipline will give you what you are asking for at the appropriate time and in calm and order? Is it worth risking a serious crisis to obtain in five years what could be obtained in seven or eight without great changes?"

All European social democrats ask this question in one way and another, and the socialist movement can only respond by stressing that there is a basic difference between its policies and those of reformism.[15] *Not a difference of degree, delay or method of realizing the same thing as social democracy, only better and quicker. But a total difference, justifying a total risk. Only to the extent that it can convey the fact that its actions and objectives are not of the same kind as those of subordinate reformism; that what is at stake is not a greater relative or partial improvement, but an absolute and global improvement, can the socialist movement advance and establish itself as the hegemonic force in the workers' movement.*

Absolute and global amelioration should not, of course, be understood to mean that the earthly paradise and the installation of socialism can be promised overnight. Rather, each partial improvement, each reform demanded, should be articulated into a general project aiming at producing a global change. The scope of this change must transcend each partial objective that illustrates one of its determined aspects: the absolute improvement at stake is the emancipation of all those who are exploited, oppressed, degraded, and crippled by capitalist relations of production in what is their social value and individual pride: their social labor.

Reformists and socialists do have some wishes in common; but not for the same purposes or in the same way. For reformism, at stake in the reforming action is merely "things"—wages, public amenities, pensions, etc.—which the state is to dispense from on high to individuals maintained in their dispersion and impotent with respect to the process of production and relations of production. For the socialist movement, the workers' sovereign power to determine for themselves the conditions of their social participation, to submit to their collective intent the content, development, and social division of their labor, is as important, if not more so, than "things."

Hence the profound difference between reformism and socialism. It is the difference between granting reforms that perpetuate the subordination of the working class in factory and society; and reforms imposed, applied, and controlled by the masses themselves, based on their capacity for self-organization and their initiative. In the last analysis, it is the difference between technical, state reforms and democratic reforms; it being understood that the latter are *necessarily* anticapitalist:

> The struggle for an authentic democracy, for any form of real participation in the management of collective interests, for any form of collective control, in particular for the workers' control of all aspects of the process of production . . . is to challenge in practice capitalism's power of decision. An essential aspect of this struggle is the struggle of the working class for the right to manage for itself the patrimony of labor power, with all the consequences which follow from this as to the organization of labor in the factories and the autonomous management of deferred payments (social insurance, etc.).[16]

Thus there is necessarily a difference in method corresponding to the difference in content separating neocapitalist reforms and anticapitalist reforms. The liberating value of reforms can only manifest itself if it is already present in the mass actions aiming to establish them. At the level of method, the difference between technical reforms and democratic reforms is that separating a bureaucratically applied institutional reform and a reform imposed in the heat of collective action. From a formal point of view, any reform whatsoever—including workers' control—may be emptied of its revolutionary significance and reabsorbed by capitalism if it is merely instituted by government fiat and administered by bureaucratic controls, i.e., reduced to a "thing."

Certain "maximalists" conclude from this that all reforms are vain as long as the capitalist state survives. They are right if they mean reforms granted from on high and institutionalized. They are wrong if they mean reforms imposed from below in the heat of struggle. A reform cannot be separated from the action which produces it. Democratic and anticapitalist reforms cannot be achieved by action that is neither the one nor the other. The emancipation of the working class can only constitute for the workers a total stake justifying a total risk if the action of struggle has already been an experiment for them in self-organization, in initiative and collective decision-making, in short, an experiment in the possibility of their own emancipation.

III. THE GLOBAL ALTERNATIVE:
THE PROBLEM OF ALLIANCES

Whenever the socialist movement works alongside a strong social democracy or a dynamic neocapitalism, it is necessary for it to shift the emphasis from partial, immediate, quantitative, and disparate demands to the presentation of the policies and program of a *global and qualitative change*. This what is implied by the many references to the "global alternative," to the "model" of development, civilization and social organization whose elaboration has been presented as the most urgent, nay, the principal task by the most advanced flank of the European Marxist movement.

Hold-all programs that take into account all demands and all subjects of discontent are no longer merely implausible; they lack a general perspective: they have none of the coherence necessary—not only economically and logically but above all politically and ideologically—to constitute a "global alternative," to forge the unity between objectively anticapitalist forces, which can only be the synthesis at a higher level (not just the sum) of their demands, interests, and immediate aspirations.

In this respect, Sweden offers a particularly pertinent illustration. The significance of the Swedish experience extends well beyond the case of Sweden itself, so frequently held up as a model by European social democracy, and as the forerunner of the type of society toward which most European neocapitalist states are evolving.

Swedish social democracy postulated the possibility of pursuing a policy of social welfare, public amenities, and high wages linked to high productivity within the framework of capitalism and without rejecting its mechanisms. Past development of social allowances, amenities, and services was based on direct taxation that increased with the level of income. But this development went hand in hand with that of a civilization of individual consumption. Eventually, an acute double contradiction manifested itself.

On the one hand, the development of social services and amenities financed by direct taxation was obtained by what was in effect the socialization of the major part of private saving. The result was a grave crisis in the capitalist mechanisms of accumulation: a decline in the capital market (the Stock Exchange) without any increase in the self-financing power of enterprise (in fact there was a decrease). But on the other hand, this crisis in the accumulation mechanisms was not offset by opulence in the social sector; on the contrary, there is an acute crisis in housing and town planning, an acute shortage of medical and educational personnel, an accelerated drift from the country to the towns, etc.

Thus the expansion of social services and public intervention, subordinated to the expansion of industrial capitalism, was not adequate to satisfy the social needs engendered by the development of the latter. But it was sufficient to make difficulties for it, by tapping certain of its sources of finance.

Social democracy thus finds itself faced with a choice. The accelerated expansion of social and collective services and the pursuit of monopolist expansion can no longer be attempted together. There are two alternatives: either 1) the stabilization, if not the reduction, of social and public expenditure (with an aggravation of the shortages listed above) so as to increase not only saving, but also private consumption, and thus give a new dynamic to capitalist accumulation; or 2) a more rapid development of social services and public intervention than in the past, demanding a much more extensive socialization of the economy, including nationalizations, collectivization of saving and the investment function, global (i.e., planned) public direction of the economy, priority of collective consumption and services rather than "luxury" consumption, etc.

The choice imposed is not a simple technical choice; it is destined to make a political impact on the modes of development, consumption and civilization, and on the style of life.

The first alternative is instinctively rejected by the majority of workers. But this does not at all mean that the second, necessary from a logical point of view even on the basis of popular demands, may automatically count on a majority.

This difficulty in passing from logical analysis to practical politics is based on the marked differentiation of the working classes (as well as on the fact that a logical analysis is never used by all the interested parties). The immediate interests of large categories of relatively highly paid manual laborers—notably building workers and those in the heavy engineering and shipbuilding industry—do not automatically coincide with the interests of workers (particularly women) in underdeveloped or "remote" regions, and in public service, who are badly paid; nor with the aspirations of technical and scientific workers.

At the level of consciousness and immediate interest, categories of workers with relatively high wages are not spontaneously attracted to an extreme policy of socialization. Trade union and social democratic ideology has induced them to give priority to consumption demands and "values": labor is regarded as a daily hell; the management's norms of productivity organization and division of labor are regarded as intolerable; but they are accepted nonetheless on the pretext that they are technical necessities, and that what *really* counts is wages. Work is regarded as the purgatory that must be passed through so that, after work, the heaven of individual consumption may be reached. Given this ideological conditioning, the first alternative—including a reduction of very heavy direct taxation and a development of "luxury" consumption to the detriment of social consumption—is much more immediately attractive to a part of the working class than a far-reaching policy of socialization.

Therefore, demands for individual consumption and wages, which remain of primary importance for poor regions and categories, cannot serve as a unifying theme for the workers' movement. The political unity of the working class, an indispensable condition for the imposition of the second alternative, can only be constructed around themes that transcend immediate interests toward a synthesis at a higher level. Thus ideological and political work, the critique of the "consumption civilization," and the elaboration of a model of change become determinant.

It becomes necessary to show that the oppression and alienation of labor accepted for the sake of liberation in non-labor can only result in alienation of consumption and leisure; that to acquire the goods for the consumption and leisure that "liberate" him from the oppression of work, the worker is led by an infernal logic to work longer and longer hours and faster and faster, to take on overtime and bonus rates to the extent that he loses all possibility, material or psychological, of any liberation whatsoever; that the man at work is *the same man* as the man not at work, and that the one cannot be liberated without the other; that the basic class interest of all workers is to put an end to their subordination in labor and in consumption, and to take over control of the organization and purposes of social production; that a rise in direct wages is a priority demand for an important mass of workers, but that satisfying it is insufficient to put an end to capitalist exploitation; that in any event there are objective limits to the wage level and objective and subjective limits to the satisfaction that can be obtained from individual income without a sufficient development of collective services and amenities.

As long as production decisions are dominated by capital, as long as consumption, culture and lifestyles are dominated by bourgeois values, the only way to live better is to earn more. But if capitalist relations of production are abolished, living better will also mean working less and less intensely, adapting work to the requirements of the workers' biological and psychological equilibrium, disposing of better collective services, greater possibilities of direct communication and culture, in and out of work, for oneself and for one's children, etc.

On the other hand, the checks and limitations imposed on scientific, technical, and cultural development by the capitalist criterion of profitability, the sterilization of economic resources and human energies implied by the process of financial and geographical concentration, the under-utilization of human capacities and the waste of energy necessitated by the authoritarian organization of labor, the contradiction between the law of maximum returns that dominates production on the one hand, and on the other the waste constituted by a marketing policy based on continual innovations with no use value and costly "sales promotion" campaigns, etc.; all these contradictions of developed capitalism are as important, if the system is to be challenged, as the subject of immediately conscious discontent: they imply a critique of the capitalist lifestyle, of capitalist values and rationality.

Obviously, from this enumeration of themes, which it is not claimed is exhaustive, we cannot proceed to the elaboration in the abstract of absolute solutions, nor to propositions of a purely speculative "model of change." The superiority of a mass revolutionary party over parties based on apparatus and clientele, preoccupied with gaining power and governing, *under existing conditions*, is that it can (and must) awaken aspirations and pose problems that presuppose the radical transcendence of the capitalist system. The mass revolutionary party exercises its directive and educational functions without pretending to know in advance the answers to the questions it will raise. Not only because these answers cannot be found within the framework of the existing system, but because their research and elaboration by permanent confrontations and debates among the rank and file is *par excellence* the way to provoke the participation, the *prise de conscience* and the self-education of the workers, to give them a direct hand in the party and the society to be constructed, and to let them grasp, through their exercise of party democracy, the profoundly authoritarian and antidemocratic character of the society in which they live.

Animating and stimulating collective reflection and democratic debate is also the best way for the party to enrich and develop the themes of struggle it proposes, to submit its general analyses to a practical test and to detect the forms of action best suited to local conditions, to the powers of initiative and sensibility of the masses.

This permanent labor of research and collective reflection, associating the rank and file of the party with the elaboration of its policy, asking it to choose amongst the various possible forms of action, must of necessity go beyond the bounds of the party structure itself. The latter cannot function in a closed circuit. Its hegemonic capacity depends on the attraction exerted by its internal life, its actions and its political positions on those working masses that are unorganized or bear the marks of different ideological or religious imprints. In an economically developed society, with a working class highly differentiated by origin (workers, peasants, petty bourgeois) and by mode of labor (manual, technical, intellectual), the party is obliged in any event to take this diversity of specific aspirations into account; it can only exercise its leading role by seeking to transcend this diversity towards a higher unity that will respect these diverse elements, in their relative autonomy.

The policy of transition to socialism, the "model" of the transitional and even of the socialist society itself, must recognize this diversity. In advanced capitalist countries, the revolutionary party can hope neither to conquer, nor to exercise, power alone. It must ally itself with all the political, social, and intellectual forces that refuse capitalist rationality, and which can be won over to a transitional policy that is clear and coherent in its socialist objectives. But at the same time, the work of elaboration of its transitional policy, and notably of the political and institutional reforms it must realize, can no longer only be initiated by the leading organs of the party, even if (or particularly if) it is by far the strongest workers' party.

Even the attraction of the unorganized masses and of the rank and file of other formations depends in intensity and potential on the attractions that the long-term or even very long-term options exercise on the actual or potential allies of the proletarian revolutionary party. Hence the necessity for the latter to recognize the other socialist tendencies as *permanent* partners in a *common* labor of research and elaboration into the programmatic content and the forms of transition to socialism, guaranteeing the rights of a plurality of tendencies and parties during the transition period and even during the construction of socialism.

The past and present electoral strength of these permanent partners is not the principal criterion of choice. What matters more than their numerical strength is the representativity of their militant rank and file, their authentically socialist orientation and their real autonomy.[17] For the mass revolutionary party to ally itself with different, even weak, formations and to conduct a common research with them is to demonstrate in practice, not merely in declarations of principle, that its respect for political pluralism and the autonomy of allies is not simply a tactical concession. And it is also a powerful attraction on the militant rank and file and left wing of social democracy and of the avant-garde Christian movements,[18] as much by the working methods adopted as by the coherence of the transition policy (or of the "global alternative") elaborated in common.

Therefore, the revolutionary party must never by a doctrinaire attitude reject the masses influenced by social democracy or traditional reformist movements; but neither must it enter into negotiations or summit dialogs with them if these will be immediately blocked by ideological or doctrinal differences, or led into the impasse of bargaining for a "minimum common program." Nor should it seek a facade of unity for the workers' movement (or for some of its components) by federating existing organizations, i.e., by *juxtaposing their party apparatus*: this attempt will rapidly exhaust itself in summit bargaining between leaders and notables, like a ghostly government or parliament, and before long it will have cut itself off from the masses or discouraged those militants who have been left without a say in the decisions and arrangements which, at the summit of the "regrouping," will respond to criteria internal to the party machines rather than to a real collective intention of the rank and file. They should rather, straight away, set in motion a process of unification of those forces that are essentially socialist, by the common elaboration of a coherent policy, affecting long-term and even very long-term solutions as much as problems of immediate concern and a medium-term program.[19] The consistency of this elaboration, the openness and transparency of the debate, their repercussion on the militant rank and file, destined to participate with its initiatives in the process of unification, will have a much greater effectiveness and attraction than overtures toward traditional reformist parties, which are always suspected of tactical opportunism. To destroy the subordinate reformism of social democracy, a dialog should be opened with the masses under its influence, not its party machine. And the best way to win them over is to propose to them the "alternative" of a socialist policy, consistent and clear in its options, and democratic methods of work that social democracy, in its essence, cannot adopt.

IV. THE IDEOLOGICAL FRONT:
NEW TASKS OF THE REVOLUTIONARY PARTY

This permanent labor of research and elaboration cannot be limited to the strictly political, programmatic realm. It is not policies that politicize the masses, nor action and struggle alone. Political commitment and choice are, in fact, the final position of a *prise de conscience* that never starts with politics, i.e., with the problem of the organization of society and social relations, but from the direct and fragmentary experience of a change *that is necessary because it is possible.*

The demand for change, in other words, does not arise from the *impossibility* of accepting what is, but from the *possibility* of no longer accepting what is. The revelation of this possibility (actual or not, translatable into practical action or not) in all the realms of social and individual life is one of the basic functions of the *ideological work* of a revolutionary movement.[20]

The domination of one class over another, in fact, is not merely exerted by political and economic power, but by its perception of the possible and the impossible, of the future and the past, of the useful and the useless, the rational and the irrational, the good and the bad, etc. This perception is carried in the whole web of social relations, by the objective future that determines their persistence, their resistance to change. But it is also carried at the specific level of language (the main tool or obstacle for the *prise de conscience*), of the means of mass communication, of the ideology and values to which the ruling class submits science, technique, and also *life* itself (i.e., the fundamental needs, called "instincts," and immediate relations, e.g., social relations, between individuals). In other words, the possibilities, aspirations, and needs (excluded from reality by the social relations), are repressed and censored (in Freud's sense, not that of the police) at the specific level of their possible *prise de conscience*, by the depth conditioning exercised on consciousness by the dominant ideology and lifestyle.

As much as a set of "values," this is a pessimistic realism, rejecting "values," typical of conservative ideology: it is "unrealistic" to believe that a healthy economy can do without competition in trade, individual profit, disciplinary constraint of labor, or the threat of unemployment; the intensification of exploitation of the workers, the mutilation of their human faculties, and their nervous exhaustion are the "inevitable" consequences of technological development; there is no "global alternative" to capitalism, the worker will always be a worker, it is a technical matter; the individual will always be "self-interested," his "instincts" will always be antisocial and must be repressed, etc.

The destruction of this ideological conditioning, rooted in material relations, is one of the essential tasks of the revolutionary movement.

Only if the possibility, even if it is not actual, of partial or total liberation in the framework of a "global alternative" can be illustrated is it possible for the repressed needs, the aspirations for change and liberation, to cease to be a diffuse and recriminatory discontent, convinced in advance of the futility of any rebellion, and to acquire confidence in their legitimacy and reality. Even the most immediately insupportable consequences of new methods of organization of labor, for example, will be accepted in bitterness, after a burst of anger, if management propaganda has been able to prove (as is usually the case) that they were technically indispensable and economically advantageous. The workers' instinctive rejection of them will not be able to transcend the level of an impotent burst of anger, gain confidence in the legitimacy and *reality* of its motives, nor translate itself into a resolute struggle, unless the union is able to oppose the management's model for the organization of labor with a different model, based on a different conception of labor and worker, integrating with the "rationality" of labor the nervous and physiological equilibrium of the individual, his relationship with his tools and with other individuals, etc.

The same kind of procedure, demonstrating the necessity of change by its possibility, revealing and reawakening thereby those needs censored and repressed by society, is valid in all aspects of the individual's relation to his labor as a profession and as social production; to society insofar as it is his immediate environment, his natural and cultural surroundings, in a web of social relations; and to others, including the family and the other sex. Therefore, this labor of ideological research and elaboration, as well as having a political sense, is a *cultural* labor aiming at the overthrow of the norms and schemata of social consciousness, the revelation of the alienations that society represses from consciousness through the possibilities that it refuses.

The revolutionary movement's capacity for action and hegemony is enriched and confirmed by its capacity to inspire autonomous research in such fields as town planning, architecture, occupational medicine, labor organization, education, psychology, sexual education, etc. In all these fields, the contradiction between the possibilities of liberation and expansion which the productive and cultural forces place at the disposal of society, and its incapacity to take advantage of them and develop them in a liberating direction, is revealed. In all these fields as well, the contradiction between the demands of social, cultural, and economic development available in the autonomous activity of town planners, architects, doctors, teachers, and psychologists, and the demands to which capitalist society enslaves them, is equally revealed.

The revolutionary party's hegemonic capacity is thus directly linked to its degree of implantation in the professions and in intellectual circles. It can counter bourgeois ideology to the extent that it is inspiring their research, that it associates their avant-garde with reflection on an "alternative model," while still respecting the autonomy of their research. The mediation of these intellectual avant-gardes is essential to its ability to contest and destroy the grip of the ruling ideology. It is even necessary to provide the ruled classes with a language and means of expression that will give them a consciousness of the reality of their subordination and their exploitation. In fact, without the possibility of expression, i.e., of objectification and reflection, a demand cannot recognize its own reality: when the experience the workers have of their condition is not reflected back to them, but on the contrary, is denied or passed over in silence by all those who—through the mass media—form the "public consciousness," it becomes dubious, even for the workers themselves.[21] The repressive (in the psychological sense) and class nature of culture does not simply, nor even primarily, spring from the social composition of the pupils at high schools and universities. It springs even more basically from the prior inexistence or extreme poverty of the "work culture," the specific workers' culture, of the *language*—presupposing a literature, a theatre and a cinema—able to take into account the experience the workers themselves have of the laboring condition.

Struggling in this manner against the class character of culture, abolishing the cultural privilege of the bourgeoisie cannot mean bringing popularized bourgeois culture to the working masses. Quite the reverse: the working class must not be impregnated with bourgeois culture: the culture must be impregnated with the experience, the values, the tasks, and the problems that the working class lives daily, in its labor, in its life outside labor, and in its struggles. The class character of culture is marked by the fact that the working class is absent from it as a subject, as a perception of society as it really is from a working-class point of view. We have abundant cultural production *about* the workers as they appear to capitalist society—technical, sociological, moral, political literature, etc.—but very little about society in its various levels as it appears *to the workers*. What we know about the reality of industrial labor and the *professional culture* found even in the least skilled trades, we take primarily from a few Soviet novels and the occasional dry sociological inquiry destined for a non-working public. An appalling silence has fallen over working-class reality; it is this silence that makes possible the daily claims that the workers' condition has become acceptable and even comfortable, that class differences have softened.

This silence cannot be broken without the mediation of intellectuals. Attempts, notably in the German Democratic Republic, to create a workers' culture by encouraging writers and artists in the factories have resulted in failure. For culture creation is a *trade*, which presupposes an apprenticeship, the perfection and mastery of specific techniques. Notably, of a language and forms of expression capable of rehabilitating the workers' experience in all the richness of its individual and collective, contemporary and historical dimensions. These forms of expression will not be utilizable by everyone as their "common heritage" until they have been established by someone. This work of elaboration largely remains to be performed. It is of necessity a collective labor, but cannot be collective immediately. For if it is a matter of revealing the existence of a workers' culture— which is in reality a series of local, professional and oral subcultures—it is at the same time a matter of providing it with the means which it does not initially have for its self-discovery and self-affirmation as a culture. At this level, the mediation of intellectuals becomes necessary. Not only the kind of mediation exemplified by Brecht's theatre, the novel or "depth reporting," but also, and primarily, that which consists of providing the working class with a voice it recognizes as its own, after the event, because it says what the workers usually experience in silence and solitude.

There have been attempts at the beginnings of this kind of work in several countries with the collaboration of students or university teachers: tape-recorded interviews with workers in factories or at factory gates; questionnaires whose answers demand individual comment as well as factual information; films shot from life; biographies of workers and militants showing how life is conditioned by the history of the firm, of the dynasty of owners, of the economy, of science, of technology and of the international workers' movement.[22] A selection and montage of the questionnaires, interviews, films, etc., is then presented to the group of workers who collaborated in them so that these collective works can be collectively discussed, and so that workers may recognize themselves as the collective subject of the cultural work, of the values, demands, and language which it brings them, and so that by the mediation of this work they may see themselves as virtual creators of a possible culture and not as underprivileged consumers of an alien culture.

Therefore, the destruction of the cultural monopoly of the bourgeoisie will not take place by the mass diffusion of previous cultural production. The mass diffusion of "culture" is merely the diffusion of one kind of consumption goods amongst others. Its various forms—television, cinema, paperbacks, press—are based on the *centralization of communication* inherent in the "mass media." In other words, the "means of mass communication" do not allow the mass of individuals to communicate *one with another*, on the contrary, they allow the central communication of information and cultural products *to a mass* of individuals, which is maintained in the state of a silent, atomized mass, destined for passive consumption by the very unilateral character of this form of "communication."

It is not mass cultural consumption, but only the creation of their own culture by the dominated classes, which will break the bourgeois cultural monopoly.[23] To animate, inspire, or guide this cultural creation, to solicit permanent free expression and collective discussion, the exchange of experience and ideas among the rank and file is an essential task of the revolutionary party. It cannot cope with this task unless it enjoys a large mass base, particularly in the sites of production and education; unless it seeks the greatest development of democracy and initiative among the rank and file, where individuals are working and living collectively; unless it permanently stimulates free debate at all levels, so that the demands repressed by the society can be expressed and take consciousness of themselves in their depth and diversity; unless it draws in the intellectual forces which can give the working class its voice and language, can detect, reveal and formulate its deepest aspirations, can unify them at higher level in an anticapitalist perspective and "alternative."

In nearly all these respects, the task of the revolutionary party and the structure this demands are sensibly different in an advanced capitalist society from the task and structure of the Bolshevik party. The Leninist, later Stalinist, type of party was adapted to periods of acute crisis, of the probable, but not necessarily imminent, collapse of the capitalist system, of clandestine struggle, and of war. It is not impossible that such periods will recur, but it is not very likely. The working hypothesis on which the revolutionary party must base its activity is no longer a sudden seizure of power, made possible by the breakdown of capitalist mechanisms or a military defeat of the bourgeois state; but that of a patient and conscious strategy aimed at provoking a crisis in the system by the masses' refusal to bend to its logic, and then resolving this crisis in the direction of their demands.

However, the renewal of the revolutionary party in accord with its present task runs up against resistance that cannot be explained as an imprint of Stalinism considered as a "historical accident." On the contrary, we have to explain why this imprint could be so deep and so durable. An explanation by external influences or historical conjunctures will not do. On the contrary, it must be admitted that the Stalinist type of party corresponds to one of the permanent tendencies, or temptations, of the workers' movement even, where it is possessed of a strong class consciousness and revolutionary tradition.

This is the temptation of the *ideological withdrawal* of the working class in regard to capitalist society. This withdrawal may well be associated on occasion with opportunist political practice. In fact, its goal is not the immediate revolutionary overthrow of capitalism, but, on the contrary, the strengthening of class consciousness and organization in a period still hardly propitious for revolutionary action. It is a form of revolutionary *attentisme*. Precisely because the working class (or its most advanced sector), although already highly politicized, powerfully organized, and certain of its ultimate victory, cannot count on an immediate seizure of power, it tends to defend itself against the relaxation of its structures, the flagging of its will, the disintegration of its unity, and the temptations and immediate advantages of reformist participation by fortifying itself in its own existence through isolation between itself and the society in which it exists.[24] It constitutes itself as an order apart. Its party incarnates the society of the future. Indeed, it prefigures the socialist state yet to be born, so much so that the party already conducts itself as a state: the hierarchical relations between the leaders are those characteristic of the relations of a head of state or government with its ministries and civil service. A protocol recalling that of official visits marks the tours and visits of party delegates. The fraternal relations between parties are governed by rules recalling those of diplomatic relations between states. The party demands of its militants the same kind of discipline as the state of the dictatorship of the proletariat, besieged by internal and external enemies, does of its citizens.

In short, the party has most of the internal characteristics of a post-revolutionary party, holding a monopoly of power. And there is some sense in this behavior: the ultimate crisis must someday break out; when it does, the socialist state must emerge, armed from head to toe, thanks to the inflexible rigor with which the party has preserved its unity and purity. Until the day comes, the conditions of the masses will inevitably deteriorate, and their action can only amount to a protest that changes little. *Attentisme* and catastrophism go hand in hand.

Stalinist dogmatism allowed this attitude to survive for a long time. By strictly identifying the USSR with socialism, socialism with Soviet society and its copies, and the world victory of socialism with the victory of the Soviet camp (which imperialism was inevitably bound to attack some day), Stalinism solved to its own satisfaction the problem of the "global alternative," of the positive "model" for the inspiration and guidance of the workers' movement. It allowed the working class to refuse the ideological and cultural hegemony of the bourgeoisie *without having to resort to the mediation of intellectuals*: it was enough to consider bourgeois society and culture from the point of view of a society and culture to come which had already materialized in another place; to oppose all the unresolved problems *here* to the solutions applied *there*, and to interpret the course of events as the inexorable decline of capitalism.

In this perspective, there is no sense in more exhaustive analysis, in the elaboration of the remedies to be applied and the action aimed at imposing them; they would only serve to prolong the life of the system; it seemed unrealistic to suppose that they might deepen the contradictions by forcing the bourgeoisie into granting concessions that could be turned against it. It was all or nothing.

Stalinism thus appears as an ideology of the withdrawal of the working class: it isolates and protects it against the surrounding society, provides it with a perspective owing nothing to bourgeois ideology, nor even to an autonomous intelligentsia. It constituted (and still, in new forms, constitutes) a typical primitivist deviation: an attempt at working-class autarchy in the fields of ideology and culture; a dogmatic rejection not only of the surrounding capitalist society, but also of the scientific, artistic, and cultural production carried on within this society, on the pretext that this production was not proletarian (which was true) and that it reflected the decadence and crisis of capitalism and had hardly any interest for the revolutionary struggle (which was sometimes true, sometimes false).[25] The subjective advantage of this primitivist deviation is that it allowed the proletariat to establish for itself *a postrevolutionary point of view* against the bourgeoisie and to reject bourgeois ideological domination in the name of a simple alternative ideology.

The sterility of this attitude in the context of advanced capitalism is generally recognized today in the European communist movement as a whole. Ideological withdrawal, which could be of value in an earlier historical conjuncture, would today tend to isolate the workers' movement not only from possible political allies but also from new generations of workers, more differentiated both in aspirations and in interests, and from the intellectual avant-garde, whose mediation is indispensable to the hegemonic capacity of the revolutionary party.

Nevertheless, it is easier to recognize the necessity of a renewal of the methods and structures of the revolutionary party than to achieve this renewal. The difficulty often derives less from the resistance of the party machine to change[26] than from the attachment of the most militant and embattled part of the proletariat to the primitivist attitude of withdrawal. For this ageing generation of working-class militants, the effectiveness and radiance of the party are of less account than its homogeneity: it is at once a homeland, a refuge, and a source of moral comfort. As it evolves; as the socialist societies of Europe evolve; as the USSR comes to abandon its function as leader-state and socialist model, as the problems of the construction of socialism, the solutions they call for, and the roads to socialism that can be envisaged in various parts of the world diversify, part of the old working-class rank and file will be tempted to see in this evolution not the consequence of objective changes, but an opportunist revision or betrayal of the basic principles of the international revolutionary movement.

This partly explains the caution and slowness with which certain parties are renewing themselves. The absolute datum line that the Stalinist model has been for the communist movement cannot be rejected all at once, particularly if there is nothing very much to put in its place.

But it is also impossible to retain this model, now that the unresolved problems with which it has saddled the socialist societies have become so obvious. Certainly, it made possible a rapid development, but it is also the source of the retardations and contradictions that must now be overcome.

From this point of view, the task of reflection on a socialist "model of development" and a socialist "alternative" adapted to the conditions of industrially developed countries has also become necessary. This demands a critical examination of the reasons for the difficulties and delays that have appeared; the ways to avoid and transcend them; the kind of civilization that the socialist movement must aim at when the development of the productive forces allows the creation of the su-perfluous, and no longer only the necessary. This examination is the business of all Marxists and socialists; by carrying it out in common, they can demonstrate the vitality of their movement and its fidelity to its original objectives.

THE MAY EVENTS AND
REVOLUTION IN THE WEST

Lucio Magri

It is true that it was a certain political and social crisis which gave birth to the May events and that they were played out to a background of that crisis. But their significance is not limited to this. In fact, they can be considered the most important revolutionary upsurge which has so far taken place in an advanced capitalist country. By studying these events, we can test many hypotheses which have been built up over the years, find many stimulating questions and even suggestions which may well be valid for many countries and for a whole historical epoch. The May events are the most well-equipped laboratory in which to do research about revolution in the West. In this concluding chapter,[1] we shall only attempt a few reflections and try to tackle some of the problems arising from the experience of May. These are, of course, just the first steps in its exploration.

I. THE IMPASSE OF THE REVOLUTION IN THE WEST

It is becoming more and more accepted that revolution is an urgent need in Western society. In the neocapitalist world, the faith in the inevitable progress of humanity toward a bright future has survived much less successfully than it did in the world of nineteenth-century capitalism. In differing ways, many people who are not Marxists have begun to be conscious that the present system is wrong. Moreover they are beginning to realize that even in its very development, its contradictions become sharper and its inhumanity increasingly evident.

Our society is characterized by the wealth of its scientific knowledge and technical resources; but these have not brought about the liberation of man; they have not made him master of all things. On

41

the contrary, they have reduced him to an instrument of production. Work, once emancipated from the most elementary forms of struggle against nature, could finally have become a free and creative expression of man's personality. But it has not: it has become more and more alienated, both in its aims and in its forms.

Consumption, once freed from the struggle for survival, could have become something more than the simple and passive act of taking possession of a number of things. It could have enriched both the individual and the community, given them new channels of expression; on the contrary, it has been degraded to a mere function of production. It has become a mass-produced form of idleness, of possessiveness and dissipation. Education is now open to a larger number of people, and the means of communication have broken down many barriers; but all this has only served to give more efficiency to nonsensical activities, or to establish new irrational myths. Political institutions seem to have become more stable, the rules of formal democracy seem safer; meanwhile, actual power is concentrated into fewer and fewer hands, repression is subtler and more efficient and reaches deep into the consciousness of the people; and again and again violence is done to all those who manage to avoid integration. The world is becoming unified, empires and religious barriers are broken, but racialism and nationalism arise again from new bases; new status and caste symbols are invented. What more is needed to establish that reformist optimism, whether liberal or socialist, has come to an end? In the West, not only art and philosophy, but even common sense, have for a long time been aware, in a confused and desperate way, of the critical state of the world surrounding them. The May movement marked a new decisive step forward in this awareness, for the first time showing how it is becoming, or at least can be transformed into, the will to struggle, political action, and social commitment.

Still, this does not bring us much closer to solving the problem of revolution in the West. In Europe itself, fascism has taught us how the fact that a society is doomed and a revolution is necessary is not of itself enough for a revolution to take place. A catastrophic outcome is always possible and in order to avoid it the existing society must produce, out of its own crisis, the "material" with which to build an alternative. Moreover, there must be forces which are capable and determined enough to make good use of the chances offered by history. From this point of view, the May experience tells us that this is no simple matter. The fact that it ended with a defeat does not really matter; it may well be only a temporary one, caused by delays and mistakes on the part of the political forces, which it is still possible to overcome and correct; what is essential, though, is that the May experience, while posing the problem of revolution in the West, has at the same time shown all the novelty and the difficulty of actually making it. In all their character-istics—the forces mobilized, the contents of the struggle, the organi-zational forms tried out—the May events teach us that the question of revolution "in its highest form" cannot just be taken up again at the point where it was interrupted in 1923.

The May movement was very radical in content and this, together with its great spontaneity, was a basic factor in its mobilizing power; at the same time, these are also basic factors in its novelty and conse-quently in the problem of analyzing it. Up to now, where the socialist revolution has taken place, it has been "socialist" of a particular kind; in fact, the proletariat has gained power by utilizing and coordinating, towards a common objective, forces and energies which arose from the inadequacies of developing capitalism (such as the peasant problem or the national question). It is not by chance that, so far, the revolution has involved the conquest of state power by a very strictly organized vanguard. Furthermore, one of the first tasks of the new society has been to secure, through years of hard work, the same level of primi-tive capital accumulation already achieved by capitalism in many other countries. As a consequence, the transition to communism has had to be delayed. So far an attempt has been made, with very little result, to reproduce this scheme in Western societies, using the frontist strategy based on the contradictions which appeared with fascism, as well as on the relative backwardness of Europe. But the experiences of May have strikingly demonstrated the worthlessness of this approach. Of course, even in its most advanced forms, capitalist society is complex and in-consistent, full of privilege, of status, of parasitism. Development and underdevelopment, the cult of productivity and Malthusianism, are constantly intertwined. The theory of "pure capitalism," so dear to the Second International, is completely disproved even within the very strongholds of the system. Still, it is now easy to see in these complex social relationships the mechanism which controls and sustains them. Each one of these phenomena, once analyzed, does not appear as a remnant from the past, nor yet as a frontier still to be conquered, but on the contrary all are indissolubly linked to the development of the system of which they are merely new and changing aspects. This means that no contradiction or cause of contention can be made to explode, nor its solution found, unless its very roots—the capitalist system—are immediately and explicitly discovered and removed. This applies to all issues, even the most traditional ones, the most "bourgeois-democratic" ones (such as antiauthoritarianism), and the most trade unionist ones (such as the elementary defense of the immediate conditions of the working class). Taking the case of authoritarianism, for example, we can find its roots in the social and economic processes—the division of labor, mass culture, the conditioning of consensus, centralized planning—which are themselves its direct presuppositions, its essential instruments.

But it is not easy to make a revolution that, right from the beginning, is explicitly antibourgeois in all its contents. First of all, in an advanced capitalist society there is not a simple polarization between capitalists on one side and proletarians on the other, where the two become increasingly antagonistic and increasingly conscious of this antagonism. On the contrary, there is an extremely complex social scheme in which a socialist transformation would harm the immediate interests of strong groups, while on the other hand the proletariat itself at present is fragmented into diverse conditions of life, work and culture.

Moreover, it has become evident that the proletariat, as well as other potentially revolutionary strata, can become really interested in a socialist revolution only on certain conditions. It is not enough for them to know that the revolution will assure a quantitative rise in the standard of living, education, and personal and social security; they want to be sure that it is the transition to a society where work is freer, where the division between the state and society no longer exists, and where the individualistic way of life and consumption no longer prevail. It is now clear that this cannot be achieved simply by transferring state power into the hands of a party which has grown out of the working class, nor merely by state ownership of the means of production. And the May movement is the best proof of how difficult it is in the heat of the struggle to direct the majority of the population toward the concrete objective of state power. It has also proved, moreover, how little the word "socialism" means even to the vanguard unless it implies, immediately and substantially, the liberation of man.

On the other hand, the very events of May have shown that we cannot hope to find a solution to the problem through the spontaneous explosion of a catastrophic crisis, or through the "inevitable progress of forces of production." Waste, parasitism and irrationality do not suffocate the dynamics of production of an advanced capitalist society: in most cases they are functional to it. Political and social struggles, however acute, do not signify a disintegrating society or a paralyzed economy; on the contrary, they often result in a dynamic reaction on the enemy's side, urging him forward rather than pushing him back. The contradiction within the system is not an expression of its arrested development but rather of social unease, of desires aroused but repressed and of emerging antagonistic forces, all of which are by-products of it. On the other hand, we can no longer talk of a positive-negative polarization between the forces involved in production and the social relations arising from it, in which the former is striving toward a better system and the latter is acting as a brake. On the contrary, the forces of production themselves (science, technology, and professional needs and capabilities) tend to surmount the confines of the system while at the same time being deeply scored by it; their shape is that imposed on them by exploitation and they are susceptible to the requirements of the system. The theory of the progression from spontaneity to consciousness, an axiom of the traditional working class movement, is sensibly being changed. Spontaneity seems less restricted, less "within the system" than Lenin thought, and more susceptible toward socialist perspectives. On the other hand, conscious political interpretation must take place, because without it the revolutionary dynamics and forces of the situation are less cogent and less disruptive, and socialism itself appears inevitably as "immature," "a leap in the dark," "an act of violence," compared with the immediate state of affairs.

This ambiguity is primarily to be found among the social classes— the most important of all forces of production. Throughout the May events, none of the social groupings proved themselves capable of arriving at a revolutionary position spontaneously—even in its vanguard, was the spontaneous movement able to do more than express an extraordinarily radical spirit of revolt?—and afterwards, the defeat has surely brought us to realize how strong the influence is in our society of those people who do feel the need of a change but who are not at all willing to accept the risks of an adventure, the pure logic of a refusal and a total crisis.

All this leads to the realization that new and major contradictions can explode in an advanced capitalist society, and a revolutionary front can be constructed, only if an alternative force is already active within the social body; this force must illuminate the socialist perspectives within the present society, consequently developing its requirements, providing solutions, unifying scattered forces and constructing a political force able to transcend the choice between Jacobinism and anarchism. This indicates, or at least encourages, the development of a revolutionary strategy that does not put a wall between "before" and "after" the conquest of state power, and which builds the "historical bloc" of forces, united through concrete struggles and positive objectives, which already contains the seeds of socialism; a strategy which conceives socialism as the immediate transition to communism. This is the road that Gramsci first tried to define and which some Western Communist parties have attempted to follow, though with limitations and prevarications, as we shall see presently.

This road, however, has been blocked by another aspect of advanced capitalism: the great rigidity of the system and its power of integration. In this integration of the various national economies within one capitalist system, the alternatives, concerning investments and the division of labor, are controlled by the international market and cannot be regulated by any one country. At the same time, in each individual country, all sectors of production become themselves integrated into a single system, which together with the expansion of investment regulates all present and future development: consumption is hence increasingly subordinated to production, and production to profit. As a result of both these processes, it becomes increasingly difficult to modify a section of the economy of a single country, or its general line of development, in a direction which endangers its equilibrium and which is other than that of the system as a whole. And it is even more difficult to find possible alternative equilibria within the system which are susceptible to reformist pressures without interrupting its development. In other words, the system is so strong and compact that reforms which are gradual and prudent are soon reabsorbed and totally distorted, and those which go beyond the permitted limits let loose a chain reaction which immediately leads to the "revolution-reaction" polarization they sought to avoid.

Because of these phenomena, the very conditions are lacking in Italy that might engender a political force capable of being autonomous vis-à-vis the system and able to strive for significant reforms that open the way to revolution. This general problem has many aspects: the increasing conditioning of the productive process upon individual personality as well as upon the collective consciousness; the growth of investments and their automatic character; the selectivity of the system as regards scientific research and the uses to which it puts technical achievements; the crisis of all culture that is not specialized and technical; the malfunctioning of representative institutions and the general debilitation of political power, prevented by its own authoritarianism from any freedom of choice. We must not therefore be deceived by any apparent public control of the economy; it does not represent a real political control exercised autonomously within the system, but demonstrates the degree of integration of the state by the society of which it is the expression.

The development of advanced capitalist society is distinguished by a continuity in which every choice is deeply conditioned by the choices which have been made beforehand or are being made contemporaneously. The system is constantly blackmailing its opponents with the threat of a crisis, and far too many social groups are extremely sensitive to this. If we really desire to oppose the system, it is not enough just to remove certain political and social power relations; we must reconstruct a complete alternative way of life, of thinking, producing, and consuming. Herein we can see the total crisis of reformism, which has become so evident in Italy and England, for instance, in recent years, and which the crisis of May so fundamentally exposed.

The contradiction facing the Western revolutionary movement is then evident. In order to achieve victory, it must gradually build an alternative to the system. But the alternative must not only be in words, in ideals; it must be a mass movement, able to anticipate a socialist future, to create new demands and new capabilities. It must be a conscious and well-organized force, able to take the lead and to change society at its roots. This is one face of the contradiction. The other is that the system, with its strength, its mechanisms of integration, and its rigidity, leaves little space for the creation of this alternative, but at the same time the question of power is posed in very radical and immediate terms. Consequently, the Left in Western Europe is always oscillating between worn-out and increasingly subordinated reformist positions and abstract dreams of extreme revolt. Thus, within Western Marxism, there are many trends which, though bitterly criticizing the system and its deformations, place most of their revolutionary hopes outside the borders of Western society, in the struggle of the oppressed people of the world (e.g., Baran and Sweezy), or, with conscious pessimism, link the destiny of the revolution to the rebellion of alienated minorities, and to a "philosophy of values" (e.g., Marcuse). Both approaches, in fact, have ceased to consider communism as a "real" movement in the West, and a necessity within the dialectics of capitalism.

II. NEW REVOLUTIONARY INCENTIVES

There is no doubt that the May events have posed the question of this "impasse" and of its accompanying contradictions in a clear and often dramatic way. Still, perhaps for this very reason, the May events have also revealed a solution and the way to it.

First of all, the May events have suddenly brought to light many objective and material pressures produced by capitalist development itself that tend to overthrow the logic of the system and are themselves the premises of a really different one. We shall here recall some of them, with no attempt at an analysis. We just wish to point to a direction for research and a hypothesis for consideration.

Why did student revolt take such a radical character? Was it only because of the revolutionary ideology which some groups borrowed from the experiences of the Third World, and from new extremist cultural fashions acting on an already acute social instability? An analysis of the facts would seem to prove the contrary. Many different currents, both in levels of contradiction and ideological positions, were to be found in the student revolt in May. An analysis of the ways in which the university crisis has exploded in various capitalist countries shows that some of these contradictions can be solved, or at least rendered less acute, by the very development of the system itself (always providing that it can overcome the present crisis). This applies particularly where the organization of education is centralized and authoritarian, and where the necessary material expenditure has not been provided, and where there is a sharp dichotomy between the university and the requirements of the labor market. Moreover, the system has at its disposal many ways to contain higher education and to use it for its own purposes; in France, as in Italy, many of these have not been utilized yet. The most important of them is the downgrading of the university degree and the setting up of increasingly differentiated courses and different standards of diplomas. This would serve to reestablish on the plane of higher education the selection between wage-earners and the ruling class, traditionally carried out in the primary and secondary schools. Once having reached a certain level of development and being assured of a scholastic structure adequate for its needs, the system can then conveniently encourage mass education as a means to contain unemployment, to augment a plethora of unproductive research and to provide personnel for the tertiary sector of the economy. But behind the question of student revolt there is a much deeper contradiction, which came out clearly in May and which is inherent to the system and to its possible development. And this overriding contradiction, which both unifies the revolt and gives it a revolutionary character, is the mass of knowledge needed by the system at an ever-increasing rate, not only at high levels of research but also for all executive and managerial roles. This high level of knowledge, though, is not matched by the actual tasks performed by the worker, nor in the development of his career, nor in his ability to participate in the decision-making processes. The students realize that even those lucky enough to find jobs will be faced with unbearable disillusionment both at work and in their social life; that their chances of advancement or improvement in either are extremely problematical. What is facing them is not the "ascent" of the self-confident bourgeois individual, but rather the progressive physical and intellectual decay in the past reserved for the proletariat. The doom pronounced by Nizan is truer than ever: at forty, a bourgeois is a dead man. Higher education is no longer the hard but safe road towards membership of the ruling class. It has now become a desperate race to enter an increasingly restricted power elite; and after a while most of the competitors will feel the serious gap between their aspirations and potentialities and the concrete reality of everyday life. This contradiction is first noticeable in a particularly acute form in France and Italy, where an old university structure is still working to produce a nineteenth-century ruling class. This aggravates the dichotomy between cultural knowledge and professional requirements, with the absurdly encyclopaedic "basic theory" taught at the university (totally useless both for research workers and technicians), in stark contrast to the backwardness of professional knowledge. This contrast is a basic and permanent element in all capitalist countries and it constitutes the objective origin of the student revolt, which was born as a rebellion against the division of labor, against the uses of science, the worship of productivity, and the restricted concentration of power. Students are extremists because they are a new revolutionary group; every step forward of the system can only aggravate the contradiction.

An even deeper contradiction may emerge from the revolt of the students and intellectuals. In May, we saw a primary role being played by some sections of the intelligentsia in the scientific field (pure sciences, sociology, and town planning), which traditionally had been among the main supports of the system. Is this only a phenomenon of the "proletarianization of the intellectuals" already mentioned? Or is it possible that this phenomenon arises, albeit in a confused and contradictory way, from the fact that by preselecting its goals and imposing its methodology, the system has now become a brake on the real development and application of scientific research? In turn, science itself, because of the logic of the force autonomously developing within it, rebels against this. May we not be approaching the end of the time when science and technology seemed closely linked to exploitation, automation, and specialization, and when they almost naturally accepted the place created for them within the system? Might not the revolt of the physicist, of the biologist, of the social scientist, economist, and town planner express something more than his protest as a new exploitee, cut off from power? Might it not also express the birth of a consciousness of the fact that it is no longer possible to conquer new fields of knowledge, to be a good physicist, biologist, etc., to criticize the structure of these disciplines now undergoing such a crisis—except within the framework of a new society and a new culture? What happened in France and what is happening in the world makes these questions valid and legitimate, although a simple reply is not possible at this stage.

It is also important to discover the basic reasons for the rebellion of the working class—so unforeseen, general, and militant. Can the return of political questions and forms of struggle forgotten for decades be simply put down to the severity of Gaullist oppression or to the agitation of small political groups? For us, the new extremism of some sections of the working class, and which affects the whole class, has deep and objective causes. In May, a leading role was played by two types of workers who had never previously been outstanding in trade union struggles: on the one hand, these were the young un-skilled workers, condemned to the most repetitive and underpaid jobs, and, on the other, the young technicians skilled enough to perform delicate tasks that control the productive process, but who have no chance of joining the managerial staff. Clearly these two categories are the most directly linked to the development of modern capitalist industry and its organization of labor; moreover, they are the groups most exploited and alienated by it. In the dynamics of social devel-opment they are the permanent reserve of misfits and rejects, which can be profitably squeezed, expended, and replaced with more young and fresh fodder. In some advanced capitalist countries, this contradic-tion has been contained by employing discriminated social minorities (Negroes and other "racially inferior" social groups) to perform the menial tasks while at the same time holding out strong social and fi-nancial inducements to encourage the integration of the technicians. But these tensions cannot be bought off for long; nor does economic development tend to alleviate them. Clearly such problems cannot be dealt with by traditional trade union methods. In various ways, they challenge the capitalist organization of labor, the relationship between education and professional requirements, the question of professional careers, and the rhythm of work and the power structure in the facto-ries themselves. And since it is not easy to raise these issues as concrete demands, a radical but confused sense of rebellion suddenly springs up spontaneously, both against the system and against the impotence of the trade unions, which cannot do anything about it. In France, as in Italy, where the relative backwardness of the economy and the absurd importance of the most parasitic sectors adds to the depreciation of the workers' salaries, the newest sectors in rebellion have discovered in the traditional channels of struggle a viable terrain on which to fight. This in turn gives to the traditional struggles a potentially radical content, which is always present even if it does not immediately manifest itself.

Finally, let us consider the phenomenon which in the May events has appeared to everyone as the most novel and least expected: the extraor-dinary need for human communication and for life in common; the enthusiasm with which the great mass, educated and conditioned by the models of consumer society, rebelled against those models, agreeing to consider them absurd and, if only for a short time, showing themselves ready to give them up without difficulty; and the ease with which, in

cover its refusal to analyze in Marxist terms the problems of the existing socialist societies and the models of socialism possible elsewhere. Perhaps, from a political point of view, this attitude may once have been understandable. Today, though, the opposite is true, since political necessity itself requires us to tackle the question seriously. State ownership of the means of production and power in the hands of the Communist parties have not been enough to avoid or contain the rise of new contradictions in the countries that have already achieved their revolution; moreover, in the countries that have not, it is clear that the revolution will not be achieved unless some theory of socialism, taking hold of the masses of the people, contributes to precipitate the crisis of the existing system. In this respect, completely new themes have to be tackled. The paths indicated by Marx in the *Critique of the Gotha Programme*, by Lenin in *The State and Revolution*, or the simpler formula of the late Lenin (soviets and industrialization) can only serve as distant guides to our work, which must be a real scientific research, involving a degree of political inventiveness for which, after all, the materials are provided only by history.

From the point of view of theory—the development of a model—two main questions condition all others. On the one hand, how to achieve the management of production by the producers, in a way that is directly socialist and irrevocable and that once and for all excludes the sovereignty of the market and the exploitation of work. The other question is how to achieve the "withering away" of the state as a separate structure and the establishment of a superior form of democracy that will finally lead to the transcending of democracy itself, as of any other form of political power. In Marx's times, these two questions seemed the fruit of a far-seeing genius; today, they are the core of a confused research arising from actual necessity—albeit in diverse forms. Some discussion and a few chance experiences in recent years have shown that there are no possible shortcuts or easy solutions. Some had fostered the illusion that simple measures of decentralization or liberalization would be enough to ensure the social management of the economy or the development of democracy in a socialist system. But the illusion did not last long. People were forced to see that such objectives imply the need to find a solution to the fundamental problems of the social order. A new technology, a new organization of labor, a new kind of consumption, new institutional forms, a new leveling of social inequalities are needed—new relationships of production, in fact. An economy cannot be managed in the real interests of society unless it has undergone a qualitative change in most of its aspects; nor can it be democratically directed if it still contains major elements of repression and stratification.

For this reason, socialist society still seems a society in a state of transition; despite great qualitative changes, this is inevitable when compared to the highest stage of capitalist development, especially where certain countries are concerned, such as those in Eastern Europe, where serious problems of scarcity still exist. And this leads to the second, fundamental series of questions: How are we to judge the efficacy of the structures, institutions and concrete alternatives operating in a given society in a given phase, in such a way as to develop a program of transition to communism in which the long-term perspective is guaranteed without damaging the immediate requirements of the actual starting point?

It must be emphasized, though, that the problems of socialism cannot be solved in advance, or abstractly around a table. The solution must come from generalizing particular experiences, from considering processes as they are taking place; by definition, therefore, precise and consistent answers can only be found in the heat of a revolutionary crisis. It is essential, though, that we remove all prejudices which might hinder or distort our research. These prejudices no longer derive from the Soviet model or from the "sacred" texts, but above all from the empiricism of the theory of "national roads." Frequently, this theory raises original questions in the concept of socialism, only to find original ways of suppressing them. In this way, any reflections or judgments on the existing socialist societies are suppressed—they are "absolved" by the principle of the autonomy of each country; and so too is the possible character of future revolutions—in the name of "specific situations" and the improvisation of history. Actually, the only principle concerning revolution in the West that has escaped this double obstacle is that of "respect for a multiparty system and the traditional forms of freedom." This, though, only serves to prove how superficial the analysis has been so far; if the existence of many parties can and must be guaranteed within a Western society, why should it not be so in a society that has known socialism for over fifty years but where it has been clearly demonstrated that internal political and social contradictions remain? Why should the views of Christian Democrats be thought useful and stimulating within Italian socialist society, while those of a "pro-Chinese" communist be thought sterile and dangerous within Soviet socialism? To go deeper: How is it possible to guarantee the existence of many parties once the roots of private property have been removed? What new mechanisms and institutions will be used for this purpose? Or let us suppose that the future socialist system is completely democratic both toward classes and ideologies: How shall the effective political leadership of the proletariat be assured, since this class has never had the social and intellectual tools at its disposal for a natural hegemony? All this is not to deny that the problem of democracy is important, even in its traditional aspects; but it does give a concrete example of how, even in the areas where it has been most comprehensive, the research into socialism has been inadequate and dominated by contradictory tactical exigencies.

For our part, the events in May have demonstrated that if this work is not brought up-to-date very soon, at least in the West, some of those who would otherwise contribute to the revolution, but who are worried by existing socialist systems, may think that it is not worth risking a revolution to achieve *that* kind of socialism. There are others who will fight a revolutionary struggle but only in terms of a complete rejection of everything, or a naïve and anarchistic desire for total and immediate freedom.

In the present stage, many of the tensions latent within the social body are bound to remain, without assuming any political relevance. This is because a viable alternative is lacking that would help people understand the real situation and the social roots of their personal unhappiness.

The necessity of developing a socialist perspective that is both theoretically accurate and politically concrete is not only required in the name of intellectual coherence, nor because of the necessity of making the long-term perspective clear and persuasive. It is needed above all to exploit the latent contradictions within this society and bring them to the boil: to ripen the revolutionary consciousness in those cases where it cannot mature spontaneously. In short, we have to create a politi-cosocial bloc that is consciously anticapitalist, homogeneous enough to embody an alternative, and strong enough to stand the test of a radical reconstruction of society. But the essence of modern capitalist society is to prevent the superstructure having any real autonomy and to absorb and distort any opposition that presents itself in a primarily ideological form. Therefore the question of a socialist perspective can only survive and operate insofar as it shifts its base from discussion, propaganda, and education to the plane of political and social practice: to that of mass struggle around specific objectives starting from the dynamic of immediate demands and progressively developing their revolutionary content.

There are those who see immediate struggles in trade union terms only and who would introduce the need for a revolutionary solution only as a propagandist and ideological addition. This scheme seems more inadequate than ever today. And more legitimate than ever is the necessity for research into intermediate objectives of struggle that would ripen the subjective and objective conditions of a revolutionary solution. In Italy this strategy is known by the rather unfortunate name of "structural reforms." Still, the May events have tended to vindicate it and given it stimulus. This vindication can be seen negatively, by the lack of intermediate objectives in May that were authentically antagonistic to the system and also strongly linked both to the consciousness of the masses and to a perspective of social transformation; their absence prevented the growth of the movement and the strengthening of its unity. But it can also be seen positively. It was proved that a mass revolutionary consciousness can develop without a general economic crisis, but through the development and growth of particular struggles linked to specific contradictions within the society. Besides, in the words of student leaders such as Dutschke and Cohn-Bendit, we can find a full understanding of the necessity of this general strategy well expressed in the slogan of "the long march through the institutions."

The diffidence of the new forces of the Left toward the "strategy of reforms"—often developing into a rejection of any concrete objectives or partial victory—is based on its frequent reduction to mere reformism, seen both in practice and by implication in many theoretical definitions. Still looking at May, we can say that these fears are not without foundation; if only because that very experience has put into relief a number of distinctive elements in the conception of the struggle for reform that had never before been clearly exposed. Besides, the existence and gravity of the problem is proved by this paradox: the student movement is totally hostile to reforms and yet it is still the first movement in Europe in twenty years to have led a real mass struggle for the reform of a social structure (the university). This struggle employed means and aims that led it to challenge the whole social system, whilst those who claim to support the concept of a "struggle for reforms," such as the Communist parties, have never in fact led a real one (although they have certainly directed decisive political and trade union battles). The diffidence mentioned previously, therefore, can only be overcome if some very simple points are finally clarified.

The first concerns the relationship between reforms and revolutionary crises. We can no longer remain sitting on the fence; we must choose. On the one side there is the strategy that envisages the revolution as the result of a long transition from capitalism to socialism through a series of reforms, while, contemporaneously, the leading sections advance on the control points of the state. On the other, there is the strategy in which the struggle for reforms provides the best possible conditions for the inevitable revolutionary crisis to ripen and for the "bloc of forces antagonistic to the system" to be created that, in the heat of the crisis, will conquer the state machine and break it. Many years' experience and the lessons of May show that only this second line can stand the test.

A struggle for reforms that introduces subjective and objective elements into society antagonistic to it will create a crisis and a polarization of forces. The system, on the one hand, tries to present itself as a well-defined entity, while the opposition forces tend to desert the institutional environment and assume the function of a living critique of the power of the existing state. This does not, of course, mean that any struggle that does not end up in revolution is doomed to sterility or only to be valued as an experience, nor that shifts in the political balance or program at state level have no relevance; but it does mean that if such a struggle has *really* achieved something, if such shifts have represented a real crisis within the balance of power, then they must have created the base for sharper antagonisms. They must have accelerated the process leading to a wider crisis, the result of which cannot but be a revolutionary leap forward, either by arms or by the "peaceful" weapons of insubordination and mass struggle.

Here we come to the second point. The struggle for reform is not the same thing as reformism, if we accept that in the present stage of capitalist society new pressures have developed within certain social groupings and aspects of society—pressures that are objectively antagonistic to the system and that pose the need for a superior one. In fact, it is as a result of capitalist development that socialism has today become a historical necessity. If this were not so, it would be impossible to refute the well-known Leninist thesis that intermediate objectives can escape a reformist fate only if proposed in a time of revolutionary crisis. In this new concept of the struggle for reforms, therefore, it is the key sectors of the system that are the vital ones; the protagonists must be the revolutionary social forces, and the objective that of introducing tensions and contradictions into the system. It is the logic of the social necessity for a reform that has to be considered and not its degree of compatibility with the system as a whole. Therefore, such struggles must not be conceived or presented to make the existing society work better, to satisfy "national interests" or a "need for modernity and rationality"; this is not because they are intended as instruments of political subversion but rather because of their own intrinsic character. Their perspectives and their political synthesis are always outside the system. For example, let us take the university that the students want. The demand does not arise out of an ideological preference, but as the true projection of their need for culture and freedom. But such a university could not function within our present system; it would be the source of waste and chaos, since it would be a living contradiction of the predominant interests of society.

For these reasons—and this is our third point—struggles for reform can only make sense as movements of direct mass insubordination to the existing legal order, and not as a form of pressure of public opinion to be directed into institutional channels and from there to be integrated. This is because the specific logic that dominates all institutions would prevail—legalism and adherence to the "national interest." This does not mean that the struggle must take place completely outside the institutions. On the contrary, the latter may be the place where compromises are reached and partial results are codified, in those cases when the confrontation has not yet gone so far as to contest the whole of society. The crucible of the struggle, however, and its real conclusions, are always to be found outside the institutions. The moment it becomes institutionalized is a moment of temporary defeat; every compromise that has been obtained, by definition, becomes ground for the new initiatives of the system and can only be valuable insofar as there are forces strong enough both to make sure of it and to challenge it. In the long term, it is evident that this general strategy raises onto a new level and with a new clarity the whole question of "dual power," that is, of new democratic organs of power at the base; i.e., since it is not such a bad expression, of soviets.

We think that the May events require reflection and work in this very direction. They have shown that it is possible to detect contradictions in the advanced sectors of society onto which to graft a struggle that is both concrete and antagonistic to the system; that in this case the radical and fully explicit nature of the anticapitalist objectives has served to enlarge the movement, not to restrict it; that authentic struggles for reform can and must be based upon mass insubordination and "violent resistance"; and finally, that a real advance in the consciousness of the masses can only be achieved as a result of their direct involvement, and in the heat of acute political and social crisis. We are sincerely convinced that the strategy of the struggle for reforms has not been negated by the May events; but we must also honestly recognize that they do constitute the ultimate critique of the way in which the question has usually been tackled, both in theory and in political practice.

Central to all revolutionary strategy is the problem of discovering and analyzing the driving forces on which it can count. The crisis in May has provided many new suggestions on this question also.

First of all, it has made us rediscover the role that can be played by the working class in the socialist revolution of an advanced capitalist country, not only as the political vanguard of an army (whose basic assault troops are to be found elsewhere) but as the direct social protagonist of the revolutionary process. Never before has it been possible to see how vast the borders of the "new working class" have become; how there is a real class continuity among the different strata of wage-earners in advanced industry, and how the pressure arising objectively from the immediate problems of defending the interests of the working class calls for a rupture with the methods of labor organization and the division of power used by capitalism.

We have also learnt, however, how difficult it is for revolutionary potentialities to be consolidated into conscious struggle. A grave delay has accumulated in the formation of political consciousness, of cadres, of forms of organization adequate to the actual needs and potentialities of today. The problems of the unity and political mobilization of the working class, of surpassing "trade unionism" and finding methods of unified political struggle in the factories is once again paramount: the very problem around which, in Italy at least, the Communist Party was created. The real cause of the May defeat was that the whole French Left was completely unprepared to face this problem. But does this apply only to France? Here in Italy, have we not become used to accepting the ever-increasing gap between the social and political maps of the country as something obvious? Or that the predominant organization of the working class in the factories should be the trade unions? Or that in the struggle to obtain reforms, the organized working class should be less predominant than other social groupings? Or finally that as a matter of course in Italy there should be a grave division, both politically and in the content of demands raised, between the traditional working class and the new strata of intellectuals of production?

New possibilities are also evident on the question of social alliances. In the traditional strategy, the social allies of the proletariat were above all the peasants and those sections of the party bourgeoisie most oppressed by the monopolies. In May, and not only in May, the decisive allies on the workers' side were intellectuals and students. Both arrived at militant positions autonomously, without any real help from any organized force, either in the form of effective solidarity or of a serious debate. But are there not, if we only start working on a new level, other latent forces to be discovered, and other tensions on which to work? Here again there is completely new ground for concrete analysis, organizational experiments and the creation of new movements.

So the problem of social alliances becomes first of all a problem of unity among different strata and sectors of the proletariat, and between the proletariat and other groupings directly linked to the most modern forms of production and relatively privileged with respect to their incomes. But if this is so, it is also clear that this unity cannot be achieved on merely trade unionist grounds and that every section must be prepared to transcend its own immediate corporate interests. Thus the very concept of alliances tends to change, and to become synonymous for the "bloc of historical forces" unified in their common interest in a revolutionary solution. In this bloc, the working class retains the leading role only because it is the only class whose immediate interest tends to coincide with the needs of the revolution and which cannot actually liberate itself except ultimately by negating itself; nevertheless, the objectives and motives that bring other social groups to rally round it are also intrinsically anticapitalist. All this, however, carries the clear implication that this unity cannot be realized except through the mediation of a consciousness and an organization, i.e., the bloc must be political and social at the same time. The experience of May marked the end of the separation of political action from social struggles. Therefore, not only the traditional strategy of social alliances has entered a crisis, but also that of political alliances.

Social democracy and petty bourgeois radicalism—the allies so diligently wooed but so seldom won—have not failed the test because of the choices or directions they have taken. They have often tried to make contact with the movement, outbidding the communists by taking up demagogic positions. But they have failed in their rapport with the actual situation in the country. They have revealed themselves as they actually are: empty and impotent power machines, able to express the conservative aspect of some intermediate social groupings, and to represent them in elections, but completely unable to interpret the creative potential of these same people and to lead them in a real movement. When they refused to accept an alliance with Mitterrand and Mendès-France, the French students made a tactical mistake but grasped a strategic truth: that such an alliance, rather than being too difficult to achieve or too costly, is useless. In the midst of a very real confrontation, these political forces appeared to the students as false alternatives, mystifying structures behind which another game was being played—the game between the system, with its power and ideology, and the revolutionary movement. This is not intended to deny the importance of existing political forces, the practical impact of ideologies, the political value of traditions, or the need to conceive the revolution as the convergence of many different political forces. It does mean that we recognize the degeneration of certain political groups, in their structure and internal mechanisms and in their links with the masses; by now, they have come to represent the instrument used by the system to congeal certain social and ideological contradictions. Therefore, any revolutionary struggle must necessarily bring about a crisis in these groups, their leaders, and their ideology. In fact, the great political and ideological, as well as social, complexity of the May movement has shown that this crisis is ripe, and that some social strata and currents of thought, traditionally organized by radicalism and social democracy, have been searching for new ways of expression which will lead them autonomously to join the revolutionary front. Unity among the parties of the Left at this stage becomes mainly a tactical element in a much deeper process wherein a new deployment of political forces has to be created.

It would certainly be arbitrary to export these lessons from one country to another; in France, the crisis of the intermediate political forces is much more serious than elsewhere. Still, similar problems and tendencies can be found elsewhere, as for example in Italy, where, despite a rich tradition of mass parties, the political structure has clearly degenerated and is organically incapable of comprehending the real movements that are developing in the country. These movements, meanwhile, have developed into forces of contestation outside the political structure, and now encompass social and ideological sectors of the people that are traditionally Catholic or socialist.[1]

However, it must be stressed that this crisis does not take the form of splits or new regroupings within the traditional political forces; everywhere it has meant the radical criticism of their very essence—delegated democracy, bureaucratic structures, allocation of power and electoralism. In May, the crisis was not one of a particular alliance between left-wing parties, but of the very concept of a political alliance as an agreement at the top, around a minimal common programme, and among organizations that themselves reflect the structure of bourgeois democracy. Such a problem cannot be solved in the space of a day, since organizations and traditions are always much more glutinous than one would imagine. However, the problem has now reached historical maturity.

This leads us to discuss what is perhaps the most delicate and complex problem posed by the French experience: that of a new concept of the revolutionary party.

Of course, there were many who obediently followed the existing Communist Party and others who only lamented the absence of a "true revolutionary party" of a Leninist type. But the May movement had quite a different effect on the consciousness of most militants, especially the young ones, which arose from the actual experience of the movement. It was not only the particular policy or particular leaders of the PCF that were challenged, but the very concept of the revolutionary party, seen in terms of an organized vanguard with a well-defined ideology and a centralized leadership.

Now, how much is this libertarian polemic against the party as such the authentic expression of a new level of struggle, conditioned by its own development, and how much did it serve to disarm the movement, crucifying it on its own spontaneity? The facts do not permit a simple answer one way or the other. On the one hand, the new conditions in which revolutionary struggle takes place in advanced capitalism seem not only to confirm the need for such a political force, but even to make it more evident. It is most needed to provide some theoretical synthesis and organizational guidance, which would harmonize many spontaneous pressures into a strategic design and elaborate the tactics to be followed. No social contradiction can reach full ripeness without the presence of an alternative, nor can the socialist revolution avoid always being "premature." If this is so, then the role of political consciousness and organization has acquired a new value. Moreover, socialism, being a society in a state of transition, still has surviving elements of repression, albeit dying out, and it has been shown how the instruments of repression in the hands of the state and the bureaucracy can be the source of great dangers within socialist society. Is it not evident, then, that only the party, seen as a force founded by consensus, with a freely accepted discipline, can really provide the only acceptable "instrument of repression"? One, moreover, able to suppress itself when necessary, not to suffocate the social dynamics and to adapt itself according to the development of the revolutionary program.

On the other hand, the revolutionary party that can fulfill this task of stimulating and coordinating the social movements rather than that of substitution and delegation is not the one we know now. Gramsci's analysis led in this direction and as a result initiated a profound re-appraisal of the theory as well as the practice of the parties of the Third International. And, in our opinion, the May movement has provided further stimulation in the same direction as Gramsci, moving the problem of party democracy away from the sterile questions of differing types of delegated democracy (monolithism or factionalism) to the very fruitful question of the relationship between the masses and the party; in fact, between the party and its social practice. Questions of unity and internal debate were thus only a phase and a means with which to achieve radical change in this fundamental relationship. The student movement, for instance, has developed both a deep sense of unity and a great freedom of discussion because it chose the necessity for struggle as its basic point of reference. Certainly it lacked the cultural and organizational means that would enable it to develop into a permanent and coherent political force; but it has already offered a great practical lesson that goes counter to a whole political tradition—in which the struggle for power among some groups at the top has been camouflaged under complex ideological polemics or ossified theoretical positions. This served to avoid the need to face up to the creative problems that arise from real action. In other words, we think it is time to abandon once and for all the concept of the party as a professional body that is the custodian and guarantor of a "science," the principles of which it carries into the working class from outside. We must move on and arrive at the point where the party is seen as the channel of communication between the day-to-day conditions of the working class and its theoretical tradition—an element of constant stimulus to and synthesis of the actual social experience of the class. This substantially modifies the relationship between the party and the movement. It is no longer enough to affirm the autonomy of particular movements with respect to the party, which itself remains the privileged center of revolutionary consciousness. It must be conceded that revolutionary praxis is many-sided, that each separate inclination tends toward the universal, and that in the process of struggle new institutions, new organs of direct democracy, are created. In respect to this varied experience, the party cannot but be a point of synthesis, of fermentation, where the universal is extracted from the particular and the strategy is elaborated—a strategy, moreover, always open to question and always being challenged. It is not the movement that serves the party, but the party that serves the movement; it is not the party that will hold state power, but the masses that use the party to prevent political power from ossifying into the traditional state form. In other words, we must say goodbye to Jacobinism and go back to the Marxian concept of the socialist revolution as a social, not a political one. On these contradictions Lenin's concept of soviets is again viable—organs of class democracy, with no delegation of power and no "specialists."

Certainly, this line of analysis must be followed seriously and prudently. The working class needs organizations that fulfill the simultaneous role of tutor and mouthpiece, and which are suspicious of the call of anarchists, who would leave it defenseless. This is why in May the majority of the working class reacted with intransigent opposition when the student movement concentrated its most destructive powers of criticism on the CGT and the PCF. In this iconoclastic rage, the working class saw, quite correctly, the expression of bourgeois privilege, of the privilege of a social group that can live and fight, in political terms, outside definite organizations. Therefore, we must try to consider, in concrete terms, how both the party and the trade unions can be positively changed. What is the structure and internal life that will equip a revolutionary force to meet the needs of the new phase of the struggle? This is a complex problem, and we do not know the perfect recipe. One thing is certain, though: the time is now ripe to pose the problem, and furthermore to abandon the three cardinal principles that characterized the life and activity of the parties of the Third International—the delegation of political decisions and day-to-day management to a body of political professionals; the selection and continuity of this body through co-option from above, directed by a leading group seldom more than ten to fifteen strong; the separation of political debate into various levels; and the systematic way of achieving unity on a scale descending from the top to the base.

Clearly, these are not merely organizational questions; they imply a whole theory of the party. Just as clearly, though, factionalism is not the answer, since it would produce the same impasse; but because of this, we must not allow ourselves to become prisoners of our own mythology. Whoever understands the working class movement in the West, with all its problems, or examines it critically but without prejudices, will be aware that an effective revolutionary position implies not only the development of a certain line, but also the revision of the revolutionary instruments themselves. It is to the credit of the May events that not only have they pointed out the problem, but also they have provided an interesting hypothesis on how to tackle it.

Undoubtedly, the experience of May has offered some rich and stimulating suggestions; but they are far from being a strategic line or a political platform. They have exposed many more problems than they have been able to solve and they have shown that the theory and practice of the working movement is badly out of date, while providing some ideas for work and research to make this up. But time and energy are needed to do this, and even then, the one aspect essential to a revolutionary strategy will still have been neglected: the concrete analysis of existing forces, the elaboration of definite objectives to be fought for—a draft program. A strategic plan, a way to work for the revolution, has been suggested, but this plan has not been tested against a concrete analysis of French society or imperialism today. What was latent in the May movement was not actually a new or different strategy, but rather some of the basic, stimulating premises to one. The vacuum resulting from its absence, however, was often filled with enticing deviations, undefined activism, and revolutionary phrasemaking, all of which could later develop into serious obstacles to prevent the most positive and vital potentialities of the movement from maturing.

Therefore, while strongly emphasizing the novelty and richness of the May movement, we have not tried to give a picture of it that is either reassuring or an apology for it; we have suggested an analysis that clearly refutes the idea that a revolution was just around the corner. On the contrary, if the French Left, and primarily the PCF, had provoked a political and social crisis, aggravated it, and then left the breech open, thus overthrowing the regime, they would have run a very serious risk. It would have meant launching a drive that could only succeed if they were capable of a tremendous renovation and if many factors ran in their favor. Within a very short time, and in the course of a bitter confrontation, a delay of many years would have had to be made up. To have undervalued the size and importance of this problem, or to have tried to solve it, as many suggested, with a few clever tactical moves and by throwing its full weight behind the movement, would have signified an irresponsible rush into an adventure. But we hope we have shown how it was quite reasonable to have run such a risk in view of the many favorable objective and subjective conditions existing nationally and internationally at the time. However, in the present world and European crisis—which is far from being solved—it is an inevitable risk that will certainly recur; especially since, in view of the state of the crisis, there is not enough time or enough forces available to build a secure and organic alternative. The problem, therefore, is how to give a realistic evaluation of this risk of an adventure, not in order to avert it, but to cope with it.

The very idea of accepting and even aggravating a confrontation without being sure of winning, of engaging in a struggle without being absolutely clear how it will end, is totally repugnant to our generation, which well remembers the antifascist struggle, and is therefore very sensitive to the dangers of activism and adventurism. It is also repugnant to the working class as a whole, which has patiently constructed itself into a political force through long hard trials, and is genuinely afraid of compromising this.

And this leads to the last, and not least, of the lessons of May: the lesson of creativity and courage. This experience is of a movement that grew out of struggle, and from that struggle provided new political data and thus new dimensions of theoretical research. It teaches us to comprehend Marxism in a less pedantic and "enlightened" way, which is such an essential lesson in a society armed with many instruments of integration that can profoundly condition the will and the intelligence. Besides, haven't revolutions always occurred in the course of a dramatic crisis in which someone had enough courage to interpret latent dynamic possibilities, and also the courage to run the inevitable risk of failing? It is not by chance that all the revolutions we know of have been made by young people and young parties.

MARX AND ENGELS
AND THE CONCEPT OF THE PARTY

Monty Johnstone

I.

The concept of a proletarian party occupies a central position in the political thought and activity of Marx and Engels. "Against the collective power of the propertied classes," they argued, "the working class cannot act as a class except by constituting itself into a political party distinct from, and opposed to, all old parties formed from the propertied classes." This was "indispensable in order to ensure the triumph of the social revolution, and its ultimate end, the abolition of classes."[1] Yet nowhere do the authors of the *Manifesto of the Communist Party* set out in systematic form a theory of the proletarian party, its nature and its characteristics, any more than they do for social class or for the state, to both of which it is closely related. Moreover, within the broad general framework of their theory of class struggle and of revolution, they evolved their ideas on the forms and functions of proletarian parties as they went along, and related them to their analyses of often very different historical situations. They did not work out in advance any "plan" for the creation of a revolutionary proletarian party to which their subsequent theoretical work was geared;[2] and at no time did they themselves establish a political party. Having already, by the beginning of 1844, come theoretically to see the proletariat as the leading force for social emancipation,[3] they were to base themselves on existing organizations created by advanced sections of that class and to condemn as sectarianism any attempt to impose preconceived organizational forms on the working class movement from outside. In the sphere of party building, Marx could have said, as Molière did of the plots of his plays: "*Je prends mon bien où je le trouve*" ("I take my property wherever I find it").

Although members and leaders of party organizations for only a few years,[4] Marx and Engels devoted a considerable amount of time, particularly in the latter parts of their lives, to giving advice on the programs and development of workers' parties in various countries, seeing themselves as occupying a "special status as representatives of *international* Socialism"[5] and of "the general staff of the Party."[6] When we examine the totality of these party activities and views on parties spread over half a century, we are faced with a considerable variety and complexity, embodying at first sight a number of contradictions. Moreover, our difficulty is increased by the fact that during the life-times of Marx and Engels the whole notion of a political party was to develop and change along with the forms of activity open to it;[7] and, as we shall see, they were to use the term in several different senses, without defining them. It has therefore been quite possible to draw selectively on their activities, and above all their writings, in support of the most opposite versions of their views.

An understanding of the ideas of Marx and Engels on proletarian parties is only possible if they are set in each case in their widely vary-ing historical and semantic contexts. This I shall attempt to do by ex-amining the major "models" of the party in their work, each of which corresponds to a stage or stages in the development of the working class movement in a given period or in given countries. These I take as: (a) the small international Communist cadres' organization (the League of Communists—1847–52); (b) the "party" without an organization (during the ebb of the labor movement—1850s and early 1860s); (c) the broad international federation of workers' organizations (the First International—1864–72); (d) the Marxist national mass party (German Social Democracy—1870s, 1880s and early 1890s); (e) the broad na-tional labor party (Britain and America—1880s and early 1890s) based on the Chartist model. I have chosen to examine the views of Marx and Engels together for they were in fundamental agreement on all the questions discussed here; and over an important period, in keeping with a division of labor agreed between them, Engels dealt on behalf of both of them with requests for political advice from all over the world, continuing and extending this work after Marx's death into the era of the Second International.

II.

Having found themselves in 1844–45 in agreement on some of the basic principles of Marxism, Marx and Engels were to embark on a lifetime collaboration, involving both the further development of their theoretical ideas and the attempt "to win over the European and in the first place the German proletariat."[8] From the beginning of 1846, based on Brussels, they initiated the setting up of Communist Correspondence Committees, notably in Belgium, Britain, France, and Germany. These were to concern themselves with the internal affairs of what Engels was later to call "the Communist Party in the process of formation";[9] though in this period both he and Marx were speaking of "the Communist Party" and "our party"[10] in the traditional sense of a *société de pensée*—however, with them, it was seen as expressing the interests of a class—rather than a political organization in anything approaching the modern sense. Among those who received the lithographed circulars and pamphlets issued from Brussels were the leaders of the League of the Just, which, formed in 1836, was a small international secret society, consisting mainly of German artisans, that in recent years had particularly concerned itself with setting up and working within workers' educational associations. This was the organization that Marx and Engels now entered on the invitation of its leaders, who indicated that they were convinced of the general correctness of their views and agreed to their stipulation that the old conspiratorial forms related to the organization's Blanquist past should be scrapped.[11] At a congress in the summer of 1847, it was reorganized as the League of Communists, adopting new rules giving it official Communist aims at a second congress at the end of the year. A new and thoroughly democratic constitution laid down that annual congresses were "the legislative authority of the League" and provided for the electivity, accountability and revocability at any time by their electors of all leading committees.[12] It was as a "detailed theoretical and practical programme" of the League that Marx and Engels were commissioned to write their famous *Manifesto of the Communist Party*.[13]

The Communist League was an international association of workers in a number of Western European countries, in which Germans predominated and which paid special attention to Germany.[14] Although "for ordinary peace times at least" it was seen by Marx and Engels as "a pure propaganda society",[15] it was forced by the conditions of the time

to operate as a secret society during most of the five years of its existence. It had its origins, wrote Engels in 1892, in "two independent currents": on the one hand "a pure workers' movement" and, on the other,
"a theoretical movement, stemming from the disintegration of Hegelian
philosophy," associated predominantly with Marx. "The *Communist
Manifesto* of 1848," he goes on, "marks the fusion of both currents".[16]

In the *Manifesto* are set out some of the basic ingredients of Marx
and Engels's conception of the party. It puts forward the Communists'
claim to leadership of the working class by virtue of their superior
theoretical consciousness, which belongs to the essence of this conception. The previous year, in his polemic against Proudhon, Marx had
described the Socialists and Communists as "the theoreticians of the
proletarian class."[17] Now he and Engels present the Communists as
the theoretical vanguard of the class, which has "no interests separate
and apart from those of the proletariat as a whole" and does not "set
up any sectarian principles of [its] own, by which to shape and mould
the proletarian movement."[18] They were distinguished from "the other
working class parties" only in that in national struggles "they point
out and bring to the forefront the common interests of the entire proletariat, independent of all nationality" and that, in the various stages
of the struggle against the bourgeoisie, "they always and everywhere
represent the interests of the movement as a whole." They were in their
practice "the most advanced and resolute section of the working class
parties of every country, that section which pushes forward all others,"
whilst in their theory they had "over the great mass of the proletariat
the advantage of clearly understanding the line of march, the conditions and the ultimate general results of the proletarian movement,"[19]
which they conceived as "the self-conscious, independent movement
of the immense majority, in the interest of the immense majority."[20]

When Marx and Engels speak in the *Manifesto* of the "organization of the proletarians into a class, and consequently into a political
party,"[21] they clearly have in mind the English model that Marx had
described in *The Poverty of Philosophy* the year before. Here he had
shown how in their struggle, first in trade unions,[22] and then also by
constituting "a large political party under the name of Chartists,"[23]
the mass of workers had developed from an amorphous, fragmented,
potential class *an sich* into a fully-fledged, national class *für sich* engaged
of necessity in political struggle.[24]

At the primitive stage of development and organization of the work-ing class on the continent at this time, with the Communist League as a tiny cadres' organization of some two to three hundred members,[25] spread throughout Western Europe, the *Manifesto* indicated that "the Communists do not form a separate party opposed to other working class parties."[26] In fact, at this time, there was only one workers' party organized on a national scale, the Chartists,[27] and the British Commu-nists, Julian Harney and Ernest Jones worked in it as leaders of its left wing.[28] In other countries, the members of the League were to join such parties as the French Social Democrats of Ledru-Rollin and Louis Blanc,[29] which Marx described as "a coalition between petty bourgeois and workers."[30] In Germany in the 1848 revolution they joined the Democratic Party, "the party of the petty bourgeoisie,"[31] whose most advanced wing they formed until the spring of 1849.[32] Whilst the form of these tactics was dictated by the circumstances of the time, they do contain an element that is common to all their party models: the avoid-ance of sectarian isolation and the finding of fields of work where the Communists can get "the ear of the working class."[33]

It must be clear from the above that the Communist League, an international secret society comprising "only a small core" of mili-tants,[34] cannot be described as a political party, even in the usual sense in which the term was most frequently used at the time and is applied in the *Manifesto* itself to the large national organizations in which the Communists were to work. As the Soviet Marx scholar E. P. Kandel argues in one of the regrettably few books published on the League, Marx and Engels saw the League only as "the germ, the nucleus" of their party, notwithstanding the fact that they called its programme the *Manifesto of the Communist Party*.[35] The conditions of the time, he writes, "did not provide possibilities for the League of Communists to turn into a real party."[36] A glance at the League's role in the revolution of 1848–49 will bear this out.

Returning to Germany in the spring of 1848 after the start of the revolution, together with the bulk of League members who had been living abroad, Marx and Engels went to Cologne. After initially get-ting the League's Central Committee operating from there, they appear to have concentrated all their efforts from about the middle of May on the production of the *Neue Rheinische Zeitung*. This famous radical daily paper, whose first number appeared on June 1, campaigned under

the editorship of Marx for a determined struggle to carry through to
the end the democratic tasks in this bourgeois democratic revolution.
Seeing the very great difficulties for the League in issuing directives
to its dispersed supporters, Marx and Engels concluded that "such directives were . . . much better disseminated through the press."[37] In
recent years, a bitter controversy has raged between Boris Nicolaevsky,
the old Menshevik who died in America in 1966, and E. P. Kandel
around the alleged dissolution of the League in the summer of 1848.[38]
Whether in fact Marx used special discretionary powers (bestowed on
him at the beginning of the revolution) to dissolve the League in June
1848, as Nicolaevsky alleges on the basis of the prison deposition of P. G.
Röser,[39] one of those sentenced at the Cologne trial of League leaders in
1852,[40] or whether, as Kandel argues, the possibility of such a dissolution
is contradicted by the "high evaluation of the past role of the League
throughout the whole period of 1847–52 given by Marx and Engels,"[41]
who never in their accounts of the League's activity referred to such a
dissolution,[42] we shall probably never know for certain. Unless further
research brings some new documents to light, we shall have to make
up our minds on the balance of probabilities. There is however no dispute on the fact that, as Engels testified later, "the few hundred League
members vanished in the enormous mass that had been suddenly hurled
into the movement."[43] Kandel accepts that in the summer of 1848 the
Cologne Central Committee ceased to function and was (in late August
or September, he now thinks) dissolved and its powers transferred to
the London District Committee.[44] Further, Soviet historians accept as
"credible" Röser's account of a meeting that he attended in the spring of
1849 between Marx and Joseph Moll,[45] who had been sent by the new
London Central Committee to reorganize the League in Germany.[46]
According to Röser, Marx "declared that with the existing freedom of
speech and of the press the League was superfluous."[47]

A number of contemporary Marxist historians have unfortunately
found it necessary to interpret these tactics in terms of a later Marxian,
and *a fortiori* Leninist, concept of the party. They therefore argue that
"the editorial staff of the *Neue Rheinische Zeitung* was the political centre
of leadership of the proletarian party in Germany, of the Communist
League,"[48] "the true general staff of the proletarian party,"[49] to which
"now fell in practice the tasks of the Central Committee of the Communist League."[50] In the accounts of the history of the League and

the *Neue Rheinische Zeitung* that Marx and Engels wrote in the 1860s and 1880s there are no such anachronistic formulations to be found. Nor for that matter are there in Lenin, a keen student of the history of Marxism, who wrote in 1905:

> It was only in April 1849, after the revolutionary newspaper had been published for almost a year . . . that Marx and Engels declared themselves in favor of a special workers' organization! Until then they were merely running an "organ of democracy" unconnected by any organizational ties with an independent workers' party. This fact, monstrous and incredible from our present-day standpoint, clearly shows us what an enormous difference there is between the German workers' party of those days and the present Russian Social-Democratic Labour Party.[51]

April 1849, as Lenin indicates in the passage quoted, was to see an important change in Marx and Engels's revolutionary strategy. Marx and other Communists issued a statement announcing their resignation from the Rhineland District Committee of the Democratic Associations and urging "a closer union of workers' associations" of which a national congress was planned.[52] They appear to have concluded that the German workers had now developed sufficient political experience for it to be a practical proposition to work for a broad mass workers' party based on the workers' associations and independent of the petty bourgeois Democrats with their "indecision, weakness and cowardice."[53] It was too late, however, for these plans to get off the ground. The outbreak of the insurrection in southern and western Germany (*Reichsverfassungskampagne*) was to begin soon afterwards and its defeat by mid-July signified the end of the German revolution.

Most of the old leaders of the League came together again in exile in London in the autumn of 1849, where the Central Committee was reconstituted, and proceeded to reorganize the League in Germany, of necessity as a secret society. On the assumption that "a new revolution is impending,"[54] Marx and Engels drew up their famous "Address of March 1850" on behalf of the League's Central Committee.[55] It notes that in the two years of revolution, although the League's members as individuals had stood in the forefront of the struggle, the "former firm organization of the League was considerably slackened." Whilst the democratic party had organized itself more and more in Germany, "the workers' party" (by which they here must mean either the labor movement as a whole or the general interest of the proletariat as a class) "lost its only firm foothold" (by which the Communist League is meant).[56] The conclusion that is drawn as the *leitmotif* of the eleven-page address is: "An end must be put to this state of affairs, the independence of the workers must be restored,"[57] and they must not allow themselves to be drawn into a large opposition party embracing all shades of democratic opinion.[58] "The workers, and above all the League," they write, "must exert themselves to establish an independent, secret and public organ-ization of the workers' party."[59] The League would clearly form the secret organization and its branches should become "the central point and nucleus of workers' associations in which the attitude and interests of the proletariat will be discussed independently of bourgeois influ-ences."[60] These workers' associations, existing throughout Germany and normally of a social, cultural and educational character, would pro-vide the broad mass basis and public organization of the independent workers' party that was to be created. After the expected democratic revolution, the workers must contest elections to a national assembly with their own independent candidates, consisting "as far as possible of members of the League."[61]

Eduard Bernstein started the fashion, now followed, among others, by Mr. George Lichtheim[62] and Professor Bertram Wolfe,[63] of describ-ing the March Address as "Blanquist".[64] Yet the concept of party and revolution is certainly very far from being Blanquist in the normally accepted sense of the term, though there are indeed points of conver-gence with Blanqui's tactics in 1848, which were in a number of ways untypical,[65] and with the forms of struggle foreseen for the forthcom-ing revolution by the emigre Blanquists with whom Marx and Engels concluded a short-lived agreement in 1850.[66] What the Address makes quite clear is that what it envisages is not a putsch carried out by a rev-olutionary elite, but the organizing of the most broadly based workers' party, which in the next revolution will march together with the petty bourgeois democrats, whom it will help bring to power and then push forward to make the maximum inroads into capitalist property.[67] In the "revolutionary excitement that the workers should keep alive as long as possible,"[68] they "must attempt to organize themselves inde-pendently as a proletarian guard" with commanders and a general staff elected by themselves.[69] It is significant, as Dr Rudolf Schlesinger has noted, that the Address, which was confidential, does not suggest that these detachments should be subordinated to Communist control, but indicates rather that they should "put themselves at the command . . . of revolutionary community councils" that the workers will have established.[70] The Address recognizes that the German workers will need to go through "a lengthy revolutionary development" before themselves taking power, and stresses the need for their "clarifying their minds as to what their class interests are,"[71] with the obvious implication that the League should function as a propaganda society.

When, in the late summer of 1850, Marx concluded that European capitalism had entered a period of prosperity and there would be no new revolution in the period ahead, he was faced with opposition from an important section of League members headed by Willich and Schapper. Combating their voluntarism, he said that, instead of studying the real conditions, they had made "the will alone into the driving force of revolution."[72] The League in London split on this issue and the Central Committee was transferred back to Cologne, where it functioned for a while until its members were arrested and, in November 1852, sentenced by a Cologne court. Shortly afterwards the League in London was dissolved on Marx's proposal and its "continuation on the continent declared to be no longer opportune."[73]

III.

After the split in the Communist League in the autumn of 1850 and even before its formal dissolution two years later, Marx and Engels had begun to withdraw into an "authentic isolation,"[74] preferring the "position of the independent writer" to that of "the so-called revolutionary party."[75] The relief expressed by Marx to Engels on February 11, 1851, at the end of "the system of mutual concessions, of inadequacies endured for the sake of appearances,"[76] was matched by Engels's joy two days later that from now on they were responsible to themselves alone.[77] "How do people like us, who flee official positions like the plague, fit into a 'party'?" he thunders. "What good to us, who spit on popularity . . . is a 'party,' i.e., a band of asses who swear by us because they take us for the likes of them?"[78] Strong words—but it would be wrong, as Franz Mehring says, to take the actual expressions used too seriously,[79] and totally indefensible to divorce them from their actual context and argue, as Bertram Wolfe does, that they represent their real private opinions about the party, to be contrasted with statements made by them thirty and forty years later (some of which he quotes), which were "written for the eyes of others."[80] They reflect the frustrations of the first difficult period of exile after the defeat of the revolution and the recognition that no new one was impending. They represent their reaction to the "petty squabbles"[81] of the emigration,[82] from which they were withdrawing in order to return to their studies, interrupted since 1848, in the hope of gaining, above all in the sphere of political economy, "a scientific victory for our party."[83]

What, however, was this "party" of which they continued to speak after the dissolution of the Communist League in 1852, in a period when, as Marx wrote to the poet Freiligrath in 1860, he "*never* again belonged . . . to any *secret* or *public* society,"[84] and considered that his "theoretical works were of greater benefit to the working class than participation in associations whose days on the continent were over"?[85] What we have here is not a party in the normal sense that Engels was using when he indicated in December 1852 that "no political party can exist without an organization,"[86] but rather, in the first instance, a return to the use of the term that we saw them make in the mid-1840s to designate Marx and the small band broadly sharing his basic views, whom the Prussian police reports as well as Marx's supporters in this period refer to as the "Marx party."[87] Already in March 1853, within four months of the dissolution of the League, Marx is writing to Engels: "We must definitely recruit our party afresh," since the few adherents that he names, despite their qualities, do not add up to a party.[88] They aimed to get this group—"our clique," as Engels calls them fairly jocularly in a letter to Weydemeyer in America in 1853[89]—to prepare themselves by study for the revolutionary struggles that they were confident lay ahead.[90] Marx was anxious to coordinate the public activities of the members of this "party embryo," as Wilhelm Liebknecht was to call it later.[91] When, in 1859, Lassalle published a pamphlet on the Italian war of that year expressing a point of view with which they disagreed, Marx wrote to Engels criticizing their wayward comrade's failure first to apprise himself of their opinion. "We must insist on party discipline or everything will land in the dirt," he added.[92]

Marx, however, also spoke of "our party" in a more transcendental sense, as when in 1860, in the letter to Freiligrath from which I have already quoted, he counterposed to the party in the "ephemeral sense," which in the shape of the Communist League had, he said, "ceased to exist for me eight years ago,"[93] "the party in the great historical sense."[94] The Communist League, like Blanqui's *Société des Saisons* and hundreds of other societies, "was only an episode in the history of the Party, which is growing everywhere spontaneously from the soil of modern society."[95] For Marx the party in this sense was the embodiment of his conception of the "mission" of the working class,[96] concentrating in itself "the revolutionary interests of society,"[97] to accomplish "the historical tasks which automatically arose" from its general conditions of existence.[98] It was in this sense also that Marx understood the term "party" when he reported to Engels in 1859 that he had told a deputation from an emigre German workers' group: "We had received our appointment as representatives of the proletarian party from nobody *but ourselves*. It was, however, endorsed by the exclusive and universal hatred consecrated to us by all the parties and fractions of the old world."[99] Does this statement indicate a "conception of charismatic election,"[100] and strains of "prophetism"[101] in Marx? Leaving aside the somewhat arrogant form in which the claim is made (and Marx could certainly be arrogant, especially when in these difficult years of poverty and ill-health he was stung by the follies of some of his fellow-exiles), there remains the idea of Marx and Engels seeing themselves, by virtue of their *scientifically* evolved theoretical understanding as a *locum tenens* for the German working-class party,[102] which for the moment enjoyed only a "theoretical existence."[103] This is however a temporary and exceptional conception for them, a special case in no way typical of the mainstream of their thought, which is found only at this early stage in the life of the still little developed German working class in the hiatus between the disappearance of the Communist League and the appearance of new working-class organizations that they were confident would emerge to take its place.[104] They were decidedly not trying to substitute themselves for such organizations, which at that time did not exist. After a real movement came once more into existence in the 1860s, they never again saw themselves as self-appointed representatives of the proletarian party. On the contrary, wherever a real working class movement existed and struggled against the existing order, even when it was led by people with whom they had strong theoretical differences, they identified themselves with it and saw it as a manifestation of the party "in the great historical sense." Thus Marx was to tell Kugelmann that the Paris Commune was "the most glorious deed of our Party since the June insurrection in Paris,"[105] in much the same way that Engels was to refer to the Commune as "without any doubt the child of the International intellectually, although the International did not lift a finger to produce it."[106] In 1892, writing for French Socialists on the movement in Germany, Engels stressed that he was speaking "only in my own name, in no wise in the name of the German party. Only the selected committees and delegates of this party have the right to do that."[107]

It is perhaps worth noting that, although in the fifties he saw no basis for an organized workers' party in Germany, he was in 1857 urging that in Britain the Chartist leader Ernest Jones should "*form* a party, for which he must go to the factory districts."[108] What he had in mind was a recruiting campaign by the National Charter Association in the industrial areas, drawing on the old Chartist traditions, to develop itself into a broadly based working-class party in which a leading role would be played by Jones himself, whom Engels was to describe on his death in 1869 as "the only educated Englishman who was, at bottom, entirely on our side."[109] Thus, even in their years in the wilderness, Marx and Engels retained and sought to realize where possible their basic concept of the party as an *organization* in which socialist theory fuses with the labor movement.

IV.

The formation of the First International in 1864 gave Marx (and somewhat later, Engels)[110] the opportunity to break out of their relative isolation and join up with the Western European labor movement that was now reviving on a much wider scale than its continental predecessor of the 1840s. Whilst not abandoning his theoretical work, Marx turned his attention more and more, right up to the Hague Congress of 1872, to organizing, uniting and leading this broad international federation of affiliated working-class organizations. Like the Communist League, the International was not founded by Marx and Engels but sprang spontaneously from the labor movement of the time,[111] to which, by virtue of their theoretical and intellectual pre-eminence,[112] they came to give direction and perspective. Unlike the Communist League,[113] however, they did not at any stage regard the International as a Communist Party. Nor did they operate with their supporters as an organized party, fraction or secret society inside the broad framework of the International.[114] Nonetheless, in speaking in the Inaugural Address of the International of "numbers . . . united by combination and led by knowledge,"[115] Marx was broadly paraphrasing his party concept of the fusion of socialist theory with the labor movement,[116] and in the International, especially after the Paris Commune, he and Engels were to develop more fully than hitherto their views on party organization. In contrast to the Communist League with its advanced theoretical programme, Marx framed the International's programme—the preamble to its Rules that he drew up[117]—"in a form acceptable from the present standpoint of the workers' movement," as he told Engels.[118] This movement had to embrace the Liberal leaders of the British trade unions, the French, Italian and Spanish Proudhonists, and the German Lassalleans.[119] It admitted both individual members and affiliated organizations.[120] The principle that it should "let every section freely shape its own theoretical programme,"[121] led Marx to propose the acceptance of the sections of Bakunin's International Alliance of Socialist Democracy into the International, which it applied to enter in 1868, despite his very strong objections to its program and suspicions from the outset of Bakunin's motives in joining.[122]

In the early years of the International, in drawing up its documents, Marx restricted himself "to those points which allow of immediate agreement and concerted action by the workers and give direct nourishment and impetus to the requirements of the class struggle and the organization of the workers into a class."[123] He realized at the start that it would "take time before the reawakened movement allows the old boldness of speech."[124] However, relying "for the ultimate triumph of the ideas set forth in the *Manifesto* . . . solely and exclusively upon the intellectual development of the working class, as it necessarily had to ensue from united action and discussion,"[125] he succeeded, as the movement developed, in gaining support for demands of an increasingly socialist character.[126] Thus by 1868, despite a dwindling Proudhonist opposition, the International, which began without any commitment to public ownership, had come out officially for collective ownership of the mines, railways, arable land, forests, and means of communication.[127]

The Paris Commune in the spring of 1871, memorably vindicated by Marx on behalf of the General Council in *The Civil War in France*, raised very sharply the question of the most effective forms of political action to secure working-class political power, which the growth of working-class suffrage,[128] as well as the "abstentionist" campaign being run by the Bakuninists in the International, had also helped to make topical. After a discussion in which both Marx and Engels participated,[129] the London Conference adopted its famous Resolution IX, quoted at the beginning of this essay, with which for the first time in its history the International officially came out in favor of the "constitution of the working class into a political party."[130] This objective was incorporated into the Rules of the International at its Hague Congress a year later. What is meant here, however, by this much quoted but little analyzed formulation? In his very stimulating and well-documented but often contentious study of the London Conference, Dr Miklos Molnar of Geneva interprets this resolution, along with those dealing with dues and statistics, as preparing the ground for the International to "become a sort of centralized international party."[131] Whilst up till then Marx had seen it as a "network of affiliated societies,"[132] Molnar argues that he later conceived and at the London Conference openly came out with "the idea of transforming all these societies and heterogeneous groupings into an international party."[133]

Molnar is unable to quote any statements from Marx or Engels to support his interpretation of the London Conference resolution and he ignores some very solid evidence indicating that they intended something quite different by it. Thus in 1893 Engels was to welcome the formation of the Independent Labour Party in Britain, saying that "this new party was the very party which the old members of the International desired to see formed" when they passed their resolution at the 1871 Conference "in favor of an independent political party."[134] Further, in the leaflet, *The Manchester Foreign Section to all Sections and Members of the British Federation*, which Engels drafted in December 1872,[135] he wrote that the resolution "merely demands the formation, in every country, of a distinct working class party, opposed to all middle class parties."[136] That is to say, he continues, "it calls here in England upon the working class to refuse any longer to serve as the fag-end of the 'great Liberal party,' and to form an independent party of their own, as they did in the glorious times of the great Chartist movement."[137] Thus we are back to the model of the mass Chartist movement—"the first working men's party of modern times"[138]—which, as explained above, was what the authors of the *Communist Manifesto* had in mind when they spoke there of the "organization of the proletarians into a class, and consequently into a political party."[139]

By 1871 Marx and Engels also had another, more recent, model in mind. This was the German Social Democratic Workers' Party, formed at Eisenach two years earlier. The antiwar stand taken by its leaders Bebel and Liebknecht in the Reichstag the previous year as cited by Marx at the London Conference as an example of the importance of having workers' representatives in national parliaments,[140] as it had been by Engels when he wrote to the Spanish Federal Council of the International on February 13, 1871.[141] In this important letter, written just before the Paris Commune, Engels argues that "experience has shown everywhere that the best way to emancipate the workers from this domination of the old parties is to form in each country a proletarian party with a policy of its own, a policy quite distinct from that of the other parties."[142]

Thus from 1871, Marx and Engels envisaged the International working for the establishment of independent national workers' parties. They had no wish to prescribe one form or another—neither the more "Marxist" type of party like the Eisenachers, who had developed "under the influence of (their) theoretical views,"[143] nor the less theoretically developed but more broadly based Chartist movement—as *the* model for all countries.[144] Nor were they aiming, as Molnar asserts, at having the International "provided with a common doctrine."[145] The "common theoretical programme" that Marx had foreseen in 1869 being created "by degrees" by the exchange of ideas throughout the International was conceived in fairly broad terms.[146] Two days after the close of the London Conference, Marx made a speech at a dinner for the delegates in which he stressed that "the International had not put forth any particular creed. Its task was to organize the forces of labor and link the various working men's movements and combine them." (Ironically enough, a full report of this speech is reproduced by Molnar as an appendix!)[147] Even at the end of August 1872, at the height of the most bitter battle with the Anarchists, to whose theories Marx and Engels personally were irreconcilably opposed, Engels made it clear that they considered that Bakunin and his followers had the right within the International to carry out "propaganda for their programme."[148]

The conflict between Marx and Bakunin, as Julius Braunthal points out in his *Geschichte der Internationale*, "was set alight not by theoretical contradictions but on the question of the organization of the International."[149] His libertarian demagogy notwithstanding, Bakunin sought

was very strongly influenced by Marxism. Commenting on the unanimous decision of its Second Congress in 1891 to exclude the representatives of the Anarchist groups, Engels wrote: "With this the old International came to an end, with this the new one begins again. It is purely and simply the ratification, nineteen years later, of the Hague Congress resolutions."[170]

V.

When in 1863 Lassalle founded the General German Workers' Union (ADAV), he performed, in Marx's view, an "immortal service" by reawakening the independent workers' movement after fifteen years of slumber.[171] Yet, although recognizing what was positive in such an independent workers' organization as the ADAV and for a short time in 1864–65 contributing to its journal, he and Engels generally described it as a "workers' sect" rather than a workers' party.[172] They saw the Lassallean attempt to prescribe to the workers the course to be followed "according to a certain dogmatic recipe."[173] its inadequate agitation (at least before 1868) for full political freedom, its leadership cult, and the "'strict' organization",[174] which the ADAV tried to carry even into the trade unions that they set up,[175] as expressions of its sectarian character. Opposing all this, Marx wrote in 1868 to ADAV President Schweitzer that, especially in Germany, "where the worker is bureaucratically disciplined from childhood up and believes in authority and the bodies placed over him, it is above all important to teach him to act independently."[176]

From 1865 Marx concentrated on the formation of sections of the International in Germany to which individual members were recruited. He saw these as preparing the ground for a national workers' party, the creation of which was being facilitated by Bismarck's surge forward to German unification.[177] An important ideological contribution to this was made by the publication, exactly a century ago, of the first volume of *Capital*, with which Marx hoped "to raise the Party as high as possible"[178] and which the next year was greeted at the national congresses the two major German workers' organizations—the ADAV[179] and the Association of German Workers' Organizations, led by Bebel and Liebknecht.[180] At a congress at Eisenach in 1869, Bebel's Association joined with opposition elements in the ADAV to form the German Social Democratic Workers' Party on the basis of a program that showed the influence of Marxism, although its demand for a "free people's state" and certain Lassallean formulations did not meet with the approval of Marx and Engels.[181] Whilst in some respects not as directly socialist as the ADAV, the new party had over it the great advantage, in Marx and Engels's eyes, of being unambiguously opposed to Bismarck's nationalism and the Prussian military state and of being organized along thoroughly democratic lines. In it, Marx and Engels came to recognize a genuine proletarian party,[182] and, for the first time since the dissolution of the Communist League in 1852, to apply the expression "our party" to an organized political party of the day.[183]

When in 1875 a unity congress was arranged at Gotha between the two German workers' organizations and a draft programme for the new party was issued, Marx and Engels wrote their famous criticisms of its theoretical insufficiencies for private consideration by leaders of the Eisenachers.[184] "Every step of real movement is more important than a dozen programmes," wrote Marx. "If, therefore, it was not possible . . . to go *beyond* the Eisenach programme, one should simply have concluded an agreement for action against the common enemy."[185] Despite these misgivings, Marx and Engels associated themselves with the new united party and before very long had come to refer to it too as "our party,"[186] and at the end of his life Engels was praising the fusion for the "immense increase in strength" that it had brought about.[187]

Whilst rejoicing at the impressive growth of the new party, Marx and Engels always took up the cudgels when they saw signs of "a vulgarization [*Verluderung*] of Party and theory"[188] in its ranks. Thus in September 1879 they sent a strongly worded circular to Party leaders criticizing their conciliatory attitude towards certain "representatives of the petty bourgeoisie"[189] who were attempting to "combat the proletarian character of the Party"[190] and thereby acting as "an adulterating element"[191] within it. They found it "incomprehensible" that the Party could "tolerate . . . in its midst any longer"[192] people who were saying that the workers were too uneducated to emancipate themselves.[193] In 1882 Engels wrote to Bebel that he had no illusions that it would "one day come to a dispute with the bourgeois-inclined elements in the Party and to a separation between the right and left wings,"[194] preferably after the Anti-Socialist Law that had been introduced in 1878 had been repealed.[195]

In the last years of his life, Engels approved in its broad essentials the line followed by the Party and the new program that it adopted, after he had criticized its first draft, at the Erfurt Congress of 1891.[196] He expressed his pride in "our" electoral successes, which in 1893 he saw approaching the two-million mark, and over-optimistically predicted an electoral majority and a Socialist government in power between 1900 and 1910.[197] In 1895, a few months before his death, he worked out in his introduction to *The Class Struggles in France 1848–1850* by Marx the theoretical justification of the "entirely new method of proletarian struggle" that had been opened up by the "successful utilisation of universal suffrage,"[198] relegating to the past "the time of surprise attacks, of revolutions carried through by small conscious minorities at the head of unconscious masses."[199] However, he stressed to Paul Lafargue that the tactics outlined there could not be followed in their entirety in France, Belgium, Italy, and Austria and that "in Germany they may become inapplicable tomorrow."[200]

Engels considered the designation Social Democratic "inappropriate for a party whose economic programme is not merely generally Socialist but directly Communist and whose ultimate political objective is the abolition of the whole state and thus also of democracy."[201] Professor Harold Laski, in his introduction to the Labour Party's centenary edition of the *Communist Manifesto*, was unable to recognize that Marx and Engels developed their concept of the party further after 1848. "The idea of a separate communist party dates from the Russian Revolution," he asserts; "it had no place in the thought of either Marx or of Engels,"[202] who, for instance, he argues, "never sought to found a separate German Communist Party."[203] He does not see that for them "German Communism," which, as Engels wrote to Sorge, in 1864 "did *not yet* exist as a workers' party"[204] gradually came to do so after 1869 in the shape of the Socialist parties led by Bebel and Liebknecht.

Nor do the views of Marx and Engels on the development of a Marxist party in France in the same period lend any support to Laski's sweeping assertion that "they will *always* support working-class parties, even when these are not communist, without forming a separate party of their own," regardless of the fact that "such a party may have an inadequate programme."[205] In fact, in 1882, Engels gave his support to Guesde and the left-wing minority when they walked out of the St. Etienne Congress of the French Workers' Party,[206] which then split into a Guesdist and a "possibilist" party. He described this separation of "incompatible elements" as "inevitable" and "good."[207] Writing to Bernstein, he reported that the "possibilist" right wing had "replaced the Communist preamble" of the 1880 party program drafted by Marx "by the Rules of the International of 1866,"[208] which, he said, "had to be framed so broadly because the French Proudhonists were so backward, and still it would not have been right to exclude them."[209] If, like the possibilists, you created "a party without a programme, which everyone can join, then it isn't a party any more," he argued. "To be for a moment in a minority with a correct programme—*quoad* organization—is still better than to have a big but thereby almost nominal semblance of a following."[210]

VI.

The idea of a broad labor party, favored by Marx and Engels in the case of Britain and the United States and developed most fully by the latter after his friend's death, would, when in the 1880s and 1890s a spontaneous labor movement sprang into life in both countries, seem to be exactly what they were opposing in Germany and France. Thus, writing to Florence Kelley Wischnewetsky at the end of 1886, Engels says that in the forthcoming American elections "a million or two of working men's votes . . . for a *bona fide* working men's party is worth infinitely more at present than a hundred thousand votes for a doctrinally perfect programme."[211] Whilst he had no illusions about the theoretical backwardness of the Knights of Labor and of Henry George, whose "banner" this party had set up,[212] he did not think the time had arrived to make a full criticism of either of them. "Anything that might delay or prevent that national consolidation of the working men's party—no matter on what platform—I should consider a great mistake," he explained.[213] This should take place through "the unification of the various independent bodies into one national labor army,"[214] he wrote in his preface to the American 1887 edition of his *Condition of the Working Class in England in 1844*. It should have "the conquest of the Capitol and the White House for its goal."[215]

In a series of articles in the "Labour Standard" in 1881 Engels had urged the British labor movement to form its own "working men's political party"[216] and send its own representatives to parliament.[217] With a brilliant anticipation of the form of organization to be adopted two decades later by the Labour Party,[218] he wrote: "At the side of, or above, the Unions of special trades there must spring up a general Union, a political organization of the working class as a whole."[219] When, out of the militant upsurge of 1888–89 and the first successes of independent labor candidates in 1892, the Independent Labour Party was formed in 1893, Engels publicly "urged all Socialists to join it, believing that, if wisely led, it would eventually absorb every other Socialist organization."[220] Although there were "all sorts of funny people" among the ILP leaders, he wrote to Sorge at this time, "the masses are behind them and will either teach them manners or throw them overboard."[221] The new party's development in the next two years, however, did not live up to his expectations and by the beginning of 1895 he saw among the British workers "nothing but sects and no party."[222] Engels was clearly judging the new party not by the criterion of its adherence to the theory of Marxism but by the extent to which it was "a distinct workers' party" promoting and reflecting the masses' "own movement—no matter in what form so long as it is only *their own* movement."[223]

Such very disparate weight given to the importance of a correct theoretical understanding, to the character of the party program and the breadth of its appeal as those given by Engels (and Marx) in relation to Germany and France, on the one hand, and to Britain and America, on the other, certainly indicate two different conceptions of the proletarian party. The differences are not, however, absolute and do not represent some inexplicable contradiction in the thought of the founders of scientific socialism.[224] On the contrary, they will be seen as logically complementary if we examine their application, in each case, on the basis of Engels's explanation, in the letter to Mrs. Kelley Wischnewetsky quoted above, that "our theory is not a dogma but the exposition of a process of evolution, and that process involves successive phases."[225] Britain and the United States were at this time both countries with substantial industrial working classes that had developed important and often militant industrial organizations, but where those who had understood anything of socialism were a tiny handful. Here then was an analogy, as Engels pointed out to Sorge, with the part "played by the Communist League among the workers' associations before 1848" in Germany.[226] And here it was therefore perfectly consistent for him to recommend that American Marxists should "act in the same way as the European Socialists have acted at a time when they were but a small minority of the working class,"[227] at the time that the *Communist Manifesto* indicated that the Communists did "not form a separate party opposed to other working class parties."[228] Since 1848, however, the position on the continent had advanced considerably. Germany in 1869, and to a lesser extent France in 1880, had reached the stage of having parties developing roots among the working class on the basis of more or less developed socialist programmes, and any attempt to fuse with other organizations or to win more votes through "adulterating" or scrapping such programs seemed to Marx and Engels to represent a "decidedly retrograde step."[229] But for Britain and America, where the workers had been bound politically to bourgeois parties, any move toward a broad united party of their own, on however backward a theoretical basis, was an advance, the "next great step to be accomplished."[230]

It was the self-imposed isolation of the main organized bodies of Marxists in the two countries that led Engels to criticize them for being and acting only like sects,[231] which "contrived to reduce the Marxist theory of development into a rigid dogma."[232] It was fundamentally his objection to such "Anglo-Saxon sectarianism,"[233] rather than pique at Hyndman's "tactless" behavior, as Cole and Postgate,[234] and after them Carew Hunt,[235] blandly assert, that was responsible for Engels dissociating himself from the Social Democratic Federation in Britain as from the Socialist Labour Party in the United States. However, he thought that these organizations, having "accepted our theoretical programme and so acquired a basis"[236] would have a role to play if they worked among the "still quite plastic mass" of workers as "a core of people who understand the movement and its aims and will therefore themselves take over the leadership"[237] at a later stage. Experience had shown that "it is possible to work along with the general movement of the working class at every one of its stages without giving up or hiding our own distinct position or even organization."[238] The Marxists would then have a big contribution to make to the emergence of the "ultimate platform"[239] of the labor movement in their countries which "must and will be essentially the same as that now adopted by the whole militant working class of Europe."[240] At such a stage, Engels doubtless foresaw the coming into being of a "new party" such as more than four decades previously he had predicted would arise from "the union of Socialism with Chartism, the reproduction of French Communism in an English manner" by the fusion of the "theoretically more backward, less developed" but "genuinely proletarian" Chartists with the "more far-seeing" Socialists, to make the working class "the true intellectual leader" of their country.[241]

VII.

Far from "discarding the notion of party . . . to return to the notion of class," as Sorel asserts, Marx and Engels saw the party as a *moment* in the development of the proletariat without which "it cannot act as a class."[242] For the working class "to be strong enough to win on the decisive day," Engels wrote to Trier in 1889, it must "form a separate party distinct from all others and opposed to them, a conscious class party," adding, with some oversimplification, that this was what "Marx and I have been arguing ever since 1847."[243] In 1865, in "The Prussian Military Question and the German Workers' Party," which he discussed with Marx before publication, Engels defines the workers' party, with which he is not in the pamphlet prepared to identify the only existing German workers' organization of the time, the Lassallean ADAV, as "that part of the working class that has attained consciousness of the separate interests of the class."[244] When they sometimes speak loosely of the proletarian party as though it were identical with the class as a whole,[245] it would seem clear from the contexts that they are referring synecdochically to the class when what they mean in fact is its "politically active portion,"[246] which more and more of the class will come to support as it "matures for its self-emancipation."[247]

Theoretical consciousness and the *Selbsttätigkeit* (spontaneous self-activity) of the working class are present, as the key elements in their conception of the proletarian party, in all periods of Marx and Engels's thought and activity from 1844 on, combining in different proportions in different conditions. They always represent complementary factors in the Marxian conception of the evolution of the proletariat to full maturity and *Selbstbewusstsein* (consciousness), rather than expressing a "'dualism'" in Marx's thought as Maximilien Rubel, of Paris, argues.[248] Rubel tries to fit Marx's conception of the party into the Procrustean bed of the highly disputable theory that there is in his work a "fundamental ambiguity" between his materialist sociology and a utopian ethic that he inherited and that serves as his "postulate" for social revolution.[249] With the aid of quotations collected totally ahistorically from a wide range of Marx and Engels's writings between 1841 and 1895, he seeks to distinguish "a double conception of the proletarian party" in their work, differentiating between "the sociological concept of the workers' party, on the one hand, and the ethical concept of the Communist party, on the other."[250] Karl Marx, asserts Rubel, "distinguishes formally between the workers' party and the body (*ensemble*) of Communists whose task is of a theoretical and educative order; the Communists are thus in no wise called to properly political functions."[251] Being "a form of non-institutionalized representation which represents the proletarian movement, in the 'historical' sense of the term," the latter "cannot identify themselves with a real organization subject to the constraints of political alienation"[252] and "obeying formally established rules and statutes."[253] The class movement of the proletariat, says Rubel, cannot be identified with the political agitation of parties. "On the contrary," he goes on, "it is represented by the trade unions if these understand their revolutionary role and fulfil it faithfully."[254] (This last assertion, endeavoring to present Marx and Engels as Syndicalists, completely ignores *inter alia* Marx and Engels's rejection before the Eisenach Congress of just such an argument by Johann Philip Becker.[255] "Old Becker must have gone right off his rocker," Engels wrote to Marx then. "How can he decree that the trades union *has* to be the true workers' association and the basis for all organization?")[256]

The *Manifesto of the Communist Party*, from which Rubel quotes, as well as the whole history of its authors' party work on which we have drawn, shows absolutely clearly and explicitly that they saw the Communists using their theoretical foresight, which for Rubel is some sort of transcendental ethical quality far removed from the corrupting political struggle, precisely to *act politically* to "push forward" and give leadership in the political struggles of their time.[257] Moreover the *Manifesto* was issued as the program of the Communist League, a political organization "obeying formally established rules and statutes"![258]

Only in the most exceptional and temporary periods did the Communists operate outside a "real organization," although—as in the case of the First International—that organization did not always need to be a Communist Party. The latter differed from "*other* working class parties" in that it had a Communist program and was guided by Communist theory.[259] However, believing that the workers "from out of their own class feeling" would "work their way up" to an acceptance of Marxist theory,[260] with the help of those "whose minds are theoretically clear" to shorten the process considerably,[261] Marx and Engels thought that sooner or later many of these other parties would either come to adopt Communist programs or be absorbed by others that had. In this belief, they were strengthened, at the end of their lives, by the example of German Social Democracy, which was developing into the type of essentially Communist mass party toward which they believed that other workers' parties, from their different starting points and in their own national forms, would ultimately advance. They saw such a fully developed proletarian party representing the fusion of socialist theory not just with a tiny handful of advanced workers, as in the Communist League, but with large and growing sections of the working class.

Marx and Engels saw the fullest possible internal democracy as an essential feature of a proletarian party. Disturbed by expulsions from the Danish Socialist Party of leading left-wing opponents of its leadership, Engels wrote to Trier in the letter quoted above: "The workers' movement is based on the sharpest criticism of existing society; criticism is its vital element; how then can it itself avoid criticism, try to forbid controversies? Is it possible for us to demand from others freedom of speech for ourselves only in order to eliminate it afresh in our own ranks?"[262] When, in 1890, the German Party leadership reacted in a high-handed way to the opposition of the so-called *Jungen* (with whom Engels disagreed politically), expressed through four Social Democratic papers that they controlled, he wrote to Sorge: "The Party is so big that absolute freedom of debate inside it is a necessity. . . . The greatest party in the land cannot exist without all shades of opinion in it making themselves fully felt."[263] For Engels, such internal democracy, diversity, and debate did not contradict, but was demanded by, German Social Democracy's existence "as the strongest, best disciplined and most rapidly growing Socialist Party,"[264] just as obversely he and Marx had at a certain stage in the history of the First International, seen a stronger General Council with disciplinary powers to use in exceptional cases as a condition for its democratic functioning.

Marx's famous principle that "the emancipation of the working classes must be conquered by the working classes themselves,"[265] on which he and Engels insisted again and again, is complemented, not contradicted, by their concept of the party. "The German Social Democratic Workers' Party, just *because* it is a *workers' party* necessarily pursues a 'class policy,' the policy of the working class," wrote Engels in 1873 in *The Housing Question*. "Since each political party sets out to establish its rule in the state, so the German Social Democratic Workers' Party is necessarily striving to establish *its* rule, the rule of the working class, hence 'class domination.'"[266] The organization by the proletariat of *its own* party was the "primary condition" of the struggle of the working class and "the dictatorship of the proletariat . . . the immediate aim."[267] Marx and Engels never went further than this in discussing the relationship of the proletarian party to their conception of proletarian dictatorship,[268] which they saw as representing a "political transition period" between capitalism and communism.[269] There is nothing in their work to justify Stalin's attempt to present as Marxist his theory that socialism demands a one-party system,[270] least of all in the form operated by him, where a small tyrannical clique substituted itself for the working class in laying some of the foundations of socialism. On the contrary, Engels's criticism of Blanqui is directed precisely against such a regime. "From Blanqui's conception of every revolution as the *coup de main* of a small revolutionary minority," he wrote in 1874, "follows of itself the necessity of a dictatorship after it succeeds: the dictatorship, of course, not of the whole revolutionary class, the proletariat, but of the small number of those who carried out the *coup* and who are themselves already in advance organized under the dictatorship of one or a few individuals."[271] Certainly the Paris Commune, which Marx described as "the conquest of the political power of the working classes"[272] and Engels as "the dictatorship of the proletariat"[273] (by which he meant the same thing), was no one-party state,[274] and was based on the election of all officials by universal suffrage,[275] and measures to "safeguard itself against its own deputies and officials, by declaring them all, without exception, subject to recall at any moment."[276]

The late Mr Carew Hunt, in his book *Marxism Past and Present*, is on peculiarly weak ground when he bases his restatement of the well-worn argument that the one-party system was "written into Marx's doctrine of dictatorship" on the assertion that "it is inconceivable that Marx, who would go to any lengths to crush a Socialist opponent," would have permitted adversaries "to organize themselves politically to defeat the objects for which the revolution had been carried out."[277] The main example that Carew Hunt obviously has in mind is that of Bakunin and his supporters, of whose appearance in the First International E. H. Carr writes: "The wooden horse had entered the Trojan citadel."[278] In a letter to Bolte in 1873 Marx wrote: "In *open opposition* to the International these people do no harm but are useful, but as hostile elements *inside* it they ruin the movement in all countries where they have got a foothold."[279] He and Engels rejected the Bakunin-ists' argument that the International, forced to meet the needs of the day-to-day struggle against capitalism, could be organized to accord as closely as possible with a future libertarian society.[280] Whilst Marx and Engels would certainly have taken exceptional authoritarian measures against reactionary opponents in a civil war or a "pro-slavery rebel-lion,"[281] there are no grounds for arguing that they would have favored the suppression of political opposition and dissent as a normal feature of the dictatorship of the proletariat.

The role of the proletarian party is circumscribed by the very con-ception of dialectics and historical development put forward by Marx and Engels. Born at a certain moment in the life of the working class, evolving in step with the different stages in the development of that class in different countries and periods, and in its turn reacting on and speed-ing up this development, its success in helping to establish working-class power would lay the basis for its own disappearance. Working-class power, by raising the consciousness of the widest sections of the popula-tion by a big educational expansion,[282] by establishing "really democratic institutions"[283] that would see "the people acting for itself by itself,"[284] could be assumed gradually to close the gap between a growing "edu-cated and trained core" of hundreds of thousands[285] in the party and the rest of the class, removing the *raison d'être* of the former conceived as a separate echelon. Finally, though Marx had no illusions that this would take place quickly,[286] the economic measures taken by the proletariat in power would end its rule by abolishing its existence as a class and, with it, the existence of the state "in the present political sense."[287] In the "association which will exclude classes and their antagonism"[288] to which Marx believed the transitional working-class dictatorship would give way, the continued existence of a proletarian party would clearly be an anachronism.

THE PRINCIPLE OF SELF-EMANCIPATION IN MARX AND ENGELS[1]

Hal Draper

There can be little doubt that Marx and Engels would have agreed with Lenin's nutshell definition of Marxism as "the theory and practice of the proletarian revolution." In this violently compressed formula, the key component is not the unity of theory and practice; unfortunately that has become a platitude. Nor is it "revolution"; unfortunately that has become an ambiguity. The key is the word "proletarian"—the class-character component.

But "proletarian revolution" too, very early, took on a considerable element of ambivalence, for it could be and was applied to two different patterns. In one pattern, the proletariat carries out its own liberating revolution. In the other, the proletariat is used to carry out a revolution.

The first pattern is new; the second is ancient. But Marx and Engels were the first socialist thinkers to be sensitive to the distinction. Naturally so: since they were also the first to propose that, for the first time in the history of the world, the exploited bottom stratum of workers in society was in a position to impress its own class character on a new social order.

When Marx and Engels were crystallizing their views on this subject, the revolutionary potentialities of the proletariat were already being recognized here and there. It was not Marx who first discovered that the proletariat was a revolutionary class. For example, Robert Owen, disappointed at the failure of his philanthropic bourgeois to become enthusiastic about the abolition of their class, turned for help to the beginnings of the working class and trade union movement in England; he thought to use them not to shift power to *that* class, but as troops, to push through his own scheme in which a philanthropic elite would "do them good." Saint-Simon, disillusioned with the failure of monarchs, bankers, scientists, etc., to understand the ineffable justice of his plans for humanity, turned, in his very last work *The New Christianity*, to the workers for the first time—appealing to them to convince their *bosses* to heed the Saint-Simonian wisdom.

THE LARGER HISTORICAL PATTERN

The first socialist view of the revolutionary proletariat was to regard its revolutionary potential as an instrument in others' hands: as a battering ram to break down the old system but not as a force fit to build a new one in its own name. These nonproletarian socialisms not only preceded Marxism, but have always been far stronger than Marxism, in the socialist movements of the world—today as yesterday.

It must be emphasized that this pattern is not something peculiar to the socialist movement, but *extends into* socialism. It extends back into all recorded history, far as the human eye can read. One section of the propertied classes, beaten on top, becomes desperate enough to resort to arousing the broader masses below both contestants, and therefore sets the plebs into motion, with appropriate promises and slogans, in order to hoist itself into the seats of power.

Hence, for example, the *tyrannoi* of ancient Greece have become *tyrants* in modern languages not because they tyrannized over the masses any more than the preceding oligarchy, but because they used the masses to "tyrannize" over that oligarchy itself. The pattern is visible in the story of the Gracchi; it is commonplace in modern history. It is a key to the dynamics of class struggle and intraclass struggle throughout time.

But it is always a gamble; there is a social risk. After you have called the masses from below onto the stage of social action, how are you going to get them off and back to their holes, after they have done the job for you? These animals are dangerous: handle with care. The intoxication of a joint victory may make them forget that you are the Natural Master. They may reach out for something for themselves, or smash things up in the process.

That danger was there even in ages when the broad working masses (slaves, laboring freemen, or serfs) could not and did not have any vision of a new social order that corresponded to their own class interests; when, therefore, their rule could not in fact mean a reorganization of society from below, but merely chaos. When that changes, what was previously a serious danger to Order becomes a mortal danger to the social order itself.

I. THE PROLETARIAN ACHERON

This is the change that takes place in history with the rise of capitalism and its shadow, the revolutionary proletariat. For the first time, there is a class below, the class on whose labor society is founded, that inherently *does* suggest a social program for its own reorganization of society. Once set in motion (in struggle), *this* class has a historical option: it is not limited to lending its services to one ruling class (or section of a ruling class) or another; it can go into business for itself. To be sure, it can still be controlled: for it is very young, and largely unformed, and often childishly stupid, and ill-educated; but how long can this adolescent giant be kept in short pants?

Because of this new type of danger, the class instinct of the bourgeoisie early made it reluctant to call the working masses into civil conflict, even as an ally in its own drive to gain power from the older feudal order, and, since then, made it interested mainly in ways and means of fragmenting and channeling the dangerous mass forces below.

But the case of individual ideologists and political adventurers is another matter; so also are the political tendencies that look in the direction of an *anti*capitalist elite.

Hence, one of the characteristic differences among the bourgeois politicians is willingness to play with this fire, to one degree or another. Marx noted this, for example, in his thumbnail sketch of the French "liberal" politician Thiers who, after serving both Louis Philippe and Bonaparte, carried out the task of massacring the Paris Commune:

> A professional "Revolutionist" in that sense, that in his eagerness . . .
> of wielding power . . . he never scrupled, when banished to the
> ranks of the opposition, to stir the popular passions and provoke a
> catastrophe to displace a rival . . . The working class he reviled as
> "the vile multitude."[2]

This political type had a Virgilian tag, which was well-enough known in Marx's day to be of interest now. It put the pattern in six vivid words: *Flectere si nequeo superos, Acheronta movebo*[3]—"If I cannot change the Powers above, I shall set the Lower Regions [Acheron] into motion."

George Brandes's book on Lassalle tells us that the would-be workers' dictator, weighing his political course, "pondering like Achilles in his tent, mentally repeated to himself for nights and days the burden of Virgil's line."[4] The motto also came to Engels's pen as he contemplated the cowardice of the French liberals of a later day:

> the *flectere si nequeo superos, Acheronta movebo* is not their business . . .
> They are afraid of the proletarian Acheron.[5]

Marx developed a new, third view of the proletariat, basically hostile both to the Olympian view of the ruling class and the Acherontic view of the would-be ruler.

THE NEW PRINCIPLE

The classic formulation of the self-emancipation principle by Marx was written down in 1864 as the first premise of the *Rules* of the First International—in fact, as its first clause.

> Considering, That the emancipation of the working classes must be conquered by the working classes themselves; . . .[6]

And it was from this source that the phrase became famous, being repeated also by various elements who did not believe a word of it.

Later on, Engels rightly predated the conception to "the very beginning": "our notion, from the very beginning, was that 'the emancipation of the working class must be the act of the working class itself,'" he wrote in a preface to the *Communist Manifesto,* slightly varying the formulation, as did Marx also in his *Critique of the Gotha Programme.*[7]

From the very beginning of Marxism, he means. But if we sketch Marx and Engels' course *before* they arrived at this keystone principle of the self-emancipation of the proletariat, we will put it into context. For it was then an unknown principle, previously almost unthinkable.[8] There was nobody from whom to adopt it. Marx had to invent it himself—or reinvent it. The probability is that it was Marx who straightened Engels out on the subject, in the course of their collaboration in 1845 on *The German Ideology.*

II. ENGELS: FROM ELITISM TO MARXISM

A good biography of Engels would recount the layers of ideas through which he had to fight his way before he could even get within reaching distance of Marx's approach. There was more standing in his way than in Marx's case.

We will only mention now that, first, Engels had to revolt against the authoritarian pietist Christianity of his family and home; then came his early intellectual development through the romanticism of "Young Germany," followed by his infatuation with the radical-liberal Ludwig Börne. Involvement in the Young Hegelian (Left Hegelian) circle in Berlin, plus an early dash of Shelley, led to his conversion to a so-called "communism" by Moses Hess, who was then in his period of *Schwärmerei* over Proudhon's newfangled "anarchism," which he understood to be similar to his own sentimental petty bourgeois socialism. In England in 1843, Engels was at first mainly in contact with the Owenites, for whose *New Moral World* he began his English writing, although he also made the acquaintance of emigre German communist workers like Karl Schapper. Then he went through a spell of enthusiasm over Wilhelm Weitling's allegedly "working class" communism, finally making contact with the Chartist movement.

The radical scene was what this sounds like, only more so: a hodge-podge of ideas, a mingle-mangle of movements. And, before Engels got to Chartism, every one of them was basically elitist to the core: "We" will bring salvation to the toilers, and consent to lead them where sheep may safely graze.

Let us pick up Engels toward the end of 1843: He is writing articles for the Owenite *New Moral World*, as a convert to "philosophical communism" by Hess, and as an admirer of Proudhon's anarchism. In a key article, he praises Proudhon's *What Is Property?* (1840) as the most important "communist" work published (for he is ignorant of the fact that Proudhon denounces "communism" since this enthusiasm came from Hess, who had adopted that label). The article emphasizes Proudhon's view

> that every kind of government is alike objectionable, no matter whether it be democracy, aristocracy, or monarchy, that all govern by force; and that, in the best of all possible cases, the force of the majority oppresses the weaknesses of the minority, he comes, at last, to the conclusion: "Nous voulons l'anarchie!" What we want is anarchy; the rule of nobody, the responsibility of every one to nobody but himself.[9]

There is more of this Proudhonism in Engels's article, radical in sound and reactionary in content. The following is pure Proudhonism:

> Democracy is, as I take all forms of government to be, a contradic-
> tion in itself, an untruth, nothing but hypocrisy . . . at the bottom.
> Political liberty is sham-liberty, the worst possible slavery; the ap-
> pearance of liberty, and therefore the reality of servitude. Political
> equality is the same; therefore democracy, as well as every form of
> government, must ultimately break to pieces . . . we must have either
> a regular slavery—that is, an undisguised despotism, or real liberty,
> and real equality—that is Communism.[10]

This reflects Proudhon's virulent hatred of democracy, using truths
about sham-democracy to damn democracy itself, not to demand that
the sham be exchanged for real democracy.

"PHILOSOPHICAL" ELITISM

To this Proudhonism is attached Hess's "philosophical communism,"
which Engels, as a disciple of Hess in this article, considers the special glory of the German mind. Unlike the economic-minded English
and the political French, the Germans became communists *philosophi-
cally,* by reasoning upon first principles," he boasts.[11] For "the Germans
are a philosophical nation" and will adopt communism "as soon as it
is founded upon sound philosophical principles." This will surely be
done; and so, no doubt,

> There is a greater chance in Germany for the establishment of a
> Communist party among the educated classes of society, than any-
> where else. The Germans are a very disinterested nation; if in Ger-
> many principle comes into collision with interest, the principle will
> almost always silence the claims of interest. The same love of abstract
> principles, the same disregard of reality and self-interest, which have
> brought the Germans to a state of political nonentity, these very
> same qualities guarantee the success of a philosophical Communism
> in that country. It will appear very singular to Englishmen, that a
> party which aims at the destruction of private property, is chiefly
> made up by those who have property; and yet this is the case in Ger-
> many. We can recruit our ranks from those classes only which have
> enjoyed a pretty good education; that is, from the universities and
> from the commercial class; and in neither we have not hitherto met
> with any considerable difficulty.[12]

This hash, which is pure Hess, gives a good idea of what some of the
better elements of the day were thinking and saying. Engels's next

contribution to the Owenite paper is especially taken from Weitling, who had also been praised in the previous article as the leader of the "working-class" wing of German communism. Engels now stresses

> the chief point in which Weitling is superior to Cabet, namely, the abolition of all government by force and by majority, and the establishment in its stead of a mere administration . . . [and] the proposal to nominate all officers of this administration . . . not by a majority of the community at large, but by those only who have a knowledge of the particular kind of work the future officer has to perform; and, one of the most important features of the plan, that the nominators are to select the fittest person, by means of some kind of prize essay.[13]

All this will give an idea of the thinking of the radical world into which Marx came. Engels's subsequent articles for the Owenites, at the end of 1844 and beginning of 1845, became gradually more ambivalent about the relation between communism and the classes.[14]

The turning point comes in late 1845—when Engels is well under way in collaboration with Marx on *The German Ideology*—and indeed in the very first article that Engels contributes, not to the Owenite organ, but to the Left Chartist paper *The Northern Star.* Engels spells out the complete turn he has made by cautioning the Chartists not to expect any revolutionary change from the middle classes:

> It is from the very heart of our working people that revolutionary action in Germany will commence. It is true, there are among our middle classes a considerable number of Republicans and even Communists, and young men too, who, if a general outbreak occurred now, would be very useful in the movement, but these men are "bourgeois," profit-mongers, manufacturers by profession; and who will guarantee us that they will not be demoralized by their trade, by their social position, which forces them to live upon the toil of other people, to grow fat by being the leeches, the "exploiteurs" of the working classes?

Those who remain "proletarian in mind" will be infinitely small in numbers, he goes on: "Fortunately, we do not count on the middle classes at all."[15]

Engels is now a Marxist.

III. MARX: THE CASE OF THE SAVIOUR-RULER

Marx's course appears to have been less complicated. Still, there are sig-nificant stages to be marked. One of the first nodal points showed him what the pursuit of an academic career would mean. As it happens, it has to do with the historic opposite of the principle of self-emancipation, viz. the illusion of the Savior-Ruler.

A common form of this illusion has always been hope for salvation from the ascent to the throne of a new, liberal monarch. Marx went through this at an early age along with the Left Hegelian circle.

In mid-1840 the old king of Prussia was succeeded by his son, Freidrich Wilhelm IV, who as Crown Prince had excited great hope in liberal circles that he would grant constitutional reforms; for he had made certain noises about liberty and national unity.[16] It seems to be a common habit of royal heirs; the same pattern had been true a century before, when Frederick the Great had uttered similar "nice phrases . . . shortly or immediately after his accession to the throne." So remarks Mehring in *The Lessing Legend*, which observes that this is "the noted liberalism of crown princes."[17] One of the leading lights of the Young Hegelians, Bruno Bauer, seized the opportunity to pay fulsome homage to "the highest idea of our State life," the spirit of the Hohenzollerns.[18]

These hopes for democratization from above collapsed quickly. Bauer's prostrations before the crown earned only a kick in the face: the new king appointed an orthodox reactionary to the university post that Bauer had his eye on.[19] Next, Bauer was even ousted from his post at the University of Bonn.[20] It was at this point that it was clear to Marx that, doctorate or no, an academic career was closed to him unless he was ready to bootlick the establishment like academia in general.

MARX AND KÖPPEN

There is indirect evidence that, with the rest, Marx had been caught up in the liberal illusion about the new king.

In April 1840, looking to the new reign, Marx's best friend,[21] Karl Friedrich Köppen, also a prominent Left Hegelian, though ten years older than Marx, had published a book on *Frederick the Great and His Opponents*.[22] One biographer of Marx describes the book as follows:

> Köppen honored Frederick, "in whose spirit we swore to live and die," as the enemy of Christian-German reaction. His basic idea was that

the state was embodied in its purest form in a monarchy ruled over by a monarch like Frederick, a philosopher, a free servant of the world spirit. Renewal could only come from the top . . .[23]

Köppen was suggesting that the new monarch should bear the torch of the Savior–Ruler like his great predecessor. Another biographer comments:

> The fact that a man like Köppen yearned for "the spiritual resurrection" of the worst despot in Prussian history in order "to exterminate with fire and sword all those who deny us entrance into the land of promise" is sufficient to give us some idea of the peculiar environment in which these Berlin Young Hegelians lived.[24]

This is unjust: there was nothing "peculiar" about this attitude. It had been dominant for a few thousand years, and essentially it still is. Frederick may have been "the worst despot" but he was a *modernizing* despot, and this variety still has mass allegiance from well-intentioned people, especially those who would like to become modernizing bureaucrats or mouthpieces for the modernizing despot. Marx's liberal friends held to the old illusion that, if only power found its way into the hands of a Good Man, he would hand down salvation from his seat of rule—and thus, incidentally, spare one all the inconveniences of having to conquer salvation for oneself in struggle against power.

Köppen's book was dedicated to "my friend Karl Heinrich Marx of Trier." There is every reason to believe that at this point Marx saw nothing "peculiar" about his friend's stance, and probably shared it.[25] In addition, the following year Marx returned the compliment with an admiring mention of Köppen's book in the planned foreword (dated March 1841) to his doctoral dissertation.[26]

The new king's failure to conform to the dream brought about a revulsion of feeling in liberal circles. Engels later described the result:

> Indeed, the middle classes, who had partly expected that the new King would at once grant a Constitution, proclaim the Liberty of the Press, Trial by Jury, etc., etc., in short, himself take the lead of that peaceful revolution which they wanted in order to obtain political supremacy—the middle classes had found out their error, and had turned ferociously against the King.[27]

In the Rhineland (continues Engels), this revulsion or exasperation produced the *Rheinische Zeitung* in Cologne, and made its bourgeois

sponsors temporarily willing to let Young Hegelian radicals edit it—
Marx becoming Editor in October 1842.

This is the place to mention that the young Engels also went through
his stage of disillusionment in benevolent royalty, before and after Friedrich Wilhelm IV. Just before, though not yet very radical, Engels had
written a friend about his disgust with Friedrich Wilhelm III's failure
to carry out his promise of a constitution:

> The same king who in 1815, beset with fear, promised his subjects in
> a Cabinet Order that they would get a constitution if they pulled him
> out of that pickle—this same shabby, lousy, god-damned king now
> lets it be known . . . that nobody is going to get a constitution from
> him . . . There is no period richer in royal crimes than 1816–1830;
> nearly every prince that reigned then deserved the death penalty . . .
> Oh, I could tell you delightful tales about the love that princes bear
> their subjects—I expect anything good only from the prince whose
> head is buzzing from the buffets of his people, and whose palace
> windows are being smashed by a hail of stones of the revolution.[28]

After the accession of the new king in 1840 and the abovementioned
"revulsion," Engels published an essay attacking the king's political and
social views and warning that a free press and a real parliament would
not be granted by the monarch but would have to be won by the people. It closed with a hint that Prussia was nearing its 1789.[29]

All this merely taught the liberals not to expect much from this
particular monarch; by nature, liberalism typically seeks reform by
seeking the ear that is connected to the hand that holds the levers of
power. But for Marx the lesson bit deeper. It was his last illusion in the
Savior-Ruler.

THE SERVILE STATE AND ACADEMIA

Marx later summarized the whole episode in hindsight at a point (May
1843) when he was in midstream of the passage from radical democracy
to communism. The king's "liberal speeches and outpourings" did
signify a desire "to bring life into the state," if only his own variety of
backward-looking life ("old German fancies"); but when even this variety of change threatened to open the gates to other changes, the old
bureaucratic-despotic system "soon killed these un-German activities."
It was a "miscarried attempt to transcend the philistine-state on its very
own basis."[30]

One was only mistaken for a while in considering it important which wishes and thoughts the King would come out with. This could not change anything in substance; the philistine is the stuff making up the monarchy, and the monarchy is always only the king of the philistines. He can make neither himself nor his people into free, real men, if both sides remain what they are.[31]

Since it was impossible for this state "to abandon its own basis and pass over to the human world of democracy," the inevitable result was

regression to the old fossilized servile state [Dienerstaat], in which the slave serves in silence and the owner of the land and the people rules as silently as possible simply through a well-trained, quietly obedient servant-staff. Neither of the two could say what they wanted—neither the former, that they wanted to become men, nor the latter that he had no use for men in his land. The only recourse, therefore, is to keep silent. Muta pecora, prona et ventri obedientia. [The herd is silent, submissive, and obeys its stomach.][32]

Therefore:

The self-reliance of men—freedom—would first have to be reawakened in the hearts of these men. Only this consciousness, which vanished from the world with the Greeks and into the blue mist of heaven with Christianity, can again turn society [Gesellschaft] into a community [Gemeinschaft] of men to achieve their highest purposes, a democratic state.[33]

For Marx, the freedom of self-reliance meant not only the abandonment of the Savior-Ruler illusion, but also the decision to abandon the road of scholarship in the university world. For that road was possible only by accepting a life of silent submission to the Servile State, refraining from giving battle to ensconced power, burying one's nose in scholarly busy-work and profound thoughts, while injustice and inhumanity reigned outside the stained glass windows.

IV. MARX: THE PROMETHEAN SPIRIT

If the course of the professional panderer to power was impossible for Marx, this was by no means simply determined by history or social forces, which do not determine this or that individual. It was demanded by Marx's total personality, combined with his intellect—the two conditioned by the times.

Marx's theories, to be sure, can be held by anyone, once developed:
but the way they were developed and the form in which they were
expressed were all heavily influenced by the impact of Marx's personal character. The steel core of that character has been portrayed
for all time by Marx's favorite poet-dramatist (alongside Shakespeare):
Aeschylus, in *Prometheus Bound*. Aeschylus does not really attempt to
explain why Prometheus, insisting on serving humanity, whom the
new gods would destroy, refuses to bow the neck to Zeus, to power—
like everyone else and as all his well-wishers advise him to do. That is
simply the fatality of his character.

It was also Marx's, and as far as anyone can tell, he seems to have
been born with it, as his intelligent father early recognized. Marx himself made the connection in preparing for publication the first child
of his thought, his doctoral dissertation. Although its subject was De-
mocritus and Epicurus, in writing the foreword, Marx handed the
center-stage over to Prometheus. The foreword ends with the invoca-
tion of Prometheus's defiance to authority:

> Prometheus' admission: "In sooth all gods I hate" is [philosophy's]
> own admission, its own motto against all gods, heavenly and earthly,
> who do not acknowledge the consciousness of man as the supreme di-
> vinity. There must be no god on a level with it . . . [Prometheus says:]
>   "I shall never exchange my fetters for slavish servility.
>   'Tis better to be chained to the rock than bound to the service of
> Zeus."
>   Prometheus is the noblest of saints and martyrs in the calendar of
> philosophy.[34]

The defiance of the closing sentence alarmed friend Bruno Bauer as
"unnecessary temerity"[35]—an unconscious echo of the very counsels of
timorous prudence to Prometheus by the leader of the chorus.

The dissertation itself had not mentioned Prometheus, although in
his workbooks for it Marx had written:

> . . . as Prometheus, who stole fire from Heaven, began to build houses
> and establish himself on the earth, so philosophy which has extended
> itself into the [real] world turns against the apparent world.[36]

Prometheus scarcely appears again in Marx's writings,[37] and the above
passages were never published in Marx's lifetime. But the comparison
was not lost upon those who knew him. When the government closed

down the *Rheinische Zeitung*, a contemporary cartoon depicted Marx as Prometheus bound to a printing press while the royal Prussian eagle gnaws at his vitals.[38] The last issue of the paper carried an unsigned farewell poem, ending on the Promethean note.

> Our mast blew down, but we were not affrighted,
> The angry gods could never make us bend.
> Columbus too at first was scorned and slighted,
> And yet he saw the New World in the end.
>
> Ye friends, who cheer us till the timbers rattle
> Ye foes, who did us honour with your strife—
> We'll meet again on other fields of battle:
> If all is dead, yet courage still is life.[39]

More amusing but not less indicative is the evidence of the impression that Marx's character made on his young associates. There is a long satiric "epic," protesting against the dismissal of Bruno Bauer, which Engels wrote *before* he knew Marx personally, containing versified portraits of the prominent Young Hegelians. The passage devoted to Marx goes approximately as follows, in limping hexameters:

> Then who, with fiercesome rage, comes rushing thereupon?
> A swarthy chap from Trier, a real phenomenon.
> He neither walks nor skips but springs up in the air,
> And storms about with red-hot fury as though to tear
>
> Down to the earth the far-hung tent of the broad sky—
> His arms he stretches up to seize the winds on high.
> With angry fist up-clenched, he rages without rest
> As if ten thousand flaming demons him possessed.[40]

The portraits in this "epic" are frankly friendly caricatures—the young Engels was a talented cartoonist—but there is no doubt of what kind of character is being caricatured.

CHOICE AND CHARACTER

And so it was history and the state of society that, in 1841, presented Marx with the choice: submit to power, or break with power. But it was Marx's character that made the choice a foregone conclusion.

Such a character will naturally always excite a variety of reactions. After all, many in the audience are in the position of Hephaestus, who, weeping salt tears very liberally, is the one who actually fetters the hero in chains, protesting that it is against his will. "The dirty job must be done," he whines to Power, "but don't push me too hard."

More are in the position of Oceanus, who delivers himself of sage advice: "I would admonish thee to prudence . . . see what are the wages of too bold a tongue. Thou hast not learned humility, nor to yield to evils . . ." He will try to negotiate peace with Zeus, but meanwhile: "Do thou keep thy peace, and restrain thy blustering speech." Others are in the position of the leader of the chorus, who has his own diagnosis of the hero's sins: "Care not for mortals overmuch, whilst you neglect your own profit."[41] (In other words: get a well-paying job instead of wasting your time in the British Museum.)

Then also in the audience are the descendants of Hermes, the "lackey of Zeus," who thinks anyone who does not cringe before power is simply stark mad—the very best frame of mind for a lackey.

V. MARX: THE EDUCATION OF THE EDUCATOR

But the Promethean rejection of injustice-by-power could be only half of Marx's road to the principle of self-emancipation; for as we have mentioned, there have been not a few who don the mask of Prometheus in order to replace Zeus as ruler. Aeschylus himself raised the question, long before Lord Acton: "Who could endure you in prosperity?" It is Zeus' lackey Hermes who directs this sneer to Prometheus.

Even after the collapse of the Savior-Ruler by 1841, Marx *must* have gone through the next stage, like everyone else: hope in some kind of intellectual elite, who, their hearts bursting with sympathy for the suffering people, would sacrifice themselves in order to lead the flock into a new and better sheepfold. The amazing thing about Marx is that there is only a single, and very ambiguous, scrap of evidence of such a state of mind even transiently, dating to the beginning of 1844. This occurs at the end of the article in which Marx first arrives at the idea that it is the emancipation of the proletariat that means the emancipation of all mankind. Then there is this sentence: "The *head* of this emancipation is *philosophy*, its *heart* is the *proletariat*."[42]

Taken by itself, this sentence is compatible with the tradition of an intellectual elite that conceives itself to be the head of the movement, with the masses making up the troops. On the other hand, this interpretation is difficult to reconcile with the whole train of thought for pages before, which it merely summarizes. Marx had already explained: "As philosophy finds its *material* weapons in the proletariat, the proletariat finds its *intellectual* weapons in philosophy," and the emancipation in question must be based "on the *theory* proclaiming that man is the highest essence of man," etc. These and many other expressions indicate that, by "philosophy," Marx literally means *theory*, and not the philosoph*ers*, that is, the intellectuals.[43]

Yet it is certain that even Engels understood this sentence in more or less the traditional elitist sense (which Engels himself still held).[44] And certainly it would have been an extraordinary feat if Marx had managed to skip this stage entirely.

But what is not in doubt is that the general trend of Marx's thinking went the other way "from the very beginning." As early as his pre-socialist writings of 1842 for the *Rheinische Zeitung*—in fact in his first published article, on freedom of the press—we find the following retort to a legislator who argued in the Diet that man is naturally imperfect and immature and needs educational guidance:

> For him true education consists in keeping man swaddled in the cradle all his life, since as soon as man learns to walk he also learns to fall, and only through falling does he learn to walk. But if we all remain children in swaddling-clothes, who is to swaddle us? If we all lie in the cradle, who is to cradle us? If we are all in jail, who will be the jailer?[45]

This extension of *Quis custodiet ipos custodes?* is already the fundamental answer to all the arguments, old and current, for "educational dictatorships." It already implies that emancipation is not a form of graduation ceremony (getting the diploma from teacher for passing the exam) but rather it is a process of struggle by people *who are not yet "ready" for emancipation*, and who can become ready for emancipation *only by launching the struggle themselves*, before anyone considers them ready for it.[46]

THEORY AND THE THEORETICIAN

This is the principle that Marx set down in the spring of 1845 in the third of his "Theses on Feuerbach"—one of the jottings in which he attempted to clarify a new world outlook for himself. The crux of the third thesis is that it asks the question: *Who will educate the educator?*

It goes directly to the elitist concept of the role of the educated "bringer of socialism" to the uneducated masses. Naturally Marx does not question the matter of *fact* that it is the educated who have raised the idea of socialism before the masses. That is how it *begins*; but it cannot be merely a one-way relationship. When Engels published his edited version of the "Theses" in 1888, he usefully concretized this meaning by introducing an example, Robert Owen, who was not in Marx's original note.

It was Owen's type of materialism which *onesidedly* emphasized that men are the products of their environmental circumstances and upbringing, and which concluded that to change men for the better, one had to change the environmental circumstances and upbringing. Marx's thesis cuts straight to the heart of the difficulty in this reasoning: *who* are the men who are going to operate this change? These men apparently stand exempt from the very law they enunciate; for they, who are also the product of their environmental conditioning, are going to act to change the world which conditioned them. Prometheus was able to change men from the outside, because he was himself a god; but Owen's (and Marx's) problem is harder than his.

Who are these "educators" to be, and how do they come into being? Owen's implied answer is very simple: they are "people like me," who just happen to get the idea, plus others whom I convince with its inexorable logic . . .

Against this, Marx's thesis points out (1) that "it is essential to educate the educator himself," and (2) that until this "educator" is himself changed ("educated"), one cannot overcome the division of society between rulers and ruled.

> The materialist doctrine concerning the changing of circumstances and upbringing [*that men are products of circumstances and upbringing and that therefore changed men are products of other circumstances and changed upbringing*] forgets that circumstances are changed by men [*themselves*], and that it is essential to educate the educator himself. Hence this doctrine must [*necessarily have the effect to*] divide society into two parts, one of which is superior to society. [*For example, in Robert Owen.*]
>
> The coincidence of the changing of circumstances and of human activity or self-changing can be conceived and rationally understood only as revolutionary practice.[47]

How then are the educators to be educated, and, for that matter, how do the uneducated become educators? How does this whole two-sided process of "self-changing" take place? Marx's answer is:

by "revolutionary practice." One learns to revolutionize society even as one revolutionizes oneself; one learns to revolutionize oneself by trying to revolutionize society. For the working class, it is a process in which two sides interpenetrate; a mountain climber, making his way up a "chimney" formation, can understand it better than a metaphysician.

This, the third thesis, is the "philosophic" formulation by Marx of the basis of the principle of self-emancipation. It represents the first time in socialist thought that theory turns around to take a hard look at the theoretician.

VI. THE REJECTION OF HUMANITARIAN-PHILANTHROPIC ELITISM

The third thesis entails, or leads right into, rejection of the whole humanitarian-philanthropic attitude toward the masses of people, which was typical not only of Owen and the utopians, but also of all the other pre-Marxian socialists to one degree or another. There are many reasons why the masses need protection from their friends, "but the greatest of these is charity." In the long run, a people can be held in subjection most effectively not by brute force but by gutting them of the capacity to fight for themselves.

St. Peter explained it long ago: "for charity shall cover the multitude of sins." It was explained also in Deuteronomy: "For the poor shall never cease out of the land: *therefore* I command thee, saying, Thou shalt open thine hand wide unto thy brother, to thy poor, and thy needy, in thy land." *Therefore* has been italicized here since it explains the practical reason for this holy injunction.

Marx's burst of indignation at this sociological strategy of Christianity was directed, in 1847, at a pious Prussian who sermonized that "if only those whose calling it is to develop the social principles of Christianity do so, the Communists will soon be put to silence":

> The social principles of Christianity have now had eighteen hundred years to develop and need no further development by Prussian councillors.
>
> The social principles of Christianity justified the slavery of Antiquity, glorified the serfdom of the Middle Ages, and equally know, when necessary, how to defend the oppression of the proletariat, although they make a pitiful face over it.

The social principles of Christianity preach the necessity of a ruling and an oppressed class, and all they have for the latter is the pious
wish the former will be charitable.

The social principles of Christianity transfer the councillors' adjustment of all infamies to heaven and thus justify the further existence of those infamies on earth.

The social principles of Christianity declare all vile acts of the
oppressors against the oppressed to be either the just punishment of
original sin and other sins or trials that the Lord in his infinite wisdom imposes on those redeemed.

The social principles of Christianity preach cowardice, self-con-
tempt, abasement, submission, dejection, in a word all the qualities of
the *canaille*; and the proletariat, not wishing to be treated as canaille,
needs its courage, its self-reliance, its pride and its sense of independence more than its bread.

The social principles of Christianity are sneakish and the proletariat is revolutionary.

So much for the social principles of Christianity.[48]

In this passage, the authentic Promethean spirit of self-reliant defiance
is transferred from the bosom of a god filled with "love of mankind"
to the proletariat itself.[49] Prometheus plus Spartacus equals the starting
point of Marxism.

THE CLASS CHARACTER OF CHARITY

From here on, Marx's war against humanitarian-philanthropic socialism is unremitting. Engels had anticipated it partly in his earlier *Condition of the Working Class in England*, in a passage attacking the charity
system—"your self-complacent, Pharisaic philanthropy"—which gives
the victim a hundredth part of what has been plundered from his labor:

> Charity which degrades him who gives more than him who takes;
> charity which treads the downtrodden still deeper in the dust, which
> demands that the degraded, the pariah cast out of society, shall first
> surrender the last that remains to him, his very claim to manhood,
> shall first beg for mercy before your mercy deigns to press, in the
> shape of an alms, the brand of degradation upon his brow.[50]

This first book of Engels's is one of those germinal works of which
it can be said, as Rupert Brooke did in another connection, that
"thoughts go blowing through them, are wiser than their own." By

1847 Engels was more direct. An article of his on the literature of the then prominent petty bourgeois "True-Socialist" tendency starts with a mortal thrust at one Karl Beck's "Songs of the Poor Man"—which begins with a poem addressed to the House of Rothschild:

> The poet does not threaten the destruction of the real power of Rothschild, the social conditions on which it is based; no, he wishes only it should be used philanthropically. He laments that the bankers are not socialistic philanthropists, not sentimental visionaries, not benefactors of humanity, but just bankers. Beck sings the praises of this cowardly, petty-bourgeois *misère*, of the "poor man," the *pauvre honteux*, with his poor, pious and contradictory desires, the "little man" in all his forms—not of the proud, menacing and revolutionary proletarian.[51]

About the same time, in *The Poverty of Philosophy*, Marx included a pungent page devoted to

> the *humanitarian school*, which . . . seeks, by way of easing its conscience, to palliate even if slightly the real contrasts; it sincerely deplores the distress of the proletariat, the unbridled competition of the bourgeois among themselves; it counsels the workers to be sober, to work hard and to have few children; it advises the bourgeois to put a reasoned ardor into production . . .
>
> The *philanthropic* school is the humanitarian school carried to perfection. It denies the necessity of antagonism; it wants to turn all men into bourgeois . . . The philanthropists, then, want to retain the categories which express bourgeois relations, without the antagonism which constitutes them and is inseparable from them. They think they are seriously fighting bourgeois practice, and they are more bourgeois than the others.[52]

The *Communist Manifesto* repeats this more concisely,[53] under the head of "bourgeois socialism," by which is meant bourgeois social reform; for in the pre-1848 period "*social*-ism" was still a common label simply for reformatory concern with the "social question." Besides Proudhon, who is specifically mentioned,

> to this section belong economists, philanthropists, humanitarians, improvers of the condition of the working class, organizers of charity, members of the society for the prevention of cruelty to animals, temperance fanatics, hole-and-corner reformers of every imaginable kind.[54]

And a little further, it is pointed out that utopian socialism, despite its positive "critical" content, tends to degenerate into this kind of social-ism too.[55] "Only from the point of view of being the most suffering class does the proletariat exist for them." And "the proletariat, as yet in its infancy, offers to them the spectacle of a class without any historical initiative or any independent political movement."[56] In contrast, the *Manifesto*'s message is that "the proletarian movement is the self-con-scious, independent movement of the immense majority, in the inter-ests of the immense majority."[57]

This is the "very beginning" to which Engels later referred, al-though the self-emancipation principle had not yet received the apho-ristic form under which it became famous.

VII. "TO WALK BY HIMSELF"

Henceforward the principle weaves through the analyses of Marx and Engels as an integral part of their thought. Here are some examples that come to hand.

During the revolutionary period that followed the *Communist Mani-festo*, Marx and Engels's articles in the *Neue Rheinische Zeitung* continu-ally appealed to action from below by the populace. In this connection Engels wrote at one point: "In Germany there are no longer any 'sub-jects,' ever since the people became so free as to emancipate themselves on the barricades."[58] At the beginning of another article, praising the resistance of the Poles to Prussian conquest, he relates a touching anec-dote about a practical philanthropist, picked up from a biography of the priest Joseph Bonavita Blank. The holy man was frequented by birds that hovered on and about him; and the people wondered mightily to see this new Saint Francis. No wonder: he had cut off the lower half of their beaks, so that they could get food only from his own charitable hands. Engels comments on his parable:

> The birds, says the biographer, *loved* him as *their benefactor.*
> And the shackled, mangled, branded Poles refuse to love their Prussian benefactors![59]

The experience of the revolution was one of the reasons why Marx was sensitized to the necessity of breaking the German people from the habit of obedience to authority from above:

> For the German working class the most necessary thing of all is
> that it should cease conducting its agitation by kind permission of
> the higher authorities. A race so schooled in bureaucracy must go
> through a complete course of "self-help."[60]

Around the same time, he embodied the same idea in a letter that we
have already quoted in the preceding chapter: "Here [in Germany]
where the worker's life is regulated from childhood on by bureaucracy
and he himself believes in the authorities, he must be taught before all
else to walk by himself."[61]

THE OCTROYAL PRINCIPLE

Of course, this applied not only to the Germans. It was ever present
to Marx's mind when he discussed the phenomenon of the state-spon-
sored "revolution from above" in connection with Bonapartism. In
pre-Bismarck Prussia, there were the Stein-Hardenberg reforms-from-
above, designed to rally support against Napoleon; in Russia there was
the tsar's emancipation of the serfs. Marx commented (in English):

> In both countries the social daring reform was fettered and limited
> in character because it was octroyed from the throne and not (in-
> stead of being) conquered by the people.[62]

"Octroyed" is a rare word in English, but deserves to be more widely
used. Its connotation—more than merely "grant" or "concede"—is
precisely the handing-down of changes from above, as against their
conquest from below. (In fact, "octroyal socialism" is a fine coinage for
the opposite of the Marxist principle of self-emancipation.)

In his book on the 1848 revolution in France, Marx recurs to a characteristic metaphor of the theatre (as in "theatre of war"): in this case,
not the contrast between "above" and "below," but rather between the
active participants on the stage of history and the passive onlookers of
the pit or the wings. On the first stage of the revolution:

> Instead of only a few factions of the bourgeoisie, all classes of French
> Society were suddenly hurled into the orbit of political power, forced
> to leave the boxes, the stalls and the gallery and to act in person upon
> the revolutionary stage![63]

On the peasantry who were momentarily set into motion—to give
Bonaparte his election victory of December 10, 1848:

> For a moment active heroes of the revolutionary drama, they could no
> longer be forced back into the inactive and spineless role of the chorus.[64]

This metaphor illuminates Marx's concept of the revolution from below as self-emancipation. Less figuratively, in another passage, Marx
mentions indicia of the proletariat's immaturity:

> As soon as it was risen up, a class in which the revolutionary interests
> of society are concentrated finds the content and the material for its
> revolutionary activity directly in it own situation: foes to be laid low,
> measures dictated by the needs of the struggle to be taken; the con-
> sequences of its own deeds drive it on . . . The French working class
> had not attained this level; it was still incapable of accomplishing its
> own revolution.[65]

The proletariat was as yet incapable of carrying through a rising from
below, under the self-impulsion of its own class drives.

After Bonaparte had consolidated his power, Engels remarked that
he hoped the old scoundrel was *not* assassinated. For in that case the
Bonapartist clique would merely make a deal with the Orleanist monarchy and go right on:

> Before the workers' districts could think about it, Morny would
> have made his palace-revolution, and although a revolution from
> below would be thereby postponed only briefly, yet its basis would
> be a different one.[66]

VIII. IN THE FIRST INTERNATIONAL

If the principle of self-emancipation had to be spelled out more formally in 1864, it was because of the problem Marx faced in drawing
up the program of the new International so as to gain the agreement of
a wide variety of political views. What programmatic statement could
delimit the organization as a *class movement* of the proletariat, yet avoid
lining up with any of the various ideological tendencies within that
class (or outside it)? The very concept of a *class program that was not a sect
programme*—not the programme of a Marxist sect either—was itself a
basic Marxist concept; but for this the movement was ready. The Preamble to the *Rules* was Marx's solution, beginning with the clause on
self-emancipation that we have already quoted.

The principle was so deceptively simple that naturally academic historians of socialism never got the point until years afterwards. Thus the

eminent Belgian historian Emile de Laveleye (one of those who, Engels rightly remarked, spread nothing but "lies and legends" about the history of the International[67]) wrote in *Le Socialisme Contemporain* in 1881:

> The International also affirmed that "the emancipation of the labourers must be the work of the labourers themselves." This idea seemed an application of the principle of "self-help"; it enlisted for the new association, even in France, the sympathies of many distinguished men who little suspected how it was to be interpreted later on. This affords a new proof of the fact frequently observed, that revolutionary movements always go on increasing in violence. The originators of the movement . . . are replaced by the more fanatical, who, in their turn, are pushed aside, until the final abyss is reached to which wild revolutionary logic inevitably leads.[68]

In contrast to this liberal ignoramus, the viciously reactionary historian of the International, Edmond Villetard, understood very quickly that the militants of the International were so wildly fanatical as to believe exactly what the principle of self-emancipation said. "No idea, without excepting perhaps their hatred of capital," he charges, "entered more passionately into their heads and hearts." He quotes one of the French militants who were arrested as Internationalists by the Bonaparte government:

> We have proclaimed sufficiently . . . that we no longer wanted deliverers, that we no longer wished to serve as instruments, and that we had the pretention to have knowledge of the situation, to understand our interests as well as any one.[69]

Once launched, the principle kept recurring in the documents of the International, whether written by Marx or others. In an official manifesto addressed to the National Labour Union of the United States, Marx went back to the "stage" metaphor:

> On you, then, devolves the glorious task to prove to the world that now at last the working classes are bestriding the scene of history no longer as servile retainers, but as independent actors, conscious of their own responsibility . . .[70]

In a manifesto denouncing the shooting of strikers in Belgium, Marx granted that the Belgian capitalist was so liberty-loving

> that he has always indignantly repulsed any factory law encroaching upon that liberty. He shudders at the very idea that a common work-

man should be wicked enough to claim any higher destiny than that of enriching his master and natural superior. He wants his workman not only to remain a miserable drudge, overworked and underpaid, but, like every other slaveholder, he wants him to be a cringing, servile broken-hearted, morally prostrate, religiously humble drudge. Hence his frantic fury at strikes. With him, a strike is a blasphemy, a slave's revolt, the signal of a social cataclysm.[71]

At a General Council discussion on the Irish question, in the course of a long speech attacking English policy, Marx put it sententiously: "The old English leaven of the conqueror comes out in the [government] statement: we will grant but you must ask."[72] In other words, the octroyal attitude of the master.

DO-IT-YOURSELF MOVEMENT

Not drafted by Marx but by other members of the Council was an address calling for an independent labor press:

> Benjamin Franklin is reported to have said, "If you want a thing done, and well done, do it yourself," and this is precisely what we must do . . . we must take the work of salvation into our own hands . . . In order to guard against deceitful friends, we require a press of our own.[73]

The historian Royden Harrison remarks that "the influence of the International and of Marx himself upon the Land and Labour League is nowhere more clearly in evidence" than in its address, modeled after Marx's, which appealed:

> There is one, and only one, remedy. Help yourselves. Determine that you will not endure this abominable state of things any longer; act up to your determination, and it will vanish . . . We are many; our opponents are few. Then working men and women of all creeds and occupations claim your rights . . . to conquer your own emancipation![74]

That combines Marx with Shelley.

Aside from manifestoes, the General Council of the International was made unaccustomedly sensitive to the question of who acted in their name. A small but symbolic point was worked out in the General Council meeting after it had adopted its well-known address to Abraham Lincoln, which was to be presented to the US embassy. The minutes record:

> A long discussion then took place as to the mode of presenting the
> address and the propriety of having a M.P. with the deputation; this
> was strongly opposed by many members who said working men
> should rely on themselves and not seek for extraneous aid.[75]

The motion that was passed limited the delegation to Council members. Marx related to Engels:

> Part of the Englishmen on the Committee wanted to have the depu-
> tation introduced by a member of Parliament since it was customary.
> This hankering was defeated by the majority of the English and the
> unanimity of the Continentals, and it was declared, on the contrary,
> that such old English customs ought to be abolished.[76]

There were other symbolic tests. In 1865 the General Council announced it had refused the proposal of a rich English lord who had
offered an annual subsidy to be the organization's "protector."[77] The
question of "Tory gold" was going to be an issue of self-emancipation
all through the century.

IX. ANTICIPATIONS OF FUTURE PROBLEMS

The outbreak of war in 1870 and the Paris Commune in 1871 brought
the question of self-emancipation out of the manifestoes and into reality. Later this is reflected in Marx's analysis of the nature of the Commune state. Here we mention some smaller but anticipatory reflections.

In the "Second Address" of the International on the war, Marx already points to that fact about the newly formed Republic of liberal
politicians that excites his "misgivings." It is the fact that it has been
engineered from above; that Bonapartism was not *subverted* (which
means overturned from below) but only replaced:

> That Republic has not subverted the throne, but only taken its place
> become vacant. It has been proclaimed, not as a social conquest, but
> as a national measure of defense.[78]

The great thing for Marx about the Commune was that it was just the
opposite: the working class of Paris took over.

> It is a strange fact. In spite of all the tall talk and all the immense
> literature, for the last sixty years, about Emancipation of Labour, no
> sooner do the working men anywhere take the subject into their
> own hands with a will, than uprises at once all the apologetic phra-
> seology of the mouthpieces of present society . . .[79]

(In fact, that very Republic of the bourgeoisie about which Marx expressed instant suspicion was the instrument for smashing the Republic of workers who took things into their own hands.)

We hear more from Marx about this in his writings on the Commune State. Here let us turn to some less familiar language, written by Marx in his first draft for *The Civil War in France*. It is a passage in which he asks: What is it that is new about this revolution? True, the workers have borne the brunt; but that has been true in all French revolutions. Then there is a second feature which is not new:

> That the revolution is made in the name and confessedly for the popular masses, that is, the producing masses, is a feature this Revolution has in common with all its predecessors. The new feature is that the people, after the first rise [rising], have not disarmed themselves and surrendered their power into the hands of the Republican mountebanks of the ruling classes, that, by the constitution of the Commune, they have taken the actual management of their Revolution into their own hands and found at the time, in the case of success, the means to hold it in the hands of the People itself, displacing the State machinery, the governmental machinery of the ruling classes by a governmental machinery of their own. This is their ineffable crime! Workmen infringing upon the governmental privilege of the upper 10,000 and proclaiming their will to break the economical basis of that class despotism which for its own sake wielded the organized State-force of society! This is it that has thrown the respectable classes in Europe as in the United States into the paroxysms of convulsions.[80]

There follows the statement, which was effectively expanded in the final version: "But the actual 'social' character of their Republic consists only in this, that workmen govern the Paris Commune!"[81] "Some patronizing friends of the working class," writes Marx,[82] ask sympathy for the Commune because it did not undertake any (utopian) "socialist enterprises." He replies:

> These benevolent patronizers, profoundly ignorant of the real aspirations and the real movement of the working classes, forget one thing. All the socialist founders of Sects belong to a period in which the working class themselves were neither sufficiently trained and organized by the march of capitalist society itself to enter as historical agents upon the world's stage.[83]

But (he goes on) it is no defect of the Commune that it refused to set up a Fourierist *phalanstère* or a little Icaria *à la* Cabet. What it did set up was the condition of its own emancipation, "no longer clouded in utopian fables"—for

> the government of the working class can only save France and do the national business, by working for its *own emancipation*, the conditions of that emancipation being at the same time the conditions of the regeneration of France.[84]

For Marx and Engels, there was a direct relationship between the revolutionary (literally subversive) nature of their socialism and the principle of emancipation-from-below, the principle that, as Engels wrote, "there is no concern for . . . gracious patronage from above."[85] By the same token, only a movement looking to class struggle from below could be a genuinely *proletarian* movement. For it was the proletariat that was "below," "the lowest stratum of our present society," which "cannot stir, cannot raise itself up, without the whole superincumbent strata of official society being sprung up into the air."[86]

Marxism, as the theory and practice of the proletarian revolution, therefore also had to be the theory and practice of the self-emancipation of the proletariat. Its essential originality flows from this source.

LENIN'S *THE STATE AND REVOLUTION*

Ralph Miliband

The State and Revolution (1918) is rightly regarded as one of Lenin's most important works. It addresses itself to questions of the utmost importance for socialist theory and practice, none of which have lost any of their relevance—rather the reverse. And as a statement of the Marxist theory of the state, both before and particularly after the conquest of power, it has, because it was written by Lenin, enjoyed an exceptionally authoritative status for successive generations of socialists, never more so than in recent years, since its spirit and substance can so readily be invoked against the hyper-bureaucratic experience of Russian-type regimes, and against official Communist parties as well. In short, here, for intrinsic and circumstantial reasons, is indeed one of the "sacred texts" of Marxist thought.

"Sacred texts," however, are alien to the spirit of Marxism, or at least should be; and this is itself sufficient reason for submitting *The State and Revolution* to critical analysis. But there is also another and more specific reason for undertaking such an analysis, namely that this work of Lenin is commonly held, within the Marxist tradition, to provide a theoretical and indeed a practical solution to the all-important question of the socialist exercise of power. My own reading of it suggests, for what it is worth, a rather different conclusion: this is that *The State and Revolution*, far from resolving the problems with which it is concerned, only serves to underline their complexity, and to emphasize something that the experience of more than half a century has in any case richly—and tragically—served to confirm, namely that the exercise of *socialist* power remains the Achilles' heel of Marxism. This is why, in a year that will witness so much legitimate celebration of Lenin's genius and achievements, a critical appraisal of *The State and Revolution* may not come amiss. For it is only by probing the gaps in the argument that it puts forward that the discussion of issues that are fundamental to the socialist project may be advanced.

The basic point upon which the whole of Lenin's argument rests, and to which he returns again and again, derives from Marx and Engels. This is that while all previous revolutions have "perfected" (i.e., reinforced) the state machine, "the working class cannot simply lay hold of the ready-made state machinery and wield it for its own purposes";[1] and that it must instead smash, break, and destroy that machinery. The cardinal importance that Lenin attaches to this idea has often been taken to mean that the purpose of *The State and Revolution* is to counterpose violent revolution to "peaceful transition." This is not so. The contraposition is certainly important and Lenin did believe (much more categorically than Marx, incidentally) that the proletarian revolution could not be achieved save by violent means. But as the Italian Marxist Lucio Colletti has recently noted, "Lenin's polemic is not directed against those who do not wish for the seizure of power. The object of his attack is not *reformism*. On the contrary, it is directed against those who wish for the seizure of power but not for the destruction of the old State as well."[2] "On the contrary" in the above quotation is too strong: Lenin is *also* arguing against reformism. But it is perfectly true that his main concern in *The State and Revolution* is to attack and reject any concept of revolution that does not take literally Marx's views that the bourgeois state must be smashed.

The obvious and crucial question that this raises is what kind of postrevolutionary state is to succeed the smashed bourgeois state. For it is of course one of the basic tenets of Marxism, and one of its basic differences with anarchism, that while the proletarian revolution must smash the old state, it does not abolish the state itself: *a* state remains in being, and even endures for a long time to come, even though it begins immediately to "wither away." What is most remarkable about the answer that Lenin gives to the question of the nature of the postrevolutionary state is how far he takes the concept of the "withering away" of the state in *The State and Revolution*: so far, in fact, that the state, on the morrow of the revolution, has not only *begun* to wither away, but *is already at an advanced stage of decomposition*.

This, it must be noted at once, does not mean that the revolutionary *power* is to be weak. On the contrary, Lenin never fails to insist that it must be very strong indeed, and that it must remain strong over an extended period of time. What it does mean is that this power is not exercised by the state in the common meaning of that word, i.e., as a separate and distinct organ of power, however "democratic"; but that "the state" has been turned from "a state of bureaucrats" into "a state of armed workers."[3] This, Lenin notes, is "a state machine nevertheless," but "in the shape of armed workers who proceed to form a militia involving the entire population."[4] Again, "all citizens are transformed into hired employees of the state, which consists of the armed workers";[5] and again, "the state, i.e., the proletariat armed and organized as the ruling class."[6] Identical or similar formulations occur throughout the work.

In *The Proletarian Revolution and the Renegade Kautsky*, written after the Bolshevik seizure of power, Lenin fiercely rejected Kautsky's view that a class "can only dominate but not govern": "It is altogether wrong, also," Lenin wrote, "to say that a class cannot govern. Such an absurdity can only be uttered by a parliamentary *cretin* who sees nothing but bourgeois parliaments, who has noticed nothing but 'ruling parties.'"[7] *The State and Revolution* is precisely based on the notion that the proletariat *can* "govern," and not only "dominate," and that it must do so if the dictatorship of the proletariat is to be more than a slogan. "Revolution," Lenin also writes "consists not in the new class commanding, governing with the aid of the *old* state machine, but in this class *smashing* this machine and commanding, governing with the aid of a *new* machine. Kautsky slurs over this *basic* idea of Marxism, or he does not understand it at all."[8] This new "machine," as it appears in *The State and Revolution*, is the state of the armed workers. What is involved here, to all appearances, is *unmediated* class rule, a notion much more closely associated with anarchism than with Marxism.

This needs to be qualified. But what is so striking about *The State and Revolution* is *how little* it needs to be qualified, as I propose to show.

Lenin strongly attacks the anarchists, and insists on the need to retain the state in the period of the dictatorship of the proletariat. "We are not utopians," he writes, "we do not 'dream' of dispensing *at once* with all administration, with all subordination."[9] But he then goes on:

> The subordination, however, must be to the armed vanguard of all the exploited and working people, *i.e., to the proletariat* [my italics]. A beginning can and must be made at once, overnight, to replace the

specific "bossing" of state officials by the simple functions of "foremen and accountants," functions which are already fully within the
ability of the average town dweller and can well be performed for
workmen's wages. *We*, the workers, shall organize large-scale production on the basis of what capitalism has already created, relying
on our own experience as workers, establishing strict, iron discipline
backed by the state of the armed workers. We shall reduce the role
of state officials to that of simply carrying out our instructions as responsible, revocable, moderately paid "foremen and accountants" (of
course, with the aid of technicians of all sorts, types, and degrees.)[10]

Clearly, some kind of officialdom continues to exist, but equally clearly,
it functions under the strictest and continuous supervision and control
of the armed workers; and officials are, as Lenin notes repeatedly, revocable at any time. "Bureaucrats," on this view, have not been altogether
abolished; but they have been reduced to the role of utterly subordinate
executants of the popular will, as expressed by the armed workers.

As for a second main institution of the old state, the standing army, it
has been replaced, in the words quoted earlier, by armed workers who
proceed to form a militia involving the whole population.

Thus, two institutions that Lenin views as "most characteristic" of
the bourgeois state machine have been radically dealt with:[11] one of
them, the bureaucracy, has been drastically reduced in size and what
remains of it has been utterly subdued by direct popular supervision,
backed by the power of instant revocability; while the other, the standing army, has actually been abolished.

Even so, Lenin stresses, the centralized state has *not* been abolished.
But it takes the form of "voluntary centralism, of the voluntary amal-
gamation of the communes into a nation, of the voluntary fusion of the
proletarian communes, for the purpose of destroying bourgeois rule
and the bourgeois state machine."[12]

Here, too, the obvious question concerns the *institutions* through
which the dictatorship of the proletariat may be expressed. For Lenin
does speak in *The State and Revolution* "of a gigantic replacement of
certain institutions by other institutions of a fundamentally different
type."[13] But *The State and Revolution* has actually very little to say about
institutions, save for some very brief references to the Soviets of Workers' and Soldiers' Deputies.

Lenin reserves some of his choicest epithets for one form of representative institution, namely "the venal and rotten parliamentarism of bourgeois society."[14] However, "the way out of parliamentarism is not, of course, the abolition of representative institutions and the elective principle, but the conversion of the representative institutions from talking shops into 'working bodies.'"[15] The institutions that embody this principle are, as noted, the Soviets of Workers' and Soldiers' Deputies. On one occasion, Lenin speaks of "the simple *organization* of the armed people (such as the Soviet of Workers' and Soldiers' Deputies. . . .)";[16] on another, of "the conversion of *all* citizens into workers and other employees of *one* huge 'syndicate'—the whole state—and the complete subordination of the entire work of this syndicate to a genuinely democratic state, the state of the Soviets of Workers' and Soldiers' Deputies";[17] and the third such reference is in the form of a question: "Kautsky develops a 'superstitious reverence' for 'ministries'; but why can they not be replaced, say, by committees of specialists working under sovereign, all-powerful Soviets and Workers' and Soldiers' Deputies?"[18] It must be noted, however, that the soviets are "sovereign and all-powerful" in relation to the "committee" of which Lenin speaks. In regard to their constituents, the deputies are of course subject to recall at any time: "representation" must here be conceived as operating within the narrow limits determined by popular rule.

The "state" of which Lenin speaks in *The State and Revolution* is therefore one in which the standing army has ceased to exist; where what remains of officialdom has come to be completely subordinated to the armed workers; and where the representatives of these armed workers are similarly subordinated to them. It is this "model," which would seem to justify the contention, advanced earlier, that the "state" that expresses the dictatorship of the proletariat is, already on the morrow of the revolution, at a stage of advanced decomposition.

The problems that this raises are legion; and the fact that they are altogether ignored in *The State and Revolution* cannot be left out of account in a realistic assessment of it.

The first of these problems is that of the *political mediation* of the revolutionary power. By this I mean that the dictatorship of the proletariat is obviously inconceivable without *some* degree, at least, of political articulation and leadership, which implies political organization. But the extraordinary fact, given the whole cast of Lenin's mind, is that the political element that otherwise occupies so crucial a place in his thought, namely the party, receives such scant attention in *The State and Revolution*.

There are three references to the party in the work, two of which have no direct bearing on the issue of the dictatorship of the proletariat. One of these is an incidental remark concerning the need for the party to engage in the struggle "against religion which stupifies the people";[19] the second, equally incidental, notes that "in revising the programme of our Party, we must by all means take the advice of Engels and Marx into consideration, in order to come nearer the truth, to restore Marxism by ridding it of its distortions, to guide the struggle of the working class for its emancipation more correctly."[20] The third and most relevant reference goes as follows: "By educating the workers' party, Marxism educates the vanguard of the proletariat, capable of assuming power and *leading the whole people* to socialism, of directing and organizing the new system, of being the teacher, the guide, the leader of all the working and exploited people in organizing their social life without the bourgeoisie and against the bourgeoisie."[21]

It is not entirely clear from this passage whether it is the *proletariat* that is capable of assuming power, leading, directing, organizing, etc.; or whether it is the *vanguard* of the proletariat, i.e., the workers' party, that is here designated. Both interpretations are possible. On the first, the question of political leadership is left altogether in abeyance. It may be recalled that it was so left by Marx in his considerations on the Paris Commune and on the dictatorship of the proletariat. But it is not something which *can*, it seems to me, be left in abeyance in the discussion of revolutionary rule—save in terms of a theory of spontaneity which constitutes an avoidance of the problem rather than its resolution. On the other hand, the second interpretation, which fits in better with everything we know of Lenin's appraisal of the importance of the party, only serves to raise the question without tackling it. That question is of course absolutely paramount to the whole meaning of the concept of the dictatorship of the proletariat: What is the relationship between the *proletariat*, whose dictatorship the revolution is deemed to establish, and *the party*, which educates, leads, directs, organizes, etc.? It is only on the basis of an *assumption* of a symbiotic, organic relationship between the two, that the question vanishes altogether; but while such a relationship may well have existed between the Bolshevik Party and the Russian proletariat in the months preceding the October Revolu-

tion, i.e., when Lenin wrote *The State and Revolution*, the assumption
that this kind of relationship can ever be taken as an automatic and
permanent fact belongs to the rhetoric of power, not to its reality.

Whether it is the party or the proletariat that is, in the passage above,
designated as leading the whole people to socialism, the fact is that
Lenin did of course assert the former's central role after the Bolsheviks had seized power. Indeed, he was, by 1919, asserting its exclusive
political guidance. "Yes, the dictatorship of one party!" he said then:
"We stand upon it and cannot depart from this ground, since this is the
party which in the course of decades has won for itself the position of
vanguard of the whole factory and industrial proletariat." In fact, "the
dictatorship of the working class is carried into effect by the party of
the Bolsheviks which since 1905 or earlier has been united with the
whole revolutionary proletariat."[22] Later on, as E.H. Carr also notes,
he described the attempt to distinguish between the dictatorship of
the class and the dictatorship of the party as proof of an "unbelievable
and inextricable confusion of thought";[23] and in 1921, he was bluntly
asserting against the criticisms of the Workers' Opposition that "the
dictatorship of the proletariat is impossible except through the Communist Party."[24]

This may well have been the case, but it must be obvious that this is
an altogether different "model" of the exercise of revolutionary power
from that presented in *The State and Revolution*, and that it radically
transforms the meaning to be attached to the "dictatorship of the proletariat." At the very least, it brings into the sharpest possible form the
question of the relation between the ruling party and the proletariat.
Nor even is it the *party* which is here in question, but rather the party
leadership, in accordance with that grim dynamic that Trotsky had pro-
phetically outlined after the split of Russian Social Democracy between
Bolsheviks and Mensheviks, namely that "the party organization [the
caucus] at first substitutes itself for the party as a whole; then the Central
Committee substitutes itself for the organization; and finally a single
'dictator' substitutes itself for the Central Committee. . ."[25]

For a time after the Revolution, Lenin was able to believe and claim
that there was no conflict between the dictatorship of the proletariat
and the dictatorship of the party; and Stalin was to make that claim
the basis and legitimation of his own total rule. In the case of Lenin,
very few things are as significant a measure of his greatness than that

he should have come, while in power, to question that identification, and to be obsessed by the thought that it could not simply be taken for granted. He might well, as his successors were to do, have tried to conceal from himself the extent of the gulf between the claim and the reality: that he did not and that he died a deeply troubled man is not the least important part of his legacy,[26] though it is not the part of his legacy that is likely to be evoked, let alone celebrated, in the country of the Bolshevik Revolution.

It is of course very tempting to attribute the transformation of the dictatorship of the proletariat, as presented in *The State and Revolution* into the dictatorship of the party, or rather of its leaders, to the particular circumstances of Russia after 1917—to backwardness, civil war, foreign intervention, devastation, massive deprivation, popular disaffection, and the failure of other countries to heed the call of revolution.

The temptation, it seems to me, ought to be resisted. Of course, the adverse circumstances with which the Bolsheviks had to cope were real and oppressive enough. But I would argue that these circumstances only aggravated, though certainly to an extreme degree, a problem which is *in any case* inherent in the concept of the dictatorship of the proletariat. The problem arises because that dictatorship, even in the most favorable circumstances, is unrealizable without political mediation; and because the necessary introduction of the notion of political mediation into the "model" considerably affects the latter's character, to say the least. This is particularly the case if political mediation is conceived in terms of single party rule. For such rule, even if "democratic centralism" is much more flexibly applied than has ever been the case, makes much more difficult, and may preclude, the institutionalization of what may loosely be called socialist pluralism. This is exceptionally difficult to achieve and may even be impossible in most revolutionary situations. But it is just as well to recognize that unless adequate provision is made for *alternative* channels of expression and political articulation, which the concept of single party rule excludes by definition, any talk of socialist democracy is so much hot air. Single party rule postulates an undivided, revolutionary proletarian will of which it is the natural expression. But this is not a reasonable postulate upon which to rest the "dictatorship of proletariat": in no society, however constituted, is there an undivided, single popular will. This is precisely why the problem of political mediation arises. The problem need not be thought insuperable. But its resolution requires, for a start, that it should at least be *recognized*.

The question of the party, however, brings one back to the question of the state. When Lenin said, in the case of Russia, that the dictator-ship of the proletariat was impossible except through the Communist Party, what he also implied was that the party must infuse its will into and assure its domination over the institutions that had, in *The State and Revolution*, been designated as representing the armed workers. In 1921 he noted that "as the governing party we could not help fusing the Soviet 'authorities' with the party 'authorities'—with us they are fused and they will be";[27] and in one of his last articles in *Pravda*, writ-ten in early 1923, he also suggested that "the flexible union of Soviet with party element," which had been a "source of enormous strength" in external policy "will be at least equally in place (I think, far more in place) if applied to our whole state apparatus."[28] But this means that if the party must be strong, so must the state that serves as its organ of rule. And indeed, as early as March 1918, Lenin was saying that "for the present we stand unconditionally for the state"; and to the question that he himself put: "When will the state begin to die away?" he gave the answer: "We shall have time to hold more than two congresses be-fore we can say, See how our state is dying away. Till then it is too soon. To proclaim in advance the dying away of the state will be a violation of historical perspective."[29]

There is one sense in which this is perfectly consistent with *The State and Revolution*; and another, more important sense, in which it is not. It is consistent in the sense that Lenin always envisaged a strong power to exist after the revolution had been achieved. But it is inconsistent in the sense that he also, in *The State and Revolution*, envisaged this power to be exercised, not by the state as commonly understood, but by a "state" of armed workers. Certain it is that the state of which he was speaking after the revolution was not the state of which he was speaking when he wrote *The State and Revolution*.

Here, too, I believe that simply to attribute the inconsistency to the particular Russian conditions that faced the Bolsheviks is insufficient. For it seems to me that the kind of all-but-unmediated popular rule that Lenin describes in the work belongs in fact, whatever the circum-stances in which revolution occurs, to a fairly distant future, in which, as Lenin himself put it, "the need for violence against people in general, for the *subordination* of one man to another, and of one section of the population to another, will vanish altogether since people will become accustomed to observing the elementary conditions of social life *without violence* and *without subordination*."[30] Until that time, a state does endure, but it is not likely to be of the kind of state of which Lenin speaks in *The State and Revolution*: it is a state about which it is not necessary to use inverted commas.

In Lenin's handling of the matter, at least in *The State and Revolution*, two "models" of the state are contraposed in the sharpest possible way: *either* there is the "old state," with its repressive, military-bureaucratic apparatus, i.e., the bourgeois state; *or* there is the "transitional" type of state of the dictatorship of the proletariat which, as I have argued, is scarcely a state at all. But if, as I believe, this latter type of "state" represents, on the morrow of a revolution and for a long time after, a short cut that real life does not allow,[31] Lenin's formulations serve to avoid rather than to meet the fundamental question, which is at the center of the socialist project, namely the kind of state, without inverted commas, that is congruent with the exercise of socialist power.

In this respect, it needs to be said that the legacy of Marx and Engels is rather more uncertain than Lenin allows. Both men undoubtedly conceived it as one of the main tasks, indeed *the* main task of the proletarian revolution, to "smash" the old state; and it is also perfectly true that Marx did say about the Commune that it was "the political form at last discovered under which to work out the economic emancipation of labour."[32] But it is not irrelevant to note that, ten years after the Commune, Marx also wrote that "quite apart from the fact that this [i.e., the Commune] was merely the rising of a city under exceptional conditions, the majority of the Commune was in no sense socialist, nor could be."[33] Nor of course did Marx ever describe the Commune as the dictatorship of the proletariat. Only Engels did so, in the 1891 Preface to *The Civil War in France*: "Of late, the Social-Democratic Philistine has once more been filled with wholesome terror at the words: Dictatorship of the Proletariat. Well and good, gentlemen, do you want to know what this dictatorship looks like? Look at the Paris Commune. That was the Dictatorship of the Proletariat."[34] But in the same year, 1891, Engels also said, in his "Critique of the Draft of the Erfurt Programme of the German Social Democratic Party," that "if one thing is certain it is that our party and the working class can only come to power in the form of the democratic republic. This is even the specific form for the dictatorship of the proletariat, as the Great French Revolution has already shown."[35] Commenting on this, Lenin states that "Engels repeated here in a particularly striking form the fundamental idea which runs through all of Marx's works, namely that the democratic republic is the nearest approach to the dictatorship of the proletariat."[36] But the "nearest approach" is *not* "the specific form"; and it may be doubted that the notion of the democratic republic as the nearest approach to the dictatorship of the proletariat is a fundamental idea which runs through all of Marx's works. Also, in the preface to *The Civil War in France*, Engels said of the state that "at best it is an evil inherited by the proletariat after its victorious struggle for class supremacy, whose *worst sides* the victorious proletariat will have to lop off *as speedily as possible*, just as the Commune had to, until a generation reared in new, free social conditions is able to discard the entire lumber of the state."[37]

It is on the basis of such passages that the Menshevik leader, Julius Martov, following Kautsky, wrote after the Bolshevik revolution that in speaking of the dictatorship of the proletariat, Engels is not employing the term "to indicate *a form of government*, but to designate the *social structure* of the State power."[38]

This seems to me to be a misreading of Engels, and also of Marx. For both men certainly thought that the dictatorship of the proletariat meant not only "the social structure of the State power" but also and quite emphatically "a form of government"; and Lenin is much closer to them when he speaks in *The State and Revolution* of "a gigantic replacement of certain institutions by institutions of a fundamentally different type."[39]

The point, however, is that, even taking full account of what Marx and Engels have to say about the Commune, they left these institutions of a fundamentally different type to be worked out by later generations; and so, notwithstanding *The State and Revolution*, did Lenin.

This, however, does not detract from the importance of the work. Despite all the questions that it leaves unresolved, it carries a message whose importance the passage of time has only served to demonstrate: this is that the socialist project is an antibureaucratic project, and that at its core is the vision of a society in which "for the first time in the history of civilized society, the *mass* of the population will rise to take an *independent* part, not only in voting and elections, but *also in the everyday administration of the state.* Under socialism *all* will govern in turn and will soon become accustomed to no one governing."[40] This was also Marx's vision; and one of the historic merits of *The State and Revolution* is to have brought it back to the position it deserves on the socialist agenda. Its second historic merit is to have insisted that this must not be allowed to remain a far-distant, shimmering hope that could safely be disregarded in the present; but that its actualization must be considered as an immediate part of revolutionary theory and practice. I have argued here that Lenin greatly overestimated in *The State and Revolution* how far the state could be made to "wither away" in any conceivable postrevolutionary situation. But it may well be that the integration of this kind of overestimation into socialist thinking is the necessary condition for the transcendence of the grey and bureaucratic "practicality" that has so deeply infected the socialist experience of the last half-century.

SOME PROBLEMS CONCERNING REVOLUTIONARY CONSCIOUSNESS

Harold Wolpe

I.

In the analysis of revolutionary change (whether by this is meant the seizure of power or the transformation of the core institutional order or both), the situations in which such change becomes possible have generally been conceived of as a complex combination of two types of conditions. These are, on the one hand, objective or structural conditions including the distribution of power, economic crises, the incapacity of the government to govern, etc., and, on the other hand, subjective factors including the political beliefs or consciousness of one or more sections of the population, political actions, etc.

Despite, however, this characterization of the revolutionary situation in terms of both objective and subjective elements, not only has systematic analysis tended to focus on the processes that produce the objective conditions of revolutionary situations, but it is also in this area that theory is most advanced. The considerable body of empirical and theoretical analysis of structural contradictions in the economic system testifies to this.

By contrast, there has been relatively little progress toward the elaboration of a theory concerning the development of the subjective conditions of revolutionary situations. In part, this is no doubt due to the inherent complexities of the issues but in addition, with notable exceptions,[1] there has been a tendency to neglect the analytical problems involved. This, in itself, is curious, given the fact that the assertion that mass revolutionary consciousness is a condition of radical social change was made long ago by writers as divergent in their approaches as Tocqueville and Marx,[2] and that the latter, in particular, provided some of

the basic propositions for the development of such a theory. Be that as
it may, the fact nevertheless remains that much of the empirical analysis of the conditions and manner in which the subjective perceptions
of the relevant groups develop is, as a consequence, either ad hoc and
unsystematic, or treats revolutionary consciousness as the unproblem-
atical outcome of certain situations and actions. In this way, the very
questions that require explanation become obscured.

Thus, to take only one example at this stage, Mandel in a recent
article ascribes the revolutionary upsurge in France in May 1968 to
the contradictions in the capitalist system coupled with the detonating
effect of the students revolting against the deficiencies of the educational system.[3] But why, given the fact that the inadequacies in the
universities arose not in 1968 but long before, did the student revolt
occur only in May 1968 and furthermore, why, given the persistence of
the contradictions of capitalism and the occurrence of earlier dramatic
events (strikes, etc.) did the workers respond as they did only in May
1968? The point is that radical changes in attitudes and action cannot
simply be ascribed to *relatively unchanged* structural conditions. What
needs to be examined is the way in which objective reality comes
to be subjectively perceived and this entails more than an analysis of
objective conditions coupled with a description of subjective reactions.

For various reasons,[4] the inadequacies of approaching the subject in
this way have been, in the recent past, increasingly subjected to scru-
tiny and it is with some of the theoretical bases of these inadequacies
that the present essay is concerned. Before turning to an examination
of the issues involved, however, the scope of the essay must be deline-
ated more explicitly.

It is necessary to emphasize, in the first instance, that the main concern here is the question of *mass* revolutionary consciousness. This
means that the focus of interest is not on the systematic ideologies
developed by intellectuals but rather on what Gramsci termed "the
philosophy of common sense . . . the philosophy of the non-philos-
opher."[5] From this perspective, formal ideologies may be regarded as
possibly constituting one of the ingredients (perhaps, in particular concrete instances, an important or even crucial one) of common sense
"philosophy."

This, it should be made clear, is not to contend that it is either a necessary or a sufficient condition of revolutionary change that the masses

should intend it. On the contrary, it is perfectly possible, for example, that large-scale action by the masses, in pursuance of goals that are themselves rather limited, may result in a situation in which it becomes feasible for a party or group intent upon the revolutionary seizure of power being able to seize it. Arguably the general strike in France in May and June 1968, which rendered the state temporarily incapable of exercising control in the face of very limited economic demands, is an illustration of this type of possibility.

Nevertheless, the preparedness or otherwise of the masses to pursue revolutionary demands is clearly an extremely important element at certain points in the process of effecting revolutionary change. It is precisely for this reason that theorists of revolution have regarded mass revolutionary consciousness as generally relevant to effective mass action and, therefore, as an important condition of revolution.

The second main limitation on the scope of the paper is that it is in no sense intended as a systematic examination of theories of revolution. It is restricted to one aspect of such theories, namely: Under what conditions and in what way does mass revolutionary consciousness develop?

Clearly, this question raises vast issues that ultimately cannot be satisfactorily resolved out of the context of not only a theory of revolution, but more generally, a theory of society—in fact, it will be argued that the failure to incorporate the analysis of revolutionary consciousness into such a theory lies at the core of many of the difficulties besetting the subject. Nevertheless, it is possible to focus on the specific elements that have direct bearing on the creation of revolutionary consciousness in such a way as to expose the links that various writers make between consciousness and other factors. Although this necessarily results in a somewhat abstract analysis, it has the advantage of bringing to light problems and weaknesses that otherwise tend to remain hidden in the discussion.

The strategy adopted in this paper is to examine what a number of writers have had to say about revolutionary consciousness. This makes it possible to show how each writer, in explaining consciousness, stresses some conditions or processes but neglects others that constitute the focus of attention of one of the other writers reviewed. At the same time, this provides the basis for the central contention in this paper, which is that an adequate approach requires that the conditions or processes that are separately discussed by each writer be brought together and incorporated into an analysis that simultaneously takes account of all of them.

II.

The notion that revolutionary consciousness emerges spontaneously from certain objective conditions is to be found in a number of approaches. The property that is common to these approaches, and that links them, is the assumption that the conditions that are necessary and sufficient to the development of mass revolutionary consciousness are to be found exclusively in the "external" environment in which the masses act; that is to say, the actions of the masses themselves are not considered relevant. What differentiates the various views within this common category is the range and nature of the conditions of the "external" environment that are specified as being operative.

It is convenient to begin with the "theory" of revolution advanced by J. G. Davies,[6] an academic sociologist, whose analysis is both fairly representative of a particular type of approach and has the merit, for present purposes, of raising sharply some of the major problems with which the paper is concerned.

Davies presents a variant of the theory that increasing impoverishment leads to revolutionary consciousness. The impoverishment thesis is widely held, although sometimes it is not easy to see that it is this view which is being advanced, because it is incorporated into a sophisticated and complex account of the way in which impoverishment occurs. Nonetheless, both the simple and complex forms suffer from the same inadequacies.

Davies's argument is that if a prolonged period of rising living standards is followed by a sharp decline in social and economic levels, then the resulting gap between the actors' expectations of need satisfaction and the actual level of satisfaction of those needs,[7] whatever they are, will come to be perceived as intolerable and that this perception amounts to revolutionary consciousness.[8]

It is apparent that the restriction of the content of revolutionary consciousness in this way flows directly from the selection of a single, isolated variable as the necessary and sufficient condition of its production. For, if the gap between expectation and satisfaction is postulated as the sole producer of revolutionary consciousness, there is no reason to suppose that the latter comprises anything other than a perception of the intolerability of the gap. While there can be no doubt that one of the constituent elements of revolutionary consciousness is a feeling of overwhelming dissatisfaction with, or an awareness of the intolerability

of, "living in the old way,"[9] it is not, however, adequate to assume, as
Davies does, that this is the only, or at least the only essential, aspect of
revolutionary consciousness.

The obvious limitations of narrowing down the concept in this
manner are related to the fact that overwhelming dissatisfaction may
also be linked with a belief that suitable changes can be effected within
the existing structure, or with a belief in the immutability of the status quo and the impossibility of change. Thus, since a perception of
the present as intolerable may be common to both revolutionary and
non-revolutionary consciousness, the former can only be differentiated
from the latter in terms of some additional factors.

Briefly, the two *specifica differentia* of revolutionary consciousness are,
it is suggested, as follows: First, there must be a belief that "revolution
is necessary."[10] That is, the oppressed classes or masses must have a
consciousness "of the irreconcilable antagonism of their interests to
the whole of the modern political and social system"[11]—a belief, that is,
that the intolerable conditions of life can be terminated only in a radically different social system. This entails, as Gramsci has shown, not
only a vision (however crude) of new economic and political structures,
but also a more or less integrated, coherent and total challenge to the
political, cultural and ideological "hegemony" of the existing order.[12]

The second distinctive quality of revolutionary consciousness, and
one which has not generally been discussed in the literature, is that
change must be perceived as possible in two different senses. In one
sense, the belief in the possibility of change involves an understanding
of the relative nature of social institutions. That is to say, institutions
that have assumed a natural, reified and immutable appearance must
come to be seen as man-made and changeable. This implies the de-re-
ification of the institutional structure in men's consciousness.[13] In the
second sense, the belief in the possibility of change is a belief in the
"physical" capacity to secure the desired change whatever the given distribution of resources, men, and material may be. This involves, above
all, a conception of the assailability of the structure of power.

If, then, revolutionary consciousness is conceived of as a conjuncture of the three abovementioned characteristics, the crucial question
relates to the conditions in which this conjuncture develops.

It follows from this characterization of revolutionary belief that if
Davies's theory is to have any substance, it must be a necessary impli-

cation of his analysis that the same conditions, that is, the objectively declining living standards, etc., which produce an awareness of the intolerability of the gap between expectations and reality, must also result in a belief in the necessity and possibility of radical change. The hard empirical fact is, however, that this *simple* conjuncture does not occur—on the contrary, extreme impoverishment may be accompanied by extreme passivity.

It is, perhaps, the unacknowledged recognition of this fact that forces Davies ultimately to "explain" revolutionary consciousness completely independently of the objective conditions with which his analysis began. This point is of considerable importance, because the relationship between objective conditions and revolutionary consciousness presents an apparently intractable problem which tends to be "solved," not only by Davies but, as I will attempt to show, by Marxist writers also, by the expedient of rupturing the relationship between objective or structural conditions and subjective responses. A further reference to Davies's analysis will help clarify this point.

As I have already indicated, Davies begins by answering the question, "Under what conditions does the gap between expectations and actual satisfaction come to be perceived as intolerable?" by referring to a particular objective development. He describes this as "when a prolonged period of objective economic and social development is followed by a short period of sharp reversal."[14] This is apparently so because under these conditions, "the all important effect on the minds of people . . . is to produce during the former period, an expectation of continued ability to satisfy needs— which continue to rise—and during the latter, a mental state of anxiety and frustration when manifest reality breaks away from anticipated reality."[15] It may be pointed out, in parenthesis, that Davies does not show on theoretical grounds why such a gap should be perceived as intolerable only after a period of *increasing* satisfaction, nor do his extremely vague case studies of specific revolutions bear out this contention.

More importantly, since the gap between expectations and actual satisfaction of needs is crucial, the question arises whether any gap whatsoever will produce revolutionary consciousness, or only gaps of a particular type or size. One answer proffered by Davies is that only gaps of a certain magnitude will have revolutionary consequences. He refers to "sharp reversals" of social and economic development and, in considering why revolutions did not occur in certain historical situations, asks: "Had expectations . . . not risen *high* enough? Had the subsequent decline not been sufficiently *sharp* or *deep*?"[16]

From this it seems to follow that, for Davies, the utility of the theory depends upon the possibility of measuring the gap, since this would enable him to predict at what point revolutionary consciousness would develop. Unfortunately, at present the gap cannot be measured, but only, he argues, because we do not yet have available the appropriate techniques of measurement.

Curiously, he fails to see that on the basis of his own further argument the measurement of the critical gap becomes, in principle, of no consequence. He says: "The actual state of socio-economic development is less significant than the expectation that past progress, now blocked, can and must continue in the future."[17] And again: "It is the dissatisfied state of mind rather than the tangible provision of 'adequate' or 'inadequate' supplies of food, equality or liberty which produces the revolution."[18]

This being the case, the objective conditions, the reality of the gap and of the decline in socioeconomic conditions, become irrelevant and need not, therefore, exist at all. Starting, then, with the conception of objective economic, etc., decline as the basis of revolutionary consciousness, the theory ends by treating the objective conditions as irrelevant to consciousness. Thus, we have to take the actors' perceptions as given, since the origins are not revealed. Unless we assume that the conditions under which revolutionary consciousness develops cannot be ascertained, we are left with the original question: under what conditions will the gap be perceived as intolerable? Presumably, for Davies this question merely begins an infinite regress.[19]

In one sense this conclusion makes it superfluous to consider any further Davies's treatment of the objective conditions, but since there is a close affinity, in certain respects, between Davies's approach and widely held views of contemporary "conflict theory,"[20] it is worth pursuing the enquiry a little further.

Briefly, the particularly important points here are whether the theory relates the relevant objective factors to the social structure and accounts for the generation of these factors on the basis of some systematic, recurrent social process, or whether it assumes that they occur at random. Conflict theory, for example, asserts that changing exigencies give rise to conflicts between actors, which result in the formation of conflict groups. But which conflicts are relevant to revolutionary change and how do the appropriate exigencies arise? To this question conflict theory has no answer, because it includes no notion of systematic structural contradictions that tend to generate the exigencies that give rise to the conflicts. Furthermore, since it has no conception of the social structure in terms of crucial groups (classes), it can only define, post hoc, those groups that actually develop in response to random conflicts.[21]

More specifically, Davies clearly has no theory about the way in which the gap between expectations and need satisfaction is systematically generated in the society; nor does he relate this factor in any way to the social or class structure. It is for this reason that his theory is unable to differentiate groups in the social structure that have a propensity to develop revolutionary consciousness, and it is thus unable to explain why only some sections of a population that is subject to declining living standards are likely to turn to revolutionary action and others not.

It is, of course, the extremely different view of the objective structure that most sharply distinguishes a Marxist approach from this type of "objective theory." This very difference serves to highlight the analytical similarities in the discussion of revolutionary consciousness that are common to Davies's approach and to some versions of Marxism, to which I now turn.

III.

Those versions of Marxism which share with the "objective approach" the notion that revolutionary consciousness emerges solely from the development of certain objective conditions seem to be derived from a one-sided selection of certain of the ideas of Marx and Engels. That is to say, they are based upon one or other of the objective consequences of the contradictions in the mode of production that Marx and Engels identified, but they exclude certain other processes that these writers stressed. To the latter point I will return later. For the present I want to distinguish a line of analysis that bases its conclusions on the objective consequences flowing from the contradictions in the economic system.

As is well known, the key proposition in Marx's scheme of social change is the following: "At a certain stage of their development, the material productive forces of society come into conflict with the existing relations of production."[22] In the stage of industrial capitalism this antagonism takes the form of the contradiction between socialized production and private appropriation.[23] The consequence of this is the general crisis of capitalism: "From forms of development of the productive forces these relations turn into their fetters. Then begins an epoch of social revolution."[24] One of the consequences of this contradiction is the increasing incapacity of the productive system to meet the material wants of the proletariat, because capitalist production for profit is incapable of utilizing the productive capacity of the socialized forces of production to the full in order to meet social needs.

While it is usually suggested that Marx and Engels identified economic deprivation with increasing absolute impoverishment of the industrial working class,[25] this overlooks their observation that deprivation could equally occur in conditions in which economic levels were rising:

> A noticeable increase in wages presupposes a rapid growth of productive capital. The rapid growth of productive capital brings about an equally rapid growth of wealth, luxury, social wants, social enjoyments. Thus although the enjoyments of the workers have risen, the social satisfaction that they give has fallen in comparison with the increased enjoyment of the capitalist which are inaccessible to the worker, in comparison with the state of development of society in general. Our desires and pleasures spring from society; we measure them, therefore, by society and not by the objects which serve for their satisfaction. Because they are of a social nature, they are of a relative nature.[26]

The point that seems to emerge from this is that for Marx and Engels the important issue was not whether economic deprivation was relative or absolute, but that it was an inherent and necessary consequence of the exploitive relations of production of the capitalist mode of production. Thus the differential economic conditions that act upon the consciousness of men are not accidental or random, they are structured by a system of production.

But although economic deprivation, whether relative or not, is an ever-present condition of life of some classes in capitalist society, revolutionary consciousness is not. In order, therefore, to account for revolutionary consciousness, additional factors have to be introduced into the analysis. As is well known, in the *Communist Manifesto*, for example,

Marx and Engels briefly drew attention to some of the factors that provide the basis for the emergence of an awareness of a common situation and interests, that is, of *class* consciousness. These are, firstly, the creation of objectively identical working conditions through the development of the productive forces and, secondly, the improved means of communication between workers through their concentration in large-scale industry.[27]

However, a class which is aware of itself is not necessarily a revolutionary class, and consequently the analysis must be pushed still further. Marx and Engels in fact did so by focusing on the struggles of the proletariat and the development of political conflict. Some writers, of whom Labriola is a sophisticated example,[28] stop, however, short of this point. The analytical consequence of this is that impoverishment is considered to be the sole producer of revolutionary attitudes. The only or main difference, then, between such an approach and Davies's theory is that in the present case economic deprivation is seen as the systematically generated experience of particular social classes.

IV.

In the previous section the material, economic consequences of the contradictory relations of production were discussed. There is, however, implicit in a passage of Engels the notion that, in addition, the "internal" structure of these contradictory relations may be of relevance. Engels says:

> On the one hand, therefore, the capitalist mode of production stands convicted of its own incapacity to further direct these productive forces. On the other, these productive forces themselves, with increasing energy, press forward to the removal of the existing contradiction, to the abolition of their quality as capital, to the *practical recognition of their character as social productive forces*. This rebellion of the productive forces, against their quality as capital, *this stronger and stronger command that their social character shall be recognized, forces the capitalist class itself to treat them more and more as social productive forces.*[29] (Second emphasis is mine.)

The idea that the actual structure of production in terms of size, technology and methods may affect the relationships and, therefore, perceptions of the working class, has been utilized in opposite ways by writers who contend that capitalism has proved capable of meeting at least the elemental "needs" of the majority.

Marcuse has argued that while the main contradiction of capitalist society is more acute than ever, it has not had the expected consequences because the society has been able to disguise its existence.[30] There is as a result no revolutionary consciousness. "Advanced capitalist society suppresses the need for a qualitative change in the system as it exists and repulses its absolute negation. This is its very basis, and on this basis it succeeds in absorbing all revolutionary potential."[31] And again: "Does it make sense to go on speaking of alienation and reification when people really feel and find themselves in this society—in their motor cars, in their T.V. sets, their gadgets, their newspapers, their politicians . . . etc. This is a world of identification: the objects which are around no longer seem alien and dead."[32] The structural conditions in which this occurs are, firstly, the massive, all-pervasive production and distribution apparatus that creates and determines needs of every kind and internalizes them in men, and *satisfies* those needs by an ever-rising supply of goods.

Secondly, the class structure tends to be "flattened" out because of three features. First, the technological changes in the character of the instruments of production lead to an "assimilating" trend in occupational stratification. Second, the development of the managerial hierarchy removes from sight the object of hatred—the capitalist boss. Third, the availability of consumer goods leads to an equalization of lifestyles.[33]

But of equal relevance here is the effect of the structure and process of the situation in production—the growing isolation accompanying mechanization, the psychotechnical rather than physical nature of work, and in addition the rhythm of the machines, which mobilizes the workers' mind at work, in the street and on holiday.[34]

The point of interest that emerges from the above brief summary is the overwhelming efficacy that Marcuse accords to the productive system. Thus, not only does the production and distribution apparatus determine every need but, in addition, its very nature preconditions people to receive the ideology propagated in the mass media:

> Our insistence on the depth and efficacy of these controls is open to the objection that we overrate greatly the indoctrinating power of the "media" . . . The objection misses the point. The preconditioning does not start with the mass production of radio-television and with the centralization of their control. But, and this is the point of importance—the people enter this stage as preconditioned receptacles of long standing.[35]

Preconditioned, that is, by the productive process.

Particularly significant, in the present context, is that it follows from Marcuse's argument that changing objective conditions do not have consequences for social change. That is to say, since the apparatus of production and distribution determines needs, there is established a moving equilibrium between needs and the objective conditions of their satisfaction. It is not too much to say that for Marcuse the system induces in men the need to need the system.

In a recent analysis, Mallet,[36] like Marcuse, has argued that the enormous development of the material forces of production in advanced capitalist society has maximized the basic contradiction between socialized production and private ownership. But, unlike Marcuse, he holds that this increases, more than ever, the potential vulnerability of the capitalist system to opposition forces that may come into existence and which will "contest the nature of the productive relations."[37] Mallet accepts that the source of revolutionary consciousness is no longer to be found in largely nonexistent material deprivation but, he contends, it is to be found in the "internal" structure of relations that reflect the development of the material productive forces. That is to say, the workers' actions that *constitute* the particular industrial relations produce a revolutionary consciousness of those relations. Mallet's argument is as follows. The technological productive forces have "parcellized" work and also induced a separation between work and private life. These factors, together with the more or less conscious diversion of workers' demands to the realm of consumption, has blocked the formation of such a revolutionary opposition. The working-class parties, the trade unions, and the mass of workers ignore the relations of production in order to concentrate on winning wage increases.[38]

However, the very developments in the productive forces have brought into existence a new working class consisting of researchers, technicians, and skilled workers and "the objective conditions in which the new working-class acts and works makes it the vanguard of the revolutionary and socialist movement."[39] What are these objective conditions? Firstly, the new working class is at the "centre of the most complex mechanisms of modern capitalism."[40] It is engaged in the increasingly more important sphere of preparation for, and organization of, production. This, Mallet argues, is an area of great initiative and responsibility and wins "back for the modern worker, at the collective level, the professional independence which he lost during the stage when work was mechanized."[41] The other objective condition is that the basic demands of the new working class within the field of consumption have been met.[42] From the above, Mallet concludes: "Thus its objective position puts it in a position both to grasp the weakness of modern capitalist organization and to reach a state where it is conscious of a new type of organization of productive relations, designed to satisfy those human needs which cannot express themselves within the present structures."[43] How does he arrive at this conclusion?

The actions in production that constitute the work of the new working class by virtue of their position at the center of modern capitalist production lead these workers to turn from demands about consumption to demands for an increased share in management and for self-management. The revolutionary content of this lies in the fact that it involves a direct, conscious confrontation with "the capitalist structure of productive relations . . . and also with the techno-bureaucratic structure of concerns."[44] Leaving aside the question of the correctness of the empirical analysis of the objective conditions, some other difficulties arise.

Why should workers who are participants in important organizational work in production, and whose material needs have been satisfied, demand managerial control? Mallet's answer here seems to flow from the notion that such workers have a "professional" interest in seeing that industry is run properly. This is presumably why he refers to the "enhanced value of initiative or responsibility" of the new working class; and why he argues that the new working class insists on two preconditions for revolution. It insists, firstly, that the transformation should not destroy or weaken the existing apparatus of production and, secondly, it "is inclined to ask 'what for?' before it shouts 'seize power.'"[45]

Given that this is so, it seems equally tenable to argue that the structural position of the new working class is as likely to engender a conservative as a revolutionary consciousness. It becomes important to ask, therefore, on what basis can it be assumed that the demand for an increased share in management also involves a consciousness that such demands cannot be satisfied within the existing system? The possibility does presumably exist that this class may develop revolutionary consciousness if it puts forward demands for greater control that are frustrated, but this will depend on the operation of additional factors (for example, the struggle for control, political organization, ideologies and so on), to which Mallet refers only obliquely. Once again, as in the case of the "objective approach," the theory makes no provision for such other factors.

Mallet's analysis shares an additional feature with Davies' theory of revolution. Having located the political attitudes of the new working class in the structure of production, Mallet then confronts the problem of accounting for the spread (as he asserts) of revolutionary ideas to those sections of the working class which are not part of the new working class and which are subject to different structural conditions. In attempting to explain this fact, Mallet relies on a process of diffusion: "The all embracing character of the economy today tends to *diffuse* demands for a share in management into sectors *which still do not have the objective conditions in which such demands could spontaneously arise*" (my italics).[46] This, of course, amounts to an abandonment of the structural argument without, however, putting anything in its place. The all-important question, "Under what conditions does diffusion successfully take place?" is neither posed nor answered by Mallet.

From the above considerations it follows that in some, unspecified, circumstances Mallet relies only on action in the industrial structure and, in other, also unspecified, circumstances he relies only on a type of ideological diffusion.

The difficulty of resting an analysis only on objective conditions of the type under discussion is illustrated, I think, by the fact that it is perfectly possible to arrive at different, even opposite, conclusions, which appear equally plausible, by simply stressing different aspects of the same structural or objective conditions. This has already emerged from a comparison of Mallet and Marcuse, but the point becomes even clearer if we look briefly at Nairn's analysis, which is very similar in some respects to Mallet's.[47]

Nairn, like Mallet, considers that the basic material needs of most people have been met, that there is a high degree of "parcellization" and an impersonal, hierarchial structure of authority in industry. But instead of stressing the position of the new working class in industry, he places great emphasis on the fragmentation of tasks.

He argues that the productive system requires educated personnel and that capitalism, therefore, has to develop the forces of mental production. There is a contradiction between the specialization demanded by industry and imposed in education and the consequences

of this education, which operates against specialization. And his conclusion about the consciousness that emanates is the following: "A simple, anonymous statement by someone from the Mouvement du 22
Mars . . . put it best of all: 'In a world of abundance, the young European of '68 wants to be a whole man.'"[48] More formally: "The revolutionary movement . . . aims at the total recuperation of what the system
drains away. The 'whole man' must feel and act, wholly."[49] Thus the
same (although differently stressed) structural conditions give rise to a
new revolutionary working class for Mallet, revolutionary students for
Nairn, and a nonrevolutionary working class for Marcuse!

Before leaving Nairn's study, it is curious to note that he, like Mallet
and Davies, also ultimately abandons the structural basis of the analysis. He says, for example: "His subjectivity is the *instinctive* assertion
of control over what happens: work, 'leisure,' life!" (my emphasis).[50] It
seems difficult to resist the conclusion that in all three cases the resort
to nonstructural explanations stems from the inadequacies of the analytical framework used.

Obviously, it has not been the intention in this section to deny the
relevance of the type of processes that these authors have stressed. On
the contrary, the search for the conflictual potentialities of contradictory structures within which people are acting is highly important.
This applies not only to the industrial sector but also to other major
spheres in the society. What is questioned, however, is the validity of
attempting to locate the sources of revolutionary consciousness only
in such terms. The issue can be put in this way: given a high degree
of systematic contradiction (as asserted by all three writers) but a low
level of revolutionary consciousness (and conflict), there is no reason to
suppose that the conditions or actions that produce consciousness are
to be found only in the systematic contradictions (particularly when
these are confined to the industrial structure).[51]

V.

The theories discussed in the preceding section limit themselves to the
effect of the action, which constitutes the relations within production,
upon attitudes and beliefs—although in the end the relevance of the
former becomes, to say the least, tenuous. Debray, on the other hand,
confines his analysis to political action—generally characterized as a
subjective factor—and in so doing fails to analyze the objective condi-

tions in which it occurs.[52] His approach, nevertheless, converges strikingly with the "objective approach" discussed in sections II and III in that both focus exclusively on factors that appear as "*external*" *objective conditions from the point of view of the masses.*

By approaching Debray's theory through his critique of Trotskyism, it will be possible both to make the above points clear and expose the limitations of his analysis. According to Debray, the underlying conception of the Trotskyists is their belief in the essential, unalterable goodness of workers and peasants. This essence involves a craving for socialism of which, however, for various reasons, the workers are not aware. What is needed, therefore, is that this "latent spontaneity" be aroused.[53] How is this to be done? The Trotskyist answer, says Debray, is a theoretical one—the constant repetition of declarations that the revolution should be a socialist one.[54]

Debray rejects this view on two grounds. The first is that mere declarations addressed to the masses do not lead to revolutionary consciousness; the second is that, in the repressive conditions of Latin America, propaganda work leads to the liquidation of political movements by the forces of the governing regime.

What is the alternative to propaganda? The alternative is revolutionary action. Of course, this raises a problem, since by definition revolutionary action involves the support of the masses and therefore presupposes revolutionary consciousness. Debray overcomes this quite simply by dismissing the "old obsession" that revolutionary consciousness and the organization of the masses must always precede revolutionary action.[55] This enables him to argue that revolutionary action by a minority can develop revolutionary consciousness in the masses. How is this effected? Debray argues that "the physical force of the police and the army is considered to be unassailable (by the masses), and unassailability cannot be challenged by words but by showing that a soldier and a policeman are no more bullet proof than anyone else. . . . In order to destroy the idea of unassailability . . . there is nothing better than combat."[56]

Now, quite obviously, *if* the only impediment to mass revolutionary action is a belief in overwhelming *power* of the state forces, that is, if there is no belief in the possibility of revolution, action that can prove that the state is vulnerable may well have significant consequences for consciousness and action. But Debray, having here discussed the effect of combat on the masses' perception of the power of the regime's security forces, later, without explanation, considerably extends the consequences of combat—fighting, he now asserts, convinces the local population that the *state forces are the enemy*. He says:

> The destruction of a troop transport truck or the public execution of a police torturer is more effective propaganda for the local population than a hundred speeches. Such conduct convinces them of the essential: that the Revolution is on the march, that the enemy is no longer invulnerable. It convinces them, to begin with, that the soldier is an enemy—their enemy— and that a war is underway.[57] (My emphasis.)

It will have been noticed that for the verbal declarations of the Trotskyists, Debray has substituted combat action by the guerilla forces.

But for all the differences between his views and those of the Trotskyists whom he criticizes, there is a remarkable similarity. Both see political consciousness as being brought from the "outside" by the actions of a small elite group—the party and the *foco*, words and combat—to the inert, passive, but receptive masses. That is to say, for both, the action of the activist minority is simply a further "external" objective condition acting upon the masses from which mass revolutionary consciousness emanates. But why should *foco* action have any greater effect than Trotskyist words? If the mere attack upon state forces persuades workers and peasants that these forces are their enemy—that is, destroys the legitimacy of the government (and not only proves it assailable)—it must be, since Debray does not point to other factors, because of the essential "goodness" of the workers and peasants who only need to have their spontaneity aroused.

An adequate explanation, however, would have to be rooted in the concrete conditions in which guerilla warfare is launched. Thus, for example, the proposition: "Revolutionary consciousness will be produced by actions that reveal the vulnerability of the security forces" can only be meaningful if it relates to the production of a consciousness of the *possibility* of revolution among people who are already convinced of its necessity, that is, among those who already believe that "the soldier is their enemy." This brings the argument full circle, for if the masses do not yet reject the legitimacy of the state, etc., it cannot be assumed that guerilla action will produce such an attitude— Guevara's Bolivian Diary shows this.

What is required, it is suggested, is an analysis of existing political consciousness, the objective conditions in which the action of the activist minority occurs, and the way in which mass action interrelates with objective conditions and the action of activist groups to affect mass consciousness.[58]

VI.

I have so far focused on two types of theories that do not make the connection between mass and minority-activist action and objective conditions and I now want to deal with two theories that do, although in different ways.

I have already touched upon the relevance of structural conditions to revolutionary struggle in Marx's writings. It is clear, however, that he also regarded mass action as a crucial factor in the development of revolutionary consciousness, although he did not deal, in a sociological sense, with this either systematically or in great detail. What he had to say was nevertheless highly pertinent.

The limitations in the analysis of Marxist writers discussed earlier stems in part from their failure to keep in mind the distinction that Marx drew between the "class in itself" and the "class for itself." Marx made the point that the objective position of a class does not necessarily involve a consciousness of that objective position. He contended that this consciousness comes about in stages, as a consequence of the conflicts and struggles that it carries out in certain conditions: "Thus this mass is already a class in relation to capital, but not yet a class for itself. In the struggle, of which we have only indicated a few phases, this mass unites and forms itself into a class for itself. The interests which it defends become class interests. But the struggle between classes is a political struggle."[59] In the *Communist Manifesto*, Marx and Engels described briefly these phases.[60] But, as I indicated previously, the theory is incomplete since there is no discussion, except in the most general terms, of the role, *inter alia*, of party and ideology.

Lenin agreed with Marx that the conditions of capitalist production directly "awaken the mind of the workers" and bring about the unification of the working class in an organized class struggle.[61] He rejected the "revisionist" contention that Marx had held that revolutionary consciousness would emanate directly either from the conditions of production or the class struggle. He quoted with approval Kautsky's criticism of the belief "that Marx asserted that economic development and the class struggle create, not only the conditions of socialist production, but also, and directly, the consciousness of its necessity."[62] It follows from this, and Lenin argued the point strongly, that "left to itself" the working class is able to develop only a trade union consciousness.[63]

Revolutionary consciousness has to be brought to the workers "from without, that is, only from outside the economic struggle."[64] The first requirement is, of course, the existence of a revolutionary party whose task it is to bring "class political consciousness" to the workers.[65] How, and under what conditions, is this task to be accomplished, according to Lenin? It is not easy to give a straightforward answer to this question. It is possible to extract from his polemical writings an approach to the problem of revolutionary consciousness which not only incorporates and synthesizes some of the central ideas contained in the different views already analyzed, but also adds to them. In the final analysis, nevertheless, he left unanswered a key question.

In his earlier writing (1898), Lenin appears to have considered that revolutionary consciousness could be brought to the working class by propaganda:

> The socialist activities of Russian Social Democrats consist in spreading by propaganda the teachings of scientific socialism, in spreading among the workers a proper understanding of the present social and economic system, its basis and its development, an understanding of the various classes . . . of the interrelation, of the struggle between these classes, of the role of the working class in this struggle.[66]

However, by 1902 he had already amended this view and in "What is to be Done?" he wrote:

> The question arises, what should political education consist in? Can it be confined to the propaganda of working class hostility to the autocracy? Of course not. It is not enough to explain to the workers that they are politically oppressed (any more than it is to explain to them that their interests are antagonistic to the interests of the employers).[67]

Since propaganda alone is not sufficient, what more is required to prepare the "socio-psychological" conditions for revolution?

Writing in 1905, Lenin argued that in 1901 and 1902 neither the call for "assault tactics" nor the "tailist" call for concentration on the economic struggle were correct.

> At that time propaganda and agitation . . . were really brought to the
> fore by the objective state of affairs. . . . At that time slogans advocat-
> ing mass agitation instead of direct armed action, preparation of the
> socio-psychological conditions for insurrection instead of pyrotech-
> nics were revolutionary. Social Democracy's only correct slogans.[68]

Here Lenin reaches a position substantially different from the writers
discussed earlier, for at this point his contention is that it is not merely
the objective conditions which are relevant, nor merely propaganda
addressed to the workers from the "outside," but propaganda addressed
to them in the course of their (the workers') confrontation with the
objective conditions.[69] Thus the crucial mode of bringing revolutionary consciousness to people is through *agitation*, that is, political explanation given, not abstractly, but to workers actually experiencing and
confronting in action a "problem":

> for the self-knowledge of the working class is indissolubly bound
> up, not solely with a full clear theoretical understanding—it would
> be even truer to say, not so much with the theoretical, as with the
> practical understanding—of the relationship between all the various
> classes of modern society, acquired through the experience of polit-
> ical life. . . . It can be obtained only from living examples. It cannot
> be obtained from any book.[70]

Thus Lenin prescribed the kind of action, of both party *and masses*,
which may be necessary to the emergence of revolutionary consciousness, but does this take the argument far enough? Since neither mass
action nor agitational activities of the party necessarily produces revolutionary consciousness, we need to know what the conditions of
"success" are.[71] Lenin, himself, made this point in another connection.
"The real question that arises in appraising the social activity of an
individual is: what conditions ensure the success of his actions, what
guarantee is there that these actions will not remain an isolated act lost
in a welter of contrary acts."[72] Whatever practical success Lenin may
have had in the particular conditions of Russia, there are a number of
theoretical difficulties that make his writings on the subject less than
satisfactory from the point of view of generalizations concerning the
relationship of different factors and conditions in the creation of revolutionary beliefs.

Thus consider, for example, his position on the issue of partial reforms. Lenin contended that Marxists were in favor of such reforms but

that, at the same time, in order to prevent reforms leading to a reform-ist consciousness it was necessary for social democrats to explain the nature of capitalism to the masses.[73] That is all very well as a statement of political policy, but what are the consequences for consciousness? If there is a correlation between improved conditions and nonrevolu-tionary consciousness, can "mere" propaganda by the party destroy the effect of the "objective" conditions?

But more importantly, the inadequacy of Lenin's treatment appears from the following argument.

It is clear from his whole attack upon spontaneity that Lenin re-jected the notion that consciousness is so determined by the mode and conditions of production that ideological factors, the conscious element, can have no effect. He argues, in fact, that workers could express either of two ideologies—"the only choice is: either bourgeois or socialist ideology. There is no middle course."[74]

What then determines which ideology will enter into the conscious-ness of workers?

At several points Lenin emphasizes that bourgeois ideology will dom-inate because there is a spontaneous tendency for the working class to adopt it: "bourgeois ideology spontaneously imposes itself upon the working-class."[75] This view, of course, accords with the thesis that the working class, "left to itself," will engage only in an economic struggle. For if the working class is spontaneously led only into a trade union struggle of a limited, reformist type, then presumably bourgeois ideology, which is reflected and inherent in this action, also emerges spontaneously.

At the same time, however, and in contradiction to the above, Lenin asserts that the objective conditions of the workers is a predisposing factor to the adoption of revolutionary consciousness. "It is often said that the working-class spontaneously gravitates towards socialism. This is perfectly true in the sense that socialist theory measures the causes of misery of the working-class more profoundly and more correctly than any other theory, and for that reason the workers are able to assimi-late it so easily."[76] It follows from the above considerations that work-ers are in a given objective situation that is equally conducive to two completely opposing ideologies. This, indeed, seems to be the logical outcome of the attack on spontaneity. But if this is so, then the objec-tive conditions themselves appear to have become irrelevant to Lenin's argument, as they did in the case of the other writers discussed earlier.

If, then, the objective conditions are to be discounted, what other factors are relevant? Here, Lenin appears to give, in general, great weight to propaganda. In the polemic against the economists, for instance, he argued that to "belittle" the role of the "conscious element" was, whether intended or not, to strengthen the influence of bourgeois ideology upon the workers by leaving the field open to bourgeois ideologists.[77]

But more specifically, while in regard to proletarian consciousness Lenin contended that mere propaganda was not enough, in the case of bourgeois ideology he asserted that its overpowering weight was sufficient to lead to its domination: "But why . . . does the spontaneous movement . . . lead to the domination of bourgeois ideology? For the simple reason that bourgeois ideology is far older in origin than socialist ideology, that it is more fully developed, and that it has at its disposal immeasurably more means of dissemination."[78] Since none of these factors, either singly or in combination, are alone, as a matter of empirical fact, always sufficient for the "success" of an ideology, we still require to have the appropriate conditions specified. This Lenin failed to do.

Thus, having rejected the view that the mode of production creates, directly, revolutionary consciousness, he assigned a determining role to ideology by means of, or through, political action of the party. But in so doing he made the objective conditions irrelevant altogether and, therefore, necessarily had to treat the ideological factors in isolation from them.[79] For an approach that suggests the basis of a solution to this problem we must turn to Gramsci's work.[80]

VII.

The starting point of Gramsci's analysis is the proposition that a distinction must be drawn between the implicit meaning or significance of action and the "theoretical" consciousness of it. More precisely, he distinguishes between the actual consequences of action and the conception actors have of the consequences or significance of that action.[81]

In "normal" times there is a contradiction or lack of congruence between the theoretical consciousness and the actual consequences of action, which is not accidental, or due to "bad faith" or suchlike, but "cannot be other than the expression of more profound contradictions of an historical or social order."[82] It is precisely this lack of "fit" between consciousness and reality that permits the continuance of the system. The explanation of this is to be found in Gramsci's notion of "hegemony" to which I referred earlier. In the first place "hegemony" that means (to quote a portion of Williams' description): "an order in which . . . one concept of reality is diffused throughout society in all its manifestations, infusing with its spirit all taste, morality, customs, religious and moral connotation."[83] In this sense the notion of "hegemony" appears to be more or less identical with Weber's conception of legitimate authority. That is to say, the content of the "concept of reality" is such as to legitimate the institutions and structures of the society.

But there is a crucial distinction between "hegemony" and "legitimate authority." Whereas for Weber legitimacy appears to be a *source* of domination, for Gramsci "hegemony" refers to the set of ideas that are dominant as a consequence of a particular structure of power. More precisely, as Williams has pointed out, "hegemony" implies a control that corresponds to power conceived of in terms of a ruling class.[84] There is clearly an implication here of the "hegemony" as a legitimating mask over the real structure of power.

In fact Gramsci argues that the hegemonic theoretical consciousness contradicts the real consequences and meaning of action; it, therefore, disguises a reality which, if its "true" significance were present to the consciousness, would result in its rejection.

This means that since the regime exists not only (and perhaps not even mainly) by means of the exercise of coercive power, but also through the common man's theoretical understanding, which obscures the actual consequences of action, revolutionary consciousness will have developed when the content of consciousness coincides with the reality of practice.

The process by which this comes about takes place in two stages. "The awareness of being part of a determined hegemonic force (i.e. political consciousness) is the first step towards a further and progressive self-consciousness in which theory and practice fully unite."[85] The second or further step is the "socializing" of truths already discovered so that they become the basis of "live" action. That is to say, the existing hegemony must be replaced by a new "ethico-politico" hegemony of the working class.[86]

The question that has to be posed is: How, in Gramsci's scheme, can this come about?

The view has been expressed that Gramsci ascribed the development of consciousness to the immanent working of "the intellect and the ethico-political" factors.[87] This seems to me to be mistaken. Gramsci himself posed the question as follows in *The Modern Prince*.

> When can the conditions for the arousing and development of a national-popular collective will be said to exist? Here an historical (economic) analysis must be made of the social structure of the given country together with a "dramatic" presentation of the attempts made throughout the centuries to arouse this will and the reasons for the successive failure.[88]

Merrington, furthermore, points out that Gramsci conceived one of the main tasks of analysis to be the discovery of the form of struggle that would activate a response in the "real historical situation," that is, in the conditions of the moment.[89]

Moreover, Gramsci directly related "the formation of a collective will" to Marx's proposition that "society does not set itself problems for whose solution the material pre-conditions do not already exist" and to economic conditions that "create a more favourable ground for the propagation of certain ways of thinking, posing and solving questions."[90] Neither, however, did he accept the contention that the superstructure in general, and mass consciousness in particular, must be seen as a simple, direct expression of the economic structure. This view he described as "primitive infantilism."[91]

It is here that Gramsci confronts the issue that led Lenin into a contradictory position. He points out that economism or ideologism results respectively from either "expounding as directly operative causes that instead only operate indirectly, or . . . asserting that immediate causes are the only operative ones."[92] This clearly implies that the relationship between base and superstructure, between ideology and economic conditions, must not be conceived of as simple and direct, but as complex and indirect.

It is in this context that Gramsci, like Lenin, laid great stress upon the activity of the party and the masses and, in particular, on the intellectual-mass dialectic, which, he argues, "bounds" the creation of consciousness.[93]

But Gramsci goes beyond Lenin in that the production or nonproduction of mass revolutionary consciousness is not for him simply the outcome of the party-mass or intellectual-mass dialectic in given political and economic conditions; it is, in addition, bound by a range of "intervening" conditions and processes that mediate between base and superstructure. These include the nature of bureaucratic organizations, the intellectual strata, the organization of culture and education, and so on.

As important as this development by Gramsci is, it nevertheless leaves open a crucial issue that has increasingly become the dominant concern of a number of Marxist writers.[94] This issue can be formulated in the following way: What elements of the superstructure must be taken into account and in what way? Thus, on what basis can it be argued that political action is more important, than, say, political speeches, or that the education system rather than the religious system is crucial, or that a particular combination of factors is more relevant than another combination?

It seems clear that such questions can only be answered in terms of an adequate theory of society, which includes a theory of the superstructure.

VIII.

Some writers have argued that no such theory of the superstructure is possible,[95] and for this view there appears to be support in the works of Marx and Engels.

In the *Preface to the Critique of Political Economy*, Marx wrote of the "ideological forms in which men become conscious" of the contradiction between the relations and forces of production, and he concluded that: "this consciousness must be explained . . . from the contradictions of material life, from the existing conflict between the social productive forces and the relations of production."[96] It is clear that, interpreted literally, as it has been in much of the work of later Marxists, this passage sets up a direct, determining relationship between the economic base and consciousness. There is no room, in such an interpretation, for the operation of factors outside the economic structure—consciousness is a mere reflection of the economic, the elements of the superstructure having no influence on one another and still less on the infrastructure.

As is well known, however, both Marx and Engels, in various theoretical passages as well as in their empirical analyses, emphasized the influence of superstructural factors upon history and consciousness. A good example is Engels's frequently referred to letter to Bloch, in which he wrote:

> According to the materialist conception of history, the ultimately
> determining element in history is the production and reproduction
> of real life. . . . The economic situation is the basis, but the various
> elements of the superstructure: political forms of the class struggle
> and its results, to wit: constitutions established by the victorious class
> after a successful battle, etc., juridical forms, and then even the re-
> flexes of all these actual struggles in the brains of the participants,
> political, juristic, philosophical theories, religious views and their
> further development into systems of dogmas, also exercise their in-
> fluence upon the course of the historical struggles and in many cases
> preponderate in determining their *form*. There is an interaction of all
> these elements in which . . . the economic movement finally asserts
> itself as necessary.[97]

The superstructure is said to have a double efficacy. On the one hand,
it acts upon the infrastructure so that the relations within the latter
always assume a specific form according to the dictates of the former.[98]
On the other hand, the infrastructure's effect upon consciousness is
not direct and immediate but is affected by the specific content of the
superstructure.

This type of general statement concerning the relationship between
base and superstructure obviously serves an important function since
it directs attention to a category of factors that must be taken into
account if an analysis is to have any utility. If, for instance, we refer
back to the section on Mallet, Nairn, and Marcuse, the onesidedness
of an analysis that is restricted to the effect of the economic structure
is underlined. At the same time, a general prescription in the above
terms does not give any guidance on the crucial problems I referred
to above—what elements of the superstructure must be taken into account and in what way?

It would seem that for Marx and Engels, no theoretical answer
can be given to these questions. Thus in the "Preface" to *A Contribution to the Critique of Political Economy* Marx specifically contrasts
"the economic conditions of production which can be determined
with the precision of natural science, and the legal, political, religious,
aesthetic and philosophic—in short ideological forms." Again, if we
reexamine the passages quoted from Engels and from Marx in note
97, it is very clear that we are simply referred to the "empirically
given circumstances." There is no attempt to delineate, except by way

of example, the specific aspects of the superstructure that should be included in an analysis.

In other words, there is an empiricist–like directive to examine the superstructure "which is there."

It hardly needs to be said that there is no superstructure available to be grasped outside of a conceptual framework. The implicit assumption that there is leads inevitably either to the arbitrary emphasis upon one or other factor and the equally arbitrary exclusion of others (in different ways both Debray and Lenin provide examples of this), or, alternatively, to the simple expedient of treating the superstructure as an undifferentiated, amorphous ideological sphere. This suggests the need to develop a theory of the superstructure. It seems clear that one requirement of a theory, if such a theory is possible, is the systematic demarcation or differentiation of the parts of the superstructure and the specification of the relationship between them. Thus, it is not enough simply to catalog the differentiated structures that make up the superstructure and to analyze them in isolation or to assume a symmetrical relationship between them.[100] In his "Introduction" to *A Contribution to the Critique of Political Economy*, Marx drew attention to the fact that within the economic structure itself it is not possible to treat the elements that make up the whole on an equal footing. He argued that production dominates over exchange and distribution.

The extension of this to the society as a whole is only a reflection of the general methodological principle that is essential to a Marxist analysis, namely that the relationship between the parts that make the whole is not symmetrical. Korsch has argued that the utility of Marx's theory lies precisely in its "onesided" emphasis on the economic structure since this "onesidedness" is of the essence of *any* theoretical analytical formulation. It is this, in fact, which sets a Marxist analysis apart from *ad hoc* empiricist, or supposedly complete, descriptions of phenomena.[101]

In order, then, to arrive at the conditions that explain the emergence of a particular form of consciousness, a range of factors in both the infrastructure and superstructure have to be taken account of simultaneously. This requires an analysis of the relationship between the differentiated superstructural factors and the infrastructure—a relationship which, however, requires not merely to be stated in general, but to be specified. But as was shown from the work of Mallet, Lenin and Debray, it is not sufficient to assume that these conditions simply act on people "from the outside." For the actions of people in and on the structural conditions—whether these be the productive or political or some other structures—simultaneously contribute to the transformation of their consciousness. This paper has attempted to do no more than point to the types of conditions as well as the kinds of actions that need to be incorporated into an adequate theory for the analysis of the development of mass revolutionary consciousness.

THEORY AND PRACTICE
IN GRAMSCI'S MARXISM

John Merrington

During the past decade there has been a growing interest among European socialists in those Marxist writers and activists of the period immediately preceding and following the October Revolution, whose theories grew out of the collapse of the Second International and the failure of the revolutionary wave that swept Europe in 1917–20. The emergence of reformist tendencies in the socialist parties in the prewar period, the subsequent capitulation of the German SPD, the failure of the socialist leaderships to combat factional tendencies within their parties, and their fatal inaction in the face of events immediately following the war created a situation in which only radical new departures could create new theoretical solutions and hence new practical possibilities. Both Lukács and Gramsci responded in different ways to this need, moving beyond the terms of the earlier "revisionist debate"—both "revolutionaries" and "reformists" had remained locked within the same basic problematic—carrying out a new diagnosis and prognosis from their experience of the postwar defeat, placing a renewed stress on the active, voluntary component of historical change, on the problem of agency in the making of a revolution.

For the increasing incapacity of European social democrat leaderships, nakedly revealed in the postwar crisis, was itself the outward manifestation of a more profound malaise; the ossification of bureaucratic structures of organization went hand in hand with an "official Marxism" based on a rigid set of categorical doctrines, "laws of social development" of the natural-scientific type. The need for a renewal of Marxism in these circumstances was urgent. Both Lukács and Gramsci reacted energetically against these positivistic inroads into Marxism, the positivist scientism that was the theoretical basis of the Second International's orthodoxy. With the imposition of the new orthodoxy of Stalinism during the thirties, however, these theories became, and have largely remained, a subordinate current within the international socialist movement, and it was only after the Twentieth Congress of the CPSU in 1956 that their rediscovery became widely possible. The recurring tendency of Marxism to become petrified into a schematic system of fixed categories, eternally valid, invoking concepts rather than rediscovering them in relation to each new conjuncture, has made the work of Gramsci particularly relevant to the problems of postwar socialism in the West. The 2,800 pages of the *Prison Notebooks*, which began to be published after the war and the collapse of Italian fascism,[1] constitute the most wide-ranging and sustained attempt to renew Marxism, reformulating old categories and inventing new concepts through the confrontation of contemporary social and cultural developments, to have come from the pen of a twentieth-century Western Marxist. Gramsci's work represents above all a model of that type of critical development, as opposed to blind exegesis, of Marxism, which "actualizes" theory in relation to each specific conjuncture, locating the changing centers of contradiction in the capitalist world and elaborating the appropriate strategy. At every point, new insights produce new theoretical solutions as a means not of rejecting all existing reality, myopically intent on retaining the purity of the original formulations, but of coming to grips with reality, revealing its contradictions, locating the focal points of change as a means to guiding and directing action toward revolutionary socialist goals. The need for an integral "rethinking" of Marxism in the post–Stalinist period, not only in economic terms but in relation to the totality of social and cultural developments in the capitalist West; the continued dependence on traditional forms of organization in the socialist movement, as well as the increasing passivity of strategic options on the Left have made incumbent a confrontation with "the one genius," as Eugene Genovese has aptly remarked, "who posed and faced western socialism's most difficult problems."[2]

I.

What were the general features of Gramsci's renewal of Marxism? A precondition for such a renewal was for Gramsci, as for Lenin or Lukács, the rejection of "economism" in all its forms, the tendency to reduce the various levels of superstructure to the status of "appearance" or "phenomenon." In the hands of the "professorial" Marxists of the Second International, this tendency had produced an evolutionary–determinist conception of history, governed by objective laws whose unfolding lay beyond the scope of active human intervention. The practical result was a catastrophic fatalism in the face of events, sustained by a blind belief in the "forces of history," in the inevitable collapse of capitalism due to its internal contradictions. It was in relation to this deviation of Marxism that Gramsci entitled an early article of November 1917 "The Revolution against 'Das Kapital,'" in which he hailed the Bolsheviks for having broken the iron timetable of the stages of history.[3] In the prison notes, fatalism is characterized as "an immediate ideological 'aroma'" of Marxism, a "form of religion and a stimulant (like a drug) necessitated and historically justified by the subordinate character of certain social strata," maintaining perseverance in periods of defeat and adversity: "'I am defeated for the moment but the nature of things is on my side in the long run,' etc." But in periods of organic crisis, when the subordinate becomes potentially "directing," it becomes a substitute for taking real initiatives; the result is vacillation, passivity, and "imbecile self-sufficiency." For this reason, "the pretension (presented as an essential postulate of historical materialism) of interpreting every fluctuation of politics and ideology as an immediate expression of the structure must be thoroughly combated as a primitive infantilism."[4] Citing Engels's remark in his correspondence that "only in the last analysis is the economy the determining force in history," he goes on to dismiss the possibility that "by themselves economic crises directly produce fundamental events. . . . The question of economic malaise or health as a cause of new historical realities is a partial question of the relation of forces on their various levels."[5]

This rejection of economism was coupled with a rejection of the positivist tendency to objectify the discrete atomistic data of immediate actuality, dissolving the totality of social processes into the fragmentary "facts" of contingent reality, thereby declaring its categories universal. In his critique of Bukharin's *Theory of Historical Materialism* (1921), Gramsci rejected the crude materialism and "false objectivity" of Bukharin's method, in which Marxism was conceived as a means of predicting future events with the exactitude of the natural sciences. Echoing an earlier critique by Lukács, Gramsci insisted on the impossibility of prediction, which diverted attention from the possibilities of active political intervention; Marxism's "laws of social development" were "laws of tendency" only. Vulgar materialism and technologism merely reproduced the categories of bourgeois science and ignored the dialectical nature of the Marxist totality.[6] Gramsci's critical effort was directed toward the restoration of the dialectic and hence the possibility of conscious praxis, the interplay between subjective and objective in the historical process, within which the specific forms of superstructure, cultural, political and ideological, have a relatively autonomous existence, irreducible to the status of "emanations" of the economic structure, conceived of as an idealist "essence." In his unwavering opposition to that deformation of Marxism represented by a long arc of official theory from Plekhanov[7] to Kautsky and Bukharin, encrusted with evolutionist determinism, Gramsci clearly prefigures more recent theoretical developments of the post-Stalin period, the recognition of the need for a more integrated and total Marxism as opposed to the eclecticism of recent tendencies, with an emphasis on the specific role of the superstructures, of historical conjuncture, and of the complexity of the Marxist totality, determined only in the last instance by the economic. As Althusser has put it: "From the first moment to the last, the lonely hour of the last instance never comes."[8]

It is therefore the range, the all-inclusive scope of Gramsci's Marxism that is its distinctive feature. Economism was not merely unable to explain crucial aspects of contemporary social and political reality, the role of Catholicism or the rise of Mussolini; not only were its theoretical insights mediocre, but it was also a partial vision of the socialist future limited to the alteration of the economic structure. In place of this, it was imperative to affirm a total vision based on a total critique. Private ownership of the means of production is a *necessary* but not a *sufficient* basis of capitalist domination; similarly, because socialism reorganizes the economic structure, this does not mean that "the problems of superstructure should be abandoned to themselves, to their spontaneous development, to a hazardous and sporadic germination."[9] Gramsci's Marxism was not limited to the material conditions of existence but included also the content of existence, the integral development of human potentialities over the whole field of experience and the vast expansion of creative possibilities that socialism would make possible. This widening of focus required a new emphasis on the role of consciousness and ideas in the transformation of society, which Gramsci developed through a lifelong confrontation with the neoidealists, represented in Italy preeminently by the philosopher-historian Benedetto Croce, the most influential spokesman of speculative liberalism throughout the period. Just as the theory of Lukács was the result of a synthesis with the antipositivist sociology of Weber and Simmel, Gramsci's Marxism developed out of his critique of Croce. The European-wide reaction against positivism from the 1880s onward thus found its dialectical response within the Marxist tradition itself. Gramsci's concept of Marxist orthodoxy is "not based on this or that follower, or this or that tendency linked to currents outside the original formulation . . . but on the fundamental conception of Marxism as 'sufficient to itself,' sufficient to create an entire civilization, total and integrated."[10]

This integral Marxism was in turn made concrete by the enormous project Gramsci set himself during his long imprisonment: to rework, to actualize theory in relation to a specific national experience and culture in order to present a global critique and challenge to existing social reality. It was his refusal to apply schematic solutions to a particular "effectual reality" that made him underline the specificity of the conjuncture of forces, national and international, which determine the form a crisis will take in any particular case and hence the strategy of the revolutionary movement. In the prison notes, he attacked "closed and definitive systems" and added that "the unity and systematic quality of a theory is to be found not in its external and architectonic structure but in its intimate coherence and fertile comprehension of each particular solution."[11] In his note *Against Byzantinism*, we read:

> The correspondence of effective reality determines the identity of thought and not vice-versa. From this we deduce that every truth, while being universal and capable of being expressed in abstract form (for the tribe of theoreticians) derives its efficacy from being expressed in the language of particular concrete situations; if it is not expressible in "particular languages," it is a byzantine and scholastic abstraction serving only as a pastime for phrasemongers.[12]

The particular requirements corresponding to each situation cannot be fixed in advance:

> Reality is rich in bizarre combinations and it is the theoretician who must out of this confusion find the proof of his theory, 'translate'

> into theoretical language the elements of historical life; not, on the
> contrary, reality which must present itself according to the abstract
> schema. This can never happen and in consequence this conception
> is the expression of passivity.[13]

Each national conjuncture is "the result of an original, unique combination (in a certain sense) and it is in the context of this originality and specificity that the combination must be understood and conceived if one wishes to overcome and direct it." There is no one road to socialism applicable for all cases: "The development is in the direction of internationalism but the point of departure is 'national' and it is from here that one must start."[14] It was this overriding concern for national conjuncture, in contrast to the formal internationalism of Trotsky and of Rosa Luxemburg,[15] that enabled Gramsci to discern the specificity of the problematic in the case of Western countries and to adapt the experience of Leninism and the Russian Revolution to the different conditions of the West.

It is all the more essential to emphasize this close link between theory and actual movements within society, since the tendency to interpret Gramsci's theories as an "idealist Marxism" overlooks the unity of theory and practice, linked indissolubly with the needs of concrete struggle, which underlay his work. Gramsci's weapon against both materialism and idealism was "the energetic affirmation of unity between theory and practice."[16] The underlying thematic of his philosophical, historical and cultural studies was a response to an essentially political problem. The traditional organizations and leadership of the working class had proved unable to surmount the dilemma that faces every socialist movement, working at once within bourgeois society and utilizing its institutions, while at the same time working for its overthrow. The result was generally a defensive and corporatist posture coupled with declamatory and utopian appeals for mass action from the Left (syndicalism and spontaneism). This was particularly true in the case of the "maximalist" leadership of the Italian Socialist Party (PSI), which, in spite of its nominal allegiance to the Third International at the Congress of Bologna (1919), proved incapable of moving beyond the twin polarities of opportunist participation in society or isolationist withdrawal from society. It therefore failed to come to grips with the situation of the postwar crisis, or to provide an active revolutionary leadership; the result was a fatal kind of inaction, barricaded behind old established positions and empty rhetoric. The same tendency towards isolationism was reproduced by the dominant faction of the Italian Communist Party (PCI) in the early period from its foundation at the Congress of Livorno in 1921. The sectarian "abstentionism" of the group led by Bordiga represented the same inability to intervene actively in the political arena, based on the same mechanistic assumptions that underlay the inaction of the PSI and in glaring contrast to the policies laid down by the Comintern. Lenin had already condemned this "Left-Wing Communism" in 1920:

> Comrade Bordiga and his "Left" friends draw from their correct criticism of Turati and Co. (the reformists) the wrong conclusion. . . . Not only in the parliamentary field, but in *all* fields of activity, communism *must introduce* (and without long, persistent and stubborn effort it will be *unable* to introduce) something new in principle that will represent a radical break with the traditions of the Second International.[17]

Gramsci's early opposition to the PSI leadership, culminating in the experience of the factory councils movement in Turin, became after 1921 a struggle against the sectarianism of the early PCI, only won with his rise to leadership of the party in 1924. This position was again accentuated by the change of Comintern policy in 1929–30. During a series of political discussions with fellow prisoners in late 1930, he is reported to have strongly criticized the recrudescence of "the old maximalist phraseology" and the failure of the party to confront fascism: "They do not know how to adjust the means to different historical situations."[18]

Against this political background, the defeat of Italian socialism and the triumph of fascism, Gramsci's lasting achievement remains that of having overcome, both in theory and in his political practice, the sterile alternatives of participation and abstention, through a radical redefinition of the essential problem, the nature of power in Western society; underlining the active work of politicization and mobilization of the masses, restoring the possibility of revolutionary initiative by a conscious political agency based on an ideological and political unity between the "intellectuals" and the "masses" making up the revolutionary bloc. The problem was to elaborate the specific character of a "collective will" that would make possible the passage from a sectoral, corporate and hence subaltern role of purely negative opposition to a *hegemonic* role of conscious action towards revolutionary goals; not seeking a partial adjustment within the system, but "posing the question of the state in its entirety."[19] For this to be possible, the partial, determined character of opposition must become a universally oriented challenge over the whole range of social relations, so that "the structure of external forces that overwhelms man and renders him passive may be transformed into a means of freedom, an instrument for creating a new ethicopolitical form, making possible new initiatives." The passage to the hegemonic moment represents the transformation of the "objective" into the realm of "intersubjectivity," from "the merely economic moment (of egoistic passion) to the ethicopolitical moment; that is, the superior elaboration of the structure into superstructure in the minds and consciousness of men."[20] This transition from the purely economic struggle required a new conception of the role of ideology, of the "intellectuals" (in a broad sense, of all those who have an organizing and educative role), an emphasis on the voluntary character of the revolutionary organization as an agency bringing about the transformation of consciousness and cultural renewal at all levels of society.

It was Gramsci's great strength that he posed these problems in terms that admitted of practical solutions. The disjunction of theory and practice was seen as the root cause of the debility of strategic options on the Left. This signified that socialism was still passing through "a relatively primitive phase, one that is still economic-corporative, in which the general framework of the structure is being transformed only in quantitative terms and the appropriate 'quality superstructure' is in the process of arising but is not yet organically formed."[21] The divorce of theory from concrete struggle, from the specific possibilities contained within society, produced "arbitrary" schema in the place of that "organic" unity that alone could restore a creative dialectical relationship between objective situation and revolutionary initiatives. Gramsci's long isolation in prison, far from leading to disinterested contemplation, was compensated by an enormous effort of political engagement. His "intellectual" and "political" roles were inextricably linked and the tendency to separate them—particularly tempting, in his case, since the division corresponds to the two periods of political activity (including political journalism), 1916–26, and imprisonment, 1926–37—can only lead to a disjunction between his theories and his intentions, which gives at best a partial view. Such schematic and unilinear interpretations do less than justice to the originality and underlying coherence of the prison notes, despite their fragmentary character. Gramsci was saved from any idealist or formal solution by his close grounding in political reality. "All concrete analyses of relations of forces cannot be ends in themselves (unless one is writing a chapter of past history); on the contrary, they only acquire meaning insofar as they serve to justify practical activity, an initiative of will."[22] His analyses are never limited to the adumbration of purely conceptual alternatives; their unity and coherence lie in the theoretical-practical framework that constituted his field of research. This involved taking into account the limits present and possibilities open; "a research into the conditions necessary for freedom of action towards certain ends. . . . It is not a question of establishing a *hierarchy of ends* but a *graduation of ends* to be attained."[23] This cannot be "the result of a rational, deductive process proper to 'pure intellectuals' (or 'pure donkeys')," but an organic process in which theory finds its authenticity in practice, in which analysis is guided towards strategy, in which analysis is "active" rather than "descriptive."[24] The final test of any analysis was its "practical efficacy" in terms of "effective reality."

To understand better the nature of this "collective will" in Gramsci, it is necessary to turn to the crucial role of ideology and the superstructures in his analysis of the power structure in Western societies.

II.

Gramsci's polemic against economism was based on the need to reformulate the "problem of the relation between structure and superstructure, which must be precisely posed and resolved if one is to achieve a true analysis of the forces operating in the history of a determined period and to define their relationship."[25] The "economist" hypothesis affirms an "immediate element of force" directly produced by the determinism of the structure. The result is the identification of "state" with "government" or repressive-coercive apparatus only, proper to a "faction of the directing group, who wish to modify not the structure of the State, but only the direction of the government," for whom "it is a question merely of the rotation of directing parties, not the foundation and organization of a new political society and even less of a new type of civil society."[26] The conception of an unmediated element of force is not enough. In this case, "the analysis of the various degrees of 'relations of forces' can only culminate in the sphere of hegemony and ethicopolitical relations."[27]

The concept of hegemony is thus linked to Gramsci's aim to redefine the nature of power in modern societies in more comprehensive terms, allowing for the articulations of the various levels or instances of a given social formation, political, cultural or ideological, in the determination of a specific power structure. In a letter from prison in 1931, he outlines the place occupied by the problem of intellectuals in his program of research, which entailed the "further elaboration of the concept of the State as the equilibrium between political society (either dictatorship or coercive apparatus to conform the popular masses according to the type of production and economy of a given moment) and civil society (or the hegemony of a social group over the entire national society by way of the so-called private organizations, such as the Church, the unions, the schools, etc.)."[28] The concept of the state thus assumes "a wider and more organic sense," which includes "elements which belong to the notion of civil society (in the sense, one could say that state = political society + civil society, that is, hegemony tempered by coercion)."[29] The state becomes, in this wider sense, "the state proper *and* civil society" or "the whole complex of practical and theoretical activities through which the ruling class not only justifies and maintains its domination, but succeeds in obtaining the active consent of the governed."[30] The conception of power is thus extended to include the whole complex of institutions through which power relations are mediated in society, ensuring the "political and cultural hegemony of a social group over the entire society, as the ethical content of the state."[31] The function of "*dominio*" (coercion) is complemented by that of "*direzione*" (leadership by consent) as the two modalities or "moments" of power relations. The significance of Machiavelli in Gramsci's research lay not only in his political realism, but in the "double nature" of his Centaur, both beast and human, containing both "degrees" of force and consent, of authority and hegemony.[32] Gramsci's conceptual approach transcends the categories of political science and sociology; the state is no longer a mere apparatus of coercion but itself has a retroactive influence in the sphere of civil society through "the multiplicity of particular associations and agencies," which constitute the "hegemonic apparatus of a social group over the rest of the population (or civil society), the basis of the 'State,' in the *narrow* sense of coercive-governing apparatus."[33]

In advanced capitalist countries the autonomous role of the super-structures is fully developed; the superstructures are "an effective and operating reality."[34] While the various political and ideological forma-tions correspond to the interests of the dominant class, they cannot be reduced to mere emanations or epiphenomena of the structure, and are susceptible to different historical forms and combinations, which in turn react upon the structure. It is through this "unity in multiplicity" that it becomes possible, by the analysis of relations in forces within a determined historical situation, to establish the objective coordinates of the political struggle as a whole, taking account of the possibility of error or unforeseen results of actions on the part of the agent.[35] Gram-sci makes a distinction between "organic" movements of the struc-ture that reveal its "incurable contradictions," giving rise to relatively permanent groupings, whole classes within society, and potentially challenging the very existence of the superstructure; and "incidental" movements of "conjuncture," which are limited to adjustments within the existing power structure. The failure to establish the precise dialec-tical relationship between these two, "either by expounding as directly operative causes that instead only operate indirectly, or by asserting that immediate causes are the only efficient causes," leads on the one hand to economism and on the other hand to ideologism, "an exalta-tion of the voluntarist and individual element."[36] On the basis of this general principle, he analyzes the various "moments" of the dialectic of structure and superstructure, from the basic social relations of produc-tion to political and organizational groupings. These depend on differ-ent degrees of homogeneity, organization, and political consciousness, from the "elementary" solidarity of the economic-corporative phase to the wider solidarity of the class "for itself," but still acting within the existing political-juridicial framework of society; and finally to the most distinctly "political" moment, "which marks the clear passage from the structure to the sphere of complex superstructure," in which a group surpasses the limits of its corporate interests. These become the interests of other allied and subordinate groups; the sectional interest is superseded and becomes politically "diffused over the whole area of society, creating a unity not only of economic and political aims, but an intellectual and moral unity, posing all the issues that arise not on the corporative level but on the 'universal' level," in which particular group interests must be conceived and "coordinated concretely with the general interests of subordinate groups."[37] The political moment, in order to become universal, must move beyond "interest," surpassing the economic categories of existing society, to constitute an integral challenge—political, cultural, ideological—a qualitative affirmation of the new social order.

Hence the crucial role of ideology and the means by which consciousness is mediated in capitalist society, preserved and protected behind the whole complex of institutions, private and public, which legitimize bourgeois dominance, rendering its values and definitions universal because accepted as the definitive values of society as such. Developing his analysis from Marx's *Preface* of 1859—that "it is in the sphere of ideology that men become conscious of this conflict and fight it out"[38]—Gramsci developed, through the Sorelian concept of *historical bloc*, a theory of the role of intellectuals as "experts in legitimation," in mediating the ideological and political unity of the existing hegemonic structure, rendering it acceptable to allied and subordinate groups, universalizing its dominance. The establishment of this intellectual and political hegemony in the nineteenth century occupies a large part of Gramsci's historical analysis, particularly in the case of post-Risorgimento Italy. Thus he dwells on the process of "molecular absorption," through which the national "revolutionary" forces, represented by the Party of Action, were cut off by their failure to mobilize mass support among the peasants of the south and, without any organic class basis, failed to challenge the dominant historical bloc formed by the northern bourgeoisie in alliance with the southern landowners. In this way, the Moderates were able to build up the hegemony of a coalition of agrarian and industrial interest groups and their clientele, exercising a "spontaneous attraction" on the southern intellectuals and functionaries.[39] This process of "*trasformismo*" represented the gradual widening of the social base of the Italian ruling class bloc, the absorption of opposition and allied groups by "private" individual initiatives, in which, as in the case of republican France from 1870, corruption and bribery played a significant role, "characteristic of certain situations in which the exercise of the hegemonic function becomes difficult, while the use of force would involve too many dangers."[40] Only in periods of organic crisis was naked coercion rendered necessary, since the ruling class stood isolated and hence vulnerable, the exercise of hegemony becoming impossible. The resolution of such a crisis would depend on the forces available; the arbitration by a charismatic mediator claiming to represent the "national interest," the Caesarist solution, was the result of a static stalemate.[41]

This resort to the "moment of force" is a sign of great weakness; normally the hegemonic equilibrium is characterized by a

> combination of force and consent which are balanced in variable proportions, without force ever prevailing too much over consent— on the contrary, making it appear that force is applied by the consent of the majority, expressed by the pretended organs of public opinion—newspapers and other associations—which to this end are sometimes multiplied artificially.[42]

In Western democracy the degree of institutionalization has made the superstructures peculiarly "dense" and "civil society has become a complex structure, resistant to catastrophic irruptions of the immediate economic element (crises, depressions, etc.)."[43] In his last report to the party on the general situation, before his arrest in 1926, Gramsci observed that in the countries of "advanced capitalism," which are the "keystones of the bourgeois edifice," "the dominant class possesses political and organizational reserves, which it did not possess, for example, in Russia. Even the gravest economic crises do not have an immediate repercussion in the political field. Politics always lag considerably behind economic development." In the more peripheral countries like Italy, the existence of "large intermediate strata" between capital and labor, with their own political and ideological influence, especially on the peasantry, creates further superstructural peculiarities.[44] In the case of democratic forms of government, the principle of the division of powers, of "impartial arbitration" by the executive "who reigns, but who does not govern," helps to ensure the consent of the governed, masking the real nature of power relations in capitalist society behind a facade of formal and abstract—juridical— notions of citizenship. Under these conditions consciousness is mediated and fragmentary, refracted through the existing hegemonic apparatus of bourgeois "direction," while conflict is regulated to ensure that disputes are kept within the narrow bounds of procedural compromise, registered by the election vote.[45]

These considerations imply, in terms of strategy, that the "war of manœuvre" becomes progressively the "war of position." Borrowing the military terminology of the first world war, Gramsci wrote: "Before 1870 . . . society was still, so to speak, in a state of fluidity . . . the apparatus of the state was relatively little developed, with a greater autonomy of civil society in relation to the state." With increasing bureaucratization, "the massive structure of modern democracies, either in terms of state organization or the complexity of associations in civil life . . . constitute 'trenches' and 'permanent fortifications' on the front in the war of position," against which an artillery attack only destroys "the exterior surface, leaving the defense lines still effective." This is a problem specific to modern states, not to backward countries or colonies, in which "the structures of national life are loose and embryonic and cannot become 'trench' or 'fortress.'" This in turn meant that the "1848 doctrine of 'permanent revolution' was superseded in political science by the formula of 'civil hegemony.'"[46] Whereas in Russia, for instance, "the state was everything, civil society was primitive . . . in the West the state was only an advanced trench, behind which lay a robust chain of fortresses." The "accurate recognition of national characteristics" made it necessary to "translate" Lenin's practice into the terms appropriate for a "war of position," the only possible one in the West, a strategy of siege to challenge and breach the hegemonic apparatus of the bourgeoisie.[47]

The passage to the "war of position" becomes increasingly the key to Western strategy in Gramsci's analysis; the "war of reciprocal siege" represents the most difficult, but the most decisive phase of the struggle, which requires an "unprecedented concentration of hegemony," a mobilization on the part of the dominant groups of "all the hegemonic resources of the state" through controls of every kind, to "organize permanently the 'impossibility' of internal disintegration."[48] In his notes on *Americanism and Fordism*, Gramsci analyzed the corresponding trend toward the rationalization of the workforce and the internalization of control over the whole area of the worker's life in the most advanced sectors of capitalist production, which represented "the final extreme point . . . in the successive attempts by industry to overcome the 'tendencial law' of the fall of the rate of profit."[49] Such developments of hegemony in the productive processes themselves, the adaptation to new forms of psychic discipline, together with the existence of a "working-class aristocracy with its bureaucratic . . . and social-democratic connections" demanded "a more complex and long-term strategy and tactics than were necessary to the Bolsheviks in . . . 1917," he wrote in a letter of 1924.[50] Under these circumstances the reliance on "conditions," on the principal contradiction of capitalism, to "produce" an opposition was a vain delusion, for the "determination which in Russia launched the masses on the revolutionary path was complicated in Western and Central Europe by all the political super-structures created by the greater development of capitalism."[51] An in-tegral opposition could only come about by the properly political work of organizing and mobilizing the masses, not in terms of corporate interest, but in terms of the hegemonic leadership of the working class organized in a revolutionary party with an active mass basis. Only in this way could that transformation of consciousness take place, which would make possible a transcendence of the existing categories of so-ciety, both in theory and in revolutionary practice, transforming both workers and intellectuals into intellectuals of a new type through the active educative and political work of the revolutionary organization. "The existence of objective conditions and possibilities of struggle is not enough; it is necessary to 'know' them, to know how to use them, to want to use them."[52] Both the sectarian and the syndicalist positions underestimated this active work of mass organization in the formation of a "collective will." Gramsci's authentic Leninism lay in his rejection of all forms of spontaneism and syndicalism, which he criticized in Sorel and Rosa Luxemburg:[53] the tendency among the critics of the Second International to assume the existence of a revolutionary agency in society and to appeal to the "direct action" of the masses, without the necessary intervention of political organization. Neither was polit-ical organization in itself sufficient; the sectarian resort to the opposite extreme reproduced the same result in practice: the divorce between the party, the intellectuals, and the masses, the failure to create that "organic" relationship that alone could establish a revolutionary he-gemony, overcoming the fragmentation created and sustained by the dominant bloc and building a new coherence, capable of responding to the needs and aspirations of all exploited groups on a national scale.

The politicizing of the worker meant the transcendence of his cor-porate interests as a wage earner, which are themselves determined by the capitalist wage relation. "The proletariat, in order to be capable of governing . . . must rid itself of every corporatist residue, of every syndicalist prejudice or incrustation."[54] The trade union, Gramsci wrote in *L'Ordine Nuovo* in 1919, is a "form of capitalist society, not a potential overcoming of capitalist society. It organizes the workers not as producers, but as wage earners, that is, as creatures of the capitalist regime of private property, as sellers of their labor as commodity."[55] The problem was therefore to develop institutions that would allow the worker to develop his autonomous initiative as a producer. In the conditions of postwar Italy, the means of mobilizing the working class in Turin as a revolutionary force was through the factory council movement, which represented the direct democratic control of the productive process by all the producers in the factory. The introduction of direct democracy of producers organized as an autonomous force, in the area of production itself, the one area where democracy was crucially denied in capitalist society, at work, was seen by Gramsci as the key to the future society, in which the producers became, "instead of simple executors, agents of the process; from being cogwheels in the mechanism of capitalist production, become subjects."[56] Cammett shows, in his recent study, how the factory council represented a means by which the "workers could educate themselves as producers"; it could not therefore be subjected to the trade union and PSI bureaucracy, but had to be organized on an autonomous basis. The tendency to see the factory councils movement as a form of syndicalism ignored their role as a politically educative institution.[57] "The dictatorship of the proletariat is incarnated in the type of organization specific to the activity proper to producers and not wage earners, slaves of capital. The factory council is the first cell of this organization,"[58] the means by which the proletariat can "educate itself, gather experience, and acquire a responsible awareness of the duties incumbent upon classes that hold the power of the state."[59] In his report of July 1920 to the Comintern, Gramsci described the Turin councils as "the transfer of the struggle . . . from the strictly corporatist and reformist domain to the sphere of the revolutionary struggle, the control of production and the dictatorship of the proletariat." This meant the direct control of the councils by the producers themselves, "not through the official channels of trade union bureaucracy."[60] In this way, the "Turinese communists posed concretely . . . the question of the 'hegemony of the proletariat', in other words of the social basis of the proletarian dictatorship and the workers' state."[61] The factory council was the means by which the party, as the conscious vanguard of the struggle, could be directly linked to the active mass participation of the working class as producers, conscious of their responsible and liberated role. The factory council was "the model of the proletarian state," in which political society itself would progressively be "organically" absorbed by civil society.[62]

It was essential that this transition from a corporate to a directing function take place before the actual conquest of power; instead of a mechanical symmetry between base and superstructure, a dialectical relation enables the revolutionary movement to exercise a de facto leadership in civil society this side of power. "A social group must already become 'directing' before the conquest of power (this is itself one of the principal conditions of the conquest of power); afterwards, when it exercises power and even while it retains a firm grasp on it as the 'dominant' group, it must continue to be 'directive.'"[63] This meant that the working class could not establish its hegemony "without some sacrifice of its immediate interests" to the interests of all its potential allies in society; in particular, in Italy, it would have to ally itself with the rural masses of the south. The "southern question" has been rightly described as the "primordial problem" of Italian socialism; to Gramsci, the Turin movement had "one undeniable merit," that of having "brought the southern question to the attention of the vanguard of the working class, formulating it as one of the essential problems of the national policy of the Italian proletariat."[64] The future of the workers' movement in the north and the peasants' movement in the south were indissolubly linked; the workers had an immediate interest in not allowing "southern Italy and the islands to become a capitalist counter-revolutionary base." At the same time, in the establishment of the workers' state lay the salvation of the peasantry.[65] If this alliance is not created, "the proletariat cannot become the 'directing' class and those strata, which in Italy represent the majority of the population, will remain under bourgeois direction, enabling the state to defeat and resist the proletarian impetus."[66] The mechanical formulae of both the PSI leadership and the Bordigan group toward any autonomous initiative, either of the workers or towards the peasants,[67] was one of the major factors in the defeat of socialism in the postwar crisis.

The problem of alliance raised the whole question of the cultural and ideological preparation of the socialist movement. For the "moment in which a subaltern group becomes hegemonic and autonomous, projecting a new type of state, demands concretely the construction of a new intellectual and moral order, that is, a new type of society, and hence demands the elaboration of more universal conceptions, more refined and decisive ideological weapons."[68] The creation of this new intellectual and cultural unity was itself a condition for the "directing" function; the integration of culture was a vital complementary task of socialism. Hence the crucial role of the intellectuals in the "cementing" of the revolutionary bloc:

> Critical self-consciousness signifies historically and politically the creation of an elite of intellectuals; a human mass does not "distinguish" itself, cannot become independent of its own accord, without organizing itself; and there is no organization without intellectuals or leaders [dirigenti], that is to say without the theoretical aspect of the theory-practice nexus being concretely distinguished in a group of people specialized in conceptual and philosophical elaboration.[69]

The theoretical-practical relation necessitated in practice a new relation between the "intellectuals" and the "mass," a new unity of consciousness through a unified political practice. In this sense, the discovery by Lenin "in the field of political organization and practice of the concept of hegemony as complementary to that of 'state-as-force'" represented "*philosophical* as well as *practical-political* progress, since it necessarily involved an ethical and intellectual unity that has surpassed 'common sense' and become . . . critical."[70] The political unity of the revolutionary alliance requires a corresponding ideological coherence, and a new "total" conception of culture, in which the party, the intellectuals and the masses are brought into an "organic" relationship, qualitatively projecting an integral vision of the new civilization in all spheres of life.

III.

The work of cultural renovation, of "intellectual and moral reform," was therefore a crucial correlate of socialist hegemony; that of "breaking up the unity founded on the traditional ideologies, a rupture without which the new force cannot acquire the consciousness of its autonomous personality."[71] Through his confrontation with Croce, Gramsci derived "the importance of the cultural moment in practical (collective) activity; every historical action cannot but be accomplished by 'collective man,' that is to say it presupposes that a cultural-social unity has been attained, which transforms a large number of scattered wills, with heterogeneous goals, into one goal, on the basis of a common conception of the world."[72] Through the existing ideological and cultural forms, the bourgeoisie is able to "universalize" its "direction" of society, to hold together disparate and even oppositional groups on the basis of a consensus. The consciousness of subordinate groups is thus mediated and partial; theory is often in contradiction with actions. This is not due to "bad faith," an explanation that would apply to individuals, but to the uncritical "borrowing of conceptions" that "binds the individual to another social group, influences the . . . direction of his will in a more or less powerful way, and this can reach the point where the contradiction of his consciousness will not permit any action, any decision or choice, producing a state of moral and political passivity."[73] Hence the vital importance of the critique of existing culture and ideology, not in the sense of negation but of revealing its partial nature, the universality of which, now distorted in metaphysical terms, will be realized in the passage to socialism.[74] Through this process of demystification on the intellectual level, the fragmentary state of "common sense" gives way to "critical self-consciousness" and the "old collective will becomes disintegrated into its contradictory elements," giving rise to a new cohesion.[75]

Gramsci's emphasis on the educative aspect of socialism, achieving through the mass transformation of consciousness the "creation of a new civilization," a universal and integrated culture, is developed from the earliest of his articles in the Turinese socialist weekly *Il Grido del Popolo*, which he edited from 1917 to 1918. In contrast to the anti-intellectualism of Bordiga ("One does not become a socialist through education, but through the real necessities of the class to which one belongs") or the traditional socialist populism of the previous editor, Maria Giudice ("When the masses feel in a socialist way . . . they will act in a socialist way"),[76] Gramsci's lucid and Socratic articles were aimed at educating the worker to his role in the leadership of the revolutionary struggle. Journalism became in his hands a means of "elaborating, making to think concretely, transforming, homogenizing according to an organic process that leads from simple common sense to systematic and coherent thought."[77] In part, this emphasis was a product of his own experience as a scholar from Sardinia, one of the

most backward provinces in Italy, and the enormous intellectual effort
it had required "to overcome a backward way of life and thought, such
as that of a Sardinian at the beginning of this century, to reach a way
of life . . . that is no longer restricted to the region and the village, but
is national."[78] Even more important, however, was the fact that he was
well placed, as a provincial newcomer in the most industrialized city
in Italy, to observe the "borrowing of conceptions" in the corporatist
and exclusive socialism of the PSI leadership, which looked upon the
south as the "backland," an obstacle to economic progress and source
of cheap labor.[79] Italian socialism had "suffered the sad fate of being
approximated to the most arid, sterile thought of the nineteenth century, to positivism."[80] In the hands of Marxists like Loria, for whom
"Facts" were "divine, principles human," or Colajanni ("in the hedon-
istic principle alone and exclusively lies the justification of the class
struggle"),[81] Marxism had become a drab evolutionism in the dress
then à la mode; to Gramsci this tendency was especially dangerous
since it sanctified the corporatism of the socialist movement. "Every
revolution," he wrote in 1916, "has been preceded by an intense work
of cultural penetration, of penetration of ideas," and he added:

> It is urgent to cease conceiving of culture as encyclopedic knowledge,
> in which man is considered only as a recipient of . . . empirical facts,
> of disconnected brute facts which he must then store in his brain as
> in the columns of a dictionary . . . responding passively to stimuli. . . .
> This form of culture is catastrophic, *especially for the proletariat.*[82]

Gramsci's struggle against positivism was at the same time a struggle
for the unity of the revolutionary bloc. "The first task of the Turinese
communists was that of changing the political orientation and general
ideology of the proletariat itself, as a national element, which lives
inside the complex life of the state and undergoes unconsciously the
influence of the schools, the newspapers, of the bourgeois tradition."
The Socialist Party had "given its blessing" to the "whole 'southernist'
literature of the clique of so-called positivist writers. . . . Once again,
'science' had turned to crushing the wretched and exploited, but this
time it was cloaked in socialist colors."[83]

The development of a revolutionary consciousness required a new
emphasis on the role of ideas in changing the objective reality of external phenomena. While Gramsci's early intellectual formation took
place under the aegis of neoidealism, he underlined his "complete

break" with this tradition, in terms of a radical historicism, shorn of transcendental and ahistorical categories. To confront Croce's speculative historicism, in which "history becomes a formal history, a history of concepts and in the last analysis an autobiographical history of the thought of Croce," it was necessary to "reduce it to its real significance as an immediate ideology, divesting it of the brilliance with which it is accredited as a manifestation . . . of serene and impartial thought, situated far above the miseries and contingencies of daily life, in disinterested contemplation."[84] Croce represented the "lay Pope" of bourgeois hegemony, comparable to the position of Erasmus in relation to the Reformation. The failure of the idealists lay in the exclusiveness of their ideas, in "not having known how to create an ideological unity between the elite and the masses, between the intellectuals and the masses." Their conception of education lacked any "organic character"; it "resembled the first contact between English merchants and negro Africans."[85] The ultimate failure of idealism was the divorce of theory from the real struggles of history, through which history became reduced to an arbitrary and abstract schema; Gramsci's method, in combating both idealism and "crude materialism," was

> the "logical" passage of every conception of the world to the morality conforming to it, from every "contemplation" to "action," from every philosophy to the political practice dependent on it. . . . One could say that this is the central link of (Marxism), the point at which it becomes "actualized," in which it lives historically, that is, socially and not any longer within individual brains, at which it ceases to be arbitrary and becomes necessary.[86]

This emphasis on the practicity of theory, the intentionality of "philosophy," is directed above all to the practical problem of the mass diffusion of Marxism as a world conception; the many references to "philosophy" passing into "real history" have this polemical-indicative sense. Althusser has recently suggested, on the grounds of the "latent" tendency of every historicist problematic, that this results in an underestimation of "theoretical practice" itself, a confusion between theory and ideology, in which "philosophy" becomes reduced to an expression of a historical "essence" in a Hegelian-type "expressive unity." Theory thus becomes a reflection of history, a "historically-determined abstraction," resulting in an empiricist approach on the one hand or an idealist voluntarism on the other.[87] Without entering into the general

sense of Althusser's discussion, it may, however, be questioned that
Gramsci represents this historicist tendency; Althusser overlooks the
theoretical-practical field of Gramsci's research, in which theory is not
a passive "reflection" of history, but an essential moment in the overcoming and surpassing of existing structures, reacting against them in
terms of conscious praxis. Gramsci's historicism represents the means
by which both theory and practice are "actualized," within the determined context. He therefore avoids both spontaneism and voluntarism;
the relationship between "philosophy" and "history" is a *critical* one,
and by no means precludes the theoretical dimension as such.[88]

Gramsci's critique of idealism was not only a confrontation with
the most significant philosophy of the time, of abstract man divorced
from his social environment; it was also above all part of his critique
of "pure intellectuals," of the "cosmopolitan" tradition in Italian culture, expressed in the supranational institutions of empire and papacy,
which in turn had determined that fundamental Italian problem of a
country whose history had long been marked by a severe disproportion
between social and economic backwardness and preeminence in the
artistic and cultural field, by the wide gap between the enlightened
lay culture of a small minority and the religious superstition of the
masses. In Italy, he noted, the term "national" had a restricted sense,
not coinciding with that of "popular," "since . . . the intellectuals are
removed from the people, that is from the 'nation,' and are on the
contrary linked to a tradition of caste . . . the tradition is 'bookish'
and abstract . . . and the typical intellectual feels more linked to Han-
nibal Caro or Hippolitus . . . than to the peasant of Apulia or Sicily."
In relation to the people, the intellectuals were "a caste and not an
element organically linked to the people themselves."[89] It was the absence of any "national-popular" culture that constituted the primordial
weakness of Italian society, which in turn had made the achievement
of national unity a "passive revolution" governed by external forces,
rather than developing its own internal dynamic.[90] Gramsci uses the
term "Jacobin" in two distinct senses: first, to refer to the intellectualist
and abstract divorce of theory from the concrete possibilities contained
within society, in the sense that "Trotsky had the Jacobin temperament
without any adequate political content," while in Lenin there was "Jacobin temperament and content not according to an intellectualist eti-
quette."[91] His criticism of the sectarian position was thus linked to that

of idealism: "The position of 'pure intellectual' becomes either a really deteriorated form of 'Jacobinism'—and in this sense 'Amadeo' (Bordiga) can, on a different intellectual level, be compared to Croce—or a disdainful Pontius-Pilatism, or even both simultaneously."[92] In the second sense, Jacobinism refers to active intervention in the creation of a "national-popular collective will," the "protagonist of a real historical drama"; in this sense, the "precocious Jacobinism" of Machiavelli is traced to his proposed reorganization of the Florentine militia, bringing the peasants "simultaneously" into political life.[93]

These considerations govern Gramsci's redefinition of the role of intellectuals and that of the hegemonic party as a "collective intellectual." There exists "no independent class of intellectuals, but every social group has its own group of intellectuals or tends to form one," to give it "homogeneity and knowledge of its function, not only in the economic field, but in the social and political field as well; the capitalist entrepreneur creates with himself the industrial technician, the political economist, the organizer of a new culture, of a new law, etc."[94] These "organic" intellectuals, who usually represent "specializations of certain partial aspects of the primitive activity of the new social type to which the new class has given birth" are distinguished from the category of "traditional" intellectuals, which are "preexisting" and which appear as "representatives of a historical continuity, uninterrupted by the most complex and radical changes in social and political forms."[95] The relation between intellectuals and the world of production is "not immediate, as in the case of [social classes], but 'mediated' in different degrees by the whole social fabric, the complexity of the superstructures, of which they are the functionaries."[96] To the intellectuals, in this broad sense—in terms of their function, which is "to direct and to organize, that is [an] educational [function], which means intellectual"—falls the role of mediating the hegemony of the dominant group, ensuring that "'spontaneous' consent given by the wide masses of the population to the orientation imprinted on social life by the dominant class," and carrying out the work of "organization and connection" as "functionaries of the dominant group for the exercise of subordinate functions of social hegemony and political government."[97] It becomes imperative therefore for the revolutionary movement not only to win over elements of the "traditional" intellectuals, but above all to develop its own "organic" intellectuals to create "favorable conditions" for the expansion of its own class from a subordinate to a directing capacity. The restoration of the theory-practice nexus required

> that organic unity of thought and cultural solidarity that can only be realized if between the intellectuals and the non-intellectuals there exists the same unity that must exist between theory and practice, that is, if the intellectuals become organically the intellectuals of these masses, elaborating and making coherent the principles and problems which the masses pose in their practical activity—thus constituting a cultural and social bloc.[98]

This involved the development of a new type of revolutionary intellectual, "who arises from the masses but remains in close contact with them, to become the 'stay of the corset.'"[99]

The essentially educative relation implied by the term "organic" becomes the basis of the hegemony of the revolutionary bloc; the dialectical relation between the "intellectuals" and the "masses," the party and the active participation of its social base. This relationship is an "active relation, a reciprocal relationship" in which "every teacher is always a pupil and every pupil a teacher."[100] In contrast with previous "world-conceptions," Marxism "does not seek to sustain the people in their primitive philosophy, but to lead them to a higher view of life," making possible "the intellectual progress of the masses and not only of a few intellectual groups."[101] All men are to a certain degree intellectuals, in that they participate in a world-conception; in this wider sense of "intellectual," Gramsci writes of changing the relationship between intellectual and muscular effort to create a "new equilibrium," and a new type of intellectual, who is "actively involved in practical life," combining specialist technique with science and humanism, thus becoming a "'leader' (specialist + politician)."[102] Society itself becomes a system of educative relationships "between individuals, between intellectuals and non-intellectuals, between governed and governing. . . . Every relation of hegemony is necessarily an educative relation."[103] One is reminded of Che Guevara's writing of the need for "the development of a consciousness in which all the old categories of evaluation become changed. Society in its complexity must become a gigantic school."[104]

In 1919 Gramsci had developed, in the factory councils program, the means through which such a relation could be expressed, "corresponding to the latent aspirations and real forms of life" among the Turin workers. "At that time," he later recalled, "no initiative was taken that was not

THEORY AND PRACTICE IN GRAMSCI'S MARXISM   189

tested in reality . . . if the opinions of the workers were not taken fully into account. For this reason, our initiatives appeared as the interpretation of a felt need, never as the cold application of intellectual schema."[105]

The task was always, for Gramsci, to find the "present form of the struggle," the form that would activate a response, since it corresponded to the "revolutionary thread" in the real historical situation; in this way making possible the passage from science to action—"not pure action," the Bergsonian abandonment to the irrational, which Gramsci criticized in Sorel, "but the real, impure action in the most profane and worldly sense."[106] While the problem of hegemony was posed in this way by the *Ordine Nuovo* group in 1919–21, they had few illusions about the likelihood of failure. The "optimism of will" was always tempered by a "pessimism of awareness," to use a phrase characteristic of Gramsci. In the absence of political leadership at the national level, the Turinese movement was isolated; "abandoned by all, the Turinese proletariat was obliged to confront alone . . . national capitalism and the power of the state."[107] The Socialist Party had become a mere "spectator of the unfolding of events"; it had failed "to give a general direction to unify and concentrate the revolutionary action of the masses." The Party had shown itself to be a "mere bureaucratic organization, without soul or will," with the result that "the working class tends instinctively to constitute another party or slides into anarchistic tendencies."[108] The factory councils could not in themselves provide a solution; as Togliatti put it in 1920: "The constitution of councils only has value if it is viewed as a conscious beginning of a revolutionary process . . . Control of production has meaning only as an act . . . in this process."[109] To Gramsci, the existence of a coherent leadership was "the fundamental and indispensable condition for the experience of the workers' councils; if this condition does not exist, every . . . experimental proposition must be rejected as absurd."[110] The need for a new conception of political leadership was the lesson to be drawn from the defeat of the Italian revolution. Gramsci's concern was to develop a leadership that would "move ahead" of events, with a coherent strategy, "maintaining the permanent confidence of the masses in such a way as to become their guide, their thinking head."[111]

Gramsci's conception of the party follows closely the general framework of his ideas on the intellectuals, hegemony, and the specificity of the superstructures. The party is not reducible to an epiphenomenon of "class"; it is the political agency of the working class responsible for developing and organizing the political conditions for the foundation of the workers' state. Gramsci developed his notion of the hegemonic party through his opposition to the sectarian tendencies of the early PCI, but already by 1921, he wrote:

> An association can be called a "political party" only insofar as it has succeeded in making concrete . . . its own notion . . . of the State, in concretizing and diffusing among the masses its own programme of government, organizing, in terms of practice, that is within determined conditions, in relation to real men and not abstract phantasma . . . a State.[112]

His long struggle against sectarianism was due to the fact that the party was not conceived "as the result of a dialectical process, in which the spontaneous movement of the revolutionary masses and the organized and directive will at the centre converge, but only as something nourished on air, which develops in itself and by itself."[113] The result was passivity and inaction, the failure to intervene actively in the work of building up the ideological and political unity of the revolutionary class and its allies. "In the modern world, a party is such—whether integral or the fraction of a larger party—when it is conceived, organized and directed in such a way as to develop into a State (in the integral and not technical-governing sense) and into a conception of the world."[114] The hegemonic party is based on a continually progressing dialectic between the proletariat and its conscious vanguard: an active, reciprocal relationship, which by far surpasses the categories of the Nennian "democratic" and the "totalitarian" interpretations of many commentators, vitiated by the language of Cold War ideology. Mr Lichtheim, for example, in his summary treatment, claims that "his (Gramsci's) own approach was quite consistent with the totalitarian assumption that revolutions are made by elites."[115] Yet no reading of Gramsci, however casual, could support such an assertion. All his opposition to sectarianism was precisely directed *against* any tendency in the party towards authoritarianism or "party vanity," against the error of regarding as self-sufficient the organization itself, "which meant only to create an apparatus of functionaries who would be 'orthodox' towards the official conceptions."[116] In the face of Stalinism, his strictures against party bureaucracy in the *Prison Notebooks* have an unambiguous ring; the bureaucratic tendency represents a "most dangerous . . . conservative force; if it ends by becoming solidified . . . and feels independent from the masses, the party becomes anachronistic and in moments of crisis becomes emptied of its social content."[117] And, writing of "the morbid manifestations of bureaucratic centralism, due to lack of initiative and responsibility from below," he described the resultant "unity" as that of a "stagnant marsh, superficially calm but 'mute.'"[118]

In contrast, Gramsci's conception of the party was based on the premise that "a party cannot exist by virtue of an internal necessity" but through an organic relationship with the class it represents, expressed by his formula of "spontaneity and conscious direction." Defending the factory councils' experience against the accusation of voluntarism, he wrote:

> This leadership was not abstract; it did not consist in repeating me-
> chanical formulas; it was applied to real men . . . in a determined
> historical situation, with certain kinds of outlook, sentiments . . .
> etc., which resulted from a certain . . . milieu of production. This
> element of spontaneity was not neglected, even less despised; it was
> *educated*, orientated . . . giving the masses a theoretical conscious-
> ness, as creators of historical and institutional values, as founders of
> states. This unity of "spontaneity" and "conscious direction" . . . is
> precisely the real political action of the subaltern classes, in so far as
> this represents mass politics and not simply an adventure by groups
> who invoke the masses.[119]

"Conscious direction" must be applied if spontaneous movements are to become a positive political factor; from the postwar experience, Gramsci learned that "the decisive element in every situation is the force permanently organized . . . which one can advance when the situation is favorable—and it is . . . only to the extent that such a force exists."[120] But this "force," the political party, was not to be organized on rigid lines, nor on the basis of a doctrine, "artificial and mechanically superimposed" but rather "organically produced . . . historically . . . in the struggle."[121] The party could only successfully move beyond the existing political framework and actively promote the surpassing of existing society and politics if it became the elaborator "of new, integrated and all-embracing intellectual systems . . . the annealing agent of the unity of theory and practice in the sense of real historical process." It was therefore necessary that the party "should be formed through individual enlistment and not in a 'Labour Party' way (through affiliation) because, if the aim is to lead organically 'the whole economically active mass,' it must be led not according to the old (existing) schemes but by creating new ones." Hence the need for a leadership, but organized on the principles of "democratic centralism," a "centralism in movement"; when the party is progressive, "it functions 'democratically' (in the sense of democratic centralism); when the party is regressive it functions 'bureaucratically' (in the sense of bureaucratic centralism)."[122] Only as an "organism in perpetual movement," rather than a rigid structure, "a continual readequation of the organization to the real movement, a constantly renewed balance between forces from below and orders from above, which . . . ensures continuity and regular accumulation of experience," could the party, while it "neither reigns nor governs juridically," represent nevertheless a *"de facto* power, exercise its hegemonic function, thus balancing the various interests in 'civil society' which, however, is so closely interwoven in fact with political society, that all the citizens feel that it reigns and governs."[123] Finally, parties come into existence within a historical context; since they represent the "nomenclature" of social classes, the ultimate goal of a party that aims progressively to educate the masses to self-management, to widen vastly the sphere of the "political" in civil society, is its own disappearance.[124]

The underlying thematic of Gramsci's Marxism thus finds its unity and coherence in his creative confrontation of the social and historical realities of his world. His renewal of Marxism was never the detached work of a "scientist" but rather the product of a lifetime of political struggle. In one of his earliest articles he wrote: "To live means to take sides,"[125] and in a letter from prison: "My whole intellectual formation was of a polemical kind and to think 'disinterestedly,' that is to study for study's sake, is difficult for me. Only occasionally, I manage to forget myself . . . and find, so to speak, the interest in things in themselves to apply myself to their analysis. Normally I have to move from a . . . dialectical standpoint; otherwise I feel no intellectual stimulus."[126] The result was a Marxism adapted to the actual problems and needs of the Italian struggle. The conception of socialism as concerned above all with the qualitative, rather than quantitative, transformation of society was never confined to an abstract level but directed towards its concrete realization, in terms of the fundamental political task, which was to "define the collective will in modern terms . . . as the working protagonist of a real historical drama"; to bring the "objective" into relation with a program to be realized; to apply the will to the creation of a new equilibrium of existing and operating forces, based on the force considered to be progressive, thereby "moving always in the field of effectual reality, but to dominate it and overcome it, or to contribute to that goal. In this way, the 'ought' becomes concrete."[127] In spite of imprisonment and appalling conditions, illness and isolation, Gramsci remained in a real sense a "political activist"; like that other exile from political life, Machiavelli, his armies were "only armies of words" and he was reduced to "concretely showing how historical forces *should have* operated to be effective."[128]

Gramsci has recently been called "the theoretician of revolution in the West."[129] Certainly it is true that no Marxist has confronted with such lucidity the problem of organizing and sustaining a socialist movement in the conditions of advanced capitalism. While it would clearly be against his whole spirit to adopt his ideas uncritically in a new and different context, the unity and range of his Marxism, the absence of fixed categories in his work, and its practical and active rather than passive approach still constitute a vital source for the corresponding development of an authentic *British* Marxism and the renewal of the socialist movement in Britain.

GRAMSCI AND LENIN 1917–1922

Alastair Davidson

I.

Antonio Gramsci was twenty-six at the beginning of 1917.[1] The "sewer of his past" on whose seething resentments he had built a "Sardist" view of the world ("Into the sea with the Italians") only showed in too many coffees and cigarettes and an enormous capacity for work. He had given up his "Sardist" worldview for what he and a great many other educated Italians regarded as a satisfactory view of the world: "Crocianism." Throughout 1917 Gramsci was still "Crocian in his views,"[2] although he had been a socialist for over three years and was working full-time for the socialist newspapers *Avanti* and *Grido del Popolo*, although his "Crocian" friends of university days had gone to war, and although he had considerable contact with workers, who were always dropping in from the nearby Casa del Popolo to see him because he "had the great gift of knowing how to talk to everybody."[3]

Theoretically, he agreed with the views in Benedetto Croce's recent *Teoria delle storia della storiografia*. In particular, these were: 1) a rejection of positivism as inverted idealism; 2) a consequent rejection of any history that claimed to relate what truly happened once and for all; and therefore 3) a belief that all immanent worldviews had been "thought up" in terms of the contemporary level of knowledge.[4] It followed that Gramsci believed that men were never the prisoners of their past in the sense that they could not free themselves through their own willful actions, but only be freed by some structural conjunction of events. They could, of course, well be the prisoners of their understanding of that past, and therefore fail to comprehend the realities of their present situation. Gramsci's theoretical and emotional beliefs are summed up in words he wrote in early 1917: "For natural laws, the fatal progress of things of pseudoscientists has been substituted the tenacious will of men," and in rather more moralizing tones: "Some people whimper pitifully, others curse obscenely, but none, or few, ask themselves: if I had done my duty, if I had attempted to impose my will, my opinion, would what has happened have happened?—I hate the apathetic."[5]

This theoretical rejection of determinism was, however, only a "starting point" for Gramsci, who proceeded through the Crocian view that contemporary levels of knowledge were based on contemporary needs, and through the theory of Giovanni Gentile of the "act," to that variety of Marxism which best accorded with the notion that the revolution would not come automatically but would have to be made in a conscious willful act by men who understood that the cause of their misery was capitalism. By 1917 he had found this in the interpretation of Antonio Labriola, who denied that Marxism described the "apocalyptic" workings of history and claimed that it was a theory based on the historical need for socialism and marked a stage in men's understanding of their situation. Labriola typified this view overall as a "philosophy of praxis," thus stressing the affinity between his concerns and those of the early Croce, who had also written a *Philosophy of Practice*.[6] Influenced by Labriola's work, Gramsci, who had read by 1917 Marx's *Holy Family*, *The Poverty of Philosophy*, *The Communist Manifesto*, *Revolution and Counter-Revolution in Germany*, and a *Contribution to the Critique of Political Economy*, was even able to dub Engels's *Anti-Dühring* a humanist work, and within a year to endorse firmly Labriola's belief that *Capital* was "not the first great book of critical theory but the last great book of political economy."[7] From the Labriolan position that the revolution would take place only when men "understood and overcame"[8] (taken directly from Hegel), Gramsci had reached the ideological concerns that really interested him in 1917: how to make men "understand and overcome."

Ideologically, Gramsci was influenced by Charles Péguy and Romain Rolland, both of whom agreed with the proposition that "fate is the excuse of men without wills" and who preached on a more practical level the same sort of views and morality as Croce. This amounted above all to the belief that it was the task of the intellectuals (and Gramsci defined himself as an intellectual) to tear the veil of misunderstanding from men's eyes and help build the "City of God."[9] Gramsci endorsed this notion, and consequently, that the main socialist task was education. After he got his first job on *Avanti* in 1916 he argued in a series of important articles that: "the problem of education is the most important class-problem" and that "the first step in emancipating oneself from political and social slavery is that of freeing the mind." This education was necessary because it was clear from history that such freedom did not come according to a "fatal law" or spontaneous evolution. Man was "above all mind, historical creation and not nature" and all his knowledge of himself had been obtained as the result of "intelligent reflection" on the nature of social oppression, first by "a few men" and only later, after "an immense labor of criticism and cultural penetration," by the many, who initially resisted the new ideas. Gramsci pointed to the enlightenment for proof of his proposition that revolutions only took place after this "immense labor"—in Italy, Napoleon had found his way paved for him "by an invisible army of books, which had prepared men." The initial labor of education which Gramsci proposed was directed not to having men acquire masses of facts but to attaining that self-knowledge which would enable them to realize their "own historical value," their "own function in life," their "rights and duties."[10]

In 1917 he was still preaching these views forcefully through *Grido del Popolo* and in the single issue of *Citta Futura*, the journal of the Youth Federation of the Italian Socialist Party, but his attention was beginning to shift to the practical application of his educational programme as well.[11] This brought him to the crucial question of the *method* or *mode* of this educative process. His answer was the completely traditional, and idealist, method of indoctrination through the press, lectures, and seminars.

Practically, he engaged in "cultural messianism" among the young members of the party. He lectured frequently to the Youth Federation and the workers of Turin, urging them to read Croce or even reflect on Marcus Aurelius's character(!). He ran study circles on Marx, and in December 1917 formed the Club di Vita Morale, whose activities he described in these terms:

> At Turin we believe that preaching about the principles and moral maxims which should necessarily become established with the coming of a socialist civilization is not enough. We have tried to give this preaching an organized form; to give new examples (for Italy) of how to work together. So the Club de Vita Morale has recently emerged.

Through it we propose to accustom young people in the socialist movement to dispassionate discussion about social and ethical problems. We want them to become used to research, to read in a methodical and disciplined fashion, to expound their convictions simply and with equanimity. It works out like this: I, who have had to accept the role of *excubitor*, because I began the association, assign a paper to some young person: a chapter of Croce's "Cultura e Vita morale"; Salvemini's "Problemi educativi e sociali" or his *French Revolution* or "Cultura e laicità," the *Communist Manifesto* or the Commentary of Croce in *Critica* or something else, which, however, reflects the existing idealist movement: then I or someone else replies.[12]

This "cultural messianism"—the practical outcome of Gramsci's "Crocian" "starting point"—was completely against the current at the time. The Club lasted three meetings. The bulk of young socialists still preferred Mussolini's and Bordiga's view that "class consciousness" came through struggle and not from any cultural policy. In 1912 Bordiga had proclaimed scornfully: "The need for study should be proclaimed in a congress of school teachers, not socialists. You don't become a socialist through instruction but through experiencing the real needs of the class to which you belong," and Mussolini proclaimed even more bluntly that it would be good riddance if all the "brains" in the Socialist Party left.[13] Faced with continuous failure, Gramsci had started by 1918 tentatively to question "cultural messianism," in principle, if not in practice.[14] But in 1917 his views on the levels of theory, ideology, and practice were still comparatively homogeneous. He was already a man with formed opinions when he first faced the implicit and explicit teachings of the Russian revolutions. He believed that men made revolutions in acts of collective will; that the main problem was to make them see that they could change the world, and he had therefore engaged in an activity of "moral reeducation," which had, however, not gone much beyond a series of "didactic homilies" that workers found difficult to stomach and which they rejected.

II.

The news of the February revolution only gradually crept through the wartime censorship and not until April 1917 did Gramsci publish his first known commentary on its significance. He denied outright that it was a bourgeois revolution. "We are persuaded that the Russian revolution is proletarian in character, as it has been so far in its deeds, and that it will naturally result in a socialist regime."[15] We need not dwell on whether this was a correct assessment or not—perhaps Gramsci already perceived that the bourgeois February revolution would develop into the proletarian October revolution. However, it is clear that in one sense he quite misunderstood what was going on. Although he had heard of Lenin before 1917, he saw Chernov as the leading practical revolutionary of the Russian "maximalists." Lenin was the "master of life, the stirrer of consciences, the awakener of sleeping souls. Chernov is the realizer, the man with the concrete program to put into practice, an entirely socialist program that permits no collaboration, that cannot be accepted by the bourgeoisie because it destroys the system of private property, because it finally begins the socialist revolution, the entry into world history of collectivist socialism."[16]

This misunderstanding was not his fault entirely, nor that of the censorship. His major source of information at this time about the revolutions and Russia generally was *Avanti*, which had started to rely on the reports of an emigre Russian, Vassily Suchomlin, for its explanation of what was occurring in Russia. Suchomlin's loyalties were to the Social-Revolutionaries of that country and not only strongly biased in their favor, but also biased against Lenin.[17] Gramsci's fundamental misunderstanding indicates, however, how little he knew about the history or contemporary developments of Russian socialism. Not only was a "Crocian" facing the implications of the February revolution, but a "Crocian" who knew very little about the men who were making the revolution. As if to make up for these errors of fact, Gramsci showed an enthusiastic preference for Lenin from July onwards, dubbing him the "tomorrow of the revolution" and ascribing to him the task of preventing any compromise between the "Idea" and the incubus of the past.[18]

It is important to note at this juncture that before he had any real idea about what was going on in Russia, he had already begun an interpretation of Lenin, identifying him in "Crocian" terms as the bearer of the "Idea." He continued to find a Lenin who shared his views even in 1918 when the more reliable Balabanoff had replaced Suchomlin as *Avanti*'s Russian correspondent. This Lenin was the "practical expression" of "our Marx," whom Gramsci described in May 1918 as "not a Messiah who left a string of parables laden with categorical imperatives and absolutely incontrovertible norms outside the categories of time and space. The only categorical imperative, the single norm, is 'workers of the world unite.'"[19] The Bolsheviks, whom he had by now identified correctly as the practitioners of revolution,

> live Marxist thought, the part of it which cannot die, that part which is the continuation of German and Italian idealism, and which in Marx himself became contaminated by positivistic and naturalistic encrustations. And this thought considers not economic facts the main force in history, but man, the society of men, of men who are close to each other, who understand each other, and develop through these contacts [civilization] a social and collective will and understand, judge and order to their wishes these economic facts, so that their wishes become the motor of the economy.

He summed up the theoretical conclusions he was drawing from the Bolshevik revolution in the title he gave to the article in which these words appeared: "The Revolt against *Capital*."[20] This view was again made clear in these lines of July 1918: "If you find Lenin a utopian, if you say that the attempt to set up the dictatorship of the proletariat in Russia is a utopian effort, you cannot be a socialist, who is aware, and who builds up his culture by studying the doctrine of historical mate-rialism: you are a Catholic, bogged down in the *Syllabus:* you are the only utopian really. "Utopia consists precisely in not being able to see history as free development." In sum, the main lesson he drew from the Bolshevik revolution, even in 1918, was that it showed that history was free development, and this lesson endorsed the educative policies he had been following in the Italian proletariat. He denied that much could be learnt from the particular facts of the Bolshevik revolution, at least until some years had gone by and it could be the object of mature reflection.[21]

Yet at about the same time he decided that "what is happening in Russia shows us the way" and started to "seek for" the works of Lenin to discover how the Russian had educated the masses to a level where a socialist revolution could be conducted when "cultural messianism" alone obviously did not work. Why? Gramsci had apparently given up his belief that the revolution could be conducted only *after* a long, slow, cultural work of freeing minds and had decided that the revolution was actual given the conditions of Italy. By the beginning of 1918 he was supporting Bordiga's demand that the Socialist Party "act now" in terms which were earning him the undeserved reputation of "bergsonian voluntarist" among the more cautious maximalist leaders of the party.[22]

But, as Togliatti recalled, "matters were neither simple nor clear" in those early days,[23] and Gramsci reputedly only saw a collection of Lenin's works for the first time in the middle of 1919, when they were shown to him by the ex-syndicalist Alfredo Poliedro.[24] Moreover, there was practically nothing of Lenin translated into Italian in May 1920, when Gramsci bitterly criticized the Socialist Party for being so remiss and arranged for the publication of the first edition of Lenin's work in Italian. This was published in July 1920. So Gramsci had to turn to the newspapers in the only language which he read without difficulty: French. Leonetti recalls that "the source was always in French." And so it was that Gramsci obtained his view of the Revolution and its implicit theory and practice through the following newspapers and journals: *Communist International*, *La Vie Ouvrière* (1919–), *Le Phare* (1919–), *Demain* (1919–), *Nouvelle Internationale* (1919–), *Bulletin Communiste* (1920–), *Revue Communiste* (1920–), and *Clarté* (1920–).[25] Readers will note that because of the censorship none of these sources were available to him until 1919. The only writings of Lenin to appear in these newspapers in 1919 were his letter to "Our American Comrades," a short article declaring that the Second International was finished, and a portion of the *Proletarian Revolution and the Renegade Kautsky*, which appeared in *Nouvelle Internationale* on April 30, 1919.[26] However, a very definite picture of Lenin and Lenin's views was given in the reports of Arthur Ransome. Some indicative lines in "Conversations with Lenin" appeared in Gramsci's most important source, *La Vie Ouvrière*, on August 20, 1919.

> He [Lenin] told me that he had read a comparison of his own theories with those of the American Daniel de Leon in an English socialist newspaper. He had immediately borrowed some of de Leon's pamphlets from Reinstein (who belongs to the party which de Leon founded in the United States) and had been struck by how much and how early the thought of de Leon had started following the same course as that of the Russians.[27]

Small wonder that the paper should claim that "our Russian comrades have carried out in practice the main theoretical objects of syndicalism," and that their main achievement had been the rejection of parliament in favor of direct action through the workers' councils.[28]

If Gramsci knew no Lenin, he certainly knew something about the theories of de Leon, whom his French sources suggested presented much the same theory as Lenin,[29] since he and Togliatti had started to study IWW theory in 1916, and had, indeed, first learned of Lenin through the *Liberator*, the IWW paper of Deleonite tendency. By mid-1919 he showed quite clearly that he had decided that the Leninist theory of revolution was a theory of the primary role played by the soviets in raising revolutionary consciousness, or, in his terms, educating the masses. Given what he felt to be the great similarity between Russia and Italy—in both he isolated the war as the single most important catalyst for revolution because the bourgeoisie "had not been able to avoid giving a terrible practical lesson in revolutionary socialism" to the predominantly peasant population—he called on the Turinese workers to "create (their) own soviets within the limits allowed."[30] He and his friends set up the newspaper *Ordine Nuovo* a month later, after discussions with interested workers, mainly from the "rigid" minority of the Metalworkers' Federation (FIOM). At first this paper was no more than a renewed venture in "cultural messianism," because Angelo Tasca (another "Crocian") had found the money for it and he was unable to envisage it as anything but "a ragbag anthology—a collection of abstract cultural items and a strong leaning towards nasty stories and well-intentioned wood-cuts."[31] But in July 1919, Gramsci, Togliatti, and Umberto Terracini conducted the editorial coup d'état that led to the paper's conversion into a promoter of the transformation of the *commissioni interne*, or shop-stewards' committees, into "workers' councils," which would eventually become an alternative state power:

> This state does not pop up by magic: the Bolsheviks worked for eight months to spread and make their slogans concrete: all power to the Soviets, and the Soviets were already known to the Russian workers in 1905. Italian communists must treasure the Russian experience and save on time and labor: the work of reconstruction alone will demand so much time and work that every act, every day must be directed towards it.[32]

Gramsci made clear that the function of this self-organization was educatory in the sense in which he had understood education in 1916–17. It would "cause a radical transformation in working-class psychology, making the working-class better prepared to exercise power, and, through spontaneously generated common historical experience, spread an awareness of the rights and duties of comrades and workers."[33]

The first documents of the Communist International to be published in Italy, and especially the manifesto drafted by Trotsky, must have encouraged Gramsci's belief that the way to power was through councils that educated men through a constant class struggle at their place of work and allowed them both to understand and have the will to change the world. In the second half of 1919 and early 1920 he and his followers began an endless round of talks and agitation in the factories in favor of the establishment of workers' councils. They found the working-class contacts he had built up among the FIOM "rigids," like Giovanni Parodi, invaluable in obtaining *entrée* for them.[34] Together they and their audiences elaborated a complicated analysis of Italy's postwar problems and their solution, which formed the basis of the articles in *Ordine Nuovo*. We may sum up this analysis as: 1) the problem of capitalist society was that it alienated men from one another, and thus destroyed the possibility of their uniting to overthrow it; 2) therefore, "associating men together can and must be assumed to be the essential fact of the proletarian revolution" and 3) as the Russian, Hungarian, and German experience showed, the one effective way to do this was to form councils to unite men together and prepare them for a successful socialist revolution.[35] Gramsci wrote years later in a catalog of the lessons of the factory council movement that "our actions always had an almost immediate and wide success, and seemed like the interpretation of a diffuse, deeply-felt need, never as the cold application of an intellectual schema" because they "never took action without sounding out the opinion of the worker in various ways."[36]

In September 1919 the workers of Fiat Brevetti met to set up the first of the factory councils, starting a movement that had spread through the Turin factories by the end of 1919. It was not, at first, a movement dominated by the socialists of *Ordine Nuovo*, although they worked hard to develop its revolutionary qualities and thus win it to their point of view through their School of Cultural and Social Propaganda.[37] It is worthwhile emphasizing the enormous effort Gramsci put into these endeavors. Tasca wrote: "We must note the intense activity of Gramsci. . . . *Avanti*, the Central Executive of the Party, *Ordine Nuovo*, *Sotto la Mole*, lectures for the factory councils . . . prodigious activity, a sickly body and a steely will . . . he is a leader."[38] These words remind us that revolutions do not make themselves, and that at the beginning of 1920 Gramsci was actively committed in a practical and organizational sense to a particular course of action. He could not therefore avoid the implications of this activity for his understanding of Leninism when he began to become more acquainted with Leninism in 1920.

By May 1920 his French sources had made available to him Lenin's work on the *Problems of Soviet Power; The Heroes of the Berne International, The Third International and its Place in History*, and some work on the economic and social problems of the transition to socialism. In June further articles by Lenin on the proposal to reconstruct the Berne International appeared, and in July *Bulletin Communiste* published Lenin's letter to Sylvia Pankhurst condemning her refusal to participate in parliamentary activity. In December the same journal carried the first two chapters of *Left-Wing Communism, an Infantile Disorder*.[39] Nearly all of these writings stressed the bankruptcy of the Second International and its mechanical Marxism and the importance of the soviets, but, with the exception of *Left-Wing Communism, an Infantile Disorder*, none are really important works of Lenin.

However, there was one account of Lenin and his theory that stood out among the rather lyrical accounts of Ransome, Goode, Sadoul, and others, for whom Lenin's major discovery was still the soviets. This was Zinoviev's speech of September 6, 1918, made after the attempt on Lenin's life, which appeared in *Vie Ouvrière* on April 16, 1920. We do not know if Gramsci read it, but it was interesting because it contained the only account of *What is to be Done?* in these sources. The article stated that the first article in the *Spark* contained the "quintessence of Bolshevism" and then gave a simple account of the contents of *What is to be Done?* making clear its stress not only on "conscious" activity being necessary on a political level if a revolution was to be made, but that it was all-important to organize a revolutionary party. Yet Zinoviev also negated this emphasis by suggesting that concern with the party was only an early development in Lenin's thought (he also skated over *Materialism and Empirio-Criticism*), which proceeded to the crucial theoretical contribution of Lenin, the theory of the role of the soviets that he had supposedly developed since 1905, and his corresponding teaching on the state: "In Lenin the government of the soviets found not only its greatest political leader, a practitioner, an organizer, a fiery propagandist, a poet, but also its greatest theoretician, a

Karl Marx." So even when the fundamental text for Lenin's teaching on the party was discussed, its importance was lost in the stress that Lenin's greatest contribution to Marxism was his theory of the State.

It is clear that at this juncture Gramsci, too, still regarded the main teaching of Lenin to be that in the *State and Revolution*,[40] since he recommended it warmly as "useful to everybody."[41] Interestingly, his knowledge of this book antedated that of his French sources, which only translated it over a year later, when they were very enthusiastic about it.[42]

How important the role of the party was in Leninist revolutionary theory only became more clear when the reports of the Second Congress of the Communist International began to be published in August and September 1920, in France and Italy. It is important to recall that the emphasis on party politics at this congress, the first at which Western revolutionary socialists were present in any numbers, was accompanied by a call for moderation in their antiparliamentarism. *Left-Wing Communism* became available in French at about the same time as the Second Comintern Congress. There was a noticeable change in the attitudes of Gramsci's French sources towards Lenin. They gave *Left-Wing Communism* a mixed reception and tended to start lending more support to Trotsky than to Lenin, whose opinions had already been dubbed "rightist," or moderate, in tendency much earlier.[43]

It is not clear whether Gramsci shared their resistance to a party Leninism rather than a "sovietist" or "syndicalist" Leninism, but he certainly continued to regard Lenin as a "conciliar" theorist throughout 1920, equating the views of Lenin, Luxemburg, and Pannekoek and writing in October 1920: "The syndicalist tendencies of *Ordine Nuovo* are also a myth: we simply make the mistake of believing that only the masses can make the revolution, that a party secretary or president cannot make it through decrees: it seems that this was the opinion of Karl Marx and Rosa Luxemburg, and the opinion of Lenin."[44] He also published a whole series of eyewitness accounts of the revolution that stressed the same view of Lenin. Moreover, in the only reference to *What is to be Done?* that appeared in *Ordine Nuovo* (in an account by Charles Rapaport), Gramsci's accompanying caption dismissed it as an "old thesis."[45]

If Lenin's theory of the party had not begun to affect Gramsci by the end of 1920, he had certainly begun to use the concept of imperialism more frequently. However, the fact that he did not realize that Lenin did not agree entirely with Hilferding, or Adler and Kautsky, suggests that he had not grasped the nuances of Lenin's theory, and was, as earlier writings indicate, developing the theory autonomously.[46] Moreover, he absolutely refused to regard such worldwide developments of capitalism as shifting the main locus of the class struggle outside the factory.

At the end of 1920, accounts of Lenin's theory of the party had obviously not become sufficiently clear or predominant to make Gramsci reconsider his belief that the Russian's main contribution was a "conciliar" theory. It was still possible to have this view of Leninism and the role accorded to a party in such a theory even late in 1920 because of ambivalences in the formulations of Lenin himself. For example, in his letter published in Italy in September 1920 condemning the Italian Socialist Party and supporting a Turinese demand that the party "renew" itself, Lenin suggested that the revolution started from below and that the task of the party was to "generalize, and give watchwords."[47] But Gramsci's own activity during that year pushed him ever more strongly in the direction of favoring a renewal of the PSI and then, *faute de mieux*, a split from the PSI and the formation of a Communist Party. He was forced to consider the problem of a revolutionary party because his factory councils threatened the hegemony of the traditional union and PSI leaders in Turin. When they attacked him, and not before, he was compelled to embark on a critique, first of the unions, and then of the party. Both, he argued, were organized not to take power, but to come to agreements within the bourgeois state, and their policies and structures were therefore determined by capitalism. In the course of their dispute each side sought their allies where they could and Gramsci turned particularly to the antiparty workers, both anarchist and "abstentionist," whose leaders now controlled the FIOM. The rupture with the PSI took place after its leaders refused to lend national assistance to the Turinese workers, who were locked out in April 1920 by their employers, who had a much greater understanding of the revolutionary implications of the councils than the PSPs leaders.[48] In May, Gramsci's bitter denunciation of the PSI was read at its Milan conference. He called upon the PSI to prepare for revolution through organization and education, since the contemporary period would mark either the success of a proletarian revolution or usher in "the most terrible of reactions." He claimed that the PSI leaders had failed to help the strikers because they did not live "immersed in the reality of the class struggle," because the party was too bureaucratic. "The existence of a strongly disciplined and cohesive Communist Party, which, through its nuclei in the factory, unions and cooperatives, co-ordinates and takes central control in its executive committee of all revolutionary actions of the proletariat, is the fundamental and indis-pensable condition for attempting any Soviet experiment."[49]

The PSI rejected this critique, denying the possibility of any im-mediate revolution, although they had committed themselves to its actuality when they joined the Comintern in December 1919. Lenin learned of the exchange through intermediaries who favored the Tu-rinese and at the Second Congress of the Comintern in July–August 1920 made clear that

> the II Congress of the Third International regards the criticism of
> the party, and the practical proposals put before the national congress
> of the Italian Socialist Party by the Turinese section of the party in
> Ordine Nuovo of 8 May 1920 as substantially correct. They correspond
> fully to the fundamental principles of the Third International.[50]

The PSI delegation was flabbergasted, and it was made quite clear to Lenin that the Turinese were considered "syndicalist," and at least im-plicitly antiparty.[51] Lenin then withdrew his blanket approval of Gram-sci's policies and limited his endorsement to the text of the document, not the intentions of its authors.[52]

What this amounts to is an endorsement by Lenin of Gramsci's views on the PSI before he knew what they really meant and before Gramsci had read any of Lenin's views on the party. From the time of this refusal by Lenin to endorse any "syndicalist" interpretation of the role of the party, we can observe a growing tension between Gramsci's and Lenin's views. For although Gramsci denied that he was a syndi-calist, he did continue to equate the Russian revolution with councils, and these with what was common in the writings of Marx, Lenin, and de Leon.[53] Not without some justification.[54] On the other hand, the Russian was making clear that the party would have primacy over the soviet both in theory and practice. By March 1921 Clarté had published Right-wing Socialism and Counter-Revolution, which made clear the lead-ing role of the party in Lenin's thought: "When people talk about the unity of the proletariat it is difficult to listen to them without smiling . . . we know through experience that the unity of the proletariat can only be ensured by a revolutionary Marxist party, and only by a struggle without mercy by this party against the others."[55] Throughout early 1921, in the preparations for the Third Comintern Congress, it was made clear that when the Leninist theory of imperialism was put together with the democratic centralism of the twenty-one conditions of admission to the Communist International, the result was a hierarchy of command in which the whole of the "world communist party" was obliged to obey the Comintern's Executive Committee in Moscow, no matter what the line laid down.

Although also pushed to consider the role of the party by the continuous failure of the PSI to lead, Gramsci was drawing very different conclusions in the second half of 1920. In July he wrote in a consideration of how the party should renew itself that it should be: "a party of the masses who wish to free themselves through their own efforts, by themselves, from political and industrial slavery, through the organization of the social economy, and not a party which uses the masses to attempt heroic imitations of the French Jacobins."[56] He set to work not to replace the existing leaders of the PSI or to split away from it, as his coeditors wished, and as the "abstentionists" in the factory councils also wished, but to organize education groups that "can offer the proletariat for its emancipation neither communal councils nor union leaders, but work in the field of mass action; for communist groups in the factory and union, for the Workers' Council, for proletarian unity in the face of menace to its cohesion."[57] This activity he typified as one that escaped from the "magic circle" of concern with political leadership and, implicitly, saw the problem of the failure of the revolution to eventuate in the nature of the existing relationship between the party and the real organic life of the masses. But the correct relationship, he proposed, was one that did away with the leading role of the party, which was to become no more than the "agent" of a process of revolution taking place on the factory floor.

> The Party and the union ought not to consider themselves the tutors or readymade superstructures of the [council]. . . . They must consider themselves the conscious agents of its liberation from the forces of oppression centred in the bourgeois state. They must organize the general (political) external conditions in which the process of revolution will develop its greatest speed and in which the liberated productive forces will find their greatest expansion.[58]

Gramsci's analysis of the role of the party did not stop at such "anti-Jacobin" formulations. New events caused him to elaborate further after July 1920. The great industrialists were determined by the second half of 1920 to smash the revolutionary pretensions of the workers once and for all. They adopted a completely uncompromising position in negotiations for better conditions. So the metalworkers' trade union federation called on the workers to occupy their factories as a defensive move aimed at making the government intervene in favor of the workers. Gramsci considered the move ill-timed and likely to foster illusions. In September 1920 the workers started to occupy their factories throughout Italy, though especially in the North. Gramsci then warned that merely occupying a factory did not bring about a revolution. He penned an important article that revealed clearly that in denying a leading role to a party he was not denying that it played an important part in making a revolution. A revolution was only made (and here the influence of *State and Revolution* on him seems obvious) when the state power of the bourgeoisie was smashed, and to do this the proletariat needed an armed force to take power and coerce the reaction. He obviously did not feel that the PSI was able to take these initiatives, but he also obviously believed that nationwide initiatives, and therefore a national party, was needed as it would have to lead the assault on the state.[59]

In this state of mind, knowing that a party was necessary for a revolution, and that councils alone could not make the revolution, he sat in factories with the workers and watched the PSI ("Barnum's circus") shilly-shally and fritter away its chances. The occupations, which had started as a defensive move, were obviously becoming more and more offensive in their nature. The trade union leaders who had sown the wind began nervously to watch the approaching whirlwind. Unity of purpose was rapidly lost among the leaders of the unions and the Socialist Party. While encouraging the belief that there could be a revolution through aggressive and demagogic sloganeering and manifestoes, they simultaneously engaged in negotiations with the industrialists and the government to prevent such an outcome. Gramsci commented wryly that the Socialist Party was "no different from the English Labour Party and revolutionary . . . only in its programme."

It was really a conglomerate of parties and had become, as a result, an organization to be exploited by adventurists and careerists, and inca-

pable of showing any initiative and responsibility.[60] Small wonder that
mutual distrust was obvious when Togliatti visited Milan to discuss
policy with the trade union leaders, just as the crisis reached its peak.
The trade union leaders asked whether the Turin workers would initiate the assault on the State by coming out into the streets. Togliatti saw
in this proposal a plot to destroy the factory council movement once
and for all and refused flatly: "to do it a simultaneous action throughout
the country is necessary, and above all a nationwide action."[61]

The responsibility was too much for the leaders of both the unions
and the Socialist Party. Some offered to resign to avoid having to make
the decision, others declared that since it was a "political matter" it did
not really involve them, as they were union leaders. Finally, the problem was resolved, to the relief of the majority, by putting the issue of
whether to extend the movement to a vote, that ultimate fetish of the
irresolute. By a majority, the "revolution was lost."

It was only after the revolution was lost that Gramsci started organizing to establish a new Communist party, though he recognized that it
was really too late to be useful, since he himself had stated in May that
either the revolution would triumph or there would begin the most
"terrible of reactions." It was only in a situation that he characterized
as the "chaos and collapse" of Italian socialism, when he felt himself
"overwhelmed by events," that he agreed to split the PSI.[62] In the desperate scramble to retrieve something from the wreckage, Gramsci
helped to create the sort of party he did not want, and the sort of party
that neither Lenin, Trotsky, nor the Comintern wanted.

III.

In 1958, at the first conference of Gramscian studies, Palmiro Togliatti, the secretary of the Italian Communist Party, stated the official
orthodoxy about the relationship between Gramsci and Lenin. He affirmed that between 1919–22, Gramsci read: *What is to be Done?*, *One
Step Forward, Two Steps Back*, *Two Tactics of Social-Democracy*, *Imperialism,
the Highest Stage of Capitalism*, *The State and Revolution*, *The Proletarian
Revolution and the Renegade Kautsky*, *The Development of Capitalism in
Russia*, and *Materialism and Empirio-Criticism*; that he accepted the theory in them and rejected his "Crocianism"; and, in particular, that he
accepted the Leninist theory of the party.[63] We have shown that up to
mid-1921 Gramsci could only have read some of the works on Togliat-

ti's list; could, necessarily, only have accepted some of the theory in the *ensemble* of those works, and did not subscribe to the Leninist theory of a leading role party before the formation of the PCI in 1921. This is not to argue that Gramsci did not wish to become a Leninist in 1917–21, or that he did not devour avidly what Lenin was available to him and spread Lenin's theory among his comrades, but merely that when we follow Gicerchia's suggestion and discover how Lenin's thought permeated through Eastern Europe to the West and how it was taken up, we are left, in Terracini's words, with the fact that "Lenin . . . was known more as a revolutionary than as a Marxist theoretician."[64] Again, this is not to argue that he did not read those works of Lenin listed by Togliatti, after 1921, and espouse them, in part, or in their entirety.

It seems from a historical reconstruction that the Leninism which Gramsci knew before 1921, and *accepted*, was a "sovietist" Leninism (or, as critics would have it, a "syndicalist" deviation), which stressed that a revolution is made from below by masses of men learning in the practice of organizing themselves for united action. His Lenin was a man who never lost sight of "the mainspring of all political and economic activity: the class struggle."[65] This class struggle—because it never lost sight of the "sole categorical imperative in Marx, 'Workers of the World Unite'"—took place in a special form—through workers' councils organized at the place of work.

Is this "sovietist" Leninism—the "translation" of Leninism into the West in 1919–21—*really* Leninism? Many commentators say no. Spriano is blunt: "We cannot identify Leninism with a conception of *revolution from below*, with a *molecular process* of the formation of the workers' State, which Gramsci places at the base of his theory of power."[66] Caracciolo, Soave, and Berti more or less agree. They thus come into agreement with the extreme left students of Gramsci who maintain that Gramsci was not a Leninist because he neglected or underestimated the role of the party.[67] Both groups of commentators, despite other abiding disagreements, share the view that Gramsci was not really a Leninist because they agree that the unifying problematic in Lenin's theory is the leading role a party must play in making a revolution. The nub of such a view of the relationship between the theory of Gramsci and that of Lenin must rest *not* on the claim that he ignored the role a party can play—we have shown that after April 1920 Gramsci clearly realized that a party is essential, not so much for raising consciousness as *What is to be Done?* argues, but for the coordination of national initiatives which begin at council level, and for the assault on the bourgeois state machine. In a whole series of articles, Gramsci and his followers called for renewal of the PSI; that it be changed by "the communist groups in the factory" from an assembly expressing the "psychology of the crowd" into an "association" based on the factory and composed of "delegates [from the factory] with imperative mandates." Rather, such a view must rest on the claim that the problematic in Gramsci's theory denies *a leading role* to the party—that Gramsci takes an "anti-Jacobin" view of the revolution. It is difficult to disagree with the claim that Gramsci was an "anti-Jacobin" up to 1921. He not only wrote in 1918 that "Jacobinism was the substitution of one authoritarian regime for another," but he claimed that the Russian revolution could not be Jacobin because it was proletarian.[68] In other words, a proletarian revolution and Jacobin positions were mutually exclusive. Gramsci understood Jacobinism in a variety of senses, but the key sense was that in 1918 Jacobinism could be equated with "cultural messianism." "Cultural messianism" had the following qualities and logic, making it the opposite of revolutionary. It believed that "the majority of men were fundamentally honest and upright, but prey to and the victims of ignorance of their own real interests and the goals that they could more usefully aim for" and therefore, "cultural messianism" proposed a work of "discussion and propaganda" in that it had "infinite faith," particularly through a newspaper that would unite and clarify the diverse aims of men; but when its reason failed to unite men, it "saw the maleficent influence of perverse wills," which are finally identified with "the leaders," who it condemns to universal execration.[69]

Two points need to be made here. First, that it is easy to show that Lenin frequently asserted the identity of Jacobinism and the proletarian revolutionary. In *One Step Forward, Two Steps Back* he wrote: "A Jacobin who wholly identifies himself with the *organization* of the proletariat—a proletariat *conscious* of its class interests—is a *revolutionary Social-Democrat.*"[70] At the same time as Gramsci condemned Jacobinism and described him as an anti-Jacobin, Lenin wrote:

> Bourgeois historians see Jacobinism as a decline. Proletarian historians see Jacobinism as one of the highest points reached by an oppressed class in the struggle for its emancipation. . . . It is a characteristic of the bourgeois class to execrate Jacobinism. It is a characteristic of the

> petty-bourgeoisie to fear it. Conscious workers and proletarians be-
> lieve that power should pass to the revolutionary class, the oppressed,
> and that is where the essence of Jacobinism lies.[71]

Second, it is easy to show that in 1902–4 Lenin meant by Jacobinism
the "cultural messianism" Gramsci condemned. The dissimilarities between the contents of *What is to be Done?* and Gramsci's "cultural messianism" are too striking to be ignored. When we add *One Step Forward,*
we see that Lenin justified the purging of the party of "opportunists"
by reference to the experience of Jacobinism. In sum, it is clear that in
1904 Lenin called himself a "present-day" Jacobin because he thought
that the role of party leadership was all-important in making a revolution, and Gramsci was an "anti-Jacobin" because he did not.

A *prima facie* case exists for the claim that Gramsci was not a Leninist
because of this fundamental difference of emphasis. It is a useful base
on which to distinguish their theory, as it directs attention to what is
novel in Gramsci's views. Unlike Lenin, Gramsci never organized to
split the party even when it needed to be renewed, because he did not
consider the fundamental problem of the "conscious" revolution to be
one of leadership, but one of the relationship between the leaders and
the masses. For him, the real weakness of the PSI as a revolutionary
force was that its leaders did not live "immersed" in proletarian life, in
the class struggle, and therefore "could not express the communist solution to contemporary problems: proletarian control of production and
distribution, disarmament of mercenary armed forces, and control of
the municipalities by the workers' organizations";[72] *and* that the workers
were not united and disciplined enough to overcome their inability to
see their problems on a national level, to overcome their tendency to
"see everything rosily and to like songs and fanfares more than sacrifices"[73] and to seize power on a national level after organizing their own
armed forces. Both sides need to step out of the "magic circle" where
each blamed the other for their failures and saw the problem as either
that of political leadership *or* mass consciousness, and instead to engage
in the process of "mass work" in the factory and the union "for Workers' Council, for proletarian unity in the face of menace to its cohesion."

This displacement of the problem of revolution in the West from
the party (theory) and the masses (practice) to the relations and links
between them is what constitutes Gramsci's novelty and explains how
and why he was already by 1922 advising a revolutionary strategy of

replacing "a bourgeois personnel . . . by a communist personnel in all vital and dynamic functions organized in the State." Such suggestions preluded the concerns developed later in his *Prison Notebooks*, in particular the concern with the intellectuals as the real expression of the link between practice and theory.

Yet, while it is obviously useful to draw the distinction between Gramsci and Lenin—"anti-Jacobin" versus "Jacobin"—as it indicates the precise locus of Gramscian theory, it is useful to make a reservation about the blunt assertion that Gramsci was not a "Leninist" before 1921. This essay has been devoted to enquiring about the degree to which the ideas of Gramsci were dependent upon those of Lenin. Most other work on the relationship between the Russian and the Italian has been devoted, in one sense, to such inquiry. We have reached common conclusions that Gramsci's ideas were not dependent on those of Lenin and that in fundamental respects their views were different up to 1921. There is, however, another way of examining the relationship, which has not been attempted here, because our object has been to demystify the relationship by breaking away from the presupposition that all revolutionaries must be "Leninists" (in the sense that their thought paraphrases that of the Russian) through using a *historical* method. The alternative way of examining their relationship should placate proponents of the view that Gramsci was a "Leninist." It examines both theories from the point of view of the history of Marxist theory as a whole, and takes as its starting point the Marxist position that the meaning of Marxist writings is determined by the *present* stage in the understanding of revolutionary Marxist theory: it looks at them from the endpoint in a historical development of which they form a part. In this enquiry the meaning of both theories is theoretically, but perhaps not practically, *outside them*, and what is significant in their work is established not by *what they thought was significant*, nor by *what they directed most of their attention to*, but *by what our present revolutionary/practical understanding renders significant* in their work. This reading is an *implicit* reading in which our perspective renders *visible* what was *latent*.

To explicate to our own satisfaction, what is involved in such *revolutionary* reading would involve writing a history of Marxism *qua* theory of practice, which we cannot hope to do here. But some interesting implications for Lenin's rather than Gramsci's theory emerge from such a reading, which *practically* means reading the former in the light of the latter. We make this last assertion because we agree with Maria-Antonietta Macciocchi in *Pour Gramsci* that Gramsci and Mao hold similar views and constitute the height of contemporary revolutionary theory, though each in their own environment, and with their own real objects.[73] As an aside, we note that contemporary theory of a "structuralist" sort does not help us make a *social* revolution, whatever its contribution to philosophy. We also concede that it is theoretically inevitable that Gramsci himself will eventually have to be subjected to the same reduction in terms of future revolutionary theory, and thus our perspective on Lenin will change.

Reading Lenin from the point of view of contemporary revolutionary Marxist thought, that is, from the point of view of Gramsci, shows that the significant development in his thought is a movement away from the positivist, fatalist views of the Second International towards a philosophy of praxis: towards the point where, if we may be permitted the image, he hands the baton on to Gramsci. In this sense his theory is a "revolt against *Capital.*" This handing on of the baton is not understood simply as a filiation of ideas—we have already shown the limitations of such a *Hegelian* view in practice—rather it is to be understood as the meeting of two separate revolutionary practices, in which the practice determines the validity of the theory. Moreover, the overall reading does not deny the established facts of Lenin's life: it reorders them to render them comprehensible.

Briefly, Lenin's starting point should be seen as that of a man trying to make a revolution—where there was no real alternative—with the tools of understanding and action provided by the Second International. His theoretical paraphernalia, readers will recall, started with *Capital* and Plekhanov's *Our Differences*, which, when read in isolation, suggested that Marx's writings had already established how this world worked. Lenin, like most Marxists of the Second International, not only read Marx backwards, but also did not read crucial sections of Marx until later, if he read them at all (*The Parisian Manuscripts*, the *Grundrisse*). Together these theoretical tools provided by the Second International contained an implicit logic, which was explicated by theoreticians like Bernstein and, later, Kautsky. This logic was that Marxism was a fatalism that described the automatic development of capitalism into its own contradictory death, and led *politically* towards an *evolutionary* practice in its conclusions.

Lenin could not accept these political *conclusions* and rejected them in *Where to Begin?* and *What is to be Done?* in 1901–2. It is important to stress that it was the *conclusions* rather than their premises that he rejected, as in retaining the premises he retained a contradiction that would vitiate the practical action he took to make a revolution. As most readers of *Socialist Register* know, he proposed to create a revolutionary consciousness among the Russian workers through "combining all the activities of the local groups" of revolutionaries who had preceded him, and had been unsuccessful in their propaganda efforts because of their lack of *organization*. Since Lenin is often misunderstood as primarily an organizer, it is important to stress that the object of this organization of fragmented groups into a *party* was to facilitate the raising of a revolutionary consciousness among the Russian workers. This political intervention to make a revolution marks a step forward from the do-nothing politics of the Second International, but it failed in its object, which was to raise a revolutionary consciousness. There is not the space in this article to go into the history of this failure. What concerns us is why there was such a failure.

The crucial problem was not merely a matter of organization for revolution in the abstract, but how and where to organize. Lenin proposed to organize, and organized, on the *political* level first, to raise what seemed a perennial social revolt to the level of a *political* revolution. More lies behind this choice than the apparent realities of Russia—which were undoubtedly compellingly present. To explain the choice we must realize that Lenin was still working on the basis of the premises of the Second International's Marxism on at least two levels: first, he still believed that conditions created *class consciousness*, as distinct from a *revolutionary consciousness*, and confined his critique of "spontaneity" to the socialist notion that *class consciousness* automatically developed into *revolutionary consciousness*; second, and this partly explained his first limitation, he still thought that Marx's works contained a final description of how the world worked, and therefore, that the problem of raising a *class consciousness* to a *revolutionary consciousness* was primarily a matter of transmission of Marx by those who knew the contents of those works to those who did not. His concept was naturally one of a revolution from *above*, where "twelve wise men" were worth a "hundred fools" and where the immediate and crucial problem was one of *leadership*. Hence the overall theme in Lenin's work up to 1905 was that theory preceded practice.

However, his political practice, and especially his observation of the 1905 revolution in Russia, called into question the belief that theory preceded practice, and hence led back to rejection of the notion that the crucial problem was that of *leadership*. The lesson he drew from 1905 was clear: "The proletariat sensed sooner than its leaders the change in the objective conditions of the struggle and the need for a transition from a strike to an uprising. As is always the case, practice marched ahead of theory."[74] This was a discovery of immense theoretical as well as practical importance, but Lenin only realized it practically at first. He refused to draw the conclusions implicit in it for Marxist theory and therefore reaffirmed categorically a residual fatalism: "the idea of seeking the salvation of the working class in anything but the further development of capitalism is reactionary."[75] After 1905 Lenin still believed that objective conditions created *class consciousness*, that is, that the process of the *class-in-itself* into the *class-for-itself* is automatic. So, while he affirmed the limited historical relevance of the notions in *What is to be Done?* after 1905, and tended to devote more attention to the problem of galvanizing struggle by direct organizational activity in the working class than to the party, he simultaneously made clear his theoretical limitations to the positions of the Second International in *Materialism and Empirio-Criticism*. What is important for his further development, which, of course, had its ups and downs, is that overall his views were informed by the following sort of notion: "The real education of the masses can never be separated from their independent political and especially revolutionary struggle. Only struggle educates the exploited class."[76] There is an enormous wealth of nuance in such a notion, which started battering down the still-present vestiges of the elitist view that education (the creation of a *revolutionary consciousness*) comes from *above*, and the corresponding view that *class consciousness* arises automatically. The whole problematic of automatic Marxism is called into question.

Since the "educative struggle" took place in specific form, that of soviets, Lenin became more and more a theoretician of the role of the soviets, though first he only theorized their role practically. While the Russian revolutionary movement remained revolutionary (up to *circa* 1921), this change in Lenin's concerns from the party to the soviet was clearly recognized by the leaders of that movement (e.g., in Zinoviev's speech of 1918 cited above), but it was later clouded by a return to concern with the leading role of the party after 1921, and particularly under Stalin. Moreover, the more rapid realization by Trotsky of what role the soviets played obscured the fact that, in a slower fashion, Lenin, too, was revising his views of how a revolution was made.

Implicitly, after 1905, the problem of organization is seen in two ways by Lenin: organization must take place on 1) a political or party level, and 2) on a prepolitical, or social and class level. The stress in *What is to be Done?* shifts as well. Instead of party organization being primarily important, and organization at the level of production being secondary, the emphasis changes. The real organization for revolution takes place at the level of the class *qua* producers and the role of the party shifts implicitly from that of *the* educator ("who knows") to that of agent of the working class, especially in its assault on the state. Indeed, when the issue of insurrection became paramount in 1917 it became clear that its role was primarily that of overthrowing the bourgeois state power. The important theoretical works of that year include not only the *State and Revolution*, but apparently more practical works like *Marxism and Insurrection*. When insurrection became the order of the day, it also became clear that the development of *class consciousness* through the soviets did not mean a corresponding readiness to overthrow the state in any concrete fashion: "the majority of the soldiers sympathized with the Bolsheviks, voted for them, elected them, but also expected them to decide things." This real reaffirmation of the essentiality of the party did not, however, prevent Lenin stating that the main lesson of 1917 was the following: "The history of the Russian revolution has shown precisely that no argument can convince the great masses of the working class, the peasants, the small employees, if they are not convinced by their own experience."[77] Did the implicit affirmation that men must change the world in order to know it—this "philosophy of practice"—mean an implicit or explicit realization by Lenin that theoretical Marxism was yet to be written? Had he himself realized the theoretical implications of such statements? The answer probably depends on what status we are to accord to the criticism he made of all previous Marxist theory, including his own, when he read Hegel's work. An affirmative answer, which we do not feel capable of supporting or denying, would have important implications for the relations between Lenin and Gramsci since it would situate a rupture in the understanding of Marxism in Lenin's life as well as in Gramsci's.

We prefer to rest with the proposition that from the point of view of the history of Marxism, Leninism at its endpoint and Gramscianism at its beginning are closely linked, and that Gramsci certainly developed many of the implications of a "philosophy of practice" from 1919 onwards. By this we mean that, just as we have described Leninism as a proving in practice of the limitations of the Second International's Marxism, so we can understand Gramscianism as the proving in practice and the exposition in theory of the relevance of the endpoint of Leninism. This very method, which allows us to see a strong convergence in 1917–21, as Lenin moves from a theory of the party to a theory of councils and Gramsci follows the reverse process, both for practical reasons rather than through the influence of the ideas of the first upon the second, also compels us to see Gramsci's thought as a development *away* from that point of convergence—once again the image of men in a relay race comes to mind. This movement *away* and *beyond* Leninism is what allows Gramsci to give a much clearer theoretical formulation of his own practice than Lenin did, especially with regard to the creation of *class consciousness* through the reorganization of social life. Later it allowed him to write the invaluable *Prison Notes*, which clothe with concrete meaning, and political advice for Western revolutionaries, Marx's words:

> The materialist doctrine that men are the products of circumstances and upbringing, and that, therefore, changed men are the products of other circumstances and changed upbringing, forgets that it is men who change circumstances and that it is essential to educate the educator himself. Hence, this doctrine necessarily arrives at dividing society into two parts, one of which is superior to society (in Robert Owen, for example).
>
> The coincidence of the changing of circumstances and of human activity can be conceived and rationally understood only as revolutionizing practice.

CLASS AND PARTY

Rossana Rossanda

It has often been said that one would seek in vain a theory of class or of the party in Marx. This is true; except for the fact that the problem of class is present throughout his work in such abundance and depth as to make possible the reconstruction of the theory that his analysis implies. The case is entirely different in regard to the party. This of course is not because the problem of the "organization" of the working class was ignored by Marx. He confronted that problem as soon as he lost his illusions—immediately after *The Holy Family* and *The German Ideology*—about the efficacy of exclusively intellectual action, divorced from concrete political action inside the working class;[1] and he reflected upon it between 1845 and 1848, while he was involved in the work of the secret societies and in the German workers' associations, and through his acquaintance with the Utopian communist Weitling. None of these contacts—with the possible exception of the bonds of esteem and occasional action that linked him to Blanqui—led Marx to accept a definite "commitment": he already had a theoretical position that cut him off radically from the secret societies, with their nebulous programs, and which also placed him in immediate opposition to Weitling. The question, for him, was a practical one: it was necessary to establish links with the workers, and the fact that the secret societies and their conspiracies tended in those years to assume a proletarian character was much more important for Marx than ideological quarrels with the societies. When the League of the Just was dissolved in 1847 and became the League of Communists, Marx was commissioned to write its Manifesto: all the ancient themes, which were dear to Weitling, were eliminated. What mattered to Marx—and this explains the nature of the Manifesto, which goes far beyond the task assigned to him—was to make the German proletariat immediately conscious not only of the possibility but of the necessity of fulfilling its historical role; and this obviously requires the passage from minority consciousness and clandestine activity to the widest possible organization, public and open to all. The accent was placed on *general* and *organized* action: it is not by chance that the old motto of the League of Communists, *All Men are Brothers*, became *Proletarians of all Countries, Unite!*

However, what separates Marx from Lenin (who, far from filling in Marx's outlines, oriented himself in a different direction) is that the organization is never considered by Marx as anything but an essentially practical matter, a flexible and changing instrument, an expression of the real subject of the revolution, namely the proletariat. The organization expresses the revolution, but does not precede it; even less does it anticipate its objectives and its actions. It was not only the restrictive and secret character of conspiratorial associations that had led Marx away from them, but also their conviction that they were able themselves to direct the revolutionary process *on behalf* of the proletariat. "One can understand," he wrote scathingly,

> why these conspirators are not content to organize the revolutionary proletariat. Their occupation consists in anticipating the development of the revolutionary process, to push it deliberately towards a crisis, to make the revolution on the spot, without the conditions of revolution being present. The only condition for them is that the insurrection should be sufficiently organized. They are the alchemists of the revolution, and they share confused ideas with the alchemists of old. Obsessed by their own anticipations, they have no other aim but the next overthrow of the existing government and they have profound contempt for activity of a more theoretical kind, which consists in explaining to the workers what their class interests are. To the degree that *the Paris proletariat advanced directly to the centre of the stage as a party*, so did these conspirators see their influence wane.

And Marx concluded: "The bombs of 1847 . . . finally dispersed the most obstinate and the most absurd of these old conspirators and precipitated their groups in the *direct proletarian movement*."[2] The italics are ours: between the proletariat and the party of the proletariat, the relationship is direct, the terms are almost interchangeable. For between the class as such and its political being, there is only a practical difference, in the sense that the second is the contingent form of the first. Moreover, Marx is convinced that the proletariat does not require a specific and autonomous mode of organization and expression, for it creates and destroys as it goes along its political forms, which are simple practical expressions, more or less adequate, of a consciousness that is synonymous with the objective position of the proletariat in the relations of production and in the struggle. Thus it is that Engels was able to write at the end of *On the History of the Communist League*:

> Today the German proletariat no longer needs any official organization, either public or secret. The simple self-evident interconnection of like-minded class comrades suffices, without any rules, boards, resolutions or other tangible forms, to shake the whole German Empire to its foundations. . . . The international movement of the European and American proletariat has become so much strengthened that not merely its first narrow form—the secret League—but even its second, infinitely wider form—the open International Working Men's Association—has become a fetter for it, and that the simple feeling of solidarity based on the understanding of the identity of class position suffices to create and hold together one and the same great party of the proletariat among the workers of all countries and tongues.

This was written in 1885. But the concepts that underlie the idea of the proletariat's self-expression, and which are much broader than appears in Engels's text above, are particularly notable in those writings of Marx where he describes the development of the class struggle. The famous passage in *The Eighteenth Brumaire of Louis Bonaparte* may be recalled here:

> But the revolution is thoroughgoing. It is still journeying through purgatory. It does its work methodically. . . . First it perfected the parliamentary power, in order to be able to overthrow it. Now that it has attained this, it perfects the executive power, reduces it to its purest expression, sets it up against itself as the sole target, in order to concentrate all its forces of destruction against it. And when it has done the second half of its preliminary work, Europe will leap from its seat and exultantly exclaim: Well grubbed, old mole!

THE MODEL OF THE COMMUNE

Revolution, in this context, is nothing but the product, simultaneously, of a material situation (the confrontation between classes), its political translation (the crisis of the institutions of power), and the formation of a consciousness. This idea of revolution does not permit an interpretation of a mechanical and evolutionary type, since it sees the motor of the revolution in the irrepressible violence of the proletariat; nor does it permit the assimilation of the revolution to a subjective plan, to a design that anticipates the ongoing material circumstances, to a consciousness of history and of class that antedate both, and which are exterior to and separate from them. The distinction that Marx makes between *social being* and *consciousness* also establishes the close link between the two. In the *Eighteenth Brumaire*, it is this link—which is by no means easy to achieve, but is itself laboriously produced by the movement—which explains why, unlike the "brilliant" bourgeois revolutions,

> proletarian revolutions, like those of the nineteenth century, criticize themselves constantly, interrupt themselves continually in their own course, come back to the apparently accomplished in order to begin it afresh, deride with unmerciful thoroughness the inadequacies, weaknesses and paltriness of their first attempts, seem to throw down their adversary only in order that he may gain new strength from the earth and rise again, more gigantic, before them, recoil ever and anon from the indefinite prodigiousness of their own aims, until a situation has been created which makes all turning back impossible, and the conditions themselves cry out: *Hic Rhodus, hic salta!.*

The accent seems placed here with particular emphasis on the objectivity of the confrontation that propels and compels the consciousness and subjective will of the class, when the latter, though the principal motor of future changes, is still affected by the inertia of the present. With Marx, the fusion between *social being* and *consciousness* (a question which, as we shall see, is at the core of the Leninist theory of the party) is obviously based upon *praxis*. In other words, the answer to the question of "how" the class becomes conscious is: "By practice, in the fact of struggle." Lelio Basso acutely notes that the key to the question is to be found in the *Theses on Feuerbach*, particularly in the third thesis: consciousness is not the product of "education," but of a "being in movement," of an active relationship with nature or with society.[3] A product of capitalism, the working class receives from it its configuration and its dimensions, and simultaneously, its alienated condition; it is therefore its real situation that leads it to reject capitalism. The class struggle has thus its material roots in the mechanism of the system itself;

and revolution—meaning the process that is intended to transcend the system—is a *social* activity that creates, over time, the political forms that the class needs and which constitute its organization—namely the party. If the party and the proletariat sometimes appear as interchangeable in Marx, this is only so in the sense that the former is the *political* form of the latter, and constitutes its transitory mode of being, with the historical imperfections of concrete political institutions; while the proletariat remains the permanent historical subject, rooted in the material conditions of the capitalist system. It is not by chance that the proletariat is destined to destroy and overcome the traditional modes of political expression, including its own, insofar as they are something else than direct social rule; and it achieves this by that unique form of revolution and of a revolutionary society which Marx depicted: the Commune of 1871. In the Commune, revolutionary violence had not only smashed bourgeois power, but the latter's structures as well (from which Lenin deduced that the proletarian power could not use the apparatus of the bourgeois state but had to destroy it); direct democracy thus appeared not as an elementary form of proletarian power, but as its *specific* form. In the model of the Commune, therefore, the revolution and the revolutionary society anticipated not only the withering away of the state, but, even more radically, the progressive disappearance of the *political* dimension as a dimension separate from (and opposed to) social being, reconstituted in its unity. The proletariat in struggle does not produce an institution distinct from its immediate being; and no more does it produce its own state, distinct from the immediate being of the new society. If, that is to say, one does not find a theory of the party in Marx, the reason is that, in his theory of revolution, there is neither need nor room for it.

LENIN'S HORIZON

The question and the theory of the revolutionary party only arise with Lenin. Their birth is historically specific: we are at the end of the epoch when Marx and Engels could anticipate a relatively near revolutionary conflagration at the heart of Europe; and a new phase is opening in that the revolution seems to require a strong subjective impulse that would, in a way, do violence to history. At the turn of the century, Lenin's horizon was delimited by two major facts: first of all, capitalism has entered into the imperialist phase, and its crisis reveals itself as more complex than had been foreseen. Monopolistic concentration reaches gigantic proportions, while the most explosive contradictions move onto another terrain. "What has changed are the forms, the order and the physiognomy of each crisis, but crises continue to be an integral part of the capitalist system."[4] The thesis of the inevitable "collapse" of capitalism will endure for a long time yet in the revolutionary wing of the working class movement; but already Lenin, throughout his life, had to face the growing resistance of the system, and a capacity for action of the working class much inferior to what could have been foreseen in the first great revolutionary phase that extended from 1848 to the Paris Commune.[5]

The years from 1872 to 1905 constituted, on the contrary, a long pacific phase, marked by the absence of revolution—the phase that ended, "paradoxically,"[6] with the revolution of 1905 and with the great awakening in Asia. The fact that this new revolutionary wave occurred on the margins of the capitalist world was not due to the attenuation of the class contradictions in the citadels of capitalism; it was due rather to what would today be called the mechanisms of "integration," foremost among which was the great "revisionist" current associated with the name of Bernstein, and the opportunism of the Second International culminating in the betrayal of 1914.

Hence two great questions arose, which marked the revolutions of the twentieth century and which are also characteristic of Leninism:

1. The capitalist and imperialist system was defeated in areas which, according to the Marxian schema, were not "ripe" for communism. The theoretical implications of this fact were, to a certain extent, obscured by the thesis that "backward" countries must necessarily pass through the stage of the democratic revolution before arriving at the stage of the socialist revolution. This thesis predominated until, in the fifties, the Chinese Communists and some revolutionary currents of the "Third World" proposed the theory of "zones of revolutionary storm." Suffice it to emphasize, in relation to so complex a problem, that these movements or revolutions did not always have the proletariat as their protagonist.

2. In this context, the problem of political organization no longer presents itself in terms of the spontaneous formation, in the heat of struggle, of a vanguard of the class. The confrontation must

be prepared: the more society lacks "maturity," the more important it is that a vanguard should provoke the telescoping of objective conditions with the intolerability of exploitation and a revolutionary explosion, by giving the exploited and the oppressed the consciousness of their real condition, by wrenching them out of ignorance and resignation, by indicating to them a method, a strategy and the possibility of revolt —by *making* them revolutionaries. A vanguard of this nature may be external to the mass that it seeks to transform: it is as such an external vanguard that it has assimilated, and that it then transmits, the strategy of struggle. Thus, the revolutionary party is, paradoxically, the bearer of the analysis and the ideals of Marx, yet foreign to the process of struggle–consciousness that Marx had sketched out. It is always through this form of organization that the revolutionary wing of the workers' movement has manifested itself, so as not to be compelled to defer the revolution to the hypothetical moment when conditions would be "ripe"; even in Europe, where the objective conditions fitted better with Marx's hypothesis, the crisis of social democracy and the incapacity to oppose to social democracy a non-Leninist model (only Gramsci and Rosa Luxemburg made the attempt) rendered impossible a practical adherence to Marx's model.

WHAT IS TO BE DONE?

Lenin gave a theoretical foundation to this model of the party in *What is to be Done?* It is impossible to read this text properly, without taking into account the polemic against gradualism and economism, and against the ideological accoutrements of opportunism as practiced by the Second International. But it is equally wrong not to see how much the text, which was intended as a strict exegesis of Marx, constitutes in fact a radical revision of the relationship between class and party, class and class consciousness. On this point, as is well known, Lenin adjudged as "profoundly true" the ideas of Kautsky, who argued against those who believed that

> economic development and the class struggle create, not only the conditions for socialist production, but also, and directly, the *consciousness* of its necessity. . . . In this connection Socialist consciousness is represented as a necessary and direct result of the proletarian class struggle.

But this is absolutely untrue. Of course, Socialism, as a theory, has its roots in a modern economic relationship in the same way as the class struggle of the proletariat has. . . . But Socialism and the class struggle arise side by side and not one out of the other; each arises out of different premises. Modern Socialist consciousness can arise only on the basis of profound scientific knowledge. Indeed, modern economic science is as much a condition for Socialist production as, say, modern technology, and the proletariat can create neither the one nor the other, no matter how much it may desire to do so. . . . The vehicles of science are not the proletariat, but the *bourgeois intelligentsia*: it was out of the heads of members of this stratum that modern Socialism originated, and it was they who communicated it to the more intellectually developed proletarians who, in their turn, introduce it into the proletarian class struggle where conditions allow that to be done. Thus, Socialist consciousness is something introduced into the proletarian class struggle from without [*von Aussen Hineingetragenes*], and not something that arose within it spontaneously [*urwuchsig*]. Accordingly, the old Hainfeld programme quite rightly stated that the task of Social-Democracy is to imbue the proletariat with the *consciousness* of its position and the consciousness of its tasks.[7]

We know that Lenin went even further than this, by adding that the workers' struggle could never by itself go beyond simple economic demands (in virtue of which the spontaneity propounded by *Rabotchaia Mysl* was nothing but the ideological alibi for an objectively "trade-unionist," non-revolutionary position); and that the workers' struggle would therefore, by its nature, be incapable of grasping the links between exploitation and the political structure of the bourgeois state, which were also links that served to explain the political contradictions between the autocracy and other classes. At that time, Lenin's objective was to liberate social democracy from "economism," to bring the proletariat into the struggle against the autocracy, and to create the organizational means appropriate to the purpose. He did not therefore get bogged down in a philosophical discussion, but confined himself to denouncing and illustrating the insurmountable limitations of class instinct, and provided on the way a curiously idealist reconstruction of the birth of Marxism as a product of culture and of nothing else.[8] From this follows a sudden break between material social being (the class, the proletariat) and the political struggle for socialism (a project expressed by culture, a generous theory of man's emancipation in modern times);

hence the justification of a vanguard, the bearer of the political project, separate from the class and external to it.

The Marxist dialectic, in which the subject is the proletariat and the object the society produced by the relations of capitalist production, thus moves toward a dialectic between class and vanguard, in which the former has the capacity of an "objective quantity," while the latter, the party, being the subject, is the locus of "revolutionary initiative." Whatever may be the consequences of posing the problem in this fashion, its idealist character is obvious. While it is true that one must guard against a "mechanical" application of Marx's thought, the question remains how it is possible to think in Marxist terms and yet maintain that consciousness has an origin other than social being—"it is not the consciousness of men that determines their being, but, on the contrary, their social being that determines their consciousness"—and if the passage from social being to consciousness *in* the proletariat presents a theoretical difficulty, that problem becomes quite insoluble if, at the risk of falling back into Hegelianism, one deduces consciousness from consciousness—worse, if one does not fear *to make the consciousness of the proletariat the product of the consciousness of intellectuals* miraculously freed from their social being and abstracted from their class.

ROSA LUXEMBURG'S APPROACH

Rosa Luxemburg also attempted, theoretically and practically, to solve the problem posed by a revolutionary development of the European proletariat slower than Marx had anticipated; but the solution, in this case, was sought in accordance with the Marxian concept of class consciousness and not according to the Leninist thesis of an external vanguard. This led to Rosa Luxemburg being accused of "spontaneism," an ideological form of "left adventurism" rather than of opportunism. In reality, Rosa Luxemburg never maintained that the masses could do without an organized vanguard which, for her, was identified with the party. However, the need for the latter was not derived from the absence of a *political* dimension of working-class struggles as such, but from the objective fragmentation of these struggles, which a unifying strategy could alone overcome. It is, in effect, the *directly political* needs of the class which require its strategic unification. Rosa Luxemburg firmly denies that the theory of class struggle can come into being independently of that struggle itself:

The proletarian class struggle is older than social-democracy; as the elementary product of class society, it already manifests itself with the appearance of capitalism in Europe. It is not social-democracy which began the education of the modern proletariat but, on the contrary, it is the proletariat which brought it into being for the purpose of embodying the consciousness of the goal to be reached and coordinating, in time and in space, the episodic and local actions of the class struggle.[9]

The history of past revolutions shows that violent popular movements, far from being the arbitrary, conscious work of so-called "leaders" and "parties" . . . are rather absolutely primary social phenomena which have their origin in the class character of modern society. The birth of social-democracy has so far made no difference to this fact, and its role does not consist in prescribing laws for the historical development of class struggles but on the contrary in submitting to its laws and in that very manner to bring them under its control.[10]

The strong link between spontaneity and organization thus resides in the laws of historical development of the class struggle, that is to say, of the material base. This cannot be assimilated to the immediate consciousness that the mass has of itself, since the latter "like Thalassa the eternal sea always harbors within itself every latent possibility: the mass is always what it *must* be by the force of circumstances and is always quick to become something entirely different from what it appears to be."[11] Nor, on the other hand, can it be considered as the pure product of culture, of that "ideology of socialism," independent of the material historical development, which Lenin opposed in *What is to be Done?* to "bourgeois ideology."

Rosa Luxemburg's position was condemned by the International at a time when it had already been condemned by the failure of the German and the European revolution, i.e., of the only revolution in relation to which it was historically plausible. This condemnation had profound organizational consequences, for theory always surrounds a practical kernel, namely the question of leadership. When, that is to say, the *subject* is located *inside the class* (however great the complexity may be between being and consciousness), the political organization, the party, appears as a simple instrument, always liable to control, When, on the contrary, the subject is embodied in the *external political vanguard*, the latter bears within itself a principle of legitimacy and self-regulation, and requires the class to submit to it.

Lenin had an extremely clear awareness of this problem; and in fact—once the battle against the Right had been won and the revolutionary party had been created—his initial conception of "induced consciousness" was contradicted by the thesis "all power to the Soviets," the soviets being the direct expression of the class obviously possessed of consciousness to the point of being able to direct the new society. The word "contradicted" is used here not only because, in practice, the relationship between soviets and party found a brief and fragile equilibrium; but also because that equilibrium revealed, in Lenin, a leap between the theory of the seizure of power and the theory of revolution, in the sense that the subject of the former would be the political vanguard, and that of the latter the class. The difference of contexts explains the partial character of the positions, shows the complexity of the relation between the class and its organization and the rapidity with which the emphasis changes from one to the other in the concrete historical development.

GRAMSCI'S ITINERARY

In Gramsci's thought, the polarity is obvious. All of the Gramsci of the "councils," with his soviet and anti-Jacobin orientations, has a Luxemburgist emphasis, to the point where he finds in the network of councils, seen as the locus of the self-government of the producers, the essence of political organization, the Italian reality of the Communist International.[12] This extreme position must no doubt be viewed in the context of the debate inside the Italian Socialist party; but it is certain that the Turin experience of Gramsci is altogether based on the hypothesis of the growth of the class as the direct political subject. The party, in this perspective and as is affirmed in the famous passage on the Russian revolution, is only the ideological point of reference, a center of coherent elaboration, an intellectual and moral vanguard: an instrument, but not the only one, of political expression. That political expression does not require mediations; in the factory councils, in the achievement by the class of its consciousness of being a revolutionary alternative, a new society is already coming into being in the heat of battle. Ten years later, in the *Notes on Machiavelli*, the emphasis changes: the accent is placed on the vanguard, on "the prince," alone capable of interpreting reality by releasing reality's yet imprecise potentialities. Without its intervention, reality cannot manage to take shape, to become recognizable. The *autonomy* of the political moment, which is precisely Machiavelli's "discovery," has large implications if it is accepted as a principle that is also valid for a revolutionary party: for that autonomy explicitly detaches the party from its material base and arrests (in the reverse sense of "direct democracy") the dialectic between class and consciousness.

It is not therefore surprising that Gramsci should have been exploited as much by the partisans of the workers' councils orientation, which reappeared after 1956, as by those who sought in him a theoretical justification for the supremacy not only of the party, but of its leading cadres.[13] The real Gramsci is in his itinerary, the theoretical echo of the crisis of revolutions of the twenties, the reflection on the complexity of the relation between spontaneity and organization in the stress of concrete history, in a period when the failure of the movement seems to leave no other hope than international reference to the Soviet Union, and the maintenance at all costs of even a restricted vanguard in each country. But the real Gramsci is also to be found in the strong awareness that he always had of the complexity of the social fabric and of its forms of expression, of the consequent necessity for any organization—whether "direct" or "vertical"—to present itself as the synthesis of a process comprising numerous levels and mediations. This basic element in Gramsci does not resolve the political opposition between the two conceptions noted earlier, but it infuses a common preoccupation into both, to the point where Gramsci, even though not condemned as was Rosa Luxemburg, always remained suspected of heresy in the communist movement.

THE PROBLEM TODAY

After Lenin, the communist movement no longer discussed the question of the relation between party and class, except in an extremely onesided and indirect way, and in order to call for a "better link of the party with the masses." The question was thus reduced to one of democratic functioning of the vanguard and of its channels of communication, and of the vanguard's degree of receptivity. In its most advanced sectors, as in the Italian Communist Party, the communist movement, inspired by Gramsci, became a complex institution, rich in possibilities, not only in its internal life, but also in the interpretation of national reality that an ever better adapted political instrument made possible. Yet, here also, the effort was exclusively related to the functioning of the instrument, to the institution and to nothing else. Even the dramatic debate on Stalinism in the European socialist societies did not go beyond this purely *political* level. This is why the debate, where it occurred, oscillated between sectarianism and right deviation: the defense of monolithic structures or proposals for a multiparty system, even inside socialist society. Only one socialist country, China, displaced in the course of its revolution—and particularly during the tumultuous "cultural revolution"—the theoretical terms of the question mass-and-party by proposing the permanent recourse to the mass, the permanent reference not only to the latter's objective needs, but to the most immediate forms of its consciousness ("the poor peasant," those most in need, becoming the axis of the construction of the movement wherever arrived the Red Army and its propagandists): it is according to these criteria that must be measured the correctness of the political process and to which the organization must be subordinated. However, this insistence on the material condition is itself conditioned by the charismatic character of the "correct thought" of Mao, the leaven for the achievement of consciousness, the guarantee of the subjective process. This duality harbors an explosive tension, which, from time to time, shatters the concrete forms of political organization or of the administration of the state, but only to reproduce immediately new such forms, just as rigidly centralized, with their specific institutions and their external relation to the mass. It seems that, rather than speak of a dialectic, it is more appropriate to speak of an unresolved antinomy, kept alive as a practical, empirical system, with its own reciprocal corrective features. It may be that this is the only system which, in a situation of immaturity of productive and up to a point social forces, allows the relation class-party not to be frozen in a hierarchical structure that would otherwise be encouraged by the immensity of the problems to be tackled. The theoretical question remains unresolved; but it also remains at least present and alive in China, while in the other socialist societies it has come to be frozen in the reiteration of a Leninist scheme revised and impoverished by Stalinist experience.

Until the last few years, the debate was continued only within marginal groups. But where it did occur—as in Italy in the debate around

the councils,[14] and in France in the polemic against Sartre, begun in
1952 by Merleau-Ponty and Claude Lefort, and then continued in the
journal *Socialisme ou Barbarie*—it revealed a fundamental inadequacy.
This inadequacy was much less theoretical than political: for it is the
political dimension that gives strength to the theoretical arguments of
Marx, Lenin, Rosa Luxemburg, and Gramsci. The discussions on the
theory of the party have, since the twenties, always had in Europe a
"leftist" tinge; and they have always brought one back to the "lateness"
of the revolutionary movement in the West. But all these discussions
also sought a solution in a "return to the sources," whether in Marx or
in Gramsci, so as to find again a "pure" relationship between the class
and its political expression in the mechanism of exploitation.

All positions which, against the weaknesses of the institutional
forces of parties and trade unions, affirmed in this period the priority
of the class as the political subject (whether they accepted or denied
the necessity of organization) lent themselves easily to the critique
that Lenin addressed to the "economism" of his own day: namely that
they reduced the class and its exploitation to the relationship between
capital and labor and paid little attention to all the political, national,
and international implications of the class struggle; while these implications were, on the contrary, recognized by the institutionalized
organizations of the working class. A rereading of the debate on workers' councils reveals a lack of historical perspective, a fragmentation of
political programs, a curiously "insurrectionary" aspect where there
should have been a rediscovery of the totality of Marx's thought. What
the debate showed was that it was impossible to define a coherent class
position without taking into account the total organization of capital
as a total system of social relations. Thus, in the discussion conducted
in *Socialisme ou Barbarie*, it was not by chance that Lefort—even though
he was concerned to criticize with good reason Sartre's reduction of
the class to the party—deemed it a matter of no importance whether
the French working class did or did not demonstrate against General
Ridgway—that was not its business. The fact that the working class
movement of the twentieth century was represented by social democracy or by Leninism (or by its Stalinist version); the existence of the Soviet Union and the relations of forces that this entailed on a world scale;
the occurrence of revolutions or of revolutionary crises in "backward"
areas where revolution, when it was not organized through Commu-

nist parties, assumed even more centralized and hierarchical forms (always justified by the objective immaturity of the revolution)—all this was left aside and thus condemned the debate to fundamental sterility.

In comparison, the communist movement had an easy task: all it needed to do was to insist on its own effective insertion in historical reality. It is true that the communist movement often tended to use this as a means of avoiding any critical reexamination of its own positions. It is also true that the organization—an organization built upon the militancy and sacrifices of innumerable men and women—is often tempted to see its own perpetuation as its goal instead of constantly verifying the correctness of its political positions. Even so, the nature of Communist parties could not be brought into question, whether on theoretical or on practical grounds, merely by *reflection* on the nature of the class, least of all by reflection vitiated by the inadequacies noted earlier. It could only be brought into question by profound changes in *real* relations, which suddenly pose to the vanguard the problem, not whether it is in accord with the theory, but whether it is in tune with the potentialities of the movement, whether it precedes the movement or follows it. Elaborated as it was in the first half of the twentieth century as an instrument of revolution in areas situated on the margin of advanced capitalism, the Leninist schema of the relation between party and class only comes to the fore again at the point when the question is posed anew of revolution in advanced societies.

The solution, or at least the working hypothesis that seems appropriate, is suggested in the conversation with Sartre that follows. A solution requires collective research and discussion with the whole of the movement. It is not an accident that the questions raised here are now being asked on all sides, and as much inside Communist parties, where these are most open and receptive to the concern engendered by the appearance of new forms of struggle, as in the groups that have come into being in the last few years and which have rapidly transcended an elementary vision of spontaneity.

We should like, in conclusion, to underline two further points. The first is that the question of class and party only has theoretical value when it is politically ripe, which is another way of saying that the only theory that has meaning is one which is formed within a praxis, a concrete historical situation: no solution to it is possible that does not start from a careful analysis of the different class contradictions in advanced societies, from the concrete forms of struggle, from the needs which the crisis of capitalism reveals *today*. What this means, in effect, is that a theory of organization is closely linked to a concept of revolution, and cannot be separated from it.

The second point is that the tensions that are present in the historic institutions of the class, whether trade unions or parties, do not only result from the subjective limitations of these institutions. They are also the product of a growth in a political dimension ever more closely linked to the achievement of consciousness, and ever less capable of being delegated. In effect, the distance between vanguard and class, which was at the origin of the Leninist party, is visibly shrinking: Marx's hypothesis finds new life in the May movement in France, in many of the confrontations that occur in our societies, and which tend to escape from the control, however elastic and attentive it may be, of purely political formations. It is in terms of this fact that the problem of organization may now be posed again. From Marx, we are now returning to Marx.

MASSES, SPONTANEITY, PARTY

Jean-Paul Sartre

Manifesto: During the May events in France, and in the course of the working-class struggle of 1968 generally, movements at the base attacked the Communist parties not only for their bureaucratic degeneration or for their reformist options; they also criticized the very notion of the *party* as the political, structured organization of the class. When these movements suffered setbacks, a number of "leftist" groups came to emphasize organization against spontaneity, and advocated a return to "pure" Leninism. Neither of these attitudes seems to us satisfactory. It seems to us that one can only properly criticize spontaneity—and this was the lesson of 1968—if it is realized that the subjective maturity of the working class requires today a new form of organization, adapted to the conditions of struggle in the societies of advanced capitalism.

We should like to focus this conversation on the theoretical bases of this problem. You have been concerned with this ever since the now classic discussion of 1952 (*Communists and Peace*) and the polemic that followed with Lefort and Merleau-Ponty, by way of *The Ghost of Stalin* of 1956 to the *Critique de la Raison Dialectique*. In 1952, you were charged with hyper-subjectivism and you were reproached with a failure to recognize any existence of the working class other than in the party. In 1956, it was the reverse accusation that was directed at you, namely that you were guilty of an objectivism that tended to explain Stalinism as the inevitable product of a particular historical situation. In actual fact, it seems to us that both positions had a common basis in the concept of "scarcity," in the structural backwardness of the country in which the October Revolution occurred, in the "necessities" imposed by the fact that the revolution was not "ripe" and that socialism had to be built in a context of primitive accumulation. In

this specific situation, you considered that the party was bound to su-
perimpose itself upon a mass that had not reached the required level of
consciousness. Do you believe that this image of the party—which we
shared with you in the fifties—must be revised because the situation
has changed; or, on the contrary, that it must be revised because the
earlier formulations were vitiated by theoretical inadequacies, which
have since then been more clearly revealed?

Sartre: There was certainly inadequacy. But this must be situated historically. In 1952, when I wrote *Communists and Peace*, the essential
political choice was the defense of the French Communist Party, and
particularly of the Soviet Union, accused as it was of imperialism. It
was essential to reject this accusation if one did not wish to find oneself on the side of the Americans. Afterwards, it was shown that the
USSR, by behaving in Budapest as Stalin (whether because of political
intelligence or for other reasons) did not behave in 1948 in relation
to Yugoslavia, and then by repeating the operation in Czechoslovakia,
was acting in the manner of an imperialist power. In saying this, I do
not intend to express a moral judgment. I am only stating that the external policy of the USSR seems essentially inspired by its antagonistic
relations with the United States, and not by a principle of respect, of
equality, vis-à-vis other socialist states. I tried to explain the point in
the *Critique de la Raison Dialectique*. This of course was still an attempt
at a formal solution, which should have been followed by an historical
analysis of the USSR in Stalin's time—an analysis which I have already
sketched out and which forms part of a second volume of the *Critique*,
but which will probably never appear.

In short, what I tried to show in relation to concepts like *mass*, *party*,
spontaneity, *seriality*, *channels*, and *groups*, represents the embryo of an
answer to this problem. In effect, I tried to show that the party, in
relation to the mass, is a *necessary* reality because the mass, by itself,
does not possess *spontaneity*. By itself, the mass remains serialized. But
conversely, as soon as the party becomes an institution, so does it also—
save in exceptional circumstances—become reactionary in relation to
what it has itself brought into being, namely the *fused group*. In other
words, the dilemma spontaneity/party is a false problem. In terms
of its self-consciousness, the class does not appear homogeneous; but
rather as an ensemble of elements, of groups, which I define as "fused."

Among the workers, we always find fused groups in this or that factory where a struggle occurs, in the course of which individuals establish relations of reciprocity, enjoy in regard to the totality of groups what I have called a "wild freedom," and acquire a definite consciousness of their class position.

But besides these fused groups, there are other workers who are not united by struggle, who remain serialized, and who are therefore incapable of spontaneity because they are not linked to the rest, except in a reified relation, in a serialized connection. Even a fused group— for instance a factory that is on strike—is continually subjected to and weighed down by serialized relations (massification, etc). The same worker who finds himself in a fused group at his place of work may be completely serialized when he is at home or at other moments of his life. We are therefore in the presence of very different forms of class consciousness: on the one hand, an advanced consciousness, on the other an almost nonexistent consciousness, with a series of mediations in between. This is why it does not seem to me that one can speak of class *spontaneity*, it is only appropriate to speak of *groups*, produced by circumstances, and which create themselves in the course of particular situations; in thus creating themselves, they do not rediscover some kind of underlying spontaneity, but rather experience a specific condition on the basis of specific situations of exploitation and of particular demands; and it is in the course of their experience that they achieve a more or less accurate consciousness of themselves.

This said, what does the party represent in relation to the series? Surely a positive factor, since it prevents a collapse into complete seriality. The members of a Communist party would themselves remain isolated and serialized individuals if the party did not turn them into a group through an organic link that enables a communist in Milan to communicate with another communist worker from any other region. Moreover, it is thanks to the party that many groups are formed in the course of struggle, because the party makes communication easier. However, the party finds itself, as a general rule, compelled either to absorb or to reject the fused group that it has itself helped to create. In comparison with the group, whose organization never goes beyond a kind of reciprocal pact, the party is much more strongly structured. A group forms itself under stress, for instance to achieve some goal ("We must take the Bastille"); as soon as the action is over, the individuals who compose the group anxiously face each other and try to establish a link that might replace the link forged in action, a kind of pact or oath, which in turn tends to constitute the beginning of a series and to establish between them a relationship of reified contiguity. This is what I have called "Fraternity-terror." The party, on the contrary, develops as an ensemble of institutions, and therefore as a closed, static system, which has a tendency to sclerosis. This is why the party is always behind in relation to the fused mass, even when it tries to guide that mass: this is so because it tries to weaken it, to subordinate it, and may even reject it and deny any solidarity with it.

The thought and action of each group necessarily reflect its structure. What occurs is therefore the following: the thought of a fused group—by virtue of the fact that it is born in the stress of a particular situation and not because of some kind of "spontaneity"—has a stronger, fresher, more critical charge than that of a structured group. As an institution, a party has an institutionalized mode of thought—meaning something that deviates from *reality*—and comes essentially to reflect no more than its own organization, in effect ideological thought. It is upon its own schema that is modeled, and deformed, the experience of the struggle itself; while the fused group thinks its experience as it presents itself, without institutional mediation. This is why the thought of a group may be vague, incapable of being theorized, awkward—as were the ideas of the students in May 1968—but nevertheless represents a *truer* kind of thought because no institution is interposed between experience and the reflection upon experience.

No doubt, we are dealing here with a contradiction that is inherent in the very function of the party. The latter comes into being to liberate the working class from seriality; but at the same time, it is a reflection—a reflection of a certain type, since the party is intended to abolish that condition—of the seriality and massification of the masses upon which it operates. This seriality of the masses finds expression in the party's institutional character. Compelled as it is to deal with what is serialized, it is itself partly inert and serialized. In order to protect itself, it thus ends up by opposing the fused groups, even though these groups are an aspect of a working class that it wants to represent and which it has itself very often brought into movement.

Here is the underlying contradiction of the party, which has emerged to liberate the masses from seriality and which has itself become an institution. As such, it harbors so many negative features (I don't mean here bureaucracy or other forms of degeneration, but rather the institutional structure itself, which is not necessarily bureaucratic) that it finds itself compelled, fundamentally and in all cases, to oppose all the new forces, whether it tries to use them or whether it rejects them. We have seen these two different attitudes adopted by the French and the Italian Communist parties vis-à-vis the students: the French party rejected them; more subtly, the PCI tried to attract them and to direct their experience by means of contact and discussion. A party can only choose between these two attitudes: this is its underlying limitation.

Let me give you another classic example, namely the question of democratic centralism. As long as democratic centralism operated in a dynamic situation, for instance during clandestinity and the organization of the struggle in Russia, that is, precisely at the time when Lenin elaborated its theory, it remained a living thing. There was a moment of centralism, because it was necessary, and a moment of real democracy, because people could argue and decisions were taken in common. As soon as it was institutionalized, as was the case in all communist countries, centralism took precedence over democracy, and democracy itself became an "institution," subjected to its own inertia: there exists, for instance, a right to speak, but the fact alone that it should be a right—and only that—empties it so much of its substance that, in reality, it becomes a non-right. The real question is therefore to know how to overcome the contradiction which is inherent in the very nature of the party, so that (not only in its relations with opponents and in its tasks as a fighting organization, but also in relation to the class that it represents) the party may constitute an active mediation between serialized and massified elements for the purpose of their unification; in other words, how the party may be able to receive the impulses that emanate from movements and, rather than claim to direct them, may be able to generalize experience for the movement and for itself.

Manifesto: The real location of revolutionary consciousness is therefore neither in the immediate class, nor in the party, but in the struggle. On this view, the party remains alive as long as it is an instrument of struggle, but exchanges the end for the means as soon as it becomes an institution, and becomes its own end. The contradiction that is inherent in the party, and which you emphasize, can perhaps be resolved to the extent that one tries to approach the problem of the political organization of the class not in general terms, but in the immediacy of specific situations. What seems impossible is a metahistorical solution. It therefore seems necessary to envisage the objective conditions in which this dilemma can be resolved on each occasion. In our view, this implies two conditions: first of all that the class should transcend the level of seriality to become effectively and totally the subject of collective action.

Sartre: This is an impossible condition; the working class can never express itself completely as an active political subject: there will always be zones or regions or sectors which, because of historical reasons of development, will remain serialized, massified, alien to the achievement of consciousness. There is always a residue. There is a strong tendency today to generalize the concept of *class consciousness* and of *class struggle* as preexisting elements antecedent to the struggle. The only *a priori* is the objective situation of class exploitation. Consciousness is only born in struggle: the class struggle only exists insofar as there exist places where an actual struggle is going on. It is true that the proletariat carries within itself the death of the bourgeoisie; it is equally true that the capitalist system is mined by structural contradictions. But this does not necessarily imply the existence of class consciousness or of class struggle. In order that there should be *consciousness* and *struggle*, it is necessary that somebody should be fighting.

In other words, the class struggle is virtually possible everywhere in the capitalist system, but really exists only where the struggle is actually being carried on. On the other hand, the struggle, even while it is being carried on, differs in terms of each situation. In France, for instance, the conditions and forms of struggle are extremely diverse: in Saint-Nazaire, the workers' struggles, which are very violent, retain the characteristics of the last century; in other, more "advanced," capitalist zones, they assume a different character, with an articulation of demands that may be greater, but in a more moderate context. This is why it is impossible, even for that part of the working class which is actually struggling, to speak of *unification*, save theoretically. The twenty-four-hour general strikes organized by the CGT are no more, at best, than the symbol of a unified struggle.

Manifesto: But are we not in a phase of capitalist unification of society, as much in terms of the infrastructure as of the superstructures (types of consumption and styles of life, language, massification)? Is it not true that the fragmentation of individual situations is accompanied by the ever more obvious "totalization" of the system? And should not this have as its consequence the formation of an objective material base for the growing unification of the class and of its class consciousness?

Sartre: In actual fact, the structure remains extremely diversified and unstable.

Manifesto: But is there a tendency towards unification or not?

Sartre: Yes and no. In France, for instance, capitalism artificially maintains alive thousands of small enterprises, for whose existence there is no reason from the point of view of economic rationality; but they are useful to capitalism, either because they represent a conservative political sector (these are the social strata which vote for de Gaulle or Pompidou), or because they provide a norm for capitalist costs of production, despite the increase in productivity. In effect, the tendencies to integration do not cancel out the profound diversities of structural situations.

Add to this that advanced capitalism, in relation to its awareness of its own condition, and despite the enormous disparities in the distribution of income, manages to satisfy the elementary needs of the majority of the working class—there remain of course the marginal zones, 15 percent of workers in the United States, the blacks and the immigrants; there remain the elderly; there remains, on a global scale, the Third World. But capitalism satisfies certain primary needs, and also satisfies certain needs that it has artificially created: for instance the need of a car. It is this situation which has caused me to revise my "theory of needs," since these needs are no longer, in a situation of advanced capitalism, in systematic opposition to the system. On the contrary, they partly become, under the control of that system, an instrument of integration of the proletariat into certain processes engendered and directed by profit. The worker exhausts himself in producing a car and in earning enough to buy one; this acquisition gives him the impression of having satisfied a "need." The system that exploits him provides him simultaneously with a goal and with the possibility of reaching it. The consciousness of the intolerable character of the system must therefore no longer be sought in the impossibility of satisfying elementary needs but, above all else, in the consciousness of *alienation*—in other words, in the fact that *this life* is not worth living and has no meaning, that this mechanism is a deceptive mechanism, that these needs are artificially created, that they are false, that they are exhausting and only serve profit. But to unite the class on this basis is even more difficult. This is why I do not agree with any of the optimistic visions presented by Communist parties or by left movements, who seem to believe that capitalism is henceforth at bay. Capitalism's means of control over classes are still powerful; and it is far from being on the defensive. As for bringing about a revolutionary *élan*, this requires a long and patient labor in the construction of consciousness.

Manifesto: Even so, this unification appeared immediate and obvious in May 1968.

Sartre: Absolutely obvious. It is one of the rare instances where everyone saw in the struggles of the local factory a model of his own struggles. A phenomenon of the same order, but of far greater dimension, occurred in 1936. But at that time the working-class institutions played a determinant role. The movement started when socialists and communists were already in power, and offering, up to a certain point, a model that allowed the class a rapid achievement of consciousness, the fusion of groups, and unification.

In May, not only were parties and unions not in power, but they were also a long way from playing a comparable role. The element that unified the struggle was something which, in my opinion, came from afar; it was an idea that came to us from Vietnam and which the students expressed in the formula: *"L'imagination au pouvoir."* In other words, the area of the possible is much more vast than the dominant classes have accustomed us to believe. Who would have thought that fourteen million peasants would be able to resist the greatest industrial and military power in the world? And yet, this is what happened. Vietnam taught us that the area of the possible is immense, and that one need not be resigned. It is this which was the lever of the students' revolt, and the workers understood it. In the united demonstration of May 13, this idea suddenly became dominant. "If a few thousand youngsters can occupy the universities and defy the government, why should we not be able to do the same?" Thus it was that from May 13 onwards, and following a model that at that moment came to them from outside, the workers went on strike and occupied the factories. The element which mobilized and united them was not a program of demands: this came later, to justify the strike, and of course there was no lack of motives for strike action. But it is interesting to note that the demands came later, after the factories had already been occupied.

Manifesto: It would therefore seem that, at the origin of May, there was no immediately material element, no particularly explosive structural contradiction?

Sartre: The preceding autumn, something had provoked a generalized discontent among the workers, namely the reactionary measures of the government in the field of social security. These measures had hit the whole working population, whatever their occupation. The unions, either because they were taken by surprise or because they did not want to expose themselves too much, did not manage to offer adequate opposition to the measures. There was, if my memory serves, a day of general strike, but that is as far as it went. However, a deep and unexpressed discontent endured; and it broke out again in strength in the May demonstrations. There is today a possible new element of unification: this is the absolutely futile character that the rise in prices, and then devaluation, have given to the increases in wages that were obtained at the time. But it is not easy to know in advance whether these unifying elements of discontent will lead to a united revolt. In May, on the other hand, this revolt occurred and in my opinion, the detonator was not so much that the workers became conscious of exploitation but that they became conscious of their own strength and of their own possibilities.

Manifesto: Yet, this revolt of May was a failure and was followed by a victory of reaction. Is that because it did not contain the elements capable of pushing the revolution to a conclusion or because it lacked political direction?

Sartre: It lacked political direction, of a kind capable of giving it the political and theoretical dimension without which the movement could not but subside, as indeed happened. It lacked a party capable of taking up completely the movement and its potentialities. As a matter of fact, how could an institutionalized structure, as in the case of the Communist parties, place itself in the service of something that took it by surprise? How could it be sufficiently receptive to react, not by saying "Let us see what we can get out of this?" or "Let us try to attract the movement to ourselves so that it does not escape from us," but by saying "Here is reality and we must serve it by trying to give it theoretical and practical generality so that it may grow and be further advanced?" Furthermore, a Communist party that is unable to adopt this attitude becomes what the French Communist Party has been in practice for twenty-five years: a brake on any revolutionary movement in France. Everything that does not emanate from it alone the party either rejects or suppresses.

Manifesto: In fact, while you criticize the Communist parties as they are, you affirm the need for a moment of unification and of organization of the movement?

Sartre: Certainly, and this is where the problem lies. We are confronted with reaction, with strong and complex capitalist rule, which has an ample capacity of repression and integration. This demands a counter-organization of the class. The problem is to know how to prevent that counter-organization from deteriorating by becoming an "institution."

Manifesto: Agreed. But it is interesting to note that the need for a political organization of the class seems to contradict a forecast of Marx, according to which the proletariat, with the growth of capitalism, would express itself immediately in a revolutionary movement, without the help of political mediation. At the origin of this thesis, there was the conviction that the crisis of capitalism would occur fairly early, and that there were growing within capitalism strains which the system could not absorb—for instance, the development of productive forces would enter into contradiction with the mechanism of capitalist development. Later on, Lenin saw in the socialization of productive forces a factor capable, up to a certain point, of laying the ground for the socialist organization of the economy, once the political apparatus of the bourgeois state had been smashed. We are forced today to recognize the inadequacy of such theses. In the first place, the productive forces do not enter directly into contradiction with the system, because they do not represent something neutral and objective, but are the product of the system and are subjected to its priorities and are affected by it.

Sartre: Yes, these forces are not necessarily fated to come into conflict; they are produced by this type of development as is shown—for instance—by the choosing of space development in the scientific field. As for the socialization of productive forces, even though it is incorrect to speak here of a "class," one must recognize that the development of these forces has brought into being a bureaucracy and a certain technocracy which have acquired a dangerous power of control over the masses and the means of integrating them into an authoritarian society.

Manifesto: In effect, the passage of capitalism into socialism does not have the same characteristics as the passage of feudalism into capitalism. Capitalist relations of production developed progressively inside feudal society, so much so that when the latter collapsed, it had become no more than the shell of a different structural reality, which had already ripened within it. This is what cannot happen with the proletariat; it cannot, inside capitalism, express itself through embryonic forms of socialist organization.

Sartre: The processes are indeed different, whether from the angle of structures, or of relations of production, or of ideas. From the Renaissance onwards, culture was no longer feudal but bourgeois; new social groups, such as the *noblesse de robe*, were bourgeois. This process preceded and accompanied the establishment of capitalist relations of production. The gestation of the bourgeoisie lasted for centuries and expressed itself in an alternative that was *present* in existing society. This cannot happen in relation to the proletariat—not even from the point of view of culture. For the proletariat does not possess a culture that is autonomous: it either uses elements of bourgeois culture, or it expresses a total refusal of any culture, which is a way of affirming the lack of existence of its own culture. It may be objected that the proletariat nevertheless possesses a "scale of values" that is proper to it. Of course, by wanting a revolution, it wants something different from what now exists. But I am suspicious of expressions such as "scale of values" which can easily be turned into their opposite. The revolt of the students was a typical expression of the problem of a counterculture: it was a refusal that, because it lacked its own elaboration, ended up by borrowing, even though it gave them a contrary meaning, a series of ideological trappings from their opponents (conceptual simplification, schematism, violence, etc).

Manifesto: The anticapitalist revolution is, therefore, both ripe and not ripe. Class antagonism produces the contradiction, but is not, by itself, capable of producing the alternative. Yet, if one is not to reduce the revolution to a pure voluntarism and a pure subjectivity, or, conversely, if one is not to fall back into evolutionism, on what precise bases can one prepare a revolutionary alternative?

Sartre: I repeat, more on the basis of "alienation" than on "needs." In short, on the reconstruction of the individual and of freedom— the need for which is so pressing that even the most refined techniques of integration cannot afford to discount it. This is why these techniques try to satisfy that need in imaginary form. All of "human engineering" is based on the idea that the employer must behave towards his subordinate *as if* the latter was his equal, because—this is implicit—no man can renounce this right to equality. And the worker who falls into the trap of the "human relations" of paternalism becomes its victim, to the very degree that he wants effective equality.

Manifesto: This is true, but then how is one to demonstrate that this need is produced by advanced capitalism and that it is not simply the residue of a "humanism" that antedates capitalism? It may be that the answer will have to be sought precisely in the contradictions inherent in the development of capital: for instance, in the fragmentation of work as opposed to a level of education much higher than is required by the role that the worker is called upon to assume; in the quantitative and qualitative development of education paralleled by inadequate job opportunities; in an increase of demands and in the obstacles to their satisfaction—in short, in a constant frustration of that productive force which is man.

Sartre: The fact is that the development of capital increases proletarianization—not in the sense of absolute pauperization, but by the steady worsening in the relation between new needs and the role played by the workers, a worsening provoked not by slump but by development.

Manifesto: The revolutionary political organization of the class therefore requires the elaboration of an alternative. It seems to us that this
problem was underestimated during May. Those who took up positions of Marcusian inspiration or of a spontaneist kind in the fashion of
Cohn-Bendit relied exclusively on negation; in so doing, they were not
even able to ensure that the struggle would be continued, because in
complex and advanced societies the majority of people want to know
what is being proposed. Even though it is oppressed and alienated, the
working class does have access to means of subsistence, and is bound to
ask what will replace what is to be destroyed.

On the other hand, those who assumed positions opposed to those
of Cohn-Bendit—for instance Alain Touraine and Serge Mallet—did
not see the necessity of proposing an alternative because, according to
them, the development of productive forces and the subjective matu-
ration of the masses would make immediately possible the self-government of society. This too seems to us mistaken: for while it is true that
the development of capitalism ripens the possibility of revolution by
creating new needs and new forces, it is also true that these reflect the
system that produces them. This is why the sudden breakdown of the
system necessarily leads to a fall in production: it is an illusion to believe that socialism is the productive system inherited from capitalism
with self-government added to it. What is involved is a system of an
altogether different kind, in a national and international context that
acts and reacts upon it. This suggests the need for a transitional model,
for the construction of an alternative, for a revolutionary *project* that
constitutes the idea of the new society. One is thus driven back to the
problem of unification, of political preparation, of the party.

Sartre: It is undoubtedly true that a theory of the passage to socialism
is necessary. Suppose that the situation quickens in France or in Italy
and leads to the achievement of power. What ideas do we have as to
how a highly industrialized country can reconstruct itself on a socialist
basis, while it is subjected to foreign boycott, to the devaluation of its
currency, and to the blockade of its exports? The USSR found itself in
such a situation after the revolution. Despite the terrible sacrifices and
the enormous losses inflicted upon it by civil war, despite the political and economic encirclement that was stifling it, the problems that
the USSR had to resolve were less complex than those which would

today be confronted by an advanced society. From this point of view, none of us—and no Communist party—are prepared. You speak of the necessity of a political perspective of transition. So be it. But what Communist party has elaborated a theory of revolutionary transition in a country of advanced and nonautarchic capitalism?

Manifesto: Since the twenties, the problem of the passage to socialism has never been placed on the agenda by Communist parties in regard to advanced capitalist countries.

Sartre: Exactly. Especially not since the war and the Yalta agreements. There has therefore been no real thinking devoted to alternatives. And this is not a secondary matter if one wishes to understand what Communist parties have become. In the book of Annie Kriegel, *Les Communistes Français*, the judgment passed on the French Communist Party is on the whole a severe one; but what remains implicit is that, despite all the errors and failings that Annie Kriegel enumerates, the party, as far as she is concerned, constitutes a given alternative, notwithstanding its actual policies. Indeed, it constitutes the proletarian alternative to capitalist society in France. This reasoning makes no sense. At the point where we reach agreement in insisting on the need for the political organization of the class, we must also realize that the "historical" institutions of the Communist Party are completely inadequate for the achievement of the tasks that we try to assign to them. We were saying just now that, without a moment of unification of the struggle, without a cultural mediation and a positive response, it is impossible to go beyond revolt; and revolt is always defeated politically. We agree on that. But this does not change in any way the fact that an institutionalized party is not capable of acting as a mediator between culture and struggles: the reason being that what is still confused and nonsystematized thought in the masses (though *true* as a reflection of experience), is completely deformed once it has been translated by the ideological mechanisms of the party, and presents a totally different relation to what we call culture. In order that the schema that you propose may operate, it would be necessary that the party should continually be able to struggle against its own institutionalization. Without this, the whole schema is falsified. If the cultural apparatus of the Communist parties is practically null, the reason is not that they lack good intellectuals, but that the mode of existence of the parties paralyzes their collective effort of thought. Action and thought are not separable from the organization. One thinks as one is structured. One acts as one is organized. This is why the thought of Communist parties has come to be progressively ossified.

Manifesto: Historically, Communist parties assumed their particular character in the context of the Third International and of political and ideological events in the Soviet Union and in the socialist camp. These parties constitute a reality that has influenced the configuration of the class and which has produced certain forms of action, certain ideologies, and certain changes in existing forces. Today, however, we are witnessing a class movement which, for the first time in Europe, tends to situate itself in a dialectical relation with the Communist parties, and to identify itself with them only in part. This movement weighs upon the parties, which must either reject it or be modified by it. (The hypothesis that the movement can simply be absorbed by the party does not seem realistic to us, as is shown by the students.) In either case, the problem that is posed is that of a new manner of being of the party, either through crisis and the renewal of existing parties, or through a new construction of the unitary political expression of the class. Is such a new manner of being possible? Is a party fated to become progressively institutionalized and to detach itself from the movement that gave birth to it, as you suggested at the beginning, or can one conceive of an organization that would be capable of fighting continually against the limitations, the sclerosis, and the institutionalization that threatens it from within?

Sartre: While I recognize the need of an organization, I must confess that I don't see how the problems that confront any stabilized structure could be resolved.

Manifesto: To summarize what you have just said, the political party would need to ensure the growth and the autonomy of mass struggles instead of restraining them; it should also ensure the development of a counterculture; and it should finally know how to oppose a global, total response to the type of rationality and to the social relations upon which society rests. These are, it seems, specific tasks of the party, insofar as their global character transcends the problems that the specific moment of struggle and the fused group can resolve.

Sartre: Yes, but these cannot be resolved without the party either.

Manifesto: Agreed. In order to get out of this, one may advance some hypotheses. Before all else, the revolutionary party must, so that it may escape institutionalization, consider itself as permanently *in the service* of a struggle that has its *own* dimensions, its own autonomous political levels. This implies the transcendence of the Leninist or Bolshevik model of the party—from its origins to the Popular Fronts—according to which there is supposed to exist a constant separation between the moment of a mass struggle purely concerned with specific demands and the political moment, which is specific to the party. In history, this transcendence has only been sketched out in the "soviets." It corresponds to a model of a *social* revolution rather than a purely *political* one, a revolution where power is taken by the soviets and not by the party. Moreover, the revolutionary movement must transcend an inadequacy of Leninism: the theory of revolution has until now been a "theory of the seizure of power" much more than a "theory of society." The result has been an inability of Communist parties to analyze advanced capitalist societies and to foreshadow the goals that the revolution must reach; in other words, an inability to understand the new needs expressed by the movement and to say how they are to be satisfied. (This is what happened with the students: there was neither understanding of nor a solution to the problems that they posed on the role of education, its relation to society, the modes and content of a nonauthoritarian type of education). Thirdly, there is the need for permanent probing so that theory should be able to encompass all features of the movement. A political organization of the class which claims to be Marxist does not merely think *a posteriori*; it interprets experience through a methodology, a grid—in regard to such categories as "capital," "class," "imperialism," etc. Thus, insofar as the relation between party and class remains open—and this alone is capable of preventing both the particularism of a fragmented experience and the institutionalization of the unifying political moment—one needs to find a solution to these three problems.

Sartre: I agree, on condition that this dialectic manifests itself as a dual power, and that one does not claim to solve it within a purely political schema. Even then, there are many problems that remain. You speak of a methodological or a theoretical "grid," provided as it were in advance and through which experience may be interpreted. But is it not the case that the concept of *capital* remains a thin and abstract notion if one does not constantly elaborate anew the analysis of modern capitalism by research and by the permanent critique of the results of research and of struggle? *True* thought is certainly *one*: but its unity is dialectical—it is a living reality in the process of formation. What is required is the construction of a relationship between men that guarantees not only freedom, but *revolutionary* freedom of thought—a relationship that enables men to appropriate knowledge completely and to criticize it. This, in any case, is how knowledge has always proceeded, but it is never how the "Marxism" of Communist parties has proceeded. So that the creative culture of its members may grow and in order to enable them to acquire a maximum of true knowledge, the party—the political organization of the class—must make it possible for them to innovate and to engage in mutual argument, instead of presenting itself as the administrator of acquired knowledge. If one looks outside the party, the debate on Marxism has never been richer than it is now because, particularly since the break-up of monolithism and the posing of the problem of the diversity of socialism, there exists a plurality of Marxist inquiries and open disagreements between them.

Manifesto: But these are disagreements on the exegesis of sacred texts, quarrels of interpretation, rather than a renewal of inventiveness and of a creative interpretation of reality.

Sartre: That is not altogether true. Of course, the discussion on the texts predominates. But take the example of Althusser: he is not simply involved in exegesis. One finds in him a theory of the concept, of autonomous theoretical knowledge, of the study of contradictions from the angle of the dominant contradiction, or "overdetermination." These are original inquiries, which cannot be criticized without a new theoretical elaboration. Personally, I have been compelled, in order to criticize Althusser, to look again at the idea of "notion" and to draw a series of conclusions in the process. The same may be said about the concept of "structure" introduced by Lévi-Strauss, which some Marxists, whether fruitfully or not, have tried to use. In other words, a real discussion always demands an effort and leads to new theoretical results. If what is wanted is genuine inquiry, one must therefore set up a structure that guarantees discussion; without this, even the theoretical model that the political organization would wish to place before the experience of the class remains inoperative. This is a permanent contradiction in the party: in fact, it is a limitation of all Communist parties.

Just as complex is the hypothesis of an "open" relation between a unifying political organization of the class, i.e., the party, and the self-government of the masses in councils or soviets. We must not forget that when this was attempted, in postrevolutionary Russia, the unitary organizations of the masses rapidly disappeared, and only the party remained. Thus a dialectically necessary process resulted, in the USSR, in the party taking the power that should have been taken and kept by the soviets. It may be that it could be otherwise today but in the years of encirclement of the USSR by capitalist countries, in conditions of civil war and dreadful internal shortages, it is not too difficult to understand the process whereby the soviets completely disappeared. This is the reason why I have occasionally written that in the USSR, it is of a dictatorship *for* the proletariat rather than *of* the proletariat that one should speak, in the sense that the party assumed the task of destroying the bourgeoisie on behalf of the proletariat. It was, moreover, unavoidable that, in order that the USSR should survive, the proletariat, as has happened wherever there has been a revolution, should find itself asked to renounce what were, before the revolution, the most specific objectives of its struggle, namely an increase in its wages and the reduction in the hours of work. It could not have been otherwise, for it would have been difficult for the workers themselves to give up these objectives, even if they had experienced self-government at their place of work. Finally, to speak of what is relevant today, it seems to me difficult for an organization of soviets or councils to be created when there exists a strong "historical" articulation of the working class, in the form of trade unions or the party. In France, we have had the experience of committees of action. But these were quickly dissolved, not because they were prohibited but because the trade unions soon resumed control of the situation.

Manifesto: This last contradiction does not seem insurmountable. Every trade union struggle that involves not only negotiations about wages but also about rhythms of work, hours, the organization of work and its control, shows the need for *direct* forms of organization of the workers. Without a unitary assembly at the base, possessed of an autonomous character and a high political level, negotiations on this scale cannot be undertaken. It is in this sense the trade union struggle that compels the rediscovery of the problem of the direct institutions of the class. This is a matter of experience, not an intellectual invention. Of course, these new forms come up against conservatism and bureaucracy. But one must also take into account certain limitations which are part of their being. From this point of view, the Italian experience is interesting: between the party or the union on the one hand and the movement on the other, the alternative is not always, as you were suggesting, either rejection or reduction to the role of a transmission belt. We are here confronted with a social tension, which assumes its own forms and which, at the same time, weighs upon the traditional institutions of the class, without finding a point of equilibrium either in the first or in the second. In fact, while the limitations of the union exist and are known, the institutions of direct democracy also have their limitations: though they do, in general, function perfectly well during a period of agitation, as happened at Fiat during the recent struggles, they run the risk of subsequently becoming, unconsciously, the instruments of a separation between one group and another, one enterprise and another, and therefore of being useful to the management. And does not the union, at that point and despite all its limitations, constitute a defense against the fragility of the new institutions? In effect, the movement appears today richer and more complex than its political expression.

Sartre: At any rate, what seems to me interesting in your schema is the duality of power that it foreshadows. This means an open and irreducible relation between the *unitary* moment, which falls to the political organization of the class, and the moments of self-government, the councils, the fused groups. I insist on that word "irreducible" because there can only be a permanent tension between the two moments. The party will always try, to the degree that it wants to see itself as "in the service" of the movement, to reduce it to its own schema of interpretation and development; while the moments of self-government will always try to project their living partiality upon the contradictory complex of the social tissue. It is in this struggle, maybe, that can be expressed the beginning of a reciprocal transformation; however, that transformation—if it is to remain revolutionary—cannot but go in the direction of a progressive dissolution of the political element in a society that not only tends toward unification but also toward self-government, that is to say, which seeks to accomplish a social revolution that abolishes, together with the state, all other specifically *political* moments. In short, this is a dialectic so oriented as to bring us back to the schema of development of Marx. Up to now, it has not happened; but it may be that the conditions for it are beginning to exist in the societies of advanced capitalism. This is, in any case, a hypothesis on which to work.

MARX AND ENGELS ON THE REVOLUTIONARY PARTY

August H. Nimtz

E ngels began his brief remarks at Marx's funeral in 1883 by describing his lifelong political companion's "scientific" accomplishments. "But he looked upon science above all things as a grand historical lever, as a revolutionary power in the most eminent sense of the word . . . For he was indeed, what he called himself, a Revolutionist."[1] As his closest collaborator, Engels knew better than anyone about this indispensable dimension of Marx's project. If it wasn't enough, as the young Marx had concluded in 1845, to "interpret the world" but it was also necessary "to change it," then action and organization were essential. Yet nowhere did Marx lay out a set of clearly articulated principles for revolutionary organization. But if all of his organized political activities are examined— along with those of Engels after Marx's death—this essay demonstrates it is possible to distill in broad outlines the norms that guided Marx's approach to revolutionary organizing.

Almost fifty years ago, in the 1967 *Socialist Register*, Monty Johnstone performed an invaluable service in synthesizing for the first time— certainly in English—Marx and Engels's views on the revolutionary party.[2] But aside from materials Johnstone didn't have access to when he published his still quite valuable essay (above all the *Marx-Engels Collected Works* [*MECW*], the most complete compilation of their writings in any language), it's now easier to verify citations of their writings and, more importantly, to see the larger context in which the citations were originally written. Also, much has passed in real world politics since 1967, not least the collapse of the Soviet Union and its satellite regimes after 1989, reigniting much-debated questions (which Johnstone didn't address) about whether the actions of Lenin, let alone Stalin and his successors, were consistent with the views of Marx and Engels. For today's activists, what are—the question Marx and Engels would have posed—the organizational lessons inspired by their example?

THE COMMUNIST CORRESPONDENCE COMMITTEES

Once the Marx-Engels partnership was formed and armed with a jointly written theoretical statement, *The German Ideology* (1845–1846), the next task, as Engels recounted four decades later, was "to win over the European, and in the first place the German, proletariat to our conviction."[3] Growing evidence that revolutionary winds were about to blow across Europe made that an urgent undertaking. Political clarity and differentiation—the need to know who was committed to a revolutionary course, potential comrades; and who not, potential opponents—was necessary. The means for doing so was the Communist Correspondence Committees, established by the Marx-Engels team at the beginning of 1846 in Brussels where the two lived, their first organizational venture.[4] Named after the internationally oriented Jacobinic Corresponding Societies, the Committees' mission was to promote communication (Jenny, Marx's wife, constituted the secretariat) and "impartial criticism" between self-styled socialist and communist currents in various European settings in order to be acquainted with one another "when the moment for action comes."[5] This international character became a hallmark of the Marx-Engels team's subsequent political activities, as did the emphasis on communication and discussion not for its own sake, but for "when the moment of action comes." There's no evidence that the Committees were guided, at least initially, by formal rules; they were clearly a work in progress.[6] The Committees, at least the Brussels chapter that Marx and Engels headed, tolerated diverse, and even contradictory, views, and disputes (such as Marx had with Wilhelm Weitling in March 1846) were settled by a simple majority vote, without the losers being expelled or even expected to leave.

A request for advice from a hopeful organizer of a German Committee branch gave Marx and Engels the opportunity to formulate their first joint political and organizational statement—positions that would forever inform their practice. Their two-and-a-half-page letter to Gustave Köttgen, dated June 15, 1846, constitutes a foundational document for what came to be called, by friend and foe, "the Marx party."

The organizational advice—the need for regular meetings where discussions and debates informed by "communist" literature could take
place, for a movement that financed itself and didn't privilege, materi-
ally, its "authors," that had a clearly defined membership, that should
convene a delegated congress only after real work at the local level,
and free of "personal considerations"—anticipated norms they'd em-
ploy in all subsequent political activities. In addition to organizational
advice, Köttgen wanted political direction—whether workers should
petition Prussian authorities to win reforms. That would only be effective, Marx and Engels replied, "if there already existed in Germany
a strong and organized Communist Party, but neither is the case." In
the postscript, they proposed a remedy—take part in the petition campaigns of the bourgeoisie:

> Join them for the time being in public demonstrations, proceed jes-
> uitically, put aside Teutonic probity, true-heartedness and decency,
> and sign and push forward the bourgeois petitions for freedom of
> the press, a constitution, and so on. When this has been achieved a
> new era will dawn for c[ommunist] propaganda. Our means will be
> increased, the antithesis between bourgeoisie and proletariat will be
> sharpened.

This idea of how the nascent communist movement in Germany
should relate to the bourgeoisie for the democratic revolution would
remain at the very core of Marx and Engels's lifelong politics. As Engels explained in 1892: "Marx and I, for forty years, repeated ad nau-
seam that for us the democratic republic is the only political form in
which the struggle between the working class and the capitalist class
can first be universalized and then culminate in the decisive victory
of the proletariat." In many ways, their letter anticipated Lenin's *What
is to be Done?* (1902), which too offered an answer for how to construct a countrywide social democratic or Communist party for the
first time in a setting where the democratic and not the socialist revolution was on the immediate agenda. The advice for regular meetings,
a determinate membership, having "communist" literature to forge
such a movement, and the need for workers to join with other classes
(including the bourgeoisie) to fight for political democracy was later
captured in the spirit of Lenin's famous pamphlet. And not the least,
in quintessential Leninist sensibility, an organization meant for "when
the moment of action comes."

THE COMMUNIST LEAGUE

The short-lived Communist Correspondence Committees' most con-sequential achievement was to bring Marx and Engels in contact with Western Europe's most class conscious workers. Having bested in de-bate the utopian ideas and schemas that many of them subscribed to, the two middle-class revolutionaries were increasingly seen as a pole of attraction. In early 1847, the League of the Just, the mainly Ger-man exile worker/artisan group founded in 1836 and with branches in London, Paris, and elsewhere, invited the two to join them. Marx and Engels agreed but on one condition—that the League end its conspira-torial modus operandi. The leadership readily agreed, since the organ-ization had already done so. In turn, the two had to make clear what their "plans" were and how they would "go about achieving" them; also, they were expected to commit to the proletarian discipline of the forces they had now fused with. Two delegated conferences in 1847 resulted, at Marx and Engels's urging, in the organization's renaming, now the Communist League.

For its organizational norms, which included the stipulation that membership entailed "revolutionary energy and zeal in propaganda" and "subordination to the decisions of the League,"[7] Marx and Engels proposed only two changes, both of which were adopted. The first was that the delegated congress, "the legislative authority" to which the League's Central Authority (its "executive organ") was subordi-nate, should be the organization's supreme authority. The second, that members be allowed to join other organizations to advance the Com-munist League's agenda, made it possible for Marx and Engels to help organize and be active in the broader workers' movement and the petit bourgeois democratic associations on behalf of the League in Brussels, Paris, and eventually Cologne. The Brussels duo was also commis-sioned to compose a theoretical/action program for the League. When Marx failed to deliver on time what came to be called the *Manifesto of the Communist Party*, fellow Central Authority leaders warned that "measures would be taken" if he didn't get it written—evidence that he was indeed subordinate to the discipline of the League. Never before in the annals of the class struggle had the toilers displayed such self-con-fidence vis-à-vis their literary representatives—powerful testimony to what distinguished the proletariat from other toilers.

The ink was barely dry on the *Manifesto* when the long-expected upheavals in Europe erupted. Once Paris exploded in February 1848, followed by Vienna, and, shortly afterwards, Berlin, it became increasingly apparent that a new era had dawned, whatever the outcome. "The European Spring" made centuries-old autocratic rule an endangered species. The League's leadership realized that it needed to supplement the *Manifesto* and commissioned, once again, Marx and Engels to compose *The Demands of the Communist Party in Germany*. As Marx explained years later, both documents were written for "the Communist Party," that is, "the party in the broad historical sense" of which the League "was simply an episode."[8] The organizational expression of "the party" could therefore take different forms and names in time and place. Marx's understanding of "the party" helps to clarify what one key sentence in the *Manifesto* actually means—that communists aren't sectarian towards the workers' movement: "The Communists do not form a separate party opposed to other working-class parties."[9]

Armed with a concrete program, the Central Authority of the League organized its forces for a return to Germany in April 1848. *The Demands*, seventeen in number and two pages in length, recognized that a bourgeois democratic revolution was on Germany's immediate agenda and not a socialist revolution. That meant aligning the worker's movement with the peasantry and the petite bourgeoisie during its course. In leading the League for the duration of the German Revolution, Marx and Engels made their first venture into the electoral arena. Having been conferred by the Central Authority with "full discretionary power" for the direction of the League until "the next congress," Marx decided sometime in the summer of 1848 to put the organization on hold.[10] Forging the "people's alliance," the worker-peasant-petit bourgeois coalition to fight for the democratic revolution, in his opinion could best be done through the editorial board of the Cologne-based *Neue Rheinische Zeitung*, the newspaper Marx began publishing on June 1. Too many of the League's members were still operating in a conspiratorial manner, or had become absorbed in the larger democratic movement, or simply had dropped out of politics. Though Marx and his comrades did all they could to push Germany's democratic revolution to fruition, it became increasingly clear in the first months of 1849 that the process was ebbing. Marx and Engels and the rest of the League leadership were forced to relocate to London by September.

An essential task was to draw a balance sheet on the previous year and a half and to prepare for an expected revival of Europe's "Spring." Marx and Engels's *Address of the Central Authority to the League, March 1850* drew the key lessons of the upheavals: first, the liberal bourgeoisie could not be counted on to push forward the bourgeois democratic revolution (the *Manifesto* held open the possibility that it could be); and second, the petite bourgeoisie could not be trusted. Yet, it would be with the latter that the still small working class would have to ally in the expected renewal to overthrow "the reactionary party." To avoid betrayal, workers would have to be organized "independently," a word that appears on virtually every one of the document's eleven pages: hence, a self-criticism of the decision to suspend the League in the course of pursuing an alliance with the petite bourgeoisie.

The *Address* advised the workers' movement and the League to have "unconcealed mistrust in the new government" that would issue from the overthrow of the old regime. "Alongside the new official governments they must immediately establish their own revolutionary workers' governments, whether in the form of . . . municipal councils . . . workers' committees etc."—what Lenin would later call "dual power." The document also advised on how the League should conduct itself in the electoral arena during the next upheaval. It should run League members, when possible, as candidates "even where there is no prospect whatever of their being elected" and not be persuaded by the petite bourgeoisie that in so doing "they are splitting the democratic party and giving the reactionaries the possibility of victory"—in other words, the time-worn wasted vote/lesser-evil argument. There was more to be gained than to be lost for the long-term interests of the workers' movement in independent electoral action—an opportunity "to count their forces and to lay before the public their revolutionary attitude and party standpoint."

That this advice followed almost immediately details on how workers should be "armed and organized" made clear why there was this need "to count their forces." Only an independently organized and armed working class could assure that the next revolution in Germany would be, in the very last words of the document, "The Revolution in Permanence"—that is, a socialist revolution.[11] Along with the letter to Köttgen and the *Manifesto*, the *Address* constitutes the third key document in the Marx-Engels arsenal on the organizational question.[12] Significantly,

Lenin committed it to memory and "used to delight in quoting" it.[13] I argue that with regard to "dual power," independent electoral action, and armed organization of the proletariat, the *Address* informed, unlike any other of their writings, the Bolshevik course in 1917. It is thus crucial in explaining the Bolsheviks' success in leading Russia's workers and peasants to power in October—the first time ever anywhere.[14]

THE INTERNATIONAL WORKINGMEN'S ASSOCIATION

After a more than decade-long lull in Europe's revolutionary process and the end of the Communist League, the United States Civil War (1861–1865) brought the Marx party back into active public political work. The precipitating issue was whether Europe's proletariat should follow their ruling classes in supporting the southern slavocracy. Textile workers in England, many of whom had been made redundant by the Union blockade of Confederate cotton, said no, much to the joy of Marx and Engels. Working-class opposition to the pro-Confederacy interventionist sentiments of Europe's ruling classes registered the growing recognition that the proletariat needed its own foreign policy—not only for the Civil War, but also for other international issues such as Polish and Italian self-determination. That sentiment spurred the establishment of the International Workingmen's Association (IWA), which would become known as the First International.[15] Since Marx had already put aside work on his long-promised magnum opus, *Capital*, to mount a "struggle in the press" against supporters of the Confederacy, it didn't take much convincing to get him on board for the project's founding in London in September 1864. This was especially so because, as he explained to his comrades, "real workers' leaders" were so centrally involved. Coming out of the broadly sponsored London meeting that called for fraternal ties among Europe's proletariat, to which Marx had been invited as the representative of the German workers' movement, was the decision that the various national representatives compose a mission statement and organizational norms. That Marx was in a position to draft the founding documents for the new body reflected the experience and skills he had acquired in the 1848–49 upsurge, as well as informal organizational ties he maintained even while concentrating during the 1850s on "scientific work." Marx was able to quickly emerge as "the acknowledged leader" of the International Workingmen's Association from 1864–72, as Engels would put it at his comrade's funeral, the "crowning effort" of his revolutionary work.

The political conclusion Marx and Engels drew from 1848 concerning the indispensability of independent working-class political action directly informed the *Inaugural Address* and the *Provisional Rules of the Association* Marx drafted. After surveying, in the former, Europe's economic reality following the demise of the 1848–49 upheavals, Marx pointed not only to the growing inequalities between "the industrial masses" and the capitalists but also to the gains workers had made, particularly in England, to defend their class interests. "Yet," in words that resonate all too well today, "the lords of the land and the lords of capital will always use their political privileges for the defense and perpetuation of their economical monopolies. So far from promoting, they will continue to lay every possible impediment in the way of the emancipation of labor." There was only one answer to this, Marx concluded: "To conquer political power has therefore become the great duty of the working classes." And in the opening sentence of the preface to the accompanying rules for the new organization, he wrote: "The emancipation of the working classes must be conquered by the working classes themselves."[16]

These claims became the axis around which Marx's work for the next decade in the IWA revolved. When his drafts were adopted unanimously by the other national representatives to the London meeting, Engels, who lived in Manchester, was surprised that his partner could write something that could pass muster with all of the diverse political tendencies represented at the initial gathering. It wasn't that difficult, Marx replied, "because we are dealing with 'workers' all the time." His modus operandi, as he described it to Engels, was *fortiter en re, suaviter en modo*, strong in deed and mild in manner—what allowed him to become the new organization's unofficial head.

Within weeks of the IWA's founding, Marx, a member of the General Council (GC), its executive and highest decision-making body in between congresses, moved to enforce the norm that introduced the body's just-adopted rules. When a prominent lawyer sought a seat on the GC, it became clear that not all had fully understood what Marx proposed. Yet Marx was able to convince other members to reject the request. "I believe him an honest and sincere man; at the same time, he is nothing and can be nothing save a Bourgeois politician." Exactly

because the suitor aspired to a seat in Parliament, "he ought to be excluded from entering our committee. We cannot become *le piedestal*
for small parliamentary ambitions. . . . [Otherwise] others of his class
will follow, and our efforts, till now successful at freeing the English
working class movement from all middle class or aristocratic patronage,
will have been in vain."[17] From its commencement Marx opposed any
attempts to turn the IWA into an electoral conduit for any class other
than the proletariat; whether it should and could be such a vehicle even
for the proletariat was a discussion and debate that lay ahead.

. Exactly because of the diverse currents and tendencies that came together to form the IWA—unlike in the case of the Communist League—
it required a fairly flexible organizational framework. To accommodate
that heterogeneity in such a way as to secure political homogeneity was
certainly Marx and Engels's long-term goal, not unlike their approach
to the Correspondence Committees. Differences about the appropriate
norms for such a framework provoked the most famous fight within
the IWA, between the "Marx party" and Mikhail Bakunin's anarchist
current.[18] It began with Bakunin's proposal to the GC in 1868 to erect
alongside the IWA a parallel body of anarchist affiliates. Marx demurred:
such an arrangement would be a threat to the IWA's sovereignty, or, as
Engels put it, "a state within the state." The rest of the GC, without exception, agreed with this, seeing that by operating independently of the
GC, Bakunin's network could avoid engaging other sections in debate
and common work—the necessary process toward political homogeneity—and could insulate his forces from the arguments of Marx's current
and, of course, the discipline of the GC.

Bakunin tried another angle in response. He was prepared to dis-
band his network if the GC was willing to approve its program—a not
too subtle attempt to have his anarchist views be made official IWA
policy. Marx saw through the ruse and responded tactfully and adroitly.
The sections of the would-be disbanded network could be admitted to
the IWA as individual affiliates. As for their programmatic views, he
pointed out that given the heterogeneous character of the forces that
comprised the organization it was to be expected that "their theoretical
notions, which reflect the real movement, should also diverge." At the
same time, "the exchange of ideas facilitated by the public organs of
the different national sections, and the direct debates at the [congresses],
are sure by and by to engender a common theoretical program." Thus,

there was no need for the GC to rule on any section's program as long as "its *general tendency* does not run against" that of the International, *"the complete emancipation of the working class."*[19]

Engels explained to a Bakunin protégé the advantages of a theoretically diverse IWA at this stage in its development:

> Our power lies in the liberality with which the [IWA's] first rule is interpreted, namely that all men who are admitted aim for the complete emancipation of the working classes. . . . Unfortunately the Bakuninists, with the narrowness of mentality common to all sects, were not satisfied with this. In their view the [GC] consisted of reactionaries, the program of the Association was too vague. Atheism and materialism . . . had to become compulsory, the abolition of inheritance and the state, etc., had to be part of our program . . . But to put all these things into our program would mean alienating an enormous number of our members, and dividing rather than uniting the European proletariat.[20]

A more programmatically open organization was the means, through discussions and debates, to "engender a common theoretical program."

Bakunin's assurances notwithstanding, he reconstituted his supposedly disbanded network as a secret organization—which explains in part his next move. At the Basel Congress of the IWA in 1869, the only one he ever attended, Bakunin vigorously campaigned to have the powers of the GC vis-à-vis the sections of the IWA be expanded—a very surprising move which, as Hal Draper convincingly shows, indicated that Bakunin was planning a takeover of the GC by his partisans.[21] The proposal, like his two other organizational initiatives, was defeated. Bakunin's machinations eventually led to the expulsion of his current from the IWA at the Hague Congress in 1872. Marx and Engels were able to present enough evidence to convince delegates that the anarchist leader had organized a covert operation against the GC, in clear violation of the international's rules. Documents discovered since then make for an even more damning case. Bakunin, Draper instructively points out, has the dubious distinction of having formed "the first leftist movement to apply its conspiratorial pattern of subversion not to assail society at large or to defend itself against the police, but to destroy other socialists' organizations."[22]

Only on two occasions were the political rather than organizational differences between the Marxists and Bakunin's current in the IWA publicly debated. One came at an expanded GC meeting in London in September 1871. Due largely to the impact of the Paris Commune five months earlier—Marx's *The Civil War in France*, written for the IWA, distilled its political significance—Marx and Engels made their most forceful case to date in favor of workers forming their own political parties and participating in the electoral and parliamentary arenas: that is, independent working-class political action, the core of their *Address of March, 1850* as well as the key point Marx wrote into the IWA's founding documents. "To preach abstention" from political action, as Engels accused the Bakuninists of doing, "would be to push [workers] into the arms of bourgeois politics. Especially in the aftermath of the Paris Commune, which placed the political action of the proletariat on the agenda, abstention is quite impossible."[23] They won not only the majority of the GC to their position but also the delegates to The Hague Congress less than a year later.

The other occasion for a public airing of political differences with the Bakuninists came when the latter, in response to one of the decisions of the 1871 London Conference—specifically, the condemnation of the covert operation—charged the GC with being "authoritarian." It argued that the International, "embryo of the future human society, must be, from now on, the faithful image of our principles of liberty and federation." Marx and Engels, on behalf of the GC, countered that the IWA or any revolutionary organization could not serve as a model for a socialist society since it was absurd to think that the working classes could organize itself to take and defend state power without the centralization of authority. Drawing on the lessons of the Paris Commune, they noted sarcastically that, according to Bakunin's logic, the "Communards would not have failed if they had understood that the Commune was 'the embryo of the future human society' and had cast away all discipline and all arms, that is, the things which must disappear when there are no more wars!"[24]

Largely in response to Bakunin's subterfuges, Marx and Engels initiated and supported moves in the GC to make it more disciplined and centralized. Both steps were not, however, ends in themselves. When in July 1872 the GC codified the IWA's administrative rules, Engels proposed that the right of the GC to suspend sections be surrounded with safeguards to ensure, as Marx said at the same meeting, that the GC "never could constitute itself a power in opposition to the Associ-

ation."[25] Whether the IWA would have become an organization with
the kind of centralization, discipline and political homogeneity of the
Communist League will never be known. The IWA's move to the
United States after The Hague gathering—Marx and Engels's solution
to keep the Bakuninists at bay—effectively meant, in hindsight, its de
facto end.[26]

Marx and Engels, especially Marx, spent more time in the IWA
than any other political formation, and it is therefore the richest source
for examining their organizational norms. It is noteworthy that during
the entire course of its existence they almost never referred to "our
party" or the "Marx party" as a faction within the IWA. This suggests
that they saw the IWA itself as *their party*, or more correctly, their party
in the making. Indeed, in a highly didactic letter to a supporter in the
United States, Marx distilled the essence of the political struggle: "The
political movement of the working class naturally has as its final object the conquest of political power for this class, and this requires, of
course, a previous organization of the working class developed up to a
certain point, which arises from the economic struggles themselves."[27]
For the working class to seize political power, in other words, it must
have an organization already in place.

AFTER THE INTERNATIONAL
WORKINGMEN'S ASSOCIATION

The victory Marx and Engels scored at The Hague in having the IWA
call for working-class political action helped plant the seeds for Europe's mass working-class political parties. While much would need to
be done to make that call a reality, it nevertheless gave those predis-
posed to move in that direction the authority (i.e., the prestige of the
IWA) to go forth boldly. The end of the IWA, Marx and Engels soon
recognized, allowed the various sections to do the necessary spadework
at the national level to make the next round in international organizing more fruitful—to recall the advice they gave to Köttgen almost
thirty years earlier, not to rush prematurely into holding a national
congress for the German sections of the Correspondence Committees.

The German movement, which was in the vanguard beginning in
1869, revealed after a decade of organizing that the "independent" in
the independent working-class political action formula was very much
a work in progress. Marx and Engels became increasingly concerned

about what was taking place and wrote a stinging critique of the leadership's conduct, above all for its opportunism (what would later be called revisionism or reformism). Generally known as the *Circular Letter of 1879*, it constitutes—after the Köttgen letter, the *Manifesto*, the *1850 Address*, the *Inaugural Address*, and the *Civil War in France*—one of their major programmatic statements. Not intended for public eyes, the letter reprimanded the German leaders for bending, as a way to make the party more popular, to petit bourgeois interests at the expense of those of the proletariat. One of the addressees was the young Edward Bernstein, who would later lead the revisionist charge against the revolutionary strategy of the two founders of the modern communist movement.

A major issue the *Circular* raised spoke to an organizational matter, specifically how to make the party's Reichstag group or *Fraktion* accountable to the party as a whole—a challenge that would bedevil many a twentieth/twenty-first-century workers' party wherever it had a parliamentary group. Engels came to the defense of a rank-and-file member who charged a Reichstag representative with having violated the party's principles by voting for one of Chancellor Otto Bismarck's capitalism-from-above ventures. But the bigger problem for Marx and Engels was the uproar among the party leadership that the critique had been issued at all: "[H]as German Social-Democracy indeed been infected with the parliamentary disease, believing that, with the popular vote, the Holy Ghost is poured upon those elected, that meetings of the [*Fraktion*] are transformed into infallible councils and factional resolutions into sacrosanct dogma?"[28] To combat the "disease" of "parliamentary cretinism," as Engels had called it in 1850, the party had to uphold the norm that parliamentary representatives be subordinate to the will of the party rank and file.

The *Circular* reveals that even before Marx's death in 1883 it fell largely to Engels, its main author, to counsel the new parties—a "bounden duty that brooks no delay," as he put it less than a year before his own death in 1895. His advice to a supporter in Denmark in 1889 about the value of internal party debate is exemplary: "No party can live and prosper unless moderate and extreme tendencies grow up and even combat one another within its ranks." In the absence of "convincing proof of *activities* harmful to the party," it would be an act of "imprudence," he opined a year later, if the leadership of the German party expelled a group of its critics. Context, as always with Marx and Engels, was primary. When Bismarck's Anti-Socialist Law, in place from 1878-90, forced the German party into a virtually underground existence while permitting its *Fraktion* room for maneuver, "the parliamentary group's dictatorship . . . was essential and excellently managed."[29] But once the prohibition ended, it was "imperative that the chaps should at long last throw off the habit of handling the party officials—their servants—with kid gloves and kow-towing to them as infallible bureaucrats, instead of confronting them critically."[30]

> The party is so big that complete freedom of discussion within its ranks is imperative. . . . [It] cannot remain in existence unless every shade of opinion is allowed complete freedom of expression. . . . Do not make martyrs unnecessarily, show that there is freedom of criticism, and if you have to throw anyone out, do so in cases where the facts—OVERT ACTS of turpitude and betrayal—are quite blatant and completely demonstrable. . . . One must give the rotten elements time to become so rotten that they defect virtually on their own accord. The discipline of a party numbered in millions is quite different from that of a sect numbered in hundreds.[31]

Freedom of expression also required "a *formally* independent party press . . . which is not *directly* dependent on the Executive or even the Party Congress, i.e. which is in a position unreservedly to oppose individual party measures *within* the programme and accepted tactics, and freely to criticize that programme and those tactics, within the limits of party decorum."[32] *Nota bene* Engels's italicized/small capitalization "activities," "facts," and "overt acts." As was true when Marx asked Andreas Gottschalk to tender his resignation from the Communist League four decades earlier, actions and not opinions were the condition for party membership.

Engels was elated when the workers' movement in England began finally in 1892 to break with the Liberal Party, allowing him to reaffirm the most basic of the Marx party's organizational principles: "We have one firm rule for all modern countries and for all times and that is to prevail upon the workers to form their own independent party in opposition to all bourgeois parties."[33] The Social Democratic Party of Germany, the largest of the workers' parties, which he and Marx helped nurture, was the paragon. But he objected, five months before his death, to what he detected as the leadership's quest for "absolute legality" at the expense of the right to armed struggle: "You have nothing to gain by advocating complete abstention from force. Nobody would believe you, *nor* would *any* party in any country go so far as to forfeit the right to resist illegality by force of arms. . . . Not legality at any price, not even as a manner of speech!"[34] In hindsight, his admonition anticipated the reformist course of twentieth-century German Social Democracy.

As national parties emerged in the wake of the IWA, there were understandable urges to resurrect the IWA. Engels declared in 1874 that "the next International," unlike the IWA, "will be directly Communist" but only "after Marx's writings have been at work for some years." Thus, it was too soon to take the leap even by 1882. Wait, he cautioned, for

> when events in Europe provoke it. . . . Such events are already taking shape in Russia where the avant-garde of the revolution will be going into battle. You should—or so we think—wait for this and its inevitable repercussions on Germany, and then the moment will also have come for a big manifesto and the establishment of an *official*, formal International which can, however, no longer be a propaganda association but simply an association for action.[35]

By 1900 a new organization, the Socialist, or Second, International, was in place, grouping affiliates in at least most European countries. The International's most consequential action was helping to nurture a Russian party, whose left wing would come to be what Engels had predicted, "the avant-garde of the revolution . . . going into battle." Notably, in Lenin's debates with the so-called Economists in 1901, he countered their view that political agitation and building revolutionary organizations weren't essential in quiescent times: "It is precisely in such periods and under such circumstances that work of this kind is particularly necessary, since it is too late to form the organization in times of explosion and outbursts; the party must be in a state of readiness to launch activity at a moment's notice."[36] In this he sounded very much like Marx had in his 1871 letter to the IWA's supporter in the US. Many of the positions Marx and Engels took about how the IWA should function—at least the GC if not the body as a whole—particularly the need for more centralization and discipline in the wake of the Bakunin operation, anticipated norms that Lenin would espouse and practice in the course of leading the Bolshevik party to the Russian Revolution of October 1917.

The defeat of the German Revolution in 1919—along with the murders of Rosa Luxemburg and Karl Liebknecht—tragically confirmed the long-term perspective that Lenin shared with Marx and Engels on party building: unless the working class had a "previous organization" to take power, it would be "too late" to try to construct one in the heat of revolutionary turbulence. In founding the Communist, or Third, International in Moscow in 1919, the Bolsheviks under Lenin's leadership did exactly what Engels foresaw: "the establishment of an official, formal International . . . an association for action" and one that "will be directly Communist." Inspired by the Bolshevik example and most cognizant of the political degeneration and betrayal of the Socialist International—specifically, the vote of the parliamentary representatives of the vast majority of its affiliates (with the German party in the lead) to fund the First World War—the Communist International at its Second Congress in 1920 adopted a set of party organizational norms required for affiliation—the so-called "Twenty-One Conditions." At the Third Congress in 1921 delegates debated and voted on a set of theses on party organizational principles, "democratic centralism" being of primary importance.[37] Regarding the "Theses on the Organizational Structure of the Communist Parties" adopted at the Third Congress, Lenin, a year later at the Fourth Congress, said the "resolution is an excellent one . . . but it is almost entirely Russian . . . too Russian, it reflects the Russian experience . . . quite unintelligible to foreigners" who "cannot be content with hanging it in a corner like an icon and praying to it."[38]

Indeed, in 1921 the Bolsheviks at their Tenth Congress had already made a fateful decision owing to the still precarious situation the Revolution faced in the immediate wake of the brutally debilitating civil war. The party overwhelming voted to temporarily suspend the right to form factions, giving more weight to centralism in the democratic centralist formula that the party had long operated under. Factions had allowed for organized challenges to the party leadership, an essential requirement for the "democratic" in the democratic centralist formula. Fifteen years later, with the advantage of hindsight, Leon Trotsky, Lenin's second in command in the October Revolution, acknowledged that the organizational means for the subsequent Stalinist counterrevolution and all of its horrors had its origins in that decision, which he too had voted for and still defended given the circumstances:

"One thing is absolutely clear: the banning of factions brought the heroic history of Bolshevism to an end and made way for its bureaucratic degeneration."

The damage went beyond the USSR. "Beginning in 1923 [Stalin's] epigones extended the banning and stifling of factional struggle from the ruling party in the USSR to the young sections of the [Communist International], thus dooming them to degeneration before they had time to grow and develop."[39] Trotsky's sober assessment, made in 1935, proved to be all too accurate: not just about the Bolshevik Party in Russia, but also about the tragic trajectory of the vast majority of parties that called themselves "Marxist," "Communist," "Leninist," or some variant in whatever corner of the planet. When the international, by then moribund, no longer served as a pawn in Stalin's diplomatic maneuvers, he unceremoniously pulled the plug on it in 1943, three years after one of his many assassins had put an ice pick into Trotsky's brain. Johnstone, in his final pages, was all too right about Stalinism in relation to the project of Marx and Engels: "There is nothing in their work to justify Stalin's attempt to present as Marxist his theory that Socialism demands a one party system, least of all in the form operated by him where a small tyrannical clique substituted itself for the working class in laying some of the foundations of Socialism."[40]

A TIMELY REVISIT?

Johnstone's classic essay in the 1967 *Socialist Register* was published amidst a swell of political agitation. Most radicalizing youth in that period chose not to embrace what they understood to be Marxist-Leninist parties—the "Old Left" versus "New Left" debate.[41] But the reality of capitalism, specifically the global financial crisis that began in 2008 and the depression-like conditions that followed in its wake, alongside the limits of the "Occupy" and other protest movements as politically effective counters to the crisis, have reawakened interest in a revolutionary party.[42]

Communist party-building in the future will involve the coming together of prior organizations that bring with them an assortment of experiences—not unlike what has happened before. Among them will be the few remaining nuclei that trace their origins to the Bolsheviks via Trotsky's Left Opposition, and who still retain Leninist organizational norms. The vast majority of those coming to the process, however, will bring very different norms and traditions (e.g., anarchists), but who increasingly recognize that protest alone isn't sufficient for real liberation. Hopefully they will be open to knowing more about the rich Marxist heritage. This is what this essay purports to aid and abet: that is, the taking and transforming of state power so as to eventually end class societies and their antagonisms, and to make it possible that, in Johnstone's final words, "the continued existence of a proletarian party would clearly be an anachronism."[43]

CLASS, PARTY, AND THE CHALLENGE
OF STATE TRANSFORMATION

LEO PANITCH AND SAM GINDIN

In 1917, not only those parties engaged in insurrectionary revolution but even those committed to gradual reform still spoke of eventually transcending capitalism. Half a century later, social democrats had explicitly come to define their political goals as compatible with a welfare-state variety of capitalism; and well before the end of the century, many who had formerly embraced the legacy of 1917 would join them in this. Yet this occurred just as the universalization of neoliberalism rendered threadbare any notion of distinct varieties of capitalism. The realism without imagination of the so-called "Third Way" was shown to lack realism as well as imagination.

However reactionary the era of neoliberal globalization has been, it has seemed to confirm the continuing revolutionary nature of the bourgeoisie, at least in terms of creating "a world after its own image."[1] Nevertheless, the financialized form of capitalism that greased the wheels not only of global investment and trade, but also of globally integrated production and consumption, was clearly crisis prone.[2] The first global capitalist crisis of the twenty-first century was rooted in the contradictions attending the new credit-dependent forms through which, amidst stagnant wages in the neoliberal era, mass consumption was sustained. Yet in sharp contrast to the two great capitalist crises of the twentieth century, as the crisis has unfolded over the past decade it did not lead to a replacement of the regime of accumulation that gave rise to it. Unlike the break with the Gold Standard regime in the 1930s and the Bretton Woods regime in the 1970s, neoliberalism persisted. This could be seen in the rescue and reproduction of financial capital, the reassertion of austerity in fiscal policy, the dependence on monetary policy for stimulus, and the further aggravation of income and wealth inequality—all of which were made possible by the continuing economic and political weaknesses of global working classes through this period.

We are now in a new conjuncture. It is a very different conjuncture than the one which led to the perception that neoliberalism, at the height of its embrace by Third Way social democracy, was "the most successful ideology in world history."[3] While neoliberal economic practices have been reproduced—as has the American empire's centrality in global capitalism—neoliberalism's legitimacy has been undermined. As the aftershocks of the US financial crash reverberated across the euro-zone and the BRICS, this deepened the multiple economic, ecological, and migratory crises that characterize this new conjuncture. At the same time, neoliberalism's ideological delegitimation has enveloped many political institutions that have sustained its practices, from the European Union to political parties at the national level. What makes the current conjuncture so dangerous is the space this has opened for the far Right, with its ultranationalist, racist, sexist, and homophobic overtones, to capture popular frustrations with liberal democratic politics in the neoliberal era.

The delegitimation of neoliberalism has restored some credibility to the radical socialist case for transcending capitalism as necessary to realize the collective, democratic, egalitarian, and ecological aspirations of humanity. It spawned a growing sense that capitalism could no longer continue to be bracketed when protesting the multiple oppressions and ecological threats of our time. And as austerity took top billing over free trade, the spirit of antineoliberal protest also shifted. Whereas capitalist globalization had defined the primary focus of oppositional forces in the first decade of the new millennium, the second decade opened with Occupy and the Indignados dramatically highlighting capitalism's gross class inequalities. Yet with this, the insurrectionary flavor of protest without revolutionary effect quickly revealed the limits of forever standing outside the state. A marked turn on the Left from protest to politics has consequently come to define the new conjuncture, as opposition to capitalist globalization shifted from the streets to the state theatres of neoliberal practice. This is in good part what the election of Syriza in Greece and the sudden emergence of Podemos in Spain signified. Corbyn's election as leader of the British Labour Party attracted hundreds of thousands of new members with the promise to sustain activism rather than undermine it. And even in the heartland of the global capitalist empire, the short bridge that spanned Occupy and Sanders's left populist promise for a political revolution "to create a government which represents all Americans and not just the 1%" was reflected in polls indicating that half of all millennials did not support capitalism and held a positive view of socialism.

This transition from protest to politics has been remarkably class oriented in terms of addressing inequality in income and wealth distribution, as well as in economic and political power relations. Yet as Andrew Murray has so incisively noted, "this new politics is generally more class-focused than class-rooted. While it places issues of social inequality and global economic power front and center, it neither emerges from the organic institutions of the class-in-itself nor advances the socialist perspective of the class-for-itself."[4] The strategic questions raised by this pertain not only to all the old difficulties of left parties maintaining a class focus once elected; they also pertain to how a class-rooted politics—in the old sense of the connection between working-class formation and political organization—could become revolutionary today. Given the manifold changes in class composition and identity, as well as the limits and failures of the old working-class parties and unions in light of these changes, what could this mean in terms of new organizational forms and practices? And what would a class-focused and class-rooted transformation of the capitalist state actually entail?

While leaders like Tsipras, Iglesias, Corbyn, and Sanders all have pointed beyond Third Way social democracy, their capacity to actually move beyond it is another matter. This partly has to do with their personal limitations, but much more with the specific limitations of each of their political parties, including even the strongest left currents within them not preparing adequately for the challenge of actually transforming state apparatuses. The experience of the Syriza government in Greece highlights this, as well as how difficult it is for governments to extricate their state apparatuses from transnational ones.

All this compels a fundamental rethink of the relationship between class, party, and state transformation. If Bolshevik revolutionary discourse seems archaic a hundred years after 1917, it is not just because the legacy of its historic demonstration that revolution was possible has faded. It is also because Gramsci's reframing, so soon after 1917, of the key issues of revolutionary strategy—especially regarding the impossibility of an insurrectionary path to power in states deeply embedded in capitalist societies—rings ever more true. What this means for socialists, however, as we face up to a long war of position in the twenty-first century, is not only the recognition of the limitations of twentieth-century Leninism. It above all requires discovering how to avoid the social democratization of even those committed to transcending capitalism. This is the central challenge for socialists today.

CLASS STRUGGLE BEFORE CLASS: THEN AND NOW

The *Communist Manifesto* of 1848 introduced a new theory of revolution. Against the conspiracies of the few and the experiments of the dreamers, an emerging proletariat was heralded with the potential to usher in a new world. The argument was not that these dispossessed laborers carried revolution in their genes; rather it pointed to their potential for organization, which was facilitated by modern means of communication as well as by the way capitalists collectivized labour. Even though their organization would be "disrupted time and again by competition amongst the workers themselves," it indeed proved to be the case that "the ever expanding union of the workers" would lead to "the organization of workers into a class, and consequently into a political party."[5]

It was this sense of class formation as process that led E.P. Thompson to argue so powerfully that class was not a static social category but a changing social relationship, which historically took shape in the form of class struggle before class. Out of the struggles of the dispossessed laborers against the new capitalist order in England in the last half of the eighteenth century and the first half of the nineteenth came the growing collective identity and community of the working class as a social force.[6] Moreover, as Hobsbawm subsequently emphasized, it was really only in the years from 1870 to 1914—as proletarianization reached a critical mass, and as workers' organizational presence developed on a national and international scale through mass socialist parties and unions—that the revolutionary potential in the working class that Marx had identified looked set to be realized.[7] However arcane the very term "workers' state" now may seem, it made sense to people in 1917—and not least to nervous bourgeoisies.

Yet there was much that made this problematic even then. The fact that so many new trade unions and workers' parties had emerged that did not aim to create socialism reflected how far even the newly organized industrial proletariat stood from revolutionary ambitions. And where there was a commitment to socialist purposes, as was ostensibly the case with the social democratic parties of the Second International, this was compromised in serious ways. The winning of workers' full franchise rights had the contradictory effect of integrating them into the nation-state, while the growing separation of leaders from led inside workers' organizations undermined not only accountability, but also the capacity to develop workers' revolutionary potentials. This was of course contested in these organizations even before Roberto Michels's famous book outlined their oligarchic tendencies.[8] But these two factors—a class-inclusive nationalism and a non-revolutionary relationship between leaders and led in class organizations—combined to determine why the catastrophic outcome of inter-imperial rivalry announced with the guns of August 1914, far from bringing about the international proletarian revolution, rather ambushed European social democracy into joining the great patriotic war and making truce in the domestic class struggle.

What made proletarian revolution ushering in a workers' state still credible after this—perhaps all the more credible—was the Russian Revolution. But what Rosa Luxemburg discerned within its first year would definitively mark the outcome: a revolutionary process which, in breaking with liberal democracy, quickly narrowed rather than broadened the scope of public participation, ending as a "clique affair." Lenin, she noted, saw the capitalist state as "an instrument of oppression of the working class; the socialist state, of the bourgeoisie," but this "misses the most essential thing: bourgeois class rule has no need of the political training and education of the entire mass of the people, at least not beyond certain narrow limits." The great danger was that:

> Without general elections, without unrestricted freedom of press and assembly, without a free struggle of opinion, life dies out in every public institution, becomes a mere semblance of life, in which only the bureaucracy remains as the active element. Public life gradually falls asleep, a few dozen party leaders of inexhaustible energy and boundless experience direct and rule. Among them, in reality only a dozen outstanding heads do the leading and an elite of the working class is invited from time to time to meetings where they are to applaud the speeches of the leaders, and to approve proposed resolutions unanimously—at bottom then, a clique affair.[9]

Isaac Deutscher, looking back some three decades later, succinctly captured the dilemma that had led the Bolsheviks to bring about a dictatorship that would "at best represent the idea of the class, not the class
itself." He insisted that in consolidating the new regime the Bolsheviks
had not "clung to power for its own sake," but rather that this reflected
a deeper quandary. Even though anarcho-syndicalists seemed "far
more popular among the working class," the fact that they "possessed
no positive political programme, no serious organization, national or
even local," only reinforced the Bolsheviks' identification of the new
republic's fate with their own, as "the only force capable of safeguard-
ing the revolution."

> Lenin's party refused to allow the famished and emotionally un-
> hinged country to vote their party out of power and itself into a
> bloody chaos. For this strange sequel to their victory the Bolsheviks
> were mentally quite unprepared. They had always tacitly assumed
> that the majority of the working class, having backed them in the
> revolution, would go on to support them unswervingly until they
> had carried out the full programme of socialism. Naive as the as-
> sumption was, it sprang from the notion that socialism was the prole-
> tarian idea *par excellence* and that the proletariat, having once adhered
> to it, would not abandon it . . . It had never occurred to Marxists to
> reflect whether it was possible or admissible to try to establish social-
> ism regardless of the will of the working class.[10]

The long-term effects of what Luxemburg had so quickly understood
would contribute to reproducing a dictatorial regime regardless of the
will of the working class—and, relatedly, also to the gaps in the "political training and education of the entire mass of the people"—were
chillingly captured by what a leader of the local trade union committee
at the Volga Automobile Plant said to us in an interview in 1990, just
before the regime established in 1917 collapsed: "Insofar as workers were
backward and underdeveloped, this is because there has in fact been no
real political education since 1924. The workers were made fools of by
the party."[11] The words here need to be taken literally: the workers were
not merely fooled, but made into fools; their revolutionary understanding and capacity was undermined.

The fillip that 1917 had given to fueling workers' revolutionary ambitions worldwide was more than offset by the failure of the revolution
in Germany and the Stalinist response to an isolated and beleaguered

Soviet Union after Lenin's death, with all the adverse consequences this entailed. Though the specter of Bolshevism hardly faded, it was the specter of fascism that dominated radical change in the interwar years. Nevertheless, there was also widespread recognition of the potential of the working class as the social force most capable of transforming state and society. This perception was not least based on worker organization and class formation in the US during the Great Depression. As the US was already the new world center of capitalism, even before the Second World War, this contributed to the sense on the part of leading American capitalists and state officials that among the barriers to the remaking of a liberal capitalist international order, "the uprising of [the] international proletariat . . . [was] the most significant fact of the last twenty years."[12]

The strength of the organized working class as it had formed up to the 1950s was registered in the institutionalization of collective bargaining and welfare reforms. The effects of this were highly contradictory. The material gains in terms of individual and family consumption, which workers secured directly or indirectly from collective bargaining for rising wages as well as from a social wage largely designed to secure and supplement that consumption, were purchased at the cost of union and party practices that attenuated working-class identity and community—especially in light of the restructuring of employment, residency, and education that accompanied these developments. To be sure, the continuing salience of working-class organization was palpable. This was increasingly so in the public sector, but it was also measurable in class struggles in the private sector that resisted workplace restructuring, as well as in the wage-led inflation that contributed to the capitalist profitability crisis of the 1970s. Yet the failure to renew and extend working-class identity and community through these struggles opened the way to the neoliberal resolution of the crises of the 1970s through a widespread assault on trade unionism and the welfare state, and the interpellation of workers themselves as "taxpayers."

By the beginning of the twenty-first century, aided by the realization of a fully global capitalism and the networked structures of production, finance, and consumption that constitute it, there were more workers on the face of the earth than ever before. New technologies certainly restricted job growth in certain sectors, but this also introduced entirely new sectors in both manufacturing and especially

high tech services. Though this weakened the leverage of class struggles in important ways, it also introduced new points of strategic potential: strikes at component plants or interruptions of supplier chains
at warehouses and ports could force shutdowns throughout a globally
integrated production network, and whistleblowing could expose vast
stores of information hidden by corporations and states.

The precarious conditions workers increasingly face today, even
when they belong to unions, speaks not to a new class division between precariat and proletariat. Precariousness rather reflects how
previous processes of working-class formation and organization have
become undone. Precariousness is not something new in capitalism:
employers have always tried to gain access to labor when they want,
dispose of it as they want and, in between, use it with as little restric-
tions as possible. There is, in this context, limited value in drawing
new sociological nets of who is or is not in the working class. Rather
than categorizing workers into different strata—nurses or baristas,
teachers or software developers, farmhands or truckers, salespeople or
bank-tellers—what needs to preoccupy our imaginations and inform
our strategic calculations is how to visualize and how to develop the
potential of new forms of working-class organization and formation
in the twenty-first century.

There are indeed multitudes of workers' struggles taking place today in the face of an increasingly exploitative and chaotic capitalism.
Yet there is no denying that prospects for working-class revolutionary
agency seem dim. It was factors internal to working-class institutions,
their contradictions and weaknesses, which allowed, in the developing as well as the developed countries, for the passage of free trade,
the liberalization of finance, the persistence of austerity, the further
commodification of labor power, the restructuring of all dimensions
of economic and social life in today's global capitalism. The inability
of the working class to renew itself and discover new organizational
forms in light of the dynamism of capital and capacities of the state to
contain worker resistance has allowed the far Right today to articulate
and contextualize a set of common sentiments linked to the crisis—
frustrations with insecurity and inequality, and anger with parties that
once claimed to represent workers' interests. Escaping this crisis of the
working class is not primarily a matter of better policies or better tactics.
It is primarily an organizational challenge to facilitate new processes of

class formation rooted in the multiple dimensions of workers' lives that encompass so many identities and communities.

This organizational challenge will have to include developing socialist parties of a new kind. As can be seen from the two examples to which we now turn, the recent shift from protest to politics has already shown the popular resonance that a renewed socialist appeal can have today, even if it has only begun to probe what a consistent socialist politics would actually entail and the barriers that will be encountered.

POLITICAL REVOLUTION TODAY?
FROM SANDERS TO SYRIZA

"Election days come and go. But political and social revolutions that attempt to transform our society never end." The speech with which Bernie Sanders closed his Democratic primary election campaign began with these sentences; it ended by pointing to future historians who would trace the success of the long effort to transform American society from oligarchy to social justice as beginning with the "the political revolution of 2016."[13] It is tempting to treat as ersatz the rhetoric of revolution deployed here, taking the meaning of the word from the sublime to the ridiculous, or from tragedy to farce. The last time an American politician vying for the presidency issued a call for a political revolution it came from Ronald Reagan. But for all the limits of Sanders's populist campaign, the national attention and massive support garnered by a self-styled democratic socialist who positively associated the term revolution with the struggle against class inequality in fact represented a major discursive departure in American political life, which can be a resource for further socialist organizing.

Of course, the specific policy measures advanced by Sanders were, as he constantly insisted, reforms that had at some point been introduced in other capitalist societies. But when the call for public medicare for all, or free college tuition, or infrastructure renewal through direct public employment, is explicitly attached to a critique of a ruling class that wields corporate and financial power through the direct control of parties, elections, and the media, this goes beyond the bounds of what can properly be dismissed as mere reformism, even if the demands hardly evoke what the call for bread, land, and peace did in 1917. And it is no less a significant departure, especially in the US, to make class inequality the central theme of a political campaign in a manner designed to span and penetrate race and gender divisions, in a way that explicitly poses the question of who stands to benefit more from high-quality public health care and education and well-compensated work opportunities than African-Americans and Latinos, while pointing to the need to move beyond the ghettoes of identity toward building a more coherent class force.

The key question is whether Sanders's campaign really could lay the grounds for an ongoing political movement capable of effecting this "political revolution." Sanders's argument during the campaign that he could be sustained in the White House amidst a hostile Congress and imperial state apparatus by a "mass movement" marching on Washington D.C. was not very convincing. Much more serious was his call after he lost the primary campaign for a shift from protest to politics at every level, including "school boards, city councils, county commissions, state legislatures and governorships." But even if this happened, such engagement would also have to be directed at the institutions in which workers have heretofore been organized.

The very fact that the Sanders campaign was class-focused rather than class-rooted may be an advantage here. It opens space for a new politics that can become "rooted" in the sense of being grounded in working-class struggles but committed to the radical transformation of the generally exhausted institutions of the labor movement. This ranges across turning union branches into centers of working-class life, leading the fight for collective public services, breaking down the oligarchic relationship between leaders and led, contributing to building the broadest member capacities, emphasizing the importance of expressing a clearer class sensibility, and even becoming ambitious enough to introduce socialist ideas. This also applies to Workers Action Centers, which have spread across the US but which are so often overwhelmed by having to reproduce themselves financially in order to continue providing vital services to Black, Latino, immigrant, and women workers. Becoming more class-rooted and effective would require building the institutional capacities to creatively organize workers in different sectors into new city-wide organizations, as well as develop a coordinating national infrastructure.

Similar challenges would need to be put to consumer and credit cooperatives, which are broadly identified with the Left, but whose primarily narrow economic activities need to be politicized, above all in the sense of opening their spaces to radical education about the capitalist context in which they operate, actively participating in left campaigns, and contributing a portion of their revenue to funding organizers to carry out such tasks. And to get beyond the frustrations so often voiced in the environmental movement with workers' defensive prioritization of their jobs, turning this into a positive rather than negative class focus by speaking in terms of "just transitions" to a clean energy economy would also mean raising the necessity for economic planning to address both environmental and social crises, with the corollary of challenging the prerogatives of private property and capitalist power structures.

A new class politics cannot emerge ex nihilo, however. The Sanders campaign, initiated by an outsider in the Democratic Party, confirmed that if you are not heard in the media you are not broadly heard. But whatever the advantages of initially mobilizing from within established institutions in this respect, the impossibility of a political revolution taking place under the auspices of the Democratic Party needs to be directly faced (even in the Labour Party, it is hard enough to imagine that what Corbyn represents could be sustained without major institutional recalibration). After it had become clear he would not clinch the nomination, Sanders and the movement that had begun to take shape around him appeared at risk of falling into a myopic strategy of internally transforming and democratizing the Democratic Party. In part, this is one of the contradictions in Sanders's choice to run as a Democrat. While the Sanders campaign showed that Democratic Party institutions offer certain bases from which to advance a left politics—lending his campaign a certain legitimacy and credibility within mainstream discourse—in the long run, an alternative political pole will have to be constructed around which social struggles can condense.

It was far from surprising that the thousands of Sanders supporters who gathered at the People's Summit in Chicago after the primary campaign ended did not come to found a new party. What happened there, as Dan La Botz described it, "was about vision, not organization or strategy," so that one could at best only hear "the sound made by the Zeitgeist passing through the meeting rooms and the halls, brushing up against us, making its way, sometimes gracefully, sometimes clumsily, to the future."[14] One key test will be whether, as it "makes its way," lessons are learned from the US Labor Party project of the 1990s, links are made with attempts already underway to spawn new socialist political formations, and traces of either Bolshevik sectarianism or "Third World" romanticism are avoided while nevertheless also abandoning the naïve admiration for Canadian and European social democracy that has long characterized so much of the US left.[15]

This takes us from Sanders to Syriza, the only party to the left of traditional social democracy in Europe that has actually succeeded in winning a national election since the current economic crisis began. Syriza's roots go back to the formation of Synaspismos, first as an electoral alliance in the 1980s, and then as an independent, although factionalized, new party in the early 1990s. This was part of the broader institutional reconfiguration inaugurated by the Eurocommunist strategic orientation, searching for a way forward in the face of Communist and social democratic parties having lost their historic roles and capacities as agencies of working-class political representation and social transformation. This search went all the way back to the 1960s and accelerated after the collapse of the Soviet bloc and social democracy's embrace of the Third Way. In Greece especially, the Eurocommunist orientation was characterized by continuing to embrace the tradition of political revolution as experienced in the Civil War after 1945, even while distancing itself from the Soviet regime; and it would increasingly be characterized by the inspiration it took from, and a willingness to work with, new social movements.

Although Synaspismos through the 1990s offered enthusiastic support of European integration, as the neoliberal form of the Economic and Monetary Union buried the promises of a European Social Charter the grounds were laid in Greece, as elsewhere on the European radical Left, for a more "Eurosceptical" orientation.[16] This new critical posture towards the European variety of capitalism was a crucial element in Synaspismos explicitly defining, by the turn of the millennium, its strategic goal as "the socialist transformation of Greek society" while increasingly encouraging "dialogue and common actions" not only with the alter-globalization movement, but with radical ecologists and political groups of a Trotskyist or Maoist lineage. The goal of the Coalition of the Radical Left, with the acronym Syriza, which emerged out of this as an electoral alliance, was designed, as Michalis Spourdalakis put it, "not so much to unify but rather to connect in a flexible fashion the diverse actions, initiatives and movements . . . and to concern itself with developing popular political capacities as much as with changing state policy." But actually turning Synaspismos, and through it Syriza, into such a party was, as Spourdalakis immediately adds, "more wishful thinking than realistic prospect."[17]

As the euro crisis broke, however, with Greece at the epicenter of the attempt to save the euro through the application of severe austerity at its weakest point, all the elements of Syriza threw themselves into the 2011 wave of protests, occupations, and strikes, while supporting the four hundred or so community solidarity networks around the country to help the worst affected cope. This prepared the ground for Syriza's electoral breakthrough of 2012. Syriza's active insertion the year before into the massive outbursts across Greece of social protest from below was a source of radical democratic energy that went far beyond what can be generated during an election campaign, however successful. What this meant was eloquently articulated at Syriza's Congress in 2013 when it finally turned itself from an electoral alliance into a single party political organization. The conclusion to its founding resolution called for "something more" than the programmatic framework that resolution set out. Since "for a Government of the Left, a parliamentary majority—whatever its size—is not enough," the something more it called for was "the creation and expression of the widest possible, militant and catalytic political movement of multidimensional subversion."

> Only such a movement can lead to a Government of the Left and only such a movement can safeguard the course of such a government . . . [which] carries out radical reforms, takes on development initiatives and other initiatives of a clear environmental and class orientation, opens up new potentials and opportunities for popular intervention, helps the creation of new forms of popular expression and claims . . . Syriza has shouldered the responsibility to contribute decisively to the shaping of this great movement of democratic subversion that will lead the country to a new popular, democratic, and radical changeover.[18]

This sort of language, articulating this sort of understanding, was rare on the European radical left, let alone anywhere else. Yet as the Syriza leadership contemplated the dilemmas it faced as it stood on the doorstep of government, its concern to appear as a viable government in the media's eyes led them to concentrate, as was evident in the Thessalonika Manifesto proclaimed just a year later, on refining and scaling down the policy proposals in the 2013 party program. This was done with little internal party consultation, with the leadership mainly concerned with there not being enough experienced and efficient personnel in the party to bring into the state to change the notoriously clientelistic and corrupt state apparatus. Little attention was paid to who would be left in the party to act as an organizing cadre in society. The increase in party membership was not at all proportionate to the extent of the electoral breakthrough, and even when new radical activists did join, the leadership generally did very little to support those in the party apparatus who wanted to develop these activists' capacities to turn party branches into centers of working-class life and strategically engage with them, preferably in conjunction with the Solidarity Networks, in planning for alternative forms of production and consumption. All this spoke to how far Syriza still was from having discovered how to escape the limits of social democracy.

SYRIZA AND THE PROBLEM
OF STATE TRANSFORMATION

[This] is not a "betrayal." It's not about the well-known scenario "they have sold out." We have seen that there was real confrontation. We have seen the amount of pressure, the blackmailing by the European Central Bank. We have seen that they want to bring the Syriza government to its knees. And they need to do that because it represents a real threat, not some kind of illusion of a reformist type. So the reality is that the representatives of the Greek government did the best they could. But they did it within the wrong framework and with the wrong strategy and, in this sense, the outcome couldn't have been different . . . The people who think that "the reformists will fail" and that somehow in the wings stands the revolutionary vanguard who is waiting to take over somehow and lead the masses to a victory are I think completely outside of reality.[19]

All this was said within a month of Syriza's election at the end of January 2015 by Stathis Kouvelakis, whose interpretation of the dramatic unfolding of events in his country garnered widespread attention on the international Left. Himself a member's of Syriza's Central Committee as a partisan of the Left Platform, he was speaking at a meeting in London and addressing the disappointments already felt when the new government agreed to new negotiations with the EU and IMF. Less than five months later, as these negotiations infamously came to a climax, he would, along with many others, leave Syriza in response to what he now called the government's "capitulation," which indeed became the most common epithet used by the international Left. Yet the need to ask whether the outcome could really have been different was now greater than ever. And while the answer did indeed hinge on the adequacy of Syriza's strategy in relation to Europe, that in turn related to deeper issues of party organization, capacity building, and state transformation—as well as the adequacy of strategies on the wider European Left, at least in terms of shifting the overall balance of forces.

The common criticism of Syriza, strongly advanced by the Left Platform, was that it had not developed a "Plan B" for leaving the eurozone and adopting an alternate currency as the key condition for rejecting neoliberal austerity and cancelling debt obligations. What this criticism recoiled from admitting was that the capital and import controls this also would require would lead to Greece being forced out of the EU as a whole. After thirty-five years of integration, the institutional carapace for capitalism in Greece was provided by the manifold ways the state apparatus became entangled with the EU. Breaking out of this would have required Syriza as a party and government to be prepared for an immediate systemic rupture. It could certainly be said that Syriza was naïve to believe that it could stop the European economic torture while remaining in the eurozone, let alone the EU. At the very least, this simultaneously posed two great challenges: could such a state as Greece be fundamentally changed while remaining within the EU, and could the EU itself be fundamentally changed from within at the initiative of that state?

For a small country without significant oil resources, a break with the EU would have entailed economic isolation (along the lines of that endured by the Cuban revolution, yet without the prospect of anything like its geostrategic and economic support from the former USSR). The Syriza government faced the intractable contradiction that to fulfill its promise to stop the EU's economic torture, it would have to leave the EU—which would, given the global as well as European balance of forces and the lack of alternative production and consumption capabilities in place, lead to further economic suffering for an unforeseeable period. Despite the massive popular mobilization the government unleashed by calling the referendum in July to support its position against that of the EU-IMF, the intractable dilemma was the same as it had been when it first entered the state. That the government managed to win reelection in the fall while succumbing to and implementing the diktats of the "Institutions" indicated that Kouvelakis's observation when it entered into the negotiations back in February still held: "People support the government because the perception they have is that they couldn't act otherwise in that very specific situation. They really see that the balance of forces was extremely uneven."

Costas Douzinas, another prominent London-based Greek intellectual newly elected as a Syriza MP in the fall of 2015, hopes the story may not be over. He outlines the "three different temporalities" through which the radical Left must "simultaneously live" once it enters the state.[20] There is "the time of the present": the dense and difficult time when the Syriza government—"held hostage" to the creditors as a "quasi-protectorate" of the EU and IMF—is required "to implement what they fought against," and thus "to legislate and apply the recessional and socially unjust measures it ideologically rejects." This raises "grave existential issues and problems of conscience" which cannot go away, but can be "soothed through the activation of two other temporalities that exist as traces of futurity in the present time." This begins with "the medium term of three to five years," when time for the government appears "slower and longer" as it probes for the space it needs to implement its "parallel program" so as not only to "mitigate the effects of the memorandum" but also to advance "policies with a clear left direction . . . in close contact with the party and the social movements." This is the bridge to the third and longest temporality, "the time of the radical left vision," which will be reached "only by continuously and simultaneously implementing and undermining the agreement policies." As this third temporality starts unfolding, freed from the neoliberal lambast, "the full programme of the left of the 21st century" will emerge. "It is a case of escaping into the future, acting now from the perspective of a future perfect, of what will have been. In this sense, the future becomes an active factor of our present."

It is indeed significant that the Syriza government's continuing ideological rejection of neoliberal logic—even as it implements the measures forced upon it—is precisely what distinguishes Syriza from social democratic governments in the neoliberal era. The crucial condition for the three temporalities to coexist, however, is precisely the "close contact with the party and the social movements," which Douzinas only mentions in passing. Even in terms of its relations to the party, let alone the social movements, the Syriza government has failed to escape from familiar social democratic patterns as it distanced itself from party pressures, and seemed incapable of appreciating the need for activating party cadre to develop social capacities to lay the grounds for temporality two and eventually three. The neglect of the party turned to offhand dismissal when the government called the second election of 2015. As so many of its leading cadre left the party in the face of this—including even the General Secretary, who also resigned rather than asserting the party's independence from the government—the promise that Syriza might escape the fate of social democracy in neoliberal capitalism was left in tatters. There are still those in Syriza, inside and outside the government, who, operating with something very like the three temporalities in mind, are trying to revive the party outside government as the key agent of transformation. But whether they can manage to create the conditions for "Syriza to be Syriza again" is now moot indeed.[21]

Yet the problem goes far broader and deeper than with those who still have hopes for Syriza. It was ironically those who advanced the ostensibly more radical Plan B who seemed to treat state power most instrumentally. Little or no attention was paid by them to how to disentangle a very broad range of state apparatuses from budgetary dependence on EU funding, let alone to the transformations the Greek state apparatuses would have to undergo merely to administer the controls and rationing required to manage the black and grey markets that would have expanded inside and outside the state if Greece exited the eurozone. This was especially problematic given the notorious clientelistic and corrupt state practices that Syriza as a party had been vociferously committed to ending, but once in government did not have the time to change, even where the inclination to do so was still there. When confronted with a question on how to deal with this, one Syriza MP who was a leading advocate of Plan B responded privately that in such a moment of rupture it is necessary to shoot people. But this only raised the bigger question of whom the notoriously reactionary coercive apparatuses of the Greek state, as unchanged as they were, would be most likely to listen to, and most likely to shoot.

Perhaps most tellingly, advocates of Plan B showed no more, and often rather less, interest in democratizing state apparatuses by linking them with social movements. This stood in contrast with the Minister of Social Services, who had herself been the key founder of the federation of solidarity networks, Solidarity4All, and openly spoke of her frustrations that Syriza MPs, even while paying over a sizeable portion of their salaries to the networks, insisted that they alone should be the conduits for contact with solidarity activists in their communities. The Minister of Education visited one school a week and told teachers, parents, and students that if they wanted to use the school as a base for changing social relations in their communities they would have his support. However, the Ministry of Education itself did not become actively engaged in promoting the use of schools as community hubs, neither providing spaces for activists organizing around food and health services, nor the technical education appropriate to this, nor other special programs to prepare students to spend periods of time in communities, contributing to adult education and working on community projects.

Yet it must be said that the social movements themselves were largely passive and immobilized in this respect, as if waiting for the government to deliver. Activists from the networks of food solidarity were rightly frustrated they could not even get from the new Minister of Agriculture the information they asked for on the locations of specific crops so they might approach a broader range of farmers. But they did not see it as their responsibility to develop and advance proposals on how the state apparatuses should be changed, even minimally, so as to cope with the economic crisis. How, for instance, the agriculture ministry could have been engaged in identifying idle land to be given over to community food production coops, and in coordinating this across subregions; or how the defence ministry might have been engaged in directing military trucks (at least those sitting idle between demonstrations) to be used to facilitate the distribution of food through the solidarity networks.

The point is this. Insofar as the Syriza government has failed the most crucial democratic, let alone revolutionary, test, of linking the administration up with popular forces—not just for meeting basic needs but also for planning and implementing the restructuring of economic and social life—there were all too few on the radical Left outside the state who really saw this as a priority either.

SIGNPOSTS TOWARD DEMOCRATIC SOCIALISM

Whatever the final outcome in Greece, it is useful to look back at Nicos Poulantzas's "Towards a Democratic Socialism," especially given its formative influence on those who founded Synaspismos in the 1980s (Syriza's research institute bears his name to this day).[22] Written in 1978 as the epilogue to his last book, what Poulantzas articulated was reflective of a much broader orientation on the European Left, already represented by Gorz, Magri, Benn, Miliband, Rowbotham, Segal, Wainwright, and others, toward trying to discover new strategic directions beyond both the Leninist and social democratic "models," which, despite taking different routes, nevertheless evinced in their practices a common distrust of popular capacities to democratize state structures.[23] As Poulantzas put it: "There is no longer a question of building 'models' of any kind whatsoever. All that is involved is a set of signposts which, drawing lessons of the past, point out the traps to anyone wishing to avoid certain well-known destinations." For Poulantzas, the "techno-bureaucratic statism of the experts" was the outcome not only of the instrumentalist strategic conception of social democratic parliamentarism, but also of the "Leninist dual-power type of strategy which envisages straightforward replacement of the state apparatus with an apparatus of councils":

> Transformation of the state apparatus does not really enter into the matter: first of all the existing state power is taken and then another is put in its place. This view of things can no longer be accepted. If taking power denotes a shift in the relationship of forces within the state, and if it is recognized that this will involve a long process of change, then the seizure of state power will entail concomitant transformations of its apparatuses . . . In abandoning the dual-power strategy, we do not throw overboard, but pose in a different fashion, the question of the state's materiality as a specific apparatus.[24]

Notably, Poulantzas went back to Luxemburg's critique of Lenin in 1918 to stress the importance of socialists building on liberal democracy, even while transcending it, in order to provide the space for mass struggles to unfold that could "modify the relationship of forces within the state apparatuses, themselves the strategic site of political struggle." The very notion to take state power "clearly lacks the strategic vision of a process of transition to socialism—that is of a long stage during which the masses will act to conquer power and transform state apparatuses." For the working class to displace the old ruling class, in other words, it must develop capacities to democratize the state, which must always rest on "increased intervention of the popular masses in the state . . . certainly through their trade union and political forms of representation, but also through their own initiatives within the state itself." To expect that institutions of direct democracy outside the state can simply displace the old state in a single revolutionary rupture in fact avoided all the difficult questions of political representation and opens the way for a new authoritarian statism.[25]

Indeed, as André Gorz had already insisted in his pathbreaking essay on "Reform and Revolution" a decade earlier, taking off from liberal democracy on "the peaceful road to socialism" was not a matter of adopting "an *a priori* option for gradualism; nor of an *a priori* refusal of violent revolution or armed insurrection. It is a consequence of the latter's actual impossibility in the European context."[26] The advancement of what Gorz called a "socialist strategy of progressive reforms" did not mean the "installation of islands of socialism in a capitalist ocean," but rather involved the types of "structural reforms" or "non-reformist reforms" that could not be institutionalized so as to close off class antagonism but which allowed for further challenges to the balance of power and logic of capitalism, and thereby introduced a dynamic that allowed the process to go further. In calling for the creation of new "centres of social control and direct democracy" outside the state, Gorz was far-sighted in terms of what this could contribute to a broad process of new class formation with revolutionary potential, not least by extending to "the labour of ideological research" and more generally to the transformative capacities of "cultural labour aiming at the overthrow of norms and schemata of social consciousness." This would be essential for ensuring that "the revolutionary movements' capacity for action and hegemony is enriched and confirmed by its capacity to inspire . . . the autonomous activity of town planners, architects, doctors, teachers and psychologists."[27]

What this left aside, however, were the crucial changes in state structures that would need to attend this process. Poulantzas went to the heart of the matter, a decade later, stressing that on "the democratic road to socialism, the long process of taking power essentially consists in the spreading, development, coordination and direction of those diffuse centres of resistance which the masses always possess within the state networks, in such a way that they become real centres of power on the strategic terrain of the state." Even Gramsci, as Poulantzas pointed out, "was unable to pose the problem in all its amplitude" since his "war of position" was conceived as the application of Lenin's model/strategy to the "different concrete conditions of the West" without actually addressing how to change state apparatuses.[28] Yet it must also be said that Poulantzas, even while highlighting the need for taking up the challenge of state transformation, did not himself get very far in detailing what actually changing the materiality of state apparatuses would entail in specific instances. Lurking here was the theoretical problem Miliband had identified of not differentiating state power from class power, and therefore not specifying sufficiently how the modalities and capacities involved in exercising capitalist state power would be changed into different modalities with structurally transformative capacities.[29] And as Goran Therborn pointed out, in envisaging an important role for unions of state employees in the process of transforming state apparatuses, it was necessary to address the problem that "state bureaucrats and managers will not thereby disappear, and problems of popular control will remain," thereby continuing to pose "serious and complicated questions" for the state transformation through socialist democracy.[30]

Socialists have since paid far too little attention to the challenges this poses.[31] While the recognition that neither insurrectionary politics to "smash the state" nor the social democratic illusion of using the extant state to introduce progressive policies were viable became more and more widespread, this was accompanied with a penchant for developing "market socialist" models in the late 1980s. This has subsequently been succeeded by a spate of radical left literature that—in almost a mirror image of neoliberalism's championing of private corporations and small business firms against the state—weakly points to examples of cooperatives and self-managed enterprises as directly bearing socialist potential.[32] Replicated here is exactly what Poulantzas identified in the conception of those for whom "the only way to avoid statism is to place oneself outside the state. The way forward would then be, without going as far as dual power simply to block the path of the state from the outside." Yet by concentrating exclusively on "breaking power up and scattering it among an infinity of micro-powers," the result is that the "movement is prevented from intervening in actual transformations of the state, and the two processes are simply kept running along parallel lines."[33]

CONCLUSIONS

Political hopes are inseparable from notions of what is possible. And possibility is itself intimately related to class formation, the role of parties in this and developing confidence in class institutions, and especially the question of potentials to transform the state. The alliances that socialist parties would have to enter into, not least in the face of the growing threat from the far right of the political spectrum, should not just be among elites but be directed at new working-class formation of the broadest possible kind; and, given the uneven capacities of the class, should also be directed at developing its actual potential to become the transformative agent in a transition to socialism. New socialist parties cannot, however, see themselves as a kind of omnipotent *deus ex machina* in society. Precisely in order not to draw back from the "prodigious scope of their own aims," as Marx brilliantly wrote in *The Eighteenth Brumaire*, they must "engage in perpetual self-criticism" and deride "the inadequacies, weak points and pitiful aspects of their first attempts."[34] Developing commitments to socialism—getting socialism seriously on the agenda—consequently requires not only addressing the question of political agency, but overcoming a prevailing sense that even sympathetic governments will either be stymied by state apparatuses hostile to the socialist project, and/or that in a globalized world the problem in any case lies beyond the nation-state.

To stress the importance of a democratic socialist strategy for entering the state through elections to the end of transforming the state is today less than ever—amidst the deep political and social as well as economic contradictions of the neoliberal era—a matter of discovering a smooth gradual road to socialism. Ruptures, or extended series of ruptures of various intensities, are inescapable. This is so because of the contradictions inherent in reaching beyond capitalism while still being of it, and the virtual inevitability of conditions being premature as the project is attempted in "circumstances not of our own choosing." The contradictions for any radical government engaged in this process will include responsibilities for managing a capitalist economy that is likely in crisis while simultaneously trying to satisfy popular expectations for the promised relief, and yet also embarking on the longer-term commitment to transform the state, i.e., not pushing the latter off to an indefinite future.

It is this tension among the various new state responsibilities that makes the role of new socialist parties that will bring such governments to office so fundamental. Given the legitimacy and resources that will inevitably accrue to those party leaders who form the government, the autonomy of the party is crucial in order to counter the pull of those leaders towards social democratization. The party must more than ever keep its feet in the movements and, far from trying to direct them, remain the central site for democratic strategic debate in light of their diverse activities. This is why strategic preparations undertaken well before entering the state on how to avoid replicating the experience with social democracy are so very important. But even with this, the process of transforming the state cannot help but be complex, uncertain, and crisis-ridden, with repeated interruptions and possibly even reversals. Beginning with election to local or regional levels of the state would allow for developing capacities for state transformation before coming to national power. Developing alternative means of producing and distributing food, health care, and other necessities depends on autonomous movements moving in these directions through takeovers of land, idle buildings, threatened factories, and transportation networks. All this, in turn, would have to be supported and furthered through more radical changes in the state that would range over time from codifying new collective property rights to developing and coordinating agencies of democratic planning. At some points in this process, more or less dramatic initiatives of nationalization and socialization of industry and finance would have to take place.

For state apparatuses to be transformed so as to play these roles, their institutional modalities would need to undergo fundamental transformations, given how they are now structured so as to reproduce capitalist social relations. State employees would need to become explicit agents of transformation, aided and sustained in this respect by their unions and the broader labor movement. Rather than expressing defensive particularism, unions themselves would need to be changed fundamentally so as to be actively engaged in developing state workers' transformational capacities, including by establishing councils that link them to the recipients of state services. Of course, the possibility of such state transformations will not be determined by what happens in one country alone. During the era of neoliberalism, state apparatuses have become deeply intertwined with transnational institutions, treaties, and regulations to manage and reproduce global capitalism. This has nothing at all to do with capital bypassing the nation-state and coming to rely on a transnational state. Both the nature of the current crisis and the responses to it have proved once again how much states still matter. Even in the most elaborate transnational institutional formation, the European Union, the center of political gravity lies not in the supranational state apparatus headquartered in Brussels. It is, rather, the asymmetric economic and political power relations among the states of Europe that really determines what the EU is and does. Any project for democratization at an international scale, such as those being advanced by many of the left for the EU in the wake of the Syriza experience, still depends on the balance of class forces and the particular structures within each nation-state. Changes in international institutions are therefore contingent on transformations at the level of nation-states. And the changes in international state apparatuses that should be pursued by socialists are those that would allow more room for maneuver within each state. What socialist internationalism must mean today is an orientation to shifting the balances of forces in other countries and in international bodies so as to create more space for transformative forces in every country. This was one of the key lessons of 1917, and it is all the more true a century later.

NOTES

Reform and Revolution

This essay is taken from André Gorz's *Le Socialisme Difficile*, published in 1967 by *Editions du Seuil*. The translation is by Ben Brewster.

1   Lelio Basso has set out this view (which is held by the majority of European Marxist theoreticians) particularly clearly:

> The passage from the antechamber of socialism to socialism . . . is only possible at a certain level of development of the social forces and relations, when consciousness of the basic antagonism has penetrated the masses and when the relation of forces permits the inversion of the situation.
>
>   The present task of the workers' movement is precisely to prepare this moment. . . . This strategy can be defined as a peaceful road to socialism on the condition that it does not prejudge the form which the final crisis will take, which may be peaceful or violent according to a series of conditions which it is absolutely impossible to foresee today.

Tendenze del capitalismo europeo (Rome: Editore Riuniti, 1966), pp. 283–84.

2   I call socialist all those forces that are actually pursuing the realization of socialism, and therefore the abolition of capitalist production relations and of the capitalist state, and not only the parties that are called socialist though they are frequently not socialist at all.

3   Karl Marx and Friedrich Engels, *1872 Preface to the Communist Manifesto.*

4   This claim is only apparently contradicted by electoral victories such as that of the British Labour Party in 1964, and tomorrow perhaps, that of the German Social Democrats. Wilson's victory was really due to an internal crisis of the Conservative Party, the fruit of long wear, and of its inability to face the downgrading of British capitalism's world position without the assistance of British trade unions. Wilson's victory was not that of a new policy, but that of the same policy, pursued by means hardly different, but with the support—the extremely reticent support, during the second phase—of the trade unions, and leading to the same results in general. A Social Democratic victory in Federal Germany would amount to the same thing.

5   Lelio Basso, "Rosa Luxemburg: The Dialectical Method," *International Socialist Journal*, no. 15, July 1966, p. 244.

6   On this point, see Kautsky (in this period supported by Lenin) in his polemic against Bernstein, *Social Reform and Revolution*:

> Those who reject on principle the political revolution as a means to social transformation; those who seek to limit this transformation to those measures which can be obtained from the ruling class are *social reformers*—however much their ideal may be opposed to that of existing society. . . . What distinguishes a social reformer from a revolutionary is not the pursuit of reforms, but being explicitly confined to the pursuit of reforms.

Cf. Lelio Basso in *Tendenze del capitalismo*, p. 264: "What characterizes reformism is not the struggle for reforms, which all Marxists propose, but . . . the separation of the reforming and the revolutionary moments. This separation means that the reforms . . . lose all anti-capitalist potential and become even instruments of the social integration of the working class into the system."

7   Cf. Lucio Magri, "Il valore e il limite delle esperienze frontiste," *Critica Marxista*, July–August 1965, p. 62:

> It is no longer possible for an economic plan which proposes a real direction of development not to be of a global character, long term, progressing through rigorous choices, not to dispose of the political and social power and the institutional framework which enable it to control the great chain reaction which it will provoke. How then can we still rely on a bloc of forces united around a minimum and immediate programme; on a mass movement defending threatened interests rather than organizing and selecting them; on a governmental formula without the cohesion, strength or ideas necessary for a programme of general transformation of society?

8   The bourgeoisie would only accept this collaboration rather than provoke a trial of strength if the victory of the left was a crushing one, if it was preceded and followed by an irresistible popular movement, and if the party or parties in power were totally united and looked like remaining in power for *a very long time*. This was the case in Sweden at the beginning of the thirties, and, in a quite different context, in China in 1950.

In the Chinese case, the bourgeoisie collaborated with the revolutionary power because any attempt at resistance would have been suicidal.

In Sweden, which at that time had only just embarked on industrialization, the bourgeoisie was of recent origin, and it came to an agreement with social democracy to the extent that the latter not only accepted but relied on the interests and reason of the capitalist class. So much has this been the case that after thirty years of social democratic power, government action shows no sign of a socialist perspective, and democratic life in the party and the unions has been stifled by bureaucratic centralization.

9   This does not take into account how extremely difficult it is for the state
      to discover the real uses to which the real profits of companies are devoted,
      unless the state sets up a very clumsy control apparatus.

10   This was demanded by one of the speakers at a conference of socialist
      intellectuals at Grenoble in May 1966. The author of this report tried
      to justify the position by a false invocation of the Swedish example. The
      Swedish state imposes no control regulations on trusts, and knows neither
      the real rates of profit nor the real nature of investment plans, which are
      concealed by industrial secrecy. This is because it knows that capitalism is
      only dynamic as long as the profit motive is left untouched. The Swedish
      state does not have a medium-term global economic plan, but limits
      itself to a strict control of *individual* income. The budgetary resources it
      derives from taxation are no greater a part of the national product than in
      other developed capitalist countries (taking account of the fact that social
      security is budgeted), and does not allow it to cope with the development
      of collective needs. The housing crisis, regional imbalances, disparities
      between public and private wages, acute poverty of collective services
      (the needs for nursery schools, notably, are only 10 percent covered) are
      all comparable to those of the rest of Western Europe, as are cultural
      inequalities and the impermeability of the "ruling elite" to newcomers.

11   Cf. Bruno Trentin in *Tendenze del capitalismo europeo*, pp. 203–4:

> The initiation of the first measures of structural transformation rapidly demands
> new reforms and new transformations in the democratic organisation of power
> (if it is to avoid their neutralisation)....Democratic planning of the development
> and transformation of the economy presupposes a social and political front
> much larger than that which today revolves around the socialist and workers'
> parties; and if the aims of this planning *are not socialism*, it is nevertheless true that
> it will be difficult to realize it completely, and above all *durably* in the capitalist
> context unless, to safeguard its existence, the initial design is transcended by
> measures of reform and the democratic transformation of society. The advanced
> sector of the movement at least must be fully conscious of this process.

12   This assimilation is fairly widespread among left-wing social democrats; it
      is also found in Lelio Basso.

13   For example, social security, whose logic is that of the socialization of medical
      and pharmaceutical consumption, becomes a source of increased profit for
      the private chemical and pharmaceutical industries. The nationalization of
      basic industries—even when they are not making losses and are therefore
      unable to obtain on the financial market the capital necessary to their
      development—ultimately frees private capital for investment in sectors
      with more rapid growth and a higher rate of profit.

      Even if it is virtually dominant at a given moment, the nationalized
      sector can only remain so if it extends its activities to industries which
      promote economic development.

14 In his previously quoted report (pp. 181, 202–3), Bruno Trentin reaches analogous conclusions at the end of an analysis which is economic rather than political:

> The experience of recent years banishes any illusions as to the possibility of a process of slow and imperceptible whittling away at the system, and shows more and more clearly the inadequacy of the sectoral disruptions inflicted on the system by the working class when these disruptions are not integrated in a global strategy. In stressing this inadequacy, we are not thinking merely of the capitalist system's power to absorb and pervert partial reforms; but also and primarily of the brutal reaction of the economic forces weakened or threatened, and the objective counterstrokes provoked even by partial reforms when they shake an economic balance as delicate as that of the '60s, if the working class cannot consolidate its original breakthroughs with the conquest of new reforms . . . *originally linked together* and with a *simultaneous transformation of the present forms of organization of power*. . . .
>
> That is why the action of the workers' movement . . . must always be able to present itself as a complete strategy, at least in its general lines, within which the *principal ties* between the various moments or aspects of the reforming action are accepted in advance by the working-class parties. That is why the reform plan, if it has to be initiated gradually, must also be able to impose, *from the initial phase of its realization onwards,* through the economic and political means supporting it, not only a general control, but also a qualitative modification of the mechanisms of accumulation, and to dispose of concrete instruments of power in society such as parliament, local and regional representative institutions, the various forms of workers' control which are revealed to be actual and necessary, agricultural co-operatives, peasant associations and unions.
>
> Without this organic strategy, without an organic plan which reflects it in its general orientation, the indispensable partial struggles of the working class will, much more than in the past, be neutralized and diverted from their original goals by the more and more rigid logic of the system in which they unfold.

15 The attempts at pulling social democracy over to the left by hushing up divergences, stressing common objectives, and offering help to achieve them, are only meaningful if the strength of unitary action among the rank and file makes social democracy available for an anticapitalist alliance. This availability only manifests itself in periods of acute crisis and internal and external danger. But the "left front" immediately takes on a *defensive* and tactical rather than offensive and strategic character. Once the reactionary danger has been avoided, strategic divergences will split the alliance. It then emerges that it was not directed against the bourgeois state, but against precapitalist and prebourgeois structures and forces deriving from the incompleteness of the bourgeois revolution.

This is correctly noted by Lucio Magri, who adds: "The cement of the frontist unity thus disappears. For this cement was the common struggle against a system of power unable to assure any development of the society at all, constrained to resort to political violence and war to hide its social failings, its inability to respond to the interests of a real majority." Magri, *Critica Marxista*, p. 61.

16 Basso, *Tendenze del capitalismo*, pp. 276–77.

17 A militant formation may be representative of a current fairly widespread among the working masses without itself being very strong. This is true, for example, of Christian socialist militants.

18 This line has been put forward and sometimes applied with partial success by the left of the Italian Communist Party (the *ingraoiani*). Applied by the Federation of Metallurgical Workers and Employees (the FIOM) of the CGIL, it is consistently and notably successful. It is one of the reasons for the spectacular growth that the Swedish Communist Party is at present undergoing under the leadership of C. H. Hermansson. It must not be confused with an attempt at reaching an understanding with the social democratic party machine.

19 One of the weaknesses of the 1966 Grenoble Conference (see note 10 above) was to limit itself to a "possibilist" short or medium-term perspective that, precisely for this reason, ignored the problems of the transition to socialism and even the forms of action aiming at preparing it. Questions essential to a socialist *prise de conscience* and socialist action *cannot even be posed* so long as a short-term perspective is maintained, that is, the capitalist system is not transcended.

20 Ideological labor is nothing but a labor of unification at a specific level, *that of the consciousness that they have of themselves*, of various aspirations and interests. An ideology therefore may be mystifying, *but it may not be*, according to whether it is syncretic or synthetic.

    In the first case, e.g., the case of neocapitalist ideologies, it aims both at unifying the heterogeneous particular interests of the bourgeoisie and unifying with these the immediate interests and aspirations of the upper strata of wage earners, by ideologically integrating them, under the appellation "middle class" or "middle strata," to the bourgeois class. If this syncretic unification is to have some semblance of solidity, it demands the mediation of numerous partial and crude analyses and explanations of the evolution of the social relations and production relations of modern capitalism.

    The synthetic unification of the interests and aspirations of the working classes rests on a material basis and strong scientific analysis to the extent that it starts from the subordinate position of these classes in capitalist society. The principal concrete aspects of this subordination are nonetheless not identical for all wage categories. Their synthetic unification thus needs a finer analysis, respecting, under pain of schematism, the specificity of the material, cultural, and professional interests and aspirations of manual and intellectual workers. This unifying synthesis can therefore only be effective at a level of perspective, transcending the immediate perception of interest toward the establishment of richer human and social relationships, i.e., at the level of common demands (or "values") capable of general application.

The synthesis remains necessarily incomplete so long as class divisions, and even the kind of social division of labor resulting from the present level of development of the productive forces, have not themselves been transcended.

As the dominant neocapitalist ideology contains a considerable part of mystification and propaganda, the efforts of the workers' movement to combat this ideology will necessarily themselves contain a part of abusive simplification and propaganda. It is this practical necessity that has led to a limiting pejorative definition of "ideological work." But if it is indispensable to translate ideological elaboration into political propaganda (slogans, polemics, etc.), it is also indispensable not to confuse the two.

Ideological propaganda, in the last analysis, will not be effective unless it popularizes an ideological elaboration based on rigorous research and analysis; it will lose its effectiveness if the demands of short-term political propaganda restrain, stifle, schematize and censor the work of research and elaboration itself.

21   Unless they can freely intercommunicate. But direct communication and the self-expression and *prise de conscience* that it provokes is not hindered merely by a repressive factory system and a housing policy that disperses workers after their day's work. It is also hindered by the conditioning of thought, language, and behavior conveyed by educational formation and mass means of communication. This finally screens off experience from the consciousness of experience. The regression of proletarian culture and its sources is, to a very large extent, due to the decrease in the possibilities of direct communication and the extension of mass culture (rather, deculturation) diffused via the mass media.

22   In Italy, Norway, and Western Germany, these isolated attempts at "*enquêtes ouvrières*" have acquired a certain notoriety by reason of the strikes or lively working-class agitation they have provoked, even though this was not their original purpose.

23   In the same way, it is not the generalization of the kind of formation dispensed in high schools and universities that will "democratize" education, but a radical and general reform of the methods and content of education, aiming to destroy the barriers—which are anyway completely arbitrary from the point of view of the acquisition and progress of knowledge— between intellectual and manual, theoretical and practical, and individual and collective labor.

24   But this does not exclude reformist opportunism in practice. On the contrary, it can be pursued with a calm conscience thanks precisely to the strength of the structures and the imperviousness of the workers' party: whatever it does, it is not tainted or corrupted by its acts and alliances. It may participate in a coalition with scrupulous loyalism, precisely because it is impermeable to external influences. Its reality is not in its public behavior, its political action *within* capitalist society; it is in its internal behavior, which

prefigures the society of the future and opposes an absolute "ontological" negation to the surrounding society. This ontological, i.e., nondialectical, character of the negation is responsible for its inability to produce action capable of mediating between present and future, capitalism and socialism: a Chinese wall separates one from the other; they are ontologically different orders; there is no route between them, no theory or strategy of transition: socialism begins when capitalism ceases.

The reflection of this position can be found in the so-called theory of the two (successive and rigorously exclusive) stages: capitalism remains completely present in the stage called democratic; socialism is complete in the following stage. The problem of the passage from one to the other is left in suspense.

25   From a Marxist point of view, the decisive question is not to know whether a certain cultural product is decadent or not, but whether it conveys a *prise de conscience*, mystified or not, from which a Marxist critique can disengage the moment of truth, and, doing so, enrich and develop its own tools of knowledge and action.

26   For example, in the case of the Austrian, Belgian, and Swedish Communist parties.

The May Events and Revolution in the West

This essay is a translation of the concluding chapter of Lucio Magri's *Considerazioni Sui Fatti di Maggio* (De Donato: Bazi, 1968). The translation is by Chiaza.

1   Translator's note: i.e., under the hegemony of the Catholic Church or of the Socialist Party.

Marx and Engels and the Concept of the Party

1   Resolution relative to the General Rules (adopted at the Hague Congress of the International Workingmen's Association, September 1872, resuming Resolution IX of the London Conference of the International in September 1871 drafted by Marx and Engels), in *The International Herald* (London), no. 37, December 14, 1872. This translation from the French original is used here in preference to that appearing in Karl Marx and Friedrich Engels, *Selected Works*, hereafter noted as *SW* (Moscow: Foreign Languages Publishing House, 1950), vol. 1, p. 325, from which it differs possibly significantly, because it is specifically referred to by Engels to clear up a misinterpretation of the meaning of the resolution. (Friedrich Engels, *The Manchester Foreign Section To All Sections and Members of the British Federation*, in Karl Marx and Friedrich Engels, *On Britain* (Moscow: Foreign Languages Publishing House, 1962, p. 500). It is also used by Marx as the English text of the resolution in a letter sent to Hermann Jung at the

end of July 1872 with the phrase "constituting . . . propertied classes" and the words "the abolition of classes" underlined. (Karl Marx and Friedrich Engels, *Werke* (Berlin: Dietz, 1966), vol. 33, p. 507.

2   Cf. M. I. Mikhailov, *Voznikovenie Marksizma. Bor'ba Marksa i Engel'sa za Sozdanie Revoliutsionnoy Proletarskoy Partii* (Moscow, 1956), p. 15, where, without offering any evidence, the author states that Marx and Engels proceeded from such a "plan."

3   See, especially, Karl Marx, *Introduction to The Critique of Hegel's Philosophy of Right*, in Thomas Burton Bottomore, ed., *Karl Marx, Early Writings* (London: McGraw-Hill, 1963), pp. 58–59.

4   Only from 1847–52 were Marx and Engels members of a party organization of a kind—the League of Communists—though from 1864 (and effectively from 1870 in the case of Engels) until 1872 they played a leading part in the International Workingmen's Association (the First International).

5   Friedrich Engels to Eduard Bernstein, February 27–March 1, 1883, Karl Marx and Friedrich Engels, *Selected Correspondence* (Moscow, n.d.—1956?), hereafter noted as *SC* (Moscow), p. 432.

6   Friedrich Engels to August Bebel, December 11, 1884, ibid., p. 457.

7   See, e.g., Maurice Duverger, *Political Parties* (London: Wiley, 1954), pp. xxii–xxx; Umberto Cerroni, "Per una teoria del partito politico," in *Critica Marxista,* vol. I, no. 5–6, pp. 18ff.

8   Friedrich Engels, "On the History of the Communist League," *SW*, vol. II, p. 312.

9   Ibid., p. 313.

10   See, e.g., Karl Marx and Friedrich Engels, *The German Ideology*, in *Gesamtausgabe* (MEGA) (Moscow-Leningrad: CPSU, 1933), vol. I, no. 5, pp. 31 and 437; Karl Marx to Pavel Vasilyevich Annenkov, December 28, 1846, Karl Marx and Friedrich Engels, *Selected Correspondence* (London: Lawrence & Wishart, 1943), hereafter noted *SC* (London), p. 18; Karl Marx and Friedrich Engels, "Circular against Kriege," *Werke* (Berlin: Dietz, 1959), vol. 4, p. 3.

11   Engels, *History*, pp. 307, 313–14; Karl Marx, *Herr Vogt*, in *Werke* (Berlin: Dietz, 1961), vol. 14, pp. 438–39; Herwig Förder, *Marx und Engels am Vorabend der Revolution* (Berlin: Akudemie-Verlag, 1960), pp. 128–35. For a different and not fully credible version, see David Ryazanoff's introduction to his ed., *The Communist Manifesto of Karl Marx and Friedrich Engels* (London: Martin Lawrence, 1930), pp. 14–20.

12   *Rules and Constitution of the Communist League*, in Ryazanoff, ed., *The Communist Manifesto*, pp. 340–45, especially p. 342.

13   Karl Marx and Friedrich Engels, Preface to the German Edition of *Manifesto of the Communist Party*, hereafter noted as *Manifesto*, in *SW*, vol. I, p. 21.

14   Ibid., p. 61.

15   Engels, *History*, p. 315; Karl Marx, *Herr Vogt*, p. 440.

16 Friedrich Engels, *Socialism in Germany*, in *Werke* (Berlin: Dietz, 1963), vol. 22, p. 248.

17 Karl Marx, *The Poverty of Philosophy* (Moscow, n.d.), p. 140.

18 The original German text uses the word "*besondern*," meaning "special," but the English edition of 1888, revised by Friedrich Engels, prefers "sectarian."

19 Marx and Engels, *Manifesto*, p. 44.

20 Ibid., p. 42.

21 Ibid., p. 41. See discussions of Marx and Engels's concept of party in this context in Förder, *Marx und Engels*, pp. 290–91.

22 Marx, *Poverty of Philosophy*, p. 194. Cf. Karl Marx, *Political Indifferentism*, in *Werke* (Berlin: Dietz, 1962), vol. 18, p. 304: "The trade unions . . . organize the working class into a class."

23 Marx, *Poverty of Philosophy*, p. 194.

24 Ibid., p. 195.

25 L. I. Gol'man, *Voznikovenie Marksizma. Bor'ba Marksa i Engel'sa za Sozdanie Revoliutsionnoy Proletarskoy Partii* (Moscow, 1962), p. 70.

26 Marx and Engels, *Manifesto*, p. 44.

27 See ibid., p. 60, where reference is also made to the Agrarian Reformers in America. The latter was however more of a farmers' agitation than a workers' party. (See Ryazanoff, ed., *Communist Manifesto*, pp. 242–45.)

28 Harney and Jones's membership of the Communist League is indicated in a letter from Karl Marx to Friedrich Engels about March 12, 1848, from which the relevant extract is printed in John Saville, *Ernest Jones: Chartist* (London: Lawrence & Wishart, 1952), p. 231. See also A. R. Schoyen, *The Chartist Challenge* (London: Heinemann, 1958), pp. 142–43, 158–59.

29 Marx and Engels, *Manifesto*, p. 60.

30 Karl Marx, *The Eighteenth Brumaire of Louis Bonaparte*, in *SW*, vol. I, p. 249. This quotation and the passage in which it is to be found make rather a mockery of Mr Robert Conquest's unsubstantiated assertion that "it is strictly contrary to (Marx's) doctrines . . . to believe that a party can represent both the proletariat and another class." Robert Conquest, *Marxism Today* (London: Ampersand, 1964), p. 42.

31 Karl Marx and Friedrich Engels, *Address of the Central Committee to the Communist League* (March 1850), hereafter noted as *March Address*, *SW*, vol. I, p. 98.

32 Friedrich Engels to Florence Kelley Wischnewetsky, January 27, 1887, *SC* (London), p. 455.

33 Ibid.

34 Friedrich Engels, *Marx and the Neue Rheinische Zeitung* (1848–1849), *SW*, vol. 2, p. 297.

35 E. P. Kandel, *Marks i Engels–Organizatory Soyuza Kommunistov* (Moscow, 1953), p. 264.

36 Ibid., p. 264. G. Winkler, of the Institute of Marxism-Leninism, Berlin, attacked this conclusion as "surprising" in his review of Kandel's book

in *Zeitschrift für Geschichtswissenschaft* (Berlin, 1954), vol. II, no. 4, p. 542, arguing that the League's congress of June 1847 concluded essentially its transformation into a proletarian party (p. 545). This is the line that has mostly been taken by the historians of the German Democratic Republic (see *Grundriss der Geschichte der deutschen Arbeiterbewegung* [Berlin: Dietz, 1963], p. 42), though the new official history (Walter Ulbricht et al., eds, *Geschichte der deutschen Arbeiterbewegung* [Berlin: Dietz, 1966], vol. I, p. 66) adds qualifications.

37   Engels, *History,* p. 318.

38   See Boris Nicolaevsky, "Toward a History of 'The Communist League,' 1847–1852," in *International Review of Social History* (Amsterdam, 1956), vol. I, no. 2, pp. 234–45, especially 237, 244; E. P. Kandel, "Iskazhenie istorii bor'by Marksa i Engelsa za proletarskuyu partiyu v rabotakh nekotorykh pravykh sotsialistov," in *Voprosy Istorii* (Moscow), 1958, no. 5, pp. 120ff; Boris Nicolaevsky, "Who is Distorting History?" in *Proceedings of the American Philosophical Society* (Philadelphia), vol. 105, no. 2, April 1961, pp. 209–36; E. P. Kandel, "Eine schlechte Verteidigung einer schlechten Sache," in *Beiträge zur Geschichte der deutschen Arbeiterbewegung,* hereafter *Beiträge* (Berlin, 1963), vol. 2, pp. 290–303.

39   The full text of this deposition, introduced by the late W. Blumenberg, is printed in *International Review of Social History* (Amsterdam, 1964), vol. IX, no. 1, pp. 81–122. See especially pp. 88–89, 96.

40   Röser did not join the Communist League until the spring of 1849 (ibid., p. 90). His evidence on its alleged dissolution in 1848 is therefore of necessity presented secondhand (ibid., pp. 88-89, 96).

41   *Voprosy Istorii*, 1958, p. 124.

42   Nicolaevsky was wrong to assert that the *March Address* of 1850 "criticized . . . in particular the decision to dissolve the League," since no mention is made there of such a dissolution! Boris I. Nicolaevsky and Otto Maenchen-Helfen, *Karl Marx: Man and Fighter* (London: Lippincott, 1936), p. 206.

43   Friedrich Engels, *Marx and the NRZ*, p. 299.

44   *Beiträge*, p. 303.

45   See, e.g., E. P. Kandel, ed., *Marx und Engels und die ersten proletarischen Revolutionäre* (Berlin: Dietz, 1965), pp. 105, 502, n.60. The relevant extracts from Röser's deposition are given in E. P. Kandel and S. Z. Leviova, eds, *Soyuz Kommunistov: sbornik dokumentov* (Moscow, 1964), pp. 218–24.

46   A positive reference is made to this action of the London Central Committee in the *March Address*, p. 99, which places Moll's visit "in the winter of 1848–49" as against Röser's setting it "in the spring of 1849." *International Review of Social History*, vol. IX, no. 1, p 89.

47   Ibid., p. 90.

48   E. P. Kandel, *Beiträge*, p. 299.

49 S. Z. Leviova on the *Neue Rheinische Zeitung*, in A. I. Malysh and O. K. Senekina, eds, *Iz istorii formirovaniya i razvitiya Marksizma* (Moscow, 1959), p. 255.

50 Ulbricht et al., eds, *Geschichte*, pp. 117–18.

51 V. I. Lenin, *Two Tactics of Social Democracy*, in his *Selected Works* (Moscow: Cooperative Publishing Soc., 1936), vol. III, pp. 131–32.

52 Marx and Engels, *Werke* (Berlin, 1959), vol. 6, pp. 426, 584.

53 Friedrich Engels, *Germany: Revolution and Counter-Revolution* (London, 1936), p. 48. See, e.g., Gerhard Becker, *Karl Marx und Friedrich Engels in Köln, 1848–1849* (Berlin: Rütten & Leonung, 1963), pp. 234–56.

54 *March Address*, p. 99.

55 Ibid., pp. 98–108.

56 Ibid., p. 98.

57 Ibid., p. 99.

58 Ibid., p. 102. Cf. *Address of Central Committee to the League,* June 1850, *Werke* (Berlin, 1960), vol. 7, pp. 308–9: "The workers' party can possibly very well use other parties and fractions of parties for its ends, but it should not subordinate itself to any other party."

59 Ibid., p. 103.

60 Ibid., p. 103. Cf. *June Address*, p. 310; M. I. Mikhailow, in I. S. Galkin, ed., *Aus der Geschichte des Kampfes von Marx und Engels für die proletarische Partei* (Berlin, 1961), pp. 132–33.

61 *March Address*, p. 105.

62 George Lichtheim, *Marxism* (London: Routledge and Kegan Paul, 1961), pp. 124–25.

63 Bertram D. Wolfe, *Marxism* (London: Dial Press, 1967), pp. 153–54, 157, 163.

64 Eduard Bernstein, *Die Voraussetzungen des Sozialismus und die Aufgaben der Sozialdemokraten* (Stuttgart, 1899), p. 29.

65 See, e.g., Alan Barrie Spitzer, *The Revolutionary Theories of L. A. Blanqui* (New York: Columbia University Press, 1957), p. 9; Stanley Moore, *Three Tactics: The Background in Marx* (New York: Monthly Review Press, 1963), p. 22.

66 See David Ryazanoff, *Zur Frage des Verhältnisses von Marx zu Blanqui,* in *Unter dem Banner des Marxismus*, vol. II, no. 1/2 (Berlin–Vienna, 1928), pp. 140–45.

67 *March Address*, pp. 101, 107.

68 Ibid., p. 103.

69 Ibid., p. 104.

70 Ibid., p. 104; Rudolf Schlesinger, *Marx: His Time and Ours* (London: Routledge and Kegan Paul, 1950), p. 270.

71 *March Address*, p. 108.

72 Karl Marx, *Revelations on the Communist Trial in Cologne*, in *Werke* (Berlin, 1960), vol. 8, p. 412.

73   Karl Marx to Friedrich Engels, November 19, 1852, *Werke* (Berlin, 1963), vol. 28, p. 195.

74   Karl Marx to Friedrich Engels, February 11, 1851, *Werke* (Berlin, 1963), vol. 27, p. 184.

75   Friedrich Engels to Karl Marx, February 12, 1851, ibid., p. 186.

76   Karl Marx to Friedrich Engels, February 11, 1851, ibid., p. 185.

77   Friedrich Engels to Karl Marx, February 13, 1851, ibid., p. 189.

78   Ibid., p. 190.

79   F. Mehring, *Karl Marx* (London: Allen & Unwin, 1936), p. 209.

80   Wolfe, *Marxism*, p. 196.

81   Karl Marx to Joseph Weydemeyer, February 1, 1859, in Karl Marx and Friedrich Engels, *Letters to Americans*, 1848–1895, hereafter noted as *LA* (New York, 1963), p. 61.

82   See M. Dommanget, *Les Idées d'Auguste Blanqui* (Paris: Rivière, 1957), p. 355.

83   Karl Marx to Joseph Weydemeyer, *LA*, p. 62.

84   Karl Marx to F. Freiligrath, February 29, 1860, *SC* (Moscow), p. 146. Italics in original.

85   Ibid., p. 147.

86   Friedrich Engels, *Germany: Revolution and Counter-Revolution*, p. 114.

87   Mehring, *Karl Marx*, pp. 218–20; Friedrich Engels to Joseph Weydemeyer, April 12, 1853, *LA*, p. 58.

88   Karl Marx to Friedrich Engels, March 10, 1853, *Werke*, vol. 28, p. 224.

89   Friedrich Engels to Joseph Weydemeyer, April 12, 1853, ibid., p. 576. (This part of the letter is not included in *LA*.)

90   See, e.g., ibid., p. 581, where Engels comments acidly on those who thought they need not bother to "swot" as it was the job of "der père Marx" to know everything! Also, Wilhelm Liebknecht's account (see his *Karl Marx: Biographical Memoirs*, Chicago, 1901, p. 85) of Marx "driving" his "party" every day into the Reading Room of the British Museum.

91   Wilhelm Liebknecht, *Karl Marx zum Gedächtnis* (Nuremberg: Wörlein, 1896), p. 113.

92   Karl Marx to Friedrich Engels, May 15, 1859, *Werke* (Berlin, 1963), vol. 29, p. 432.

93   *SC* (Moscow), p. 146.

94   *Werke* (Berlin, 1964), vol. 30, p. 495. (This part of the letter is not included in the English *SC*.)

95   *SC* (Moscow), p. 147.

96   See, e.g., *Manifesto*, p. 42.

97   Karl Marx, *The Class Struggles in France*, 1848–1850, *SW*, vol. I, p. 136.

98   Karl Marx, *Revelations*, p. 458.

99   Karl Marx to Friedrich Engels, May 18, 1859, *SC* (London), p. 123. Italics in original.

100 Maximilien Rubel, "Remarques sur le concept de parti prolétarien chez Marx," in *Revue française de Sociologie*, vol. II, no. 3 (Paris, 1961), p. 176.

101 R. Quilliot, "La conception du parti ouvrier," in *La Revue Socialiste* (Paris), February–March, 1964, p. 172.

102 Half a century later such a conception was dubbed as "substitutism" by Trotsky, who imputed it to Lenin and attacked him in the name of Marxism for allegedly favoring the party substituting itself for the working class which, he argued, would lead to a single "dictator" substituting himself for the party. See Isaac Deutscher, *The Prophet Armed* (London: Oxford University Press, 1954), pp. 90–91.

103 Friedrich Engels, *Karl Marx: Critique of Political Economy*, in *Werke* (Berlin, 1960), vol. 13, p. 469.

104 For an unwarranted generalization from this historically determined special case, see Roger Garaudy, *Humanisme Marxiste* (Paris: Éditions Socialies, 1957), p. 299. To the question (asked in relation to a situation such as that which arose in Hungary in 1956): "Where then is the working class?" Garaudy, who quotes Marx's statement, writes: "A Marxist can only reply: it is wherever a man or a group of men is conscious of the historical mission of the working class and fights to accomplish it." Garaudy's more recent writings would suggest that he is today more conscious of the dangers implicit in such a paternalistic approach than he was ten years ago when he wrote these lines.

105 Karl Marx to L. Kugelmann, April 12, 1871, *SC* (London), p. 309.

106 Friedrich Engels to F. A. Sorge, September 12 (and 17), 1874, ibid., p. 330.

107 Engels, *Socialism in Germany*, p. 247.

108 Karl Marx to Friedrich Engels, November 24, 1857, *SC* (London), p. 101. Italics in original.

109 Friedrich Engels to Karl Marx, January 29, 1869, in Saville, *Ernest Jones: Chartist,* p. 247.

110 Engels was only able to come on to the General Council of the International when he moved from Manchester to London in the autumn of 1870. See Gustav Mayer, *Friedrich Engels: A Biography* (London: Alfred A. Knopf, 1936), p. 197.

111 See David Ryazanoff, *Die Entstehung der Internationalen Arbeiterassoziation,* in *Marx-Engels Archiv* (Frankfurt n.d.—either 1925 or 1926), vol. I, pp. 119–202.

112 See Karl Marx to F. Bolte, November 23, 1871, *SC* (London), pp. 317–18.

113 See Walter Schmidt, *Zum Verhältnis zwischen dem Bund der Kommunisten und der I. Internationale,* in *Beiträge,* 1964, vol. VI, S.

114 See Karl Marx to M. Barry, January 7, 1872, *Werke* (Berlin, 1966), vol. 33, p. 370. Bakunin apparently believed, on the strength of nothing more than a jesting remark made to him by Marx in 1848 that at the time of the International, the Communist League still existed as a secret society. See *Michel Bakounine et l'Italie, 1871–1872, Pt. 2, Archives Bakounine* (Leiden, 1963), vol. I, no. 2, p. 127, and A. Lehning, Introduction to *Michel Bakounine et les Conflits dans l'Internationale, 1872,* ibid., vol. II, p. xix.

115 *SW*, vol. I, p. 348.

116 Emst Engelberg, in his *Johann Philipp Becker in der I. Internationale* (Berlin: Dietz, 1964), p. 30, is however going much too far when he asserts that by this formulation of 1864 Marx meant "the disciplined, centralized party" with its "scientific theory."

117 *SW*, vol. I, pp. 350–53.

118 Karl Marx to Friedrich Engels, November 4, 1864, *SC* (London), p. 163.

119 See Friedrich Engels, Preface to the German edition (1890) of the *Manifesto*, p. 30.

120 "General Rules of the I.W.M.A.," *SW*, vol. I, pp. 351–53.

121 Documents of the First International (Moscow, n.d.—1966?), vol. III, p. 311.

122 See Marx's marginal notes on the Alliance's Programme and Rules, December 15, 1868 in ibid., pp. 273–77. (Beside the words "fondue entièrement dans la grande Association Internationale des Travailleurs" in the program, Marx writes: "fondue dans, et fondée contre!"—p. 273.)

123 Karl Marx to L. Kugelmann, October 9, 1866, *SC* (London), p. 214.

124 Karl Marx to Friedrich Engels, November 4, 1864, ibid., p. 163.

125 Friedrich Engels, Preface to the German edition of the *Manifesto*, p. 30.

126 See, e.g., Jacques Freymond's Introduction to *La Première Internationale: Recueil de Documents* (Geneva, 1962), vol. I, pp. x–xi.

127 *La Première Internationale*, vol. I, pp. 405–6.

128 In 1867 Bismarck had introduced universal manhood suffrage into the North German Confederation and extended it to the new German Reich in 1871. Urban workers in Britain had been given the vote under the Second Reform Bill of 1867.

129 See *La Première Internationale*, vol. II, pp. 191ff. A fuller report of Engels's speech, which alone refers specifically to the need for the workers to form an independent party, is given in *Werke* (Berlin, 1962), vol. 17, p. 416.

130 *The International Herald*, no. 37, December 14, 1872. (See, above, note 1.)

131 Miklos Molnar, *Le Déclin de la Première Internationale* (Geneva, 1963), p. 137. A number of Soviet historians have in the past interpreted the London Conference decisions in the same way that Molnar does here. See, e.g., Igor M. Kriwogus and Stanislav M. Stezkewitsch, *Abriss der Gegrhichte der I. und II. Internationale* (Berlin: Dietz, 1960), p. 130: "In the decisions on the organizational question were expressed the aim of making the International into an international political party of the working class." Cf. K. L. Seleznev, *K. Marks i F. Engels' o revoliutsionnoy partii proletariata* (Moscow, 1955), p. 26; A.Y. Koroteeva, "The Hague Congress of the First International," in Galkin, ed., *Aus der Geschichte*, p. 596. G. Stekloff, in his *History of the International* (London, 1928), p. 181, argued that Marx was thinking in terms of making the IWMA into an international workers' party with the General Council as its executive committee in the absence of national parties that could oppose this. (Molnar, p. 134, n.18, dissociates himself from this extreme view.) In recent years, however, Soviet colleagues have come more correctly

to see the London Conference decisions as aiming at "the creation in each country of an independent proletarian party." See B. E. Kunina, "Iz Istorii deyatel'nosti Marksa v General'nom Sovete I. Internatsionala, 1871–72," in L. I. Gol'man, ed., *Iz Istorii Marksizma i Mezhdunarodnogo rabochego Dvizheniya* (Moscow, 1963), p. 349; I. A. Bakh, ed., *Pervyi Internatsional* (Moscow, 1965), vol. II, p. 137.

132 Interview with Karl Marx, in the *World* (New York), July 18, 1871, reproduced in *New Politics*, vol. II, no. 1 (New York, 1962), p. 130.

133 Molnar, *Le Déclin*, p. 35.

134 *The Workman's Times*, March 25, 1893. The report carried there of this important speech made by Engels on March 18, 1893 at a London meeting commemorating the Paris Commune does not appear in the *Werke*, or in the Russian *Sochineniya* whose second edition they follow, whose tables of dates from Engels's life do not make any reference to it. (See *Werke*, vol. 22, p. 673.) It is, however, quoted by Siegfried Bünger, *Friedrich Engels und die britische Sozialistische Bewegung von 1881–1895* (Berlin: Rütten & Loening, 1961), p. 207. This latter work draws on a wide range of original sources and gives an extremely valuable factual and analytical treatment of this period. It is to be hoped that with the growth of studies in labor history in this country it will soon find an English translator and publisher.

135 His authorship is indicated in letters to F. A. Sorge from Karl Marx on December 21, 1872 and from Friedrich Engels on January 4, 1873, in *Briefe und Auszüge aus Briefen von Ioh. Phil. Becker, J. Dietzgen, Friedrich Engels, Karl Marx, u.A. an F.A. Sorge u. Andere* (Stuttgart, 1906), pp. 86, 88.

136 Marx and Engels, *On Britain*, p. 500.

137 Ibid., p. 500.

138 Friedrich Engels, *Socialism: Utopian and Scientific* (London: Allen & Unwin, 1932), p. xxx.

139 *SW*, vol. I, p. 41.

140 *La Première Internationale*, vol. II, pp. 195, 224.

141 *SC* (Moscow), p. 315.

142 Ibid., pp. 314–15.

143 Friedrich Engels to August Bebel, November 14, 1879, *Werke* (Berlin, 1966), vol. 34, p. 421. (The translation in *SC*, Moscow, p. 398, is poor.)

144 "The Association does not dictate the form of political movements," said Marx two months before the London Conference. "In each part of the world some special aspect of the problem presents itself, and the workmen there address themselves to its consideration in their own way." The *World*, July 18, 1871, p. 130.

145 Molnar, *Le Déclin*, p. 137.

146 *Documents of the First International*, vol. III, p. 310.

147 Report published by the *World* (New York), October 15, 1871, reproduced in Molnar, *Le Déclin*, p. 237.

148 Friedrich Engels, *Report on the Alliance of Socialist Democracy*, in *Werke*, vol. 18, p. 141.

149 Julius Braunthal, *Geschichte der Internationale* (Hannover: Dietz, 1961), vol. I, p. 186.

150 *La Revue de Paris*, 1896, p. 131, quoted by A. Lehning in his Introduction to *Michel Bakounine et l'Italie*, Part 2, *Archives Bakounine*, vol. I, no. 2, p. xxxvi. Italics in original, cf. ibid., pp. 251–52, and *La Première Internationale*, vol. II, pp. 474–75.

151 Karl Marx to Paul Lafargue, April 19, 1870, in Istituto G. Feltrinelli, *Annali* (Milan, 1958), vol. I, p. 176.

152 See, e.g., *Circulaire à toutes les fédérations de 1'Association Internationale des Travailleurs* (from the Sonvillier Congress, 1871), in *Archives Bakounine*, vol. I, no. 2, especially p. 405, which rejects "any leadership endowed with authority [*toute autorité directrice*] even if it has been elected and consented to by the workers."

153 See E. H. Carr, *Michael Bakunin* (London: MacMillan, 1937), pp. 420–23; Max Nettlau, *Michael Bakunin* (London, 1898, privately produced by autocopyist), part 3, p. 724.

154 See, e.g., Mehring, *Karl Marx*, pp. 429, 491–92.

155 See, e.g., *Archives Bakounine*, vol. I, no. 2, pp. 124–26, where Bakunin refers to the Jews as "an exploiting sect, a bloodsucking people, a unique devouring parasite, tightly and intimately organized . . . cutting across all the differences of political opinion," and Marx and the Rothschilds are said to hold each other in high esteem!

156 Karl Marx to Friedrich Engels, November 4, 1864, *SC* (London), p. 161. Italics in original.

157 Edouard Vaillant et al., *Internationale et Révolution*, in *Archives Bakounine*, vol. II, pp. 363, 366.

158 *Der Vorbote* (Geneva), March 1870, pp. 41–42; *Archives Bakounine*, vol. I, no. 2, pp. 211–12, 214–15; James Guillaume, *L'Internationale: Documents et Souvenirs* (Paris: Société nouvelle de librarie et d'édition, 1905), vol. I, pp. 207–8.

159 Hans Gerth, ed., *The First International: Minutes of the Hague Congress of 1872* (Madison: University of Wisconsin Press, 1958), p. 287.

160 *Address of the British Federal Council*, drafted by Karl Marx, *Werke*, vol. 18, p. 205.

161 Henry Collins and Chimen Abramsky, *Karl Marx and the British Labour Movement* (London: MacMillan, 1965), pp. 248ff.

162 Friedrich Engels to F. A. Sorge, September 12 (and 17), 1874, *SC* (London), p. 330.

163 Ibid., p. 330.

164 Molnar, *Le Déclin*, p. 188.

165 Roger P. Morgan, *The German Social Democrats and the First International* (Cambridge: Cambridge University Press, 1965).

166 Ibid., pp. 182–88, 204, 219–28. See also *Werke* (Berlin, 1965), vol. 33, pp. 287, 322–23, 361–62, 461–62, 467, 567; Mehring, *Le Déclin*, pp. 482–83; Braunthal, *Geschichte*, p. 195.

167 *SW*, vol. II, p. 323.

168 See Friedrich Engels, *The Sonvillier Congress and the International*, in *Werke* (Berlin, 1962), vol. 17, pp. 477–78. Also D. Lekovic, "Revolucionarna delatnost Prve intemacionale kao faktor razvitka marksizma," *Prilozi za istoriju socijalizma,* vol. II (Belgrade, 1964), esp. pp. 37–50, which deals with some very important problems of Marx and Engels's ideas on organization in this period, such as the relationship between centralism and autonomy, majority and minority and their concept of sectarianism. See, further, B. E. Kunina, in L. I. Gol'man, ed., *Iz Istorii Marksizma*, pp. 347–51.

169 See Friedrich Engels to F. A. Sorge, July 17, 1889, in *Briefe und Auszüge*, pp. 316–18.

170 Friedrich Engels, Paul and Laura Lafargue, *Correspondence* (Moscow, n.d.), vol. III, p. 103.

171 Karl Marx to J. B. Schweitzer, October 13, 1868 (draft), *SC* (London), p. 250.

172 See, e.g., Friedrich Engels to L. Kugelmann, July 10, 1869, *Werke* (Berlin, 1965), vol. 32, p. 621.

173 Marx to Schweitzer, *SC* (London), p. 250.

174 Friedrich Engels to Karl Marx, September 24, 1868, *Werke*, vol. 32, p. 161.

175 Friedrich Engels to Karl Marx, September 30, 1868, ibid., p. 170.

176 Karl Marx to J. B. Schweitzer, October 13, 1868, ibid., p. 570.

177 Friedrich Engels to Karl Marx, July 25, 1866, *SC* (London), p. 211.

178 Karl Marx to L. Kugelmann, October 11, 1867, in Karl Marx, *Letters to Kugelmann* (London: Lawrence & Wishart, 1941), p. 50.

179 M. M. Mikhailova, "Kistorii raspostraneniya I.toma 'Kapitala,'" in Gol'man, ed., *Iz Istorii Marksizma*, p. 425.

180 Wilhelm Liebknecht's closing speech at Nuremberg Congress of the Association of German Workers' Associations, 1868, in *Die 1. Internationale in Deutschland* (Berlin: Dietz, 1964), p. 245.

181 See, e.g., Karl Marx, *Notes on Bakunin's "Statism and Anarchy"* in *Werke*, vol. 18, p. 636.

182 See Friedrich Engels, *Prefatory Notes* (1874) to his *Peasant War in Germany*, *SW*, vol. I, pp. 590–91.

183 See, e.g., Friedrich Engels to August Bebel, March 18–28, 1875, *SC* (London), pp. 332, 333.

184 *Critique of the Gotha Programme*, *SW*, vol. II, pp. 13–45.

185 Ibid., pp. 15–16. Italics in original.

186 Karl Marx to F. A. Sorge, October 19, 1877, *SC* (London), p. 350.

187 Friedrich Engels, *Socialism: Utopian and Scientific*, p. v.

188 Karl Marx to F. A. Sorge, September 19, 1879, *SC* (Moscow), p. 396.

189 Karl Marx and Friedrich Engels to August Bebel, Wilhelm Liebknecht, W. Bracke, and others (Circular Letter), Middle of September 1879, *SC* (London), p. 374.

190 Ibid., p. 370.

191 Ibid., p. 376.

192 Ibid.

193 Ibid., p. 377.

194 Friedrich Engels to August Bebel, June 21, 1882, in Friedrich Engels, *Briefe an Bebel* (Berlin: Dietz, 1958), p. 64.

195 Ibid., p. 64. Cf. *Briefe und Auszüge*, pp. 203–4; *SC* (London), pp. 439–40.

196 Friedrich Engels to F. A. Sorge, October 24, 1891, *LA*, pp. 237–38. Carlo Schmid, in his article "Ferdinand Lassalle und die Politisierung der deutschen Arbeiterbewegung," in *Archiv für Sozialgeschichte* (Hanover: Verlag für Literatur und Zeitgeschehen, 1963), vol. III, p. 6, notes that it was especially at the Erfurt Congress that the party "officially dissociated itself ideologically from the opinions of Lassalle."

197 Interview with the "Daily Chronicle," July 1, 1893, in Friedrich Engels, Paul and Laura Lafargue, *Correspondence*, vol. III, p. 400.

198 *SW*, vol. I, p. 120.

199 Ibid., p. 123.

200 Friedrich Engels to Paul Lafargue, April 3, 1895, *SC* (Moscow), p. 569.

201 Friedrich Engels, *Foreword* (to the pamphlet *International Questions in the "Volksstaat"*), *Werke* (Berlin, 1963), vol. 22, p. 418.

202 Harold J. Laski, *Communist Manifesto: A Socialist Landmark* (London: Allen & Unwin, 1948), p. 75.

203 Ibid., p. 39.

204 Friedrich Engels to F. A. Sorge, September 12 (and 17), 1874, *SC* (London), p. 329. My emphasis.

205 Laski, *Communist Manifesto*, p. 57. My emphasis.

206 See Paul Lafargue to Friedrich Engels, August 10, 1882, Engels–Lafargue *Correspondence* (Moscow: Foreign Languages Publishing House, 1959), vol. I, pp. 102–3.

207 Friedrich Engels to Eduard Bernstein, October 20, 1882, *SC* (Moscow), p. 424.

208 Actually the possibilist preamble, of which presumably at that stage Engels had only seen limited reports, went much further than the 1866 Rules to the International. (See its text in Engels–Lafargue *Correspondence*, vol. I, p. 108.)

209 Engels to Bernstein, ibid., p. 424.

210 Friedrich Engels to Eduard Bernstein, November 28, 1882, in Eduard Bernstein, *Die Briefe von Friedrich Engels und Eduard Bernstein* (Berlin: Dietz, 1925), pp. 102–3.

211 Friedrich Engels to F. K. Wischnewetsky, December 28, 1886, *SC* (London), p. 454.

212 Friedrich Engels to F. A. Sorge, November 29, 1886, ibid., p. 450.

213 Engels to Wischnewetsky, ibid., p. 454.

214 *LA*, p. 290.

215 Ibid., p. 286.

216 Marx and Engels, *On Britain*, p. 481.

217 Ibid., p. 477.

218 See, e.g., Bünger, *Friedrich Engels*, p. 29.

219 *On Britain*, p. 477.

220 *The Workman's Times*, March 25, 1893.

221 Friedrich Engels to F. A. Sorge, March 18, 1893, *LA*, p. 249.

222 Friedrich Engels to H. Schlüter, January 1, 1895, *On Britain*, pp. 537–38.

223 Friedrich Engels to F. A. Sorge, November 29, 1886, *SC* (London), p. 450. Italics in original.

224 See discussion of these differences as "a sample of materialist dialectics" by V. I. Lenin, *Preface to Letters to Sorge*, in his *Selected Works* (Moscow, 1939), vol. XI, pp. 722–25, 732–33.

225 *SC* (London), p. 453.

226 Ibid., p. 450.

227 *Preface* (1887), *LA*, p. 290.

228 Ibid., p. 291.

229 Friedrich Engels, *Foreword* (1891) to *Critique of the Gotha Programme*, *SW* vol. II, p. 14.

230 *LA*, p. 290.

231 In respect of the S.D.F., see, e.g., Interview with "Daily Chronicle," p. 397; re. S.L.P., see, e.g., Friedrich Engels to F. A. Sorge, November 10, 1894, *LA*, p. 263.

232 Friedrich Engels to F. A. Sorge, May 12, 1894, *On Britain*, p. 536.

233 *LA*, p. 263.

234 G. D. H. Cole and Raymond Postgate, *The Common People 1746–1938* (London: Methuen & Co., 1938), p. 403.

235 R. N. Carew Hunt, *The Theory and Practice of Communism* (London: Penguin, 1963), p. 147, and *Marxism Past and Present* (London: G Bles, 1954), p. 157.

236 Friedrich Engels to August Bebel, August 30, 1883, *On Britain*, p. 516.

237 *SC* (London), p. 450.

238 Ibid., p. 455.

239 *LA*, p. 290.

240 Ibid.

241 Friedrich Engels, *The Condition of the Working Class in England*, in *On Britain*, p. 273.

242 Georges Sorel, *La décomposition du marxisme* (Paris, 1910), p. 51.

243 Friedrich Engels to G. Trier, 18 December 1889, *SC* (Moscow), p. 492.

244 Friedrich Engels, *Werke* (Berlin, 1962), vol. 16, p. 68. (See also pp. 66–78.) The implications of this for Marx and Engels's concept of the party are discussed in Ernesto Ragionieri's very valuable essay, "Il marxismo e la Prima Internazionale," in *Critica Marxista*, vol. III, no. 1 (Rome, 1965),

especially pp. 127–28, 149–50. See also Heinz Hümmler, *Opposition gegen Lassalle* (Berlin: Rütten & Loening, 1963), p. 142.

245 See, e.g., Karl Marx, "A Servile Government," in *New York Daily Tribune*, January 28, 1853. Also *SW*, vol. I, p. 556; *SW*, vol. II, p. 291.

246 Karl Marx, *The Chartists*, in T. B. Bottomore and Maximilien Rubel, eds, *Karl Marx: Selected Writings in Sociology and Social Philosophy* (London: Penguin, 1963), p. 206.

247 Friedrich Engels, *The Origin of the Family, Private Property and the State*, in *SW*, vol. II, p. 291.

248 Maximilien Rubel, "Introduction à l'Ethique Marxienne," in Karl Marx, *Pages Choisies pour une Ethique Socialiste* (Paris: Marcel Rivière, 1948), p. xxix.

249 *Revue française de Sociologie*, p. 168; Maximilien Rubel, *Karl Marx: Essai de Biographie Intellectuelle* (Paris: M Rivière, 1957), p. 250; Maximilien Rubel, "De Marx au bolchévisme: partis et conseils," in *Arguments* (Paris, 1962), no. 25–26, p. 33; Maximilien Rubel, "Mise au Point non Dialectique," in *Les Temps Modernes* (Paris, December 1957), no. 142, p. 1138. Lucien Goldmann gives a biting criticism of Rubel's views in his *Recherches Dialectiques* (Paris: Gallimard, 1959), pp. 280–301, to which the last noted article by Rubel was intended as a reply.

250 *Revue française de Sociologie*, p. 175.

251 Rubel, *Karl Marx: Biographie*, p. 288.

252 *Revue française de Sociologie*, p. 174.

253 Ibid., p. 176.

254 "Introduction à l'Ethique Marxienne," p. xvii.

255 Resolution of the Central Committee of the German language group of the I.W.M.A., signed by Becker, in *Der Vorbote* (Geneva), July 1869, pp. 103–5.

256 Friedrich Engels to Karl Marx, July 30, 1869, *Werke*, vol. 32, p. 353. Italics in original.

257 *SW*, vol. I, p. 44. See, e.g., *The Demands of the Communist Party in Germany*, in Ryazanoff, ed., *Manifesto*, pp. 345–47, written by Marx and Engels at the outbreak of the 1848 Revolution as a program of immediate demands for which the members of the Communist League were to campaign politically.

258 See *Rules and Constitution of the Communist League*, pp. 340–45.

259 *Manifesto*, in *SW*, vol. I, p. 44. My emphasis.

260 Friedrich Engels to F. A. Sorge, May 12, 1894, *Briefe und Auszüge*, p. 412. The translation of this passage, whose phrasing has considerable significance for an understanding of Marx and Engels's conception of the sources of revolutionary consciousness, is not entirely satisfactory in either *On Britain*, p. 536, or *LA*, p. 263.

261 Friedrich Engels to F. A. Sorge, November 29, 1886, *SC* (London), p. 451.

262 Friedrich Engels to G. Trier, December 18, 1889, Karl Marx and Friedrich Engels, *Sochineniya* (Moscow, 1965), vol. 37, p. 276. To the best of my

knowledge this part of the letter, first published in Russian in 1932, has never been published either in its German original or in English. (At the time of going to press, the *Werke* have only reached Volume 34, carrying the Marx–Engels correspondence with third persons up to the end of 1880.)

263 Friedrich Engels to F.A. Sorge, August 9, 1890, *Briefe und Auszüge*, pp. 343–44. Cf. Engels' letters on the same theme to Wilhelm Liebknecht, August 10, 1890 (Wilhelm Liebknecht, *Briefwechsel mit Karl Marx und Friedrich Engels* [The Hague, 1963], pp. 375–76), to Karl Kautsky of February 3, February 11, and February 23, 1891, September 4, 1892 (*Friedrich Engels' Briefwechsel mit Karl Kautsky* [Vienna, 1955], pp. 272, 278, 283, 363), and to August Bebel, 1(-2) May 1891 (*Briefe an Bebel*, pp. 177–78.) Also his and Marx's condemnation in 1873 of "unity of thought and action" (a principle inscribed in the program of Bakunin's Revolutionary Organization of International Brothers) as a Jesuit conception meaning "nothing other than orthodoxy and blind obedience." (*L'Alliance de la Démocratie Socialiste et l'Internationale*, in *La Première Internationale*, vol. II, p. 393.)

264 Friedrich Engels, *Introduction* (1895) to Karl Marx, *The Class Struggles in France, 1848–1850, SW*, vol. I, p. 118.

265 Karl Marx, *General Rules of the I.W.M.A., SW*, vol. I, p. 350.

266 Friedrich Engels, *The Housing Question, SW*, vol. I, p. 556. Italics in original.

267 Ibid., p. 556.

268 On the fundamentally antiauthoritarian and antibureaucratic nature of Marx's conception of this "dictatorship," see Ralph Miliband, "Marx and the State," in *Socialist Register* 1965 (London), pp. 289–93. See also Hal Draper, "Marx and the Dictatorship of the Proletariat," in *Cahiers de l'Institut de Science Economique Appliquée*, Série S, *Etudes de Marxologie*, no. 6 (Paris, 1962), pp. 5–73, where the author reproduces the principal Marx-Engels loci on this question.

269 Karl Marx, *Critique of the Gotha Programme, SW*, vol. II, p. 30.

270 Joseph V. Stalin, Interview with Roy Howard, in *The Communist International* (London), March–April, 1936, p. 14. "Where several classes do not exist," argues Stalin, "there cannot be several parties, since (a) party is part of (a) class." Marx and Engels never took such a crude view of the class basis of parties. Whilst Engels described parties as "the more or less adequate political expression of . . . classes and fractions of classes" (*Introduction to Class Struggles in France, SW*, vol. I, p. 110), he noted that, due to the uneven political development of the working class, "the 'solidarity of the proletariat' is everywhere realized in different party groupings which carry on life and death feuds with one another." (Friedrich Engels to August Bebel, June 20, 1873, *SC*, London, p. 327.) Moreover, Marx saw exclusively "ideological" factors as the *raison d'être* of the republican faction of the bourgeoisie," for instance, that in 1848 stood in opposition to the Party of Order representing the monarchist section of that class (*Eighteenth Brumaire, SW*, vol. I, p. 234), just as Engels forty years later was to see the anti-

Prussian regional particularism of the Catholic areas as the basis for the then rising German Centre Party comprising a mixture of class elements. (Friedrich Engels, *What Next?*, *Werke*, vol. 22, p. 8.)

271 Friedrich Engels, *Programme of the Blanquist Commune Refugees*, *Werke*, vol. 18, p. 529.

272 Karl Marx's speech at dinner to delegates of London Conference of I.W.M.A. in Molnar, p. 238.

273 Friedrich Engels, *Introduction* (1891) to *Karl Marx, The Civil War in France, SW*, vol. I, p. 440.

274 Members of the Commune were divided into a Blanquist majority and a mainly Proudhonist minority of members of the International. (See Engels, p. 436.) Various political groups, including the middle-class Union Républicaine, functioned freely. It is however significant that Marx and Engels, after the experience of the Commune, stressed more strongly than ever before the need for independent working-class parties to give the kind of conscious leadership and direction that had been lacking in Paris. In this connection it should be borne in mind, as Engels was to write to Bernstein on January 1, 1884, that in Marx's *Civil War in France* "the unconscious tendencies of the Commune were put down to its credit as more or less conscious plans." *SC,* Moscow, p. 440. Italics in original.

275 Karl Marx, *The Civil War in France*, hereafter *Civil War, SW*, vol. I, p. 471.

276 Engels, *Introduction* (1891), p. 438.

277 Carew Hunt, *Marxism*, p. 155.

278 Carr, *Michael Bakunin*, p. 360.

279 Karl Marx to F. Boite, February 12, 1873, *Werke* (Berlin, 1966), vol. 33, p. 566. Italics in original, cf. also Marx and Engels's Circular Letter, 1879, on the "right" of "the representatives of the petty bourgeoisie" to form their own independent party outside the German Social Democratic Workers' Party. *SC*, London, p. 376.

280 See, e.g., Engels, *The Sonvillier Congress*, p. 477.

281 Friedrich Engels, *Preface* (1886) to *Capital*, vol. I (London: Allen & Unwin, 1938), p. xiv.

282 *Civil War*, p. 471.

283 Ibid., p. 473.

284 First draft of *Civil War*, in *Arkhiv Marksa i Engel'sa*, vol. III (VIII) (Moscow, 1934), p. 208.

285 Friedrich Engels to J. P. Becker, April 1, 1880, *Werke* (Berlin, 1966), vol. 34, p. 441. (The translation in *SC*, London, p. 381, is inaccurate.)

286 Karl Marx, *Notes on Bakunin's "Statism and Anarchy,"* *Werke*, vol. 18, p. 636.

287 Ibid., p. 634.

288 *The Poverty of Philosophy*, p. 197.

The Principle of Self-Emancipation in Marx and Engels

English translations are cited, wherever possible, from the two-volume Marx-Engels *Selected Works* (Moscow: Foreign Languages Publishing House, 1955), abbreviated *SW*. Untranslated German texts are cited, wherever possible, from the Marx-Engels *Werke* (Berlin: Dietz, 1961–68), abbreviated *W*.

1   The following essay is one chapter of a larger work in progress, on *Karl Marx's Theory of Revolution*, and concerns itself with only one aspect of Marx's views on the nature of proletarian revolution. Taken by itself, isolatedly, there is a danger that it may be interpreted in a one-sided way, as *counterposing* "self-emancipation" to class organization and political leadership.

    Such a conclusion is utterly baseless, in my own opinion. And that such a counterposition has nothing in common with Marx's approach is, I think, proved to the hilt by Monty Johnstone's admirable study, "Marx and Engels and the Concept of the Party" (*Socialist Register*, 1967). I agree unreservedly with Johnstone's passing remark: "Marx's famous principle that 'the emancipation of the working classes must be conquered by the working classes themselves,' on which he and Engels insisted again and again, is complemented, not contradicted, by their concept of the Party."

    What is true, certainly, is that the "principle of self-emancipation" *conditions*, and interacts with, one's concept of class party and vanguard organization. What is true is that the principle does contradict, is quite incompatible with, a number of well-known party concepts held by self-styled "Marxist" parties, including both the classic and contemporary social democratic parties and the Stalinist-type parties, both of which are elitist in different ways. But this is a question that requires a separate and extensive treatment of its own.

2   Karl Marx, First Draft of *The Civil War in France,* in *Arkhiv Marksa i Engel'sa,* vol. 3, no. 8, 1934, p. 270.

3   From the *Aeneid*, vol.VII, 312.

4   George Brandes, *Ferdinand Lassalle* (New York: Macmillan, 1911), p. 108. The Virgilian line is also used as the title-page motto for the whole book.

5   Letter, Engels to Paul Lafargue, February 13, 1886, in *Engels-Lafargue: Correspondence* (Moscow: Foreign Languages Publishing House, 1959), vol. 1, pp. 338–39.

6   Marx, *Provisional Rules of the Association*, in *The General Council of the First International: Minutes, 1864–66*, vol. 1, p. 288. This remained the same in the later revisions; the 1871 version is in *SW*, vol. 1, p. 386.

7   Engels, Preface to 1888 English edition of the *Communist Manifesto*, in *SW*, vol. 1, p. 28; Marx, *Critique of the Gotha Program*, in *SW*, vol. 2, p. 25.

8   As usual, there are possible exceptions. A prominent candidate is the remarkable Gerrard Winstanley (and "The Diggers," the left wing of the English Revolution); but he was entirely unknown to the early socialists, completely forgotten. Then there was Thomas Münzer (who was therefore

the subject of Engels's first serious work after the 1848 revolution); and Spartacus—"the most splendid fellow that all ancient history has to show; great general—no Garibaldi—noble character, real representative of the ancient proletariat," wrote Marx. But we know too little about the last two. Letter, Marx to Engels, February 27, 1861, in *W*, vol. 30, p. 160; on Spartacus, see also Marx's well-known "Confession" (question game) in which Spartacus and Kepler are listed as his "favorite heroes"; in David Riazanov, ed. *Karl Marx: Man, Thinker and Revolutionist* (New York: International Publishers, 1927), p. 269; or *W*, vol. 31, p. 597.

9   Friedrich Engels, "Progress of Social Reform on the Continent," *New Moral World*, no. 4, November 18, 1843, in Marx and Engels, *Gesamtausgabe (MEGA)* I, vol. 2, p. 442.

10   Ibid., p. 436.

11   Ibid., p. 435.

12   Ibid., p. 449.

13   It is amusing to find Fabianism's Bernard Shaw, in the next century, rediscovering Weitling's idea of "civil service" examinations to select an oligarchy: Shaw's pet suggestion on how to replace democracy.

13   Friedrich Engels, "The 'Times' on German Communism," *New Moral World*, January 20, 1844, in Marx and Engels, *Gesamtausgabe* I, vol. 2, p. 452.

14   This change can be followed through several steps in the English-language articles reprinted in Marx and Engels, *Gesamtausgabe* I, vol. 4.

15   Friedrich Engels, "The late Butchery at Leipzig—The German Working Men's Movement," *Northern Star*, September 13, 1845, in Marx and Engels, *Gesamtausgabe* I, vol. 4, p. 477.

16   Boris Nicolaievsky and Otto Maenchen-Helfen, *Karl Marx: Man and Fighter* (Philadelphia: Lippincott, 1936), p. 43.

17   Franz Mehring, *The Lessing Legend* (New York: Critics Group, 1938), p. 29.

18   Franz Mehring, *Karl Marx* (New York: Covici Friede, 1935), p. 50.

19   Mehring, *Karl Marx*, p. 51; Nicolaievsky and Maenchen-Helfen, *Karl Marx*, p. 44.

20   Nicolaievsky and Maenchen-Helfen, *Karl Marx*, pp. 45–46.

21   Cf. Helmut Hirsch, "Karl Friedrich Koppen, der intimste Berliner Freund Marxens," *International Review for Social History* (Amsterdam), vol. 1.

22   Karl Friedrich Köppen, *Friedrich der Grosse und seine Widersacher* (Leipzig: Wigund, 1840).

23   Nicolaievsky and Maenchen-Helfen, *Karl Marx*, p. 39.

24   Mehring, *Karl Marx*, p. 47.

25   Ibid., p. 49; Nicolaievsky and Maenchen-Helfen, *Karl Marx*, p. 39.

26   In Marx and Engels, *On Religion* (Moscow: Foreign Languages Publishing House, 1957), p. 14.

27   Friedrich Engels, *Germany: Revolution and Counter-Revolution* (New York: International Publishers, 1933), pp. 22–23.

28   Letter, Engels to F. Graeber, December 9, 1839/February 5, 1840; in *W* Erg. Bd., vol. 2, p. 443.

29   Engels, "Freidrich Wilhelm IV, König von Preussen," 1843, in *W*, vol. 1, p. 446, especially p. 453.

30   Marx, Second letter, May 1843, in the "Exchange of Letters," in *Deutsch-Französischer Jahrbücher*, 1844, in *W*, vol. 1, pp. 341–42; translation largely based on *Marx: Writings of the Young Marx on Philosophy and Society*, eds Lloyd Easton and Kurt Guddat (Garden City: Doubleday, 1967), pp. 209–10.

31   Ibid., p. 341; Marx, *Writings of the Young Marx*, p. 208.

32   Ibid., p. 342; Marx, *Writings of the Young Marx*, p. 210.

33   Ibid., pp. 338–39; Marx, *Writings of the Young Marx*, p. 206.

34   In Marx and Engels, *On Religion*, p. 15.

35   Mehring, *Karl Marx*, p. 59.

36   In *W*, Erg. Bd., vol. 1, p. 215.

37   The only significant reference comes soon after, in Marx's 1844 manuscripts. See *Karl Marx, Economic and Philosophic Manuscripts of 1844* (Moscow: Foreign Languages Publishing House, n.d.), p. 117. In his *Poverty of Philosophy*, Marx has to handle Proudhon's use of Prometheus as a sort of economic Robinson Crusoe, but he does not make any Promethean analogies himself. See Karl Marx, *The Poverty of Philosophy* (Moscow: Foreign Languages Publishing House, n.d.), pp. 98–102. (There is an echo of this in Karl Marx, *A Contribution to the Critique of Political Economy*, translated by N. I. Stone [Chicago: Kerr, 1904], Appendix, "Introduction," p. 268. This "Introduction" is a section of the *Grundrisse der Kritik der Politischen Economie*.) Later come only passing references of no present interest. One might wonder if Marx knew Shelley's *Prometheus Unbound* (1819), but there is no sign of it; in fact, Marx never mentioned Shelley in writing; it is Engels who was a Shelley fan from youth to old age.

38   The cartoon may be seen in Mehring, *Karl Marx*, facing p. 296, with a detailed explanation of the verso. (Not in the later paperback edition.)

39   From the German text as given in Nicolaievsky and Maenchen-Helfen, *Karl Marx*, p. 60. Since the author seems to be thoroughly anonymous (cf. Auguste Cornu, *Karl Marx et Friedrich Engels* [Paris: P.U.F., 1958], vol. 2, p. 102), one might wonder whether this was not a last flare-up of Marx's temptation to write verse. Seven years later, when Marx's *Neue Rheinische Zeitung* was closed up in the same city in 1849, a farewell poem by Ferdinand Freiligrath was published in the final issue, naturally striking the same note.

40   The poem has a long title, usually shortened to *Der Triumph der Glaubens*, written and published in 1842; here translated from *W*, Erg. Bd., vol. 2, p. 301.

41   Most of the quotations are from the Paul Elmer More translation of *Prometheus Bound*. The first (Hephaestus) is a colloquialized adaption.

42   Marx, "Toward the Critique of Hegel's Philosophy of Law: Introduction," *Deutsch-Französischer Jahrbücher*, 1844; written end of 1843 to January 1844; in Marx, *Writings of the Young Marx*, p. 264.

43   Ibid., pp. 260–64.

44   In March 1845 Engels referred, in the Owenite paper, to the prediction
     of Marx's "a year ago" of the union of "the German philosophers" and
     the German workers, a union now "all but accomplished." He adds:
     "With the philosophers to think, and the working men to fight for us,
     will any earthly power be strong enough to resist our progress?" Engels,
     "Communism in Germany," *New Moral World*, March 8, 1845, in Marx and
     Engels, *Gesamtausgabe* I, vol. 4, p. 344.

45   Marx, "Debatte über Pressfreiheit," *Rheinische Zeitung*, May 5, 1842; in *W*,
     vol. 1, p. 49.

46   In the same article, here is how Marx refutes the opponents of a free
     press who imply that only the government—i.e. themselves—are inspired
     by God sufficiently to be guardians of the press: "But English history has
     quite sufficiently proved that the assertion of divine inspiration from above
     begets the counter-assertion of divine inspiration from below, and Charles
     I mounted the scaffold as a result of divine inspiration from below." Ibid.,
     p. 51.

47   If read without the bracketed italics, this is Marx's formulation of 1845.
     The bracketed italics are some of the editorial explanations introduced
     by Engels in his 1888 edited version. For the two versions in English, see
     Marx and Engels, *The German Ideology* (Moscow: Progress Publishers, 1964),
     pp. 646, 651–52; for the two in German, see *W*, vol. 3, pp. 5–6, 533–34. In
     the second paragraph of the thesis, Engels introduced two changes that we
     have omitted entirely, as unnecessary or misguided. He deleted the words
     "or self-changing," and altered "revolutionary practice" [*revolutionäre Praxis*]
     to "transformatory [or revolutionizing] practice" [*umwälzende Praxis*].

48   Marx, "The Communism of the Paper *Rheinischer Beobachter*," in Marx and
     Engels, *On Religion*, pp. 82–83; translation modified after *W*, vol. 4, p. 200.

49   In the same article, Marx included a powerful echo of the revulsion against
     the Savior-Ruler, as he attacked the pious Prussian's appeal for "a monarchy
     relying on the support of the people"—unaware, of course, that this was going
     to be, two decades later, the subject of Lassalle's pourparlers with Bismarck:

> We shall make but a few well-meaning remarks to those gentlemen who wish to
> save the imperilled Prussian monarchy by a *Somersault* into the people.
>
> Of all political elements the people is the most dangerous for a king . . . But
> the real people, the proletariat, the small peasants and the populace, there you
> have, as Hobbes said, *puer robustus, sed malitiosus*, a sturdy but knavish boy, who
> will not let himself be made a fool of either by thin kings or fat ones.
>
> This people would first and foremost force His Majesty to grant a constitution
> with universal suffrage, freedom of association, freedom of the press and other
> unpleasant things.
>
> And having obtained all that, it would use it to show as quickly as possible
> how it understands the *power* . . . of the monarchy.

Ibid., p. 85; translation modified after *W*, vol. 4, p. 202.

50   In Marx and Engels, *On Britain*, 2nd ed. (Moscow: Foreign Languages Publishing House, 1962), p. 315.

51   Friedrich Engels, "Deutscher Sozialismus in Versen und Prosa," September 1847, in *W*, vol. 4, p. 207.

52   Marx, *The Poverty of Philosophy*, pp. 124–25.

53   But note that Engels's draft for the Manifesto ("Principles of Communism") does not suggest that there is any incompatibility; it is simply not taken up. Nor does it appear in the Schapper-Wolff draft (published under the title "The Communist Credo" and ascribed by some to Engels) which preceded Engels's "Principles of Communism." Friedrich Engels, *Der Bund der Kommunisten. Dokumente* (Berlin: Dietz, 1970), vol. 1, pp. 1470ff.

54   In *SW*, vol. I, p. 60.

55   Ibid., pp. 63–64.

56   Ibid., p. 62.

57   Ibid., p. 44.

58   Friedrich Engels, "Berliner Vereinbarungsdebatten," *Neue Rheinische Zeitung*, June 7, 1848, in *W*, vol. 5, p. 45.

59   Engels, "Die Polendebatte in Frankfurt," *Neue Rheinische Zeitung*, August 9, 1848, in *W*, vol. 5, p. 319.

60   Letter, Marx to Engels, September 26, 1868, in Marx and Engels, *Selected Correspondence* (New York: International Publishers, 1935), p. 249.

61   Letter, Marx to J. B. Schweitzer, October 13, 1868, in Marx and Engels, *Selected Correspondence* (Moscow: Foreign Languages Publishing House, n.d.), p. 259.

62   Marx, First Draft of *Civil War in France*, p. 280.

63   Marx, *Class Struggles in France 1848–1850*, in *SW*, vol. 1, p. 146.

64   Ibid., p. 174.

65   Ibid., p. 148.

66   Letter, Engels to Marx, March 17, 1858; in *W*, vol. 29, p. 305.

67   Letter, Engels to Wl. J. Schmuilow, February 7, 1893, in *W*, vol. 39, p. 24.

68   Quoted here from the English translation, *The Socialism of Today* (London: Leadenhall Press, n.d.), p. 152. (Translation first published 1884.)

69   Edmond Villetard de Prunières, *History of the International,* translated by S. M. Day (New Haven, 1874), pp. 65–66. The speaker quoted was Chalain. The original, *Histoire de l'Internationale*, was published in Paris, 1872.

70   "The International Working Men's Association to the National Labor Union of the United States," May 12, 1869; written by Marx; adopted by the General Council; in *General Council First International 1868–70*, vol. 3, pp. 102, 321.

71   "The Belgian Massacres," May 4, 1869; manifesto written by Marx, approved by the General Council; in ibid., pp. 314–15.

72   At meeting of the General Council, November 16, 1869; in ibid., p. 182.

73   "To the Working Men of Great Britain and Ireland," September 1865; in *General Council First International 1864–66*, vol. 1, p. 299.

74 Royden Harrison, "The Land and Labour League," International Institute for Social History, *Bulletin*, vol. 8, 1953, no. 3, pp. 174, 195.

75 Minutes of November 29, 1864, in *General Council of the First International 1864–66*, vol. 1, p. 54.

76 Letter, Marx to Engels, December 2, 1864, in Marx and Engels, *The Civil War in the United States* (New York: International Publishers, 1937), p. 273.

77 Jules L. Puech, *Le Proudhonisme dans l'Association Internationale des Travailleurs* (Paris: Alcan, 1907), p. 103n.

78 Marx, "Second Address of the General Council," September 9, 1870; in *SW*, vol. I, p. 496.

79 Marx, *Civil War in France*, in *SW*, vol. I, pp. 522–23.

80 Marx, First Draft of *Civil War in France*, pp. 346–48.

81 Ibid., p. 348. Cf. *Civil War in France*, in *SW*, vol. I, p. 522.

82 Marx is here doubtlessly referring to the followers of Comte; for the English Comtists, while antisocialist, did defend the Commune against the press slander campaign; especially Prof. Edward Beesly (who had chaired the meeting that founded the First International). In a caustic paragraph just before this, Marx had distinguished the English Comtists from the French "co-religionists," and attacked Comtism as follows: "Comte is known to the Parisian workmen as the prophet in politics of Imperialism [Bonapartism] (of personal Dictatorship), of capitalist rule in political economy, of hierarchy in all spheres of human action, even in the sphere of science, and as the author of a new catechism with a new pope and new saints in place of the old ones." Ibid., p. 346. This attack did not appear in the final version, either because of respect for the courage of the English Comtists in defending the Commune, or because of space, or both.

83 Ibid., p. 348.

84 Ibid., p. 352.

85 Engels, *Ludwig Feuerbach*, in *SW*, vol. 2, pp. 400–1.

86 Marx and Engels, *Communist Manifesto*, in *SW*, vol. I, p. 44.

Lenin's *The State and Revolution*

This article was written for a special issue of *Monthly Review* commemorating the centenary of Lenin's birth, and is published here by kind permission of the editors of *Monthly Review*. Unless otherwise specified, all italics are in the text.

1 V. I. Lenin, *The State and Revolution*, in his *Selected Works* (London: Lawrence and Wishart, 1969), page unknown. Hereafter SR. [Editor's note: Here Lenin is in fact quoting Marx and Engels in their 1872 preface to the *Communist Manifesto*.]

2 Lucio Colletti, "Power and Democracy in Socialist Society," in *New Left Review*, no. 56, July–August 1969, p. 19. For another interesting assessment of *The State and Revolution*, see Lucio Magri, "'L'Etat et la Révolution' Aujourd'hui," *Les Temps Modernes*, August–September 1968, pp. 266–67.

3   Lenin, *SR*, p. 334.
4   Ibid., p. 336.
5   Ibid.
6   Ibid., p. 308.
7   V. I. Lenin, *The Proletarian Revolution and the Renegade Kautsky* (London, 1941), p. 24.
8   Lenin, *SR*, p. 347.
9   Ibid., p. 298.
10   Ibid.
11   Ibid., 283.
12   Ibid., p. 301.
13   Ibid., p. 293.
14   Ibid., p. 297.
15   Ibid., p. 296.
16   Ibid., p. 329.
17   Ibid., p. 334.
18   Ibid., p. 346.
19   Ibid., p. 318.
20   Ibid., p. 310.
21   Ibid., p. 281.
22   E. H. Carr, *The Bolshevik Revolution 1917–1923* (London: MacMillan, 1950), vol. I, p. 230.
23   Ibid., p. 230.
24   Robert V. Daniels, "The State and Revolution: A Case Study in the Genesis and Transformation of Communist Ideology," in *The American Slavic and East European Review* (February, 1953), vol. 12, no. 1, p. 24.
25   Isaac Deutscher, *The Prophet Armed* (London: Oxford University Press, 1954), p. 90.
26   See, e.g., Moshe Lewin, *Lenin's Last Struggle* (London: Faber & Faber, 1969).
27   Carr, *The Bolshevik Revolution*, p. 223.
28   Ibid., p. 224.
29   Ibid., p. 246.
30   Lenin, *SR*, p. 328.
31   This may need qualification in the following sense: *on the morrow of revolution*, the problem does often appear to have vanished. The real problems begin to emerge the day after, and the day after that, when the initial impetus and enthusiasm begin to wane and vast new problems and dangers have to be confronted.
32   Karl Marx, "The Civil War in France," in *Selected Works* (Moscow: Foreign Languages Publishing House, 1950), vol. I, p. 473.
33   Karl Marx to F. Domela-Niewenhuis, February 22, 1881, in *Karl Marx and Friedrich Engels: Selected Correspondence* (Moscow: Foreign Languages Publishing House, 1953), p. 410.
34   *Selected Works*, vol. I, p. 440.

35   Quoted by Lenin, *SR*, p. 314.

36   Ibid.

37   Quoted by Lenin, *SR*, p. 320. My italics.

38   Julius Martov, *The State and the Socialist Revolution* (New York: International Review, 1938), p. 41.

39   Lenin, *SR*, p. 293.

40   Ibid., p. 348.

Some Problems Concerning Revolutionary Consciousness

1   Among the most important of the exceptions referred to are Lenin, Gramsci, and Lukács. See in this connection particularly the following: V. I. Lenin, "What Is to Be Done?" in *Selected Works* (Moscow: Foreign Languages Publishing House, 1961), vol. 5, p. 347; Antonio Gramsci, "The Study of Philosophy and Historical Materialism," "Critical Notes on an attempt at a Popular Presentation of Marxism by Bukharin," and "The Modern Prince" collected in *The Modern Prince and Other Writings*, translated by L. Marks (London: Lawrence & Wishart, 1967); Georg Lukács, *Geschichte und Klassenbewusstsein* (Berlin: Malik-Verlag, 1923).

2   See, for example: Karl Marx and Frederick Engels, "The Manifesto of the Communist Party," in *Karl Marx and Frederick Engels: Selected Works* (Moscow: Foreign Languages Publishing House, 1962), vol. 1, p. 34; Alexis de Tocqueville, *The Old Regime and the French Revolution*, translated by Stuart Gilbert (Garden City: Doubleday and Co., 1955).

3   Ernest Mandel, "The Lessons of May," *New Left Review*, no. 52, November–December, 1968, p. 9.

4   The analysis of these reasons does not fall within the scope of this paper but no doubt includes the Cuban revolution, the failure of revolutionary consciousness to develop in the advanced capitalist states (France notwithstanding) and the revitalization of Marxist thought following upon de-Stalinization.

5   Antonio Gramsci, "Critical Notes," p. 90; André Gorz, "Reform and Revolution," in Ralph Miliband and John Saville, eds, *Socialist Register 1968* (London: Merlin Press, 1968), p. 111; VG Kiernan, "Notes on Marxism 1968," in ibid., p. 177; Tom Nairn, "Why it Happened," in Angelo Quattrochi and Tom Nairn, *The Beginning of the End* (London: Panther Books, 1968), p. 103.

6   James C. Davies, "Towards a Theory of Revolution," *American Sociological Review*, vol. 27, no. 1, 1962, p. 5. See also: Raymond Tanter and Manus Midlarsky, "A Theory of Revolution," *Journal of Conflict Resolution*, vol. II, 1967, p. 264.

7   With regard to the nature of the relevant needs the author says (p. 8): "A revolutionary state of mind requires the . . . expectation . . . to satisfy basic needs, which may range from merely physical (food, clothing, shelter,

health, and safety from bodily harm) to social (the affectional ties of family and friends) to the need for equal dignity and justice."

Similar in this respect is the approach of David Wilier and George K. Zollschan, "Prolegomenon to a Theory of Revolution," in George K. Zollschan and Walter Hirsch, *Explorations in Social Change* (London: Routledge and Kegan Paul, 1964), p. 125. Relevant here is the definition by these authors (p. 130) of their term "exigency" as "a feeling of unease in the person and the occurrence of unrest in a collectivity stemming from a differential between the person's definition of the relevant social situation as it is and as it should be. Typically an exigency as such is on a pre-verbal level." In their view the relevant discrepancies have an even wider source than in Davies's theory. See p. 130 and the following on p. 89: "whereas sources of exigencies are diffuse—all manner of discrepancies exist that have the potentiality of presenting themselves to the awareness – three types of discrepancy may be distinguished . . . affective or cathectic, evaluative and cognitive." See also Ralph Dahrendorf, *Class and Class Conflict in an Industrial Society* (London: Routledge, 1959).

8   Davies, "Towards a Theory," represents this point graphically in Figure 1 on page 6.

9   V. I. Lenin, "Left Wing Communism," 1920, in *Selected Works* (Moscow: Foreign Languages Publishing House), vol. 3, p. 430.

10   Ibid.

11   V. I. Lenin, "What is to be Done?" in *Collected Works*, vol. 5, pp. 374–75.

12   I will return to the notion of hegemony later in the paper. Briefly, hegemony can be defined as the consensual aspect of the dominant position of the ruling classes: it is the set of guiding ideas that permeate consciousness and legitimate the social arrangements. The notion of hegemony seems to have much in common with the concept of a "symbolic universe" as used by Berger and Luckmann; see Peter Berger and Thomas Luckmann, *The Social Construction of Reality* (London: Allen Lane, 1967), part 2, section 2. The central concern of these authors is with the social-psychological mechanism by which symbolic universes develop and consequently in general they take the power structure as given. They do, however, draw attention to the possible development of alternative symbolic universes. "The confrontation of alternative symbolic universes implies a problem of power—which of the conflicting definitions of reality will be 'made to stick' in the society." (pp. 126–27).

It is precisely in this aspect that Gramsci is primarily interested. One of his central concerns is with the conditions in, and processes by which, fragmented, partial, and incoherent "alternative definitions" develop into integrated, coherent hegemonies that confront and oppose the existing hegemony. The development of such an opposing hegemony implies, of course, the subjective breakdown of the institutional separation of life into encapsulated spheres and the consequent understanding that the rejection of any of the apparently discrete spheres involves the rejection of the whole of the society.

13   On this aspect see: Berger and Luckmann, *The Social Construction of Reality*; Peter Berger and Stanley Pullberg, "The Concept of Reification," *New Left Review*, no. 35, January–February, 1966, p. 56; M. Harrison, "A Critique of the Social-Psychological Assumptions in Contemporary Functionalism" (unpublished seminar paper).

14   Davies, "Towards a Theory of Revolution," p. 5.

15   Ibid., pp. 5–6.

16   Ibid., p. 19. My emphasis.

17   Ibid., p. 6.

18   Ibid.

19   In addition to the studies that are examined later in the present paper, the same type of problem seems to arise in: Harry Eckstein, "On the Etiology of Internal Wars," in George H. Nadel, ed., *Studies in the Philosophy of History* (New York: Harper Torchbooks, 1965), p. 117; and Wilier and Zollschan, *Explorations in Social Change* (note 7 above).

20   The theories of Wilier and Zollschan, *Explorations in Social Change*, Tanter and Midlarsky, "A Theory of Revolution," among others, show the same characteristics. See also: Ralf Dahrendorf, *Class and Class Conflict in an Industrial Society* (London: Routledge, 1959).

21   Compare on this point: David Lockwood, "Social Integration and System Integration," in Wilier and Zollschan, *Explorations in Social Change*, p. 244.

22   Karl Marx, "Preface to the Critique of Political Economy," in *Marx-Engels Selected Works*, vol. I, p. 363.

23   Friedrich Engels, "Socialism: Utopian and Scientific," in *Marx-Engels Selected Works*, vol. 2, p. 143.

24   Marx, "Preface."

25   Marx and Engels, "The Manifesto of the Communist Party," Friedrich Engels, *Anti-Dühring* (Moscow: Foreign Languages Publishing House, 1954).

26   Karl Marx, "Wage Labour and Capital," in *Marx-Engels Selected Works* (Moscow: Foreign Languages Publishing House, 1962), p. 94.

27   Marx and Engels, "The Manifesto of the Communist Party," pp. 42–43.

28   Antonio Labriola, *Essays in the Materialistic Interpretation of History* (New York: Monthly Review Press, 1966).

29   Engels, "Socialism," pp. 146–47.

30   Herbert Marcuse, *One Dimensional Man* (London: Routledge and Kegan Paul, 1964); "Socialism in the Developed Countries," *International Socialist Journal*, no. 8, 1965, p. 139.

31   Marcuse, "Socialism," p. 140.

32   Ibid., p. 142; see also p. 8.

33   On the points in this paragraph see: Marcuse, "Socialism," pp. 147, 148; Marcuse, *One Dimensional Man*, pp. 9, 24, 25.

34   See Marcuse, "Socialism," pp. 142–43; Marcuse, *One Dimensional Man*, p. 32.

35   Marcuse, *One Dimensional Man*, p. 8.
36   Serge Mallet, "The New Working Class," *International Socialist Journal*, no. 8, April, 1965, p. 156.
37   Ibid., p. 161.
38   Ibid., pp. 156–57.
39   Ibid., p. 163.
40   Ibid., p. 164.
41   Ibid., p. 163.
42   Ibid., p. 164.
43   Ibid.
44   Ibid., p. 163.
45   Ibid., pp. 162–63.
46   Ibid, p. 165.
47   Nairn, "Why It Happened," p. 122.
48   Ibid., p. 119.
49   Ibid., p. 122.
50   Ibid.
51   For discussion of this point see: Lockwood, "Social Integration & System Integration"; Maurice Godelier, "System, Structure and Contradiction in Capital," in *Socialist Register*, 1967 (London: Merlin Press).
52   Régis Debray, "Revolution in the Revolution," *Monthly Review*, vol. 19, no. 3, July–August, 1967, on which the discussion in this paper is entirely based. In his earlier English publications Debray took a very different position. It will be seen from my analysis in the paper that the following passage from an earlier article by Debray is quite contrary to the position criticized here: "The appearance of a guerilla centre is to be subordinated to a vigorous political analysis of the situation: the selection of the moment at which to launch the action and of the right place for it presumes a searching analysis of national contradictions understood in class terms." Régis Debray, "Latin America: The Long March," *New Left Review*, no. 33, 1965, p. 37. See also his "Problems of Revolutionary Strategy in Latin America," *New Left Review*, no. 45, 1967.
53   Debray, "Revolution in the Revolution," p. 36.
54   Ibid., pp. 36–37.
55   Ibid., p. 83.
56   Ibid:, n. 51.
57   Ibid., pp. 53–54.
58   For an assessment of Debray generally see: Leo Huberman and Paul M. Sweezy, eds, "Régis Debray and the Latin American Revolution," in *Monthly Review*, vol. 20, July–August, 1968. There is a particularly perceptive article on the issue of consciousness and the role of the *foco* by E. Ahman (p. 70), although he seems to miss the main point of his own analysis. He shows that Debray himself contended that the peasants recognized the legitimacy of the government and regarded the guerilla as alien. This being

the case, there seems to be no warrant at all for the assumption that combat will undermine the government's legitimacy in the eyes of the peasant.

59 Karl Marx, "Poverty of Philosophy," quoted in T. B. Bottomore and Maximilien Rubel, *Karl Marx* (London: Pelican Books, 1961), p. 195.

60 Marx and Engels, *Communist Manifesto*, pp. 41–43.

61 E.g.,V. I. Lenin,"What the 'Friends of the People' Are" (1905), in *Collected Works* (London: Lawrence and Wishart), vol. I, p. 236.

62 Lenin,"What is to be Done?" (1902), *Selected Works*, vol. 5, p. 383.

63 See, for example, ibid., pp. 375–76.

64 Ibid., p. 422, 375.

65 Ibid.

66 V. I. Lenin,"The Tasks of the Russian Social Democrats" (1898), in *Collected Works*, vol. 2, p. 346. See also "What is to be Done?" p. 425.

67 Ibid., pp. 400-401. See also: V. I. Lenin, "Left Wing Communism: An Infantile Disorder" (1920), *Selected Works,* vol. 3, p. 437.

68 "What the 'Friends of the People' Are," p. 535.

69 "What is to be Done?" pp. 400–1. See also "The Tasks of the Russian Social Democrats," p. 329.

70 "What is to be Done?" pp. 412–13.

71 The doubtful view that Lenin was not concerned with this problem at all has been put forward by Zbigniew A. Jordan, *The Evolution of Dialectical Materialism* (London: Macmillan, 1967), pp. 355–56.

72 "What the 'Friends of the People' Are," p. 159.

73 V. I. Lenin, "The Economic Content of Narodism" (1895), *Selected Works*, vol. I, p. 370. For an interesting discussion of this question see: Gorz, "Reform and Revolution."

74 Ibid.

75 Ibid., p. 386 note.

76 Ibid.

77 "What is to be Done?" pp. 382–84.

78 Ibid., p. 386.

79 At one point Lenin appears to attempt to escape from the difficulties by relying on the proletariat's instinctive realization of its needs for political liberty. See: "Two Tactics of Social Democracy in the Democratic Revolution" (1905), in *Selected Works*, vol. I, p. 571.

80 I attempt this brief examination of Gramsci's ideas with a great deal of hesitation. So little of his writing is available in English that it is naturally impossible to form a full and coherent view of his work. However, the importance of his insights for the present paper seem to me to justify the risk involved in basing an argument on the essays published in *The Modern Prince and Other Writings*. (See note above).

81 Ibid., pp. 61, 66–67.

82 Ibid., p. 61.

83   Gwynn A. Williams, "The Concept of 'Egemonia' in the Thought of Antonio Gramsci: Some Notes on Interpretation," *Journal of the History of Ideas*, vol. 21, no. 4, 1960, p. 586.

84   Ibid., p. 587.

85   Gramsci, *The Modern Prince*, pp. 66–67.

86   See on this point: Gramsci, the essays referred to in note 80; Williams "The Concept of 'Egemonia,'" p. 594; John Merrington, "Theory and Practice in Gramsci's Marxism," *Socialist Register*, 1968 (London: Merlin Press), p. 145, particularly pp. 154, 157.

87   Williams, "The Concept of 'Egemonia,'" p. 590.

88   Gramsci, *Modern Prince*, 138.

89   Merrington, "Theory and Practice," pp. 165–66.

90   Gramsci, *Modern Prince*, pp. 172, 185–86.

91   Quoted by Merrington, "Theory and Practice," pp. 146, 147.

92   Quoted by Merrington, ibid., p. 154.

93   See, for example: Gramsci, *The Modern Prince*, pp. 67–69, 95–96; Williams, "The Concept of 'Egemonia,'" p. 592; Merrington, "Theory and Practice," pp. 151, 157, 165–66.

94   For example: Louis Althusser, "Contradiction and Overdetermination," *New Left Review*, no. 41, January–February, 1967, p. 15.

95   Korsch, among others, has argued that no such theory is possible. He says: "Marx's materialistic social science is not sociology, but economics. For the other branches of the so-called social science there remains then, according to the materialistic principles of Marxism, a scale of phenomena which become in proportion to their increasing distance from the economic foundation, less and less accessible to a strictly scientific investigation, less and less 'material', more and more 'ideological', and which, finally, cannot be treated in a theoretical manner at all, but only critically in the closest connection with the practical tasks of the proletariat." Karl Korsch, *Karl Marx* (New York: Russell & Russell, 1963), pp. 234–35.

96   Marx, "Preface to the Critique of Political Economy," p. 363.

97   Friedrich Engels, "Letter to J. Bloch," *Marx-Engels Selected Works*, vol. 2, p. 488. Also see: Karl Marx, *Capital* (Moscow: Foreign Languages Publishing House, 1959), vol. 3, p. 722: "This does not prevent the same economic bases—the same from the standpoint of its main condition—due to innumerable different empirical circumstances, natural environment, racial relations, external historical influences, from showing infinite variations and graduations in appearance, which can be ascertained only by analysis of the empirically given circumstances." See also Althusser, "Contradiction and Overdetermination," p. 31.

98   Althusser, "Contradiction and Overdetermination," p. 27.

99   *Marx-Engels Selected Works*, vol. 1, p. 361.

100 Karl Marx, "The Introduction to the Critique of Political Economy," reprinted in David Horowitz, *Marx and Modern Economics* (London: MacGibbon and

Kee, 1968), p. 21; Ben Brewster, "Presentation of Althusser," *New Left Review*, no. 41, January–February, 1967; Korsch, *Karl Marx*, chapters VI and VII.

101　Korsch, *Karl Marx*.

Theory and Practice in Gramsci's Marxism

The author acknowledges the help and advice of John C. Cowley during all stages of the preparation of this article. He also expresses gratitude for the services provided by the Gramsci Institute, Rome, during a period of study in 1964.

1　All references to the *Prison Notebooks* in this article are to the edition of Gramsci's collected works: *Opere di Antonio Gramsci* (Turin: Einaudi); 12 volumes, including articles from *L'Ordine Nuovo* 1919–21 (2 vols.), *Lettere dal Carcere* and *Scritti giovanili*.

2　In Britain, Gramsci's work has been particularly drawn on in articles in the *New Left Review*. For translations of Gramsci's writings, see the anthology translated by Louis Marks, *The Modern Prince* (New York: International Publishers, 1957); "In Search of the Educational Principle," translated and introduced by Quentin Hoare, *New Left Review*, vol. 32, July/August 1965, pp. 52–62. A new and more comprehensive anthology of the prison writings is being prepared by Quentin Hoare and Geoffrey Noel-Smith for publication by Lawrence and Wishart in 1969. For commentaries in English, see Gwyn Williams: "Gramsci's Concept of 'Egemonia,'" *Journal of the History of Ideas*, vol. 21, no. 4, October/December 1960, pp. 586ff. See also the important recent study *Antonio Gramsci and the Origins of Italian Communism* by John M. Cammett (Stanford: Stanford University Press, 1967), which, while somewhat unbalanced and subject to limitations of approach, provides much useful information, especially for the immediate postwar period of the Turinese factory councils, and a good bibliography. Cf. Review of Cammett's book by Eugene Genovese, *Studies on the Left*, vol. 7, no. 2, 1967, p. 83ff. For a good recent biography see Giuseppe Fiori, *Vita di Antonio Gramsci* (Bari: Laterza, 1966).

3　"La Rivoluzione contro 'Il Capitale,'" *Avanti!*, November 24, 1917, reprinted in the anthology *Duemila pagine di Gramsci*, 2 volumes, (Milan: Il Saggiatore, Milano, 1964), eds, Giansiro Ferrata and Niccolò Gallo, vol. I, pp. 265–68.

4　Gramsci, *Opere* II, *Il Materialismo Storico e la filosofia di Benedetto Croce* (henceforward "*MS*"), pp. 13–14, 96.

5　Gramsci, *Opere*, vol. IV, *Note sul Machiavelli; sulla politica e sullo Stato Moderno* (henceforward *Machiavelli*), pp. 32, 48–49.

6　*MS*: pp. 132–33, *Machiavelli*, pp. 37–39. For Gramsci's critique of Bukharin's popular textbook see *MS*, pp. 119–68. "When the question is put thus (by Bukharin) one cannot understand the significance of the dialectic which becomes degraded into a formal system of logic, an elementary scholasticism," p. 132. Cf. The informative article by Aldo Zanardo: "Il Manuale di Bukharin vista dai comunisti tedeschi e da Gramsci," *Studi Gramsciani* (Rome: Riuniti,

1958), pp. 337–68; in which Gramsci's position is compared to that of Lukács, who similarly pointed out "the closeness of Bukharin's theory to bourgeois, natural-scientific materialism" derived "from his use of 'science' (in the French sense) as a model." See the translation of Lukács's "Technology and Social Relations," *New Left Review*, vol. 39, 1966, pp. 27–34.

7   *MS*, p. 80.
8   Louis Althusser, "Contradiction et Surdétermination," *Pour Marx* (Paris: Maspéro, 1966), p. 133; *New Left Review*, vol. 41, 1967, p. 32.
9   *Machiavelli*, p. 88.
10 *MS*, p. 157. Cf. Lukács in 1923: "It is not the primacy of economic motives in historical explanation which decisively distinguishes Marxism from bourgeois science, it is the view-point of the totality." *Histoire et Conscience de Classe*, translated by Kostas Alexos and Jacqueline Bois (Paris: Minuit, 1960), p. 47.
11 *MS*, p. 180.
12 Gramsci, *Opere*, vol. VII, *Passato e presente* (henceforward "*P*"), pp. 62–63.
13 *P*, pp. 58–59.
14 *Machiavelli*, p. 114.
15 See Nicolas Krassó, "Trotsky's Marxism," *New Left Review*, vol. 44, 1967, p. 81, and for Gramsci's comments on Trotsky's internationalism, *Machiavelli*, pp. 67, 114–15.
16 *MS*, p. 232.
17 Lenin, *Left-wing communism, an infantile disorder* (Moscow: Progress Publishers, n. d.); Addenda pp. 92–93 (original italics).
18 Athos Lisa, "Discussione politica con Gramsci in carcere," *Rinascita*, vol. XXI, no. 49, p. 12; vol. XII, no. 64, 1964, pp. 17–21; a report by one of Gramsci's fellow prisoners at Turi. For the early history of the PCI, see the recent and competent history by Paolo Spriano, *Storia del Partito comunista italiano*, vol. 1, *Da Bordiga a Gramsci* (Turin: Einaudi, 1967). Cf. also Cammett, *Antonio Gramsci*, chapter 8.
19 *Machiavelli*, p. 46.
20 *MS*, p. 40.
21 Ibid., p. 12.
22 *Machiavelli*, p. 49.
23 *MS*, p. 98. Williams, in the article quoted above, appears to make this disjunction, as a result concluding with the suggestion that Gramsci represented a purely "moral socialism." *Antonio Gramsci*, pp. 598–99.
24 *Machiavelli*, p. 77; *P*, p. 56. Cf. Gramsci's distinction between a purely "literary" theory, the monopoly of isolated thinkers, and that of Machiavelli, who represents a "man of action," a "politico in atto." *Machiavelli*, pp. 9, 39, 119.
25 Ibid., p. 41
26 Ibid., pp. 29–30.
27 Ibid., p. 36.

28   Antonio Gramsci, Letter to Tatania, September 7, 1931, *Lettere dal Carcere*, pp. 479–83.
29   *Machiavelli*, p. 132.
30   Ibid., p. 79.
31   *P*, pp. 164–65.
32   *Machiavelli*, pp. 37, 141. "Russo in his 'Prolegomeni' interprets *The Prince* as a treatise on dictatorship (moment of authority and of the individual) and *The Discourses* as one of hegemony (the moment of the universal . . .). Russo's observation is correct; except that even in *The Prince* there are references to the moment of hegemony and consent as well as that of authority and force." p. 141.
33   *Machiavelli*, pp. 79–80, 128, 133.
34   *MS*, pp. 236, 237.
35   *Machiavelli*, pp. 35–36.
36   Ibid., pp. 42–43.
37   Ibid., pp. 45–46.
38   Karl Marx, "Preface," *Selected Works* (Moscow: Foreign Languages Publishing House, 1958), vol. 1, p. 363.
39   Gramsci, *Opere*, vol. VII, *Risorgimento*, p. 69ff.; *Machiavelli*, pp. 70–71.
40   *Machiavelli*: p. 103. The point is made in reference to the Third Republic in France. It equally applies to the Reform League in the 1868 election in England; see Royden Harrison, *Before the Socialists* (Abingdon: Routledge & Kegan Paul, 1965), chapter 4.
41   *Machiavelli*, pp. 58–59. Gramsci distinguishes between "progressive" and "regressive" Caesarism. He also refers to a "degree" of Caesarism within parliamentary regimes, the MacDonald coalition of 1931 being a solution of this kind.
42   Ibid., p. 103.
43   Ibid., pp. 65–69.
44   "Un rapporto inedito al partito, 1926," ed. Franco Ferri, *Rinascita—Il Contemporaneo*, April 14, 1967, p. 23. The report is entitled "Situazione interna italiana; elementi per la linea politica del partito."
45   *Machiavelli*, pp. 20, 81, 87–88, 160.
46   Ibid. p. 84, 65–68. Trotsky's theory of "permanent revolution" is related to the "war of manœuvre," appropriate to an earlier period. "In this case one can say that 'Bronstein' (Trotsky) who seems to be a Westerner was in fact a cosmopolitan, that is, superficially national and superficially western or European. 'Ilici' (Lenin) on the other hand, was both profoundly national and European." p. 67. Trotsky's theory, a "retention of the political theory of frontal attack in a period in which this can only be a cause of defeat," is thus a "typical manifestation of sectarian thought. . . . The belief in the capacity to always do the same thing even when the 'politico-military situation' has changed" (pp. 70–71).
47   *Machiavelli*, pp. 67–68.

48 *P*, p. 71.

49 "Americanismo e Fordismo," *Machiavelli*, p. 312. The special conditions of American life, which make this degree of rationalization possible, mean that "hegemony is based in the factory and only has need, for its exercise, of a minimal quantity of professional intermediaries in the political and ideological spheres." The elaboration of the new type of man "conforming to the new type of work and productive process" was still (before the crisis of 1929) at its initial phase "of adaptation . . . through high salaries; . . . the fundamental question of hegemony has not yet been posed," p. 317.

50 Antonio Gramsci, Letter to Togliatti of February 9, 1924, marking Gramsci's decisive break with the Bordigan faction. In Ferrata and Gallo, eds, *Duemila pagine di Gramsci*, vol. I, p. 673.

51 Ibid.

52 *MS*, p. 35.

53 For Gramsci's critique of syndicalism, which is "addressed to a subaltern class, preventing it by this theory from becoming dominant, from developing beyond the economic-corporative phase to reach the hegemonic and ethicopolitical phase in civil society," see *Machiavelli*, p. 30. For the critique of Luxemburg's theory of "mass strike," see *Machiavelli*, pp. 4, 65.

54 "La quistione meridionale," 1926, in Ferrata and Gallo, eds, *Duemila pagine di Gramsci*, vol. I, p. 805. Cf. "Lettera di Gramsci al comitato centrale del PCUS nel 1926," *Rinascita* vol. 22, 1964; reprinted in Ferrata and Gallo, eds, *Duemila pagine di Gramsci*, vol. 1, pp. 824–25.

55 Gramsci, "Sindicalismo e consigli," *L'Ordine Nuovo*, November 8, 1919, vol. 1, p. 45.

56 Gramsci, *L'Ordine Nuovo*, vol. I, pp. 67, 123–27.

57 Cammett, *Antonio Gramsci*, pp. 79–88. Sorel expressed his admiration of the movement. For a "syndicalist" interpretation see N. Matteucci "Partito e consiglio di fabbrica nel pensiero di Gramsci," *Il Mulino*, vol. IV, April 4, 1955, pp. 350–59. Gramsci traced the defeat of the German revolutionary movement to the failure to move outside the traditional institutions of the working class, imposing external controls on the workers; hence the revolution was "shackled and domesticated." "Il Partito e la rivoluzione," *L'Ordine Nuovo*, vol. I, p. 68.

58 Gramsci, "Sindacati e consigli," *L'Ordine Nuovo*, October 11, 1919, vol. 1, p. 36.

59 Gramsci, *L'Ordine Nuovo*, vol. I, p. 46.

60 Gramsci, "Il Movimento torinese dei consigli di fabbrica" (report of July 1920), *L'Ordine Nuovo*, vol. I, p. 182. The dispute between Gramsci and Angelo Tasca was over this issue of the autonomous role of the councils. Cf. Spriano ed., *L'Ordine Nuovo*, articles of June–July 1920, and vol. 1, pp. 130–31.

61 "Alcuni temi della quistione meridionale," 1926, Ferrata and Gallo, eds, *Duemila pagine di Gramsci*, vol. I, p. 799.

62 Gramsci, *L'Ordine Nuovo*, vol. I, pp. 37, 183. *Machiavelli*, p. 132.

63   Gramsci, *Risorgimento*, pp. 70-71. *Machiavelli*, p. 94.

64   Gramsci, "Quistione meridionale," pp. 799, 825.

65   Gramsci, "Operai e contadini," *L'Ordine Nuovo*, January 1920. "The Northern bourgeoisie has subjected southern Italy and the islands and reduced them to exploited colonies; the Northern proletariat, emancipating itself from capitalist slavery, will emancipate the peasant masses of the South, at the mercy of the banks and parasitic industrialism of the North."

66   Gramsci, "Quistione Meridione," p. 805. Cf. *L'Ordine Nuovo*, vol. I, p. 90: "In Germany and Hungary the proletarian movement was not accompanied by any movement of the poorer peasant strata; the city in revolt was isolated, surrounded by the incomprehension and indifference of the countryside."

67   Cammett, *Antonio Gramsci*, pp. 91, 132. Bordiga regarded the factory councils as founded on the "error that the proletariat can emancipate itself by gaining ground in economic relations, while capitalism still holds political power." Serrati expressed the maximalist position on the peasants' movement: "Everybody knows that the movement for the occupation of lands . . . was a demagogic and petty bourgeois movement aimed at *entrancing the agricultural masses.*" (My italics.)

68   *MS*, pp. 80–81.

69   Ibid., p. 12.

70   Ibid., pp. 11, 201. *Lettere dal Carcere,* p. 185.

71   *Machiavelli*, p .10.

72   *MS*, p. 26.

73   Ibid., pp. 6, 11.

74   Ibid., pp. 94, 96. "Many idealistic conceptions, or at least *some aspects* of them, which are utopian in the reign of necessity, could become 'truth' after the passage, etc."

75   *Machiavelli*, p. 83. *MS*, pp. 3–5.

76   Giuseppe Fiori, *Vita di Antonio Gramsci* (Bari: Laterza, 1966), p. 120.

77   Gramsci, *Opere*, vol. III, *Gli intellettuali e l'organizzazione della cultura*, p. 142.

78   *P*, p. 3.

79   Cf. Fiori, *Vita di Antonio Gramsci*, pp. 109–10.

80   "Bergsoniano!" *L'Ordine Nuovo*, January 3, 1921, vol. 2, p. 13. Cf. article of May 1925: "It was the fate of Marxism in Italy to have been used as a parsley for all the indigestible sauces that the most imprudent adventurers . . . wanted to put up for sale." Ferrata and Gallo, eds, *Duemila pagine di Gramsci*, vol. I, p. 747.

81   Enzo Santarelli, *La Revisione del Marxismo in Italia* (Milan: Feltrinelli, 1964), pp. 34, 36. The astute prime minister, Giolitti, in a speech to the Chamber of Deputies (April 18, 1911) declared that the Socialist Party had "so moderated its principles that Karl Marx has been relegated to the attic." Ibid., p. 33n. For the influence of positivism on the Reformists, especially Turati, see Lelio Basso, "Turati, il riformismo e la via democratica," *Problemi del socialismo*, February 1958.

82 Gramsci, "Socialismo e cultura," *Il Grido del Popolo*, January 29, 1916. Ferrata and Gallo, eds, *Duemila pagine di Gramsci*, vol. I, p. 190. My italics. Cf. "La città futura," February 11, 1917: "To the *natural laws,* the *fatal course of things* of the pseudo-scientists, has been substituted *the tenacious will of man.*" Ibid., p. 239.

83 Gramsci, "La quistione meridionale," ibid., p. 800. On the positivist literature, sustaining the belief in "southern backwardness" and "inferiority" see *Risorgimento,* pp. 79–80.

84 For Gramsci's early idealism see the article of 1918, "Misteri della cultura e della poesia," *Scritti giovanili,* pp. 325ff, in which "the essentials" of Marxism are traced to "philosophical idealism" and history appears as the teleological "becoming" of a proletarian consciousness-subject. This is possibly the closest Gramsci came to the idealist position of Lukács in *Geschichte und Klassenbewusstem* (1923). Cf. Nicos Poulantzas, "Marxist Political Theory in Britain," *New Left Review,* vol. 43, 1967. For the critique of Croce, see *MS,* pp. 174, 189, 191, 217, 221. While Croce's "instrumental value" is recognized for having drawn attention to the "cultural front as essential," "it is necessary to carry out with regard to Croce's conception the same reduction that (Marx) carried out for the Hegelian conception," p. 199. See also Norberto Bobbio, "Nota sulla dialettica in Gramsci," *Studi Gramsciani* (Rome: Riuniti, 1958), p. 81.

85 *MS,* pp. 8–9, 84–85. See also Quentin Hoare's translation, "In search of the Educational Principle," *New Left Review,* vol. 32, 1965, pp. 56–57.

86 *MS,* p. 41.

87 Althusser et al., *Lire le Capital* (Paris: Maspero, 1965), vol. 2, "L'objet du Capital." See especially pp. 90–96.

88 For discussions of Gramsci's "historicism," see Nicola Badaloni, "Gramsci storicista," *Critica Marxista* Quaderni, no. 3, 1967, and Cesare Luporini, "Realtà e storicità: economia e dialettica nel marxismo," *Critica Marxista* no. 1, 1966. "The identification of theory and practice is a *critical act,* through which practice is demonstrated to be rational and necessary or theory realistic and rational," *MS* p. 39. It remains true, however, that at times Gramsci comes close to a pan-ideologism, reminiscent of Mannheim. See for example *MS,* p. 7, on the "lay-faith" derived from the Crocean conception of religion.

89 Gramsci, *Opere,* vol. V, *Letteratura e vita nazionale,* pp. 105–6; *P,* p. 15; *Machiavelli,* p. 7; Cf. Gramsci's linguistic studies, *Gli Intellettuali,* pp. 21–29.

90 *Risorgimento,* pp. 91–95, 100–4. *Machiavelli,* pp. 70–71.

91 *Risorgimento,* pp. 89–90, n.

92 *MS,* pp. 174–75.

93 *Machiavelli,* pp. 7, 14, 16. Cf. The failure of the intellectuals of the Party of Action to develop an "organic" rural base, "to be 'Jacobin,' not only in external 'form,' in temperament, but especially in economic-social content." *Risorgimento,* p. 81.

94 *Risorgimento*, p. 71, *Gli intellettuali*, p. 3. Cf. *Machiavelli*, p. 121, where the failure of the medieval Italian communes is traced to their not having developed their own organic intellectuals. "Religion was the basis of consent; the Church was civil society, the apparatus of hegemony of the directing group, which did not have its own apparatus, did not have its own cultural and intellectual organization." Cf. *Lettere dal carcere*, pp. 479–83.

95 *Gli intellettuali*, pp. 4-5.

96 Ibid., p. 9.

97 Ibid., pp. 9, 12. *MS*, pp. 13–14.

98 *MS*, pp. 8–9. Cf. p. 9 n., "This cannot come about unless there is a continually felt need for cultural contact with the non-intellectuals [*semplici*]." See also the need for an "organic rupture" among the intellectuals "to break up the intellectual bloc, which forms the flexible but resistent armour of the Southern agrarian bloc." "La Quistione Meridionale," in Ferrata and Gallo, eds, *Duemila pagine di Gramsci*, vol. I, p. 819.

99 *MS*, p. 17.

100 Ibid., p. 26.

101 Ibid., p. 11.

102 *Gli intellettuali*, p. 7.

103 *MS*, p. 26.

104 Che Guevara, "Socialism and Man in Cuba," March 1965. Accessible at www.marxists.org.

105 Gramsci, Letter to Togliatti, March 27, 1924, Ferrata and Gallo, eds, *Duemila pagine di Gramsci*, vol. I, p. 677. *Gli intellettuali*, p. 7.

106 Gramsci, *L'Ordine Nuovo*, vol. I, pp. 71, 148–49; *MS*, pp. 44–45.

107 Antonio Gramsci, "Il Movimento torinese," Report of July 1920, *L'Ordine Nuovo*, vol. I, p. 185.

108 Gramsci, "Per un rinnovamento del partito socialista," *L'Ordine Nuovo*, vol. I, pp. 118–20. Cf. "Il partito comunista," vol. I, pp. 159–62. The Socialist Party "which proclaims itself head of the working class, has become nothing but the *impedimenta* of the proletarian army," p. 162.

109 Cammett, *Antonio Gramsci*, p. 82.

110 Gramsci, *L'Ordine Nuovo*, vol. I, p. 122.

111 Ibid., p. 118.

112 Gramsci, "Lo Stato operaio," *L'Ordine Nuovo*, vol. II, p. 3.

113 Letter to Togliatti, February 9, 1924, Ferrata and Gallo, eds, *Duemila pagine di Gramsci*, vol. I, p. 672.

114 *Machiavelli*, pp. 147–48.

115 Cf. also: Gramsci developed "a doctrine more totalitarian than that of his goalers" [sic]: George Lichtheim, *Marxism: An Historical and Critical Study* (Abingdon: Routledge & Kegan Paul, 1961), pp. 368–69. Or H. Stuart Hughes in *Consciousness and Society* (New York: Vintage, 1959), who writes: "As so often in Gramsci's writings, a totalitarian thought was clothed in liberal guise," p. 101; a slightly more subtle variant. For a typically "Nennian"

interpretation see Giuseppe Tamburrano, *Antonio Gramsci, la vita, il pensiero, l'azione* (Bari: Laterza, 1963).

116 Ferrata and Gallo, eds, *Duemila pagine di Gramsci*, vol. I, p. 671.

117 *Machiavelli*, p. 51. For Gramsci's political position in prison in the early 1930s, see the testimony of his brother Gennaro Gramsci in Fiori, *Vita di Antonio Gramsci*, pp. 291–92; Athos Lisa's report, published in *Rinascita*, vol. 12, no. xii, 1964, and Giuseppe Ceresa's testimony, in which Gramsci is described as "combating those abstract, mechanical, antimarxist positions, which were based on the 'misery' factor." In Lisa's report, Gramsci puts forward the need for a hegemonic alliance against fascism: "without winning over these allies, the proletariat is precluded from any serious revolutionary movement." Fiori, p. 296. See also his report to the central committee of the CPSU on the eve of his arrest in 1926, in which he criticized the way in which party disputes were being handled, while not taking the side of the "opposition." Ferrata and Gallo, eds, *Duemila pagine di Gramsci*, vol. I, pp. 820–26. "Unity and discipline cannot be mechanical and coercive," he wrote. The Soviet party was "running the risk of annulling the directing function which the Communist Party of the USSR had conquered through the work of Lenin," pp. 823, 825.

118 *Machiavelli*, pp. 76–77.

119 *P*, pp. 57–58.

120 *Machiavelli*, p. 49.

121 Ibid., p. 296.

122 Ibid., p. 26; *MS*, p. 13.

123 Ibid., p. 94.

124 Ibid., p. 23.

125 *Scritti giovanili*, p. 78. See also the article "L'indifferenza," *Avanti!*, August 26, 1916, Ferrata and Gallo, eds, *Duemila pagine di Gramsci*, vol I, pp. 217–18; quoted from "Indifferenti" in "La città futura," February 11, 1917, ibid., pp. 233–35.

126 *Lettere dal Carcere*, p. 390.

127 *Machiavelli*, p. 39.

128 Ibid., pp. 39–40. Eugenio Garin "Antonio Gramsci nella cultura italiana," *Studi Gramsciani* (Rome: Riuniti, 1958).

129 Achille Occhetto, "Un teorico della rivoluzione in occidente," *Rinascita*, April 14, 1967, pp. 25–27.

Gramsci and Lenin 1917–1922

1 This section of this essay is covered at much greater length in my *The Young Gramsci: Towards an Intellectual Biography* (London: Merlin Press, 1977). Gramsci was born at Ales, Sardinia, on January 23, 1891. His father, Francesco, was a civil servant employed in the Land Registry. His mother, Giuseppina, was a member of a local landowning family, the Corrias. Gramsci had a

privileged life by Sardinian standards until he was injured in a fall at the age of four and started to develop a hunchback. Then his life became a cycle of misery: first his father was jailed in the course of a political feud; then, because he was a fallen member of the middle class in a society where the middle class had usually brutally oppressed the peasantry, he was mercilessly persecuted by his peasant school companions. He lived a life of physical and emotional deprivation—like a "bear" looking out of his lair, "convinced that no-one could love him." For compensation he turned to reading, and by the time he had finished high school in Cagliari he had moved to the top of his class. In 1910 he won a scholarship to Turin University, where once again he lived the life of a withdrawn scholar, whose brilliant potential was thwarted by starvation and a body racked by illness. His social outlook was affected by this life. As Garuglieri puts it, "being mocked at because of his deformity developed in him a great love for all those who suffer unjustly, and the need to give them succor, drove him to sacrifice himself generously in their cause." As a child he blamed the miseries of life on the Italian imperialism which exploited Sardinia, a view shared by many Sardinians, and he associated himself emotionally with the Sardinian nationalist movement known as Sardism. But under the influence of his university teachers he was attracted to socialism, joined the Italian Socialist Party in 1913, and became a full-time journalist on the socialist newspapers *Avanti* and *Grido del Popolo.* This began a long career of revolutionary militancy, first as a Socialist, and then as a leader of the Communist Party of Italy formed in 1921. In his political practice he evolved the ideas that found their culmination in the now famous *Prison Notebooks.*

2   In 1916 Gramsci stated that the views in Croce's *Teoria e storia della storiografia* constituted his "starting point," and in 1918 that they were still "undoubtedly right." *Sotto la Mole* (Turin: Einaudi, 1960), pp. 145, 365.

3   Giovanni Amoretti, "Con Gramsci sotto la Mole," in *Gramsci, Scritti di Paimiro Togliatti ed altri,* ed., Paimiro Togliatti (Rome: Unita, 1945), p. 44.

4   For Gramsci's expression of these principles see *Sotto la Mole,* p. 365 where he wrote: "To be history, and not merely graphic marks, or source material, or aids to memory, past events must be thought up again, and this rethinking brings them up to date, since the evaluation or ordering of those facts necessarily depends on the 'contemporary' knowledge of the person rethinking the past event, about who makes history, and who made it in the past." It followed that Gramsci maintained that men were never the prisoners of their past in the sense that they could not fire themselves through their own willful action. Indeed, he denied that men could only be freed by some structural conjunction of events.

5   *La Citta futura,* February 11, 1917. See reprint in Giansiro Ferrata and Niccolo Gallo, eds, *Due mila pagine di Gramsci* (Milan: Il Saggiatore, 1964), vol. I, pp. 233–35.

6   Antonio Labriola, *La concezione materialistica della storia* (Bari: Laterza, 1953), pp. 31, 151.
7   Ibid., p. 73; *Sotto la Mole,* April 3, 1916, pp. 101–2.
8   Ibid., p. 76.
9   See Alfonso Leonetti, "Romain Rolland e Gramsci," in *Note su Gramsci* (Urbino: Argalia, 1971[?]), pp. 209–21; Romain Rolland, *Jean-Christopher* (Paris: Michel, 1956), p. 22; *Au-dessus de la melée* (Michel: Paris, 1953), pp. 64, 80, 88, 124.
10 "Socialismo e cultura," *Il Grido del Popolo,* January 29, 1916, in Ferrata and Gallo, *Duemila pagine di Gramsci,* vol. I, pp. 189–93; *Avanti* (Turin), December 9, 1916, in S. Caprioglio, *Scritti 1915–1921* (Milan: Il Corpo, 1968), pp. 23–25.
11 Petro Gobetti, "Storia dei comunisti torinesi scritto da un liberale," *Rivoluzione liberale,* vol. IV, no. 2, 1922.
12 For the lectures and the strongly pro-Crocian tone of the suggested reading see Amoretti, "Con Gramsci sotto la Mole," p. 45; for the club, see the letter from Gramsci to Giuseppe Lombardo-Radice (March[?] 1918) in *Rinascita,* March 7, 1964; Leonetti, "Romain Rolland e Gramsci," pp. 105–8.
13 See *Avanguardia,* October 20, 1912, for Bordiga's statement and Luigi Cortesi, ed., *Il Socialismo italiano tra riforme e rivoluzione 1892–1921 Atti congressuali del PSI* (Bari: Laterza, 1969) for the full report of Mussolini's opinions at the 1914 Ancona conference of the PSI; for the attitude of young workers at that time see Mario Montagnana, *Ricordi di un operaio torinese* (Rome: Rinascita, 1949), p. 28; Angelo Tasca in *Il Mondo,* August 18, 1953.
14 In 1918, in an article rejecting the positivism of his former hero, Gaetano Salvemini, which is also interesting for other reasons, Gramsci wrote:

> Jacobinism is a messianic view of history: it always speaks in abstractions: evil/good; oppression/liberty; light/shade; which exist absolutely, generically, and not in historical forms. Jacobin messianism is completed by cultural messianism, which is represented in Italy by Gaetano Salvemini and has given birth to idealist movements like that of *La Voce* in the past and *V Unita* at the present time.... Even cultural messianism abstracts from the concrete forms of economic and political life, and proposes an absolute outside time and space ... and ends up being utopian.

See *Scritti giovanili* (Turin: Einaudi, 1958), pp. 271–73.
15 *Il Grido del Popolo* (April 29, 1917), in Ferrata and Gallo, *Duemila pagine di Gramsci,* vol. I, pp. 251–52.
16 Antonio Gramsci (September 29, 1917) in Caprioglio, *Scritti,* pp. 31–36. Victor Mikhailovitch Chernov (1876–1952) was one of the leaders and theoreticians of the Socialist-Revolutionary Party. After the February 1917 revolution, he was Minister for Agriculture in the Provisional Government; organizer of severe repressive measures against peasants who seized landed estates. After the October Revolution, Chernov was one of the organizers of anti-Soviet revolts. In 1920, he emigrated and continued his anti-Soviet activities from abroad.

17 Sergio Caprioglio, "Un articolo di Gramsci alla vigilia di Ottobre," *Rinascita,* October 13, 1967; Paolo Spriano, *Torino operaia nella grande guerra 1914–1918* (Turin: Einaudi, 1960), p. 210.

18 Antonio Gramsci, "Il Grido del Popolo" (July 29, 1917), in *Scritti giovanili,* pp. 122–24.

19 Antonio Gramsci, "Il Nostro Marx," in *II Grido del popolo,* May 4, 1918, in *Scritti giovanili,* pp. 217–21.

20 Antonio Gramsci, "La rivoluzione contro il *Capitale,*" *Avanti* (Milan), November 24, 1917 in ibid., pp. 149–53.

21 Antonio Gramsci, "L'utopia russa," *Il Grido del Popolo,* July 27, 1918 in Ferrata and Gallo, *Duemila pagine di Gramsci,* vol. I, p. 317.

22 Giovanni Germanetto, *Memoirs of a Barber* (Moscow-Leningrad: Co-operative Publishing Society of Foreign Workers in the USSR, 1934), p. 138; Spriano, *Torino operaia,* pp. 286–87.

23 Palmiro Togliatti, *Trentanni di vita e lotte del PCI,* vol. 2 (Rome: Quaderni di Rinascita, 1950), p. 37; Marcella and Mourizio Ferrara, *Conversando con Togliatti* (Rome: Edizioni di Cultura culturali, 1952), p. 43.

24 Sergio Caprioglio in *Rinascita,* October 13, 1967. Alfonso Leonetti casts doubt on this account in a letter to me dated March 14, 1974. He writes: "All relations between Gramsci and Poliedro were broken off after the latter became a 'social-patriot,' that is to say, in 1914. Perhaps you mean Gobetti, who took Russian lessons from Polledro's wife. That is possible."

25 Alfonso Leonetti, Letter to Rinascita, February 22, 1964; *Note su Gramsci,* p. 109. The sources were also apparently sometimes in English and German, which Togliatti translated, but this was rarely so after 1919. The contents of Leonetti's anthology, which he claims in his letter to me of March 14, 1974 "contains everything essentially important among Lenin's writings then known in Italy" are: *The Third International, Bourgeois Democracy or Proletarian Democracy, The Victory of the Soviets, The Proletarian Revolution and the Renegade Kautsky, The Heroes of the Berne International, Can exploiters and exploited be equal?, Democracy and Dictatorship in Germany, To the Workers in the Field, The National and Colonial Question, The Young International, Voluntary and Obligatory Work, The Emancipation of Women, The Struggle for Bread, The Political and Economic Situation in the World and the Task of the Third International.* See Nicola Lenin, *Pagine scelte, A cura di A. Leonetti* (Milan: Facchi, 1920), pp. 190.

26 I have been able to check the complete files of all these newspapers and journals for 1919, 1920, and 1921, mainly at the magnificent Bibliothèque de documentation internationale contemporaine at the University of Paris -X (Nanterre).

27 Arthur Ransome, *La Vie Ouvrière,* August 20, 1919.

28 *La Vie Ouvrière,* July 2, 1919.

29 Ibid., also ibid., November 21, 1919; *Clarté,* November 2, 1919.

30 The quotation is from an article by one of his close associates. See the "Dawn of Ordine Nuovo," *Avanguardia,* March 9, 1919.

31 Angelo Tasca, "Il programma dell Ordine Nuovo," *Ordine Nuovo* (Turin: Einaudi, 1955), p. 148.

32 See "Democrazia operaia" (June 21, 1919), in ibid., pp. 10–15.

33 Ibid. He also wrote that through the factory councils "began that education and that change in psychology, which, according to Karl Marx, must be considered the most promising symptom of the incipient realization of communism." Resoconto in *Avanti,* June 25, 1919, republished in Alberto Caracciolo, "Il movimento torinese dei consigli di fabbrica," *Mondo operaio,* February 2, 1958, pp. 16–27.

34 Giovanni Parodi, "Gramsci con gli operai," in Palmiro Togliatti, ed., *Gramsci,* p. 67; Umberto Terracini, "I consigli di fabbrica: vicende e problemi dall'Inghilterra alla Russia, dalla Germania a Torino," *Almanacco socialista 1920.*

35 For a fuller account see my forthcoming essay in *Australian Left Review.*

36 Gramsci to Togliatti, March 27, 1924, in Palmiro Togliatti, ed., *La formazione del gruppo dirigente del PCI* (Rome: Riuniti, 1962), p. 255.

37 Paolo Spriano, *l'Ordine Nuovo* (Turin: Einaudi, 1963), p. 37, n. 1.

38 Quoted in Giuseppe Berti, "I primi dieci anni vita del PCI," *Documenti inediti dall'Archivio Tasca* (Milan: Feltrinelli, 1969), p. 67.

39 *Bulletin Communiste*, December 23, 1920.

40 Antonio Gramsci, "Per un rinnovamento del Partito Socialista italiano," May 8, 1920, *Ordine Nuovo,* pp. 117–21; Leonetti, "Romain Rolland e Gramsci," p. 24.

41 Gramsci, "Per un rinnovamento."

42 *La Vie Ouvrière*, November 25, 1921.

43 See e.g., *Clarté,* November 29, 1919: the association with Trotsky dated back many years in the case of *La Vie Ouvrière.* See Edouard Dolléans, *Histoire du Mouvement Ouvrier 1871–1920* (Paris: Colin, 1957), vol. II, p. 234.

44 Gramsci, *Ordine Nuovo,* June 5, 1920; October 9, 1920, pp. 130, 489.

45 See *Ordine Nuovo,* January 10, 1920; Leonardo Paggi, *Gramsci e il Moderno Principe* (Rome: Riuniti, 1970), vol. I, p. 303, suggests that this indicates that Gramsci did not understand its significance in Lenin's thought at this time.

46 See *Ordine Nuovo,* pp. 130, 153, 490.

47 Ibid.; *Korrispondenz Internationale,* no. 13, 1920, col. 260.

48 See my article in *Australian Left Review.*

49 Gramsci, "Per un rinnovamento."

50 V. I. Lenin, *Sul Movimento Operaio Italiano* (Rome: Rinascita, 1952), p. 140; see *Communist International,* II, no. 15, August 1920, cols. 2487-2492 for the republication of the Turinese criticism.

51 *Il Soviet,* vol. III, no. 24, October 1920, cited by Paolo Spriano, *Storia del Partito Comunista italiano* (Turin: Einaudi, 1967), vol. I, p. 73.

52 Ibid.

53   Gramsci, "Il programma dell'Ordine Nuovo," *Ordine Nuovo*, pp. 146ff; "La relazione Tasca e il congresso camerale di Torino," *Ordine Nuovo*, June 5, 1920, in *Ordine Nuovo*, pp. 27ff.

54   *Korrispondenz internationale*, no. 13, 1920, col. 260.

55   *Clarté*, March 11, 1921.

56   Gramsci, "Due Rivoluzioni," July 3, 1920 in *Ordine Nuovo*, p. 140.

57   *Avanti*, August 12, 1920 reprinted in F. Ferri, "La situazione interna della sezione socialista torinese nell'estate del 1920," *Rinascita,* April 1958.

58   Gramsci, "Il Consiglio di Fabbrica," June 5, 1920, in *Ordine Nuovo*, p. 127.

59   Gramsci, "L'Occupazione," September 2, 1920, in Caprioglio, *Scritti*, pp. 130–32.

60   Gramsci, "Il Partito comunista," September 4–9, 1920, in *Ordine Nuovo*, p. 161.

61   Cited in Paolo Spriano, *l'Occupazione delle fabbriche* (Turin: Einaudi, 1964), p. 103.

62   Gramsci, "Contro il pessimismo," March 15, 1924 in Spriano, *Gramsci Scritti politici* (Turin: Einaudi, 1967), p. 546.

63   Palmiro Togliatti, "Il Leninismo nel pensiero e nell'azione di A. Gramsci," in *Studi Gramsciani, Atti del convegno tenuto a Roma nei giorni 11-13 gennaio 1958* (Rome: Riuniti, 1969), pp. 16–19.

64   Umberto Terracini, "Three Meetings with Lenin," in S. F. Bezveselny and D.Y. Grunberg, *They Knew Lenin* (Moscow: Foreign Languages Publishing House, 1968), p. 211.

65   Antonio Gramsci, "L'Opera di Lenin," September 14, 1918, in *Scritti giovanili 1918–1919* (Turin: Einaudi, 1958), p. 308.

66   Spriano, *Storia del Partito Comunista Italiano*, vol. I, p. 62.

67   See Alberto Caracciolo, "A proposito di Gramsci, la Russia, e il movimento bolscevico," in *Studi Gramsciani*, pp. 95–105; Emilio Soave, "Appunti sulle origini teoriche e pratiche dei consigli di fabbrica a Torino," *Rivista storica del socialismo*, vol.VII, no. 21, January–April 1964; Berti, "I primi delci anni vita del PCI." The best representative "left" article is Andreina de Clementi, "La politica del partito comunista d'Italia nel 1921–1922 e il rapporto Bordiga-Gramsci," *Rivista storica del socialismo*, no. 28, 1966.

68   Antonio Gramsci, "Note sulla rivoluzione russa," April 29, 1917, in *Scritti giovanili*, p. 106.

69   Antonio Gramsci, "La Politica del 'se,'" June 29, 1918, in ibid., pp. 272–73.

70   V. I. Lenin, *Selected Works* (Moscow: Progress Publishers, 1967), vol. I, p. 412.

71   Lenin, *Oeuvres complètes*, vol. XXV, pp. 124–25.

72   Antonion Gramsci, "I Gruppi comunisti," July 17, 1920, in *Ordine Nuovo*, pp. 140–43; "Due rivoluzioni," July 3, 1920, in ibid., pp. 135–40.

73   Maria-Antonietta Macciocchi, *Pour Gramsci* (Paris: Seuil, 1974).

74   Letter to Zino Zini in *Rinascita*, vol. XXI, p. 17, April 25, 1964; *Avanti,* September 2, 1920 in Caprioglio, *Scritti*, pp. 130–32, 134.

75   Lenin, *Selected Works*, vol. I, p. 579.

76   Ibid., p. 486.

77 Ibid., p. 792.
78 V. I. Lenin, *Sul movimento operaio* (Rome: Rinascita, 1947), p. 146.

Class and Party

This text first appeared in the Italian journal *Il Manifesto*, no. 4, which was edited by Rossana Rossanda and Lucio Magri. Both editors, as well as Aldo Natoli and Luigi Pintor, were excluded from the Italian Communist Party at the end of 1969 for refusing to cease publication of the journal. The present translation is from the French version, which appeared in the January 1970 issue of *Les Temps Modernes*.

1   "Now, we were by no means of the opinion that the new scientific results should be confided in large tomes exclusively to the 'learned' world. Quite the contrary. We were both of us already deeply involved in the political movement." Thus wrote Engels in his *On the History of the Communist League* in relation to this period.

2   Karl Marx, in *Aus dem literarischen Nachlass von Karl Marx, Friedrich Engels und Ferdinand Lassalle*, ed. Franz Mehring (Stuttgart: Dietz, 1902), vol. 3, p. 426.

3   See Lelio Basso's Introduction to Rosa Luxemburg's *Political Writings* (Rome: Editori Reuniti, 1967), p. 107.

4   V. I. Lenin, *Marxism and Revisionism*, in *Lenin: Collected Works* (Moscow: Progress Publishers, 1973 [1908]).

5   V. I. Lenin, "The Historical Destiny of the Doctrine of Karl Marx," *Pravda*, no. 50, March 1, 1913.

6   V. I. Lenin, "Backward Europe and Advanced Asia," *Pravda*, no. 113, May 18, 1913.

7   This passage is cited *in extenso* in V. I. Lenin, "What Is to Be Done?" *Lenin's Collected Works*, vol. 1 (Moscow: Foreign Language Publishing House, 1961 [1902]).

8   "In Russia too the theoretical doctrine of social-democracy was born altogether independently from the spontaneous development of the movement; it was born as the *natural and inevitable result of the development of thought* among revolutionary socialist intellectuals." Ibid. (Our italics.)

9   Rosa Luxemburg, *The Crisis of Social Democracy* (Zurich, February 1916).

10 Rosa Luxemburg, *Und zum drittenmal das belgische Experiment*, in *Die Neue Zeit*, May 14, 1902.

11 Rosa Luxemburg, Letter to Matilde Wurm, February 1917.

12 On this point, see particularly *Ordine Nuovo* (Turin: Einaudi, 1954). On the nature of the revolution, see particularly "The Party and the Revolution," pp. 67–68.

13 See especially the article by Allesandro Natta and Gian Carlo Pajetta in no. 5–6 of *Critica Marxista* (1963), p. 113, in which the "primary responsibility" of the leadership is deduced from Gramsci's thesis (in the *Notes on Machiavelli*) of a difference in political involvement.

14   The most interesting contribution to the debate was made by Raniero
      Panzieri and Lucio Libertini in 1958 and 1959 under the title *Tesi sul
      controllo operaio et Tesi sul partito di classe.*

Masses, Spontaneity, Party

This text first appeared in the Italian journal *Il Manifesto*, no. 4, which was edited
by Rossana Rossanda and Lucio Magri. Both editors, as well as Aldo Natoli and
Luigi Pintor, were excluded from the Italian Communist Party at the end of 1969
for refusing to cease publication of the journal. The present translation is from
the French version which appeared in the January 1970 issue of *Temps Modernes*.

This conversation was recorded on August 27, 1969, in Rome.

Marx and Engels on the Revolutionary Party

1   Karl Marx and Friedrich Engels, *Karl Marx and Frederick Engels: Collected
     Works,* vol. 24 (New York: International Publishers, 1975), p. 464.
2   Monty Johnstone, "Marx and Engels and the Concept of the Party," *Socialist
     Register* 1967 (New York: Monthly Review Press, 1967).
3   Karl Marx and Friedrich Engels, *MECW*, vol. 26, pp. 318–19.
4   Both had a role in founding in London, in September 1845, the short-lived
     Society of Fraternal Democrats, the first international proletariat organization.
5   Marx and Engels, *MECW*, vol. 38, pp. 38–39.
6   See my *Marx and Engels: Their Contribution to the Democratic Breakthrough*
     (Albany: State University of New York Press, 2000), pp. 30–38, for details.
7   Bolshevik archivist and biographer of Marx and Engels, David Riazanov, claims
     that with this stipulation the CL had adopted the "democratic centralism"
     usually associated with Leninist norms, in his *Karl Marx and Friedrich Engels*
     (New York: Monthly Review Press, 1973), p. 75. I have argued, as Riazanov
     admits, that owing to how the League's "executive authority" was elected by
     the local organization—as opposed to by the congress, the Bolshevik norm—
     there was effectively more democratic content to the Bolshevik modus
     operandi than that of the League. See my *Marx and Engels*, p. 54.
8   Marx and Engels, *MECW*, vol. 41, pp. 87, 82.
9   See Hal Draper, *The Adventures of the Communist Manifesto* (Berkeley: Center
     for Socialist History, 1994), pp. 236–39, on the translation and meaning of
     the passage.
10   Regarding the debate about the decision, see John Cunliffe, "The
     Communist League and the 'Dissolution Question,'" *Journal of Modern
     History*, vol. 53, no. 1 (March 1981).
11   Marx and Engels, *MECW*, vol. 10, pp. 283–87.
12   Hal Draper convincingly argues that Marx and Engels, contrary to some
     claims, never disowned the document: *Karl Marx's Theory of Revolution,*

vol. 1 (New York: Monthly Review Press, 1977), pp. 599–612. See also Johnstone, "Marx and Engels," pp. 127–28.

13 Riazanov, *Karl Marx and Friedrich Engels*, p. 100.

14 See my *Lenin's Electoral Strategy from 1907 to the October Revolution of 1917: The Ballot, The Streets—Or, Both* (New York: Palgrave Macmillan, 2014), especially chapter three. Absent in the *Address* is the worker-peasant alliance, all so vital in the success of the Bolsheviks. That omission was partly corrected in the subsequent Central Authority *Address of June, 1850*, that Marx and Engels wrote. For details see my *Marx and Engels*, p. 106.

15 On Marx and Engels's role and the organizational issues see my *Marx and Engels*, and "Marxism Versus Anarchism: The First Encounter," *Science & Society*, vol. 79, no. 2 (April 2015).

16 Marx and Engels, *MECW*, vol. 20, pp. 5–14.

17 Ibid., vol. 42, pp. 92–93. For how Marx dealt with the fact of his own class origins in his role in the IWA, see my *Marx and Engels*, pp. 185–88.

18 Much more is now known about this conflict since Johnstone penned his brief comments.

19 Marx and Engels, *MECW*, vol. 21, pp. 45–46.

20 Ibid., vol. 44, pp. 162–63.

21 Draper, *Karl Marx's Theory of Revolution*, vol. 4, pp. 270–304 makes the most detailed case against the anarchist.

22 Ibid., p. 271.

23 Marx and Engels, *MECW*, vol. 22, pp. 417–18.

24 Ibid., vol. 23, pp. 115, 121.

25 *General Council of the IWA, 1871–1872: Minutes* (Moscow: Progress Publishers, 1974), p. 242.

26 Regarding the charge that a more centralized and disciplined IWA effectively meant its demise because it resulted in the expulsion of the Bakuninists, see my "Marxism versus Anarchism," pp. 171–73.

27 Marx and Engels, *MECW*, vol. 44, p. 258.

28 Ibid., vol. 45, p. 400.

29 Ibid., vol. 49, p. 135.

30 Ibid., p. 131.

31 Ibid., vol. 48, p. 425; and vol. 49, pp. 11, 16–17, 516–17.

32 Ibid., vol. 50, p. 33.

33 Ibid., vol. 49, p. 515.

34 Ibid., vol. 50, pp. 457–59. Engels's reprimand had to do with the most famous bowdlerization in the annals of Marxism—Wilhelm Liebknecht's cut and paste job on his "Introduction" to the 1895 edition of Marx's *Class Struggles in France*, done "in such a way as to present me as a peace-loving proponent of legality quand même" (*MECW*, vol. 50, p. 486).

35 Ibid., *MECW*, vol. 46, p. 198. It is true, as Johnstone notes, that Engels gave "enthusiastic support" (p. 135) to the 1889 meeting that inaugurated what would be the Second International. But that's a hindsight observation.

There is nothing in the record that suggests Engels saw the meeting as in fact an inauguration. His counsel to "wait," I argue, was still operative.

36   Vladimir Lenin, *Collected Works*, vol. 5 (Moscow: Progress Publishers, 1977), p. 18.

37   For details on the Second Congress, see John Riddell, ed., *Workers of the World and Oppressed Peoples, United!: Proceedings and Documents of the Second Congress, 1920* (New York: Pathfinder Press, 1991).

38   Vladimir Lenin, *Collected Works*, vol. 33, p. 431. There is no mention of this crucially important fact about Lenin's understanding of party organization in Tamás Krausz's *Reconstructing Lenin: An Intellectual Biography* (New York: Monthly Review Press, 2015). What he does supply isn't necessarily erroneous but mainly inadequate and largely bereft of historical context, such as his too brief discussion of "democratic centralism" (p. 118). See my *Lenin's Electoral Strategy*, vol. 1, for understanding of how the norm developed.

39   Leon Trotsky, *Writings of Leon Trotsky, 1935–36* (New York: Pathfinder Press, 1977), p. 186.

40   Johnstone, "Marx and Engels," p. 144.

41   Notably, the new Communist party, with no organic links to the Bolsheviks, that was birthed in 1965 in Cuba, arguably the most significant revolutionary breakthrough in the second half of the twentieth century, largely escaped the opprobrium of the New Left. Despite having been born with a Stalinist defect—one of the three currents that came together for its formation after the overthrow of the old regime—the party's revolutionary wing led by Fidel Castro was, despite Moscow's embrace, able to avoid the degeneration that had occurred elsewhere. It was because the Cuban revolution was healthy enough at birth that it was able to survive for so long after the collapse of the Stalinist regimes.

42   Jodi Dean makes the most cogent case in her latest book, *Crowds and Party: How Do Mass Protests Become an Organized Activist Collective* (New York: Verso, 2016).

43   Johnstone, "Marx and Engels," p. 145. My *Marx and Engels* and *Lenin's Electoral Strategy* were written just for that reason.

Class, Party, and the Challenge of State Transformation

1   As *The Communist Manifesto* put it in elaborating on the bourgeoisie's "highly revolutionary role" historically, "the bourgeoisie cannot exist without constantly revolutionizing the instruments of production, and thereby relations of production, and with them the whole relations of society . . . In a phrase, it creates a world in its own image." Karl Marx, *Later Political Writings*, edited and translated by Terrell Carver (Cambridge, UK: Cambridge University Press, 1996), pp. 3–5. For a discussion of the continuing implications of this, see Leo Panitch, "Capitalism, Socialism and Revolution," in Ralph Miliband, Leo Panitch, and John Saville, eds,

Socialist Register 1989 (London: Merlin Press, 1989); and *Renewing Socialism: Transforming Democracy, Strategy and Imagination* (London: Merlin Press, 2009).

2   Between the 1987 American stock market crash and the investment banking collapse two decades later, there were upwards of a hundred distinct currency and banking crises as a direct outcome of global capital mobility. States were no longer in the business of "crisis prevention" through regulations that might impede the free flow of capital; rather they were in the business of "crisis containment," as the US Treasury itself put it in explaining why its central role had become "firefighting." See Leo Panitch and Sam Gindin, *The Making of Global Capitalism: The Political Economy of American Empire* (London: Verso, 2012), Chapters 10–12.

3   Perry Anderson, "Renewals," *New Left Review* 1 (January/February), 2000, pp. 7, 13. "Whatever limitations persist to its practice, neo-liberalism as a set of principles rules undivided across the globe: the most successful ideology in world history."

4   Andrew Murray, "Jeremy Corbyn and the Battle for Socialism," *Jacobin*, February 7, 2016.

5   Marx, *Later Political Writings*, pp. 9–10.

6   See E. P. Thompson, *The Making of the English Working Class* (New York: Pantheon, 1964), pp. 9–11; and "Eighteenth Century English Society: Class Struggle Without Class," *Social History*, vol. 3, no. 2, May 1978, pp. 133–65.

7   E. H. Hobsbawm, "The Making of the Working Class, 1870–1914," *Uncommon People: Resistance, Rebellion and Jazz* (New York: The New Press, 1999), pp. 58–59. See, especially, Geoff Eley, *Forging Democracy: The History of the Left in Europe, 1850–2000* (New York: OUP, 2002).

8   Robert Michels, *Political Parties: A Sociological Study of the Oligarchical Tendencies of Modern Democracy* (New York: Free Press, 1962).

9   Rosa Luxemburg, "The Russian Revolution," in Peter Hudis and Kevin Anderson, eds, *The Rosa Luxemburg Reader* (New York: Monthly Review Press, 2004), pp. 304–6.

10 Isaac Deutscher, *The Prophet Armed* (London: OUP, 1954), pp. 505–6.

11 Quoted in Leo Panitch and Sam Gindin, "Moscow, Togliatti, Yaroslavl: Perspectives on Perestroika," in Dan Benedict et al., eds, *Canadians Look at Soviet Auto Workers' Unions* (Toronto: CAW, 1992), p. 19.

12 "An American Proposal," *Fortune*, May 1942. See Leo Panitch and Sam Gindin, *The Making of Global Capitalism: The Political Economy of American Empire* (London: Verso, 2012), pp. 67–68.

13 Bernie Sanders, "Prepared Remarks: The Political Revolution Continues," June 16, 2016. Available at: https://berniesanders.com/political-revolution-continues.

14 Dan La Botz, "Life After Bernie: People's Summit Searches for the Movement's Political Future," *New Politics*, June 21, 2016. Available at: http://newpol.org.

15   See Steve Williams and Rishi Awatramani, "New Working-Class Organizations and the Social Movement Left," and Mark Dudzic and Adolph Reed, Jr., "The Crisis of Labour and the Left in the United States," in Leo Panitch and Greg Albo, eds, *Socialist Register 2015: Transforming Classes* (London: Merlin Press, 2014).

16   See Costas Eleftheriou, "The Uneasy 'Symbiosis': Factionalism and Radical Politics in Synaspismos," paper prepared for 4th Hellenic Observatory PhD Symposium, n.d.

17   Michalis Spourdalakis, "Left Strategy in the Greek Cauldron: Explaining Syriza's Success," in Leo Panitch, Greg Albo, and Vivek Chibber, eds, *Socialist Register 2013: The Question of Strategy* (London: Merlin Press, 2012), p. 102.

18   Available at: https://left.gr/news/political-resolution-1st-congress-syriza.

19   "Syriza and Socialist Strategy," *International Socialism*, no. 146, April 2015 (transcript of a debate between Alec Callinicos and Stathis Kouvelakis, London, February 25, 2015).

20   Costas Douzinas, "The Left in Power? Notes on Syriza's Rise, Fall and (Possible) Second Rise," *Near Futures Online*, March 2016. Available at: http://nearfuturesonline.org.

21   Michalis Spourdalakis, "Becoming Syriza Again," *Jacobin*, January 31, 2016.

22   Nicos Poulantzas, "Towards a Democratic Socialism," *State, Power, Socialism* (London: NLB, 1978).

23   André Gorz, "Reform and Revolution," in Ralph Miliband and John Saville, eds, *Socialist Register 1968* (London: Merlin Press, 1968); Lucio Magri, "Problems of the Marxist Theory of the Revolutionary Party," *New Left Review*, vol. 60, 1970; Tony Benn, *The New Politics: A Socialist Reconnaissance*, Fabian Tract vol. 402, September 1970; Ralph Miliband, "Moving On," in Ralph Miliband and John Saville, eds, *Socialist Register 1976* (London: Merlin Press, 1976); Ralph Miliband, *Marxism and Politics* (Oxford: OUP, 1977); Sheila Rowbotham, Lynne Segal, and Hilary Wainwright, *Beyond the Fragments: Feminism and the Making of Socialism* (London: Merlin, 1979).

24   Poulantzas, "Towards," pp. 257-58, 260–61.

25   Ibid., pp. 256, 258, 261.

26   Gorz, "Reform and Revolution," p. 112.

27   Ibid., pp. 132–33. Lucio Magri similarly called for new workers councils "right across society (factories, offices, schools), with their own structures as mediating organizations between party, union, and state institutions, for which all of the latter needed to act as elements of stimulus and synthesis." And even though he presented this in terms of the "need for a creative revival of the theme of *soviets* [as] essential to resolve the theoretical and strategic problems of the Western Revolution," this was directed at offsetting the total dominance of the party, and emphatically did not mean re-endorsing a dual power strategy for smashing the state. Magri, "Problems," p. 128.

28   Poulantzas, "Towards," pp. 256, 258.

29   Ralph Miliband, *Class Power and State Power* (London: Verso, 1983), especially chapters 2–4.
30   Goran Therborn, *What Does the Ruling Class Do When it Rules? State Apparatuses and State Power under Feudalism, Capitalism and Socialism* (London: NLB, 1978), pp. 279–80.
31   See, however, Greg Albo, David Langille, and Leo Panitch, eds, *A Different Kind of State: Popular Power and Democratic Administration* (Toronto: OUP, 1993).
32   See the critique of recent books in this vein by Alperowitz, Wolff, and Wright in Sam Gindin, "Chasing Utopia," *Jacobin*, March 10, 2016.
33   Poulantzas, "Towards," p. 262.
34   Marx, *Later Political Writings*, p. 35.

ABOUT HAYMARKET BOOKS

Haymarket Books is a radical, independent, nonprofit book publisher based in Chicago. Our mission is to publish books that contribute to struggles for social and economic justice. We strive to make our books a vibrant and organic part of social movements and the education and development of a critical, engaged, international left.

We take inspiration and courage from our namesakes, the Haymarket martyrs, who gave their lives fighting for a better world. Their 1886 struggle for the eight-hour day—which gave us May Day, the international workers' holiday—reminds workers around the world that ordinary people can organize and struggle for their own liberation. These struggles continue today across the globe—struggles against oppression, exploitation, poverty, and war.

Since our founding in 2001, Haymarket Books has published more than five hundred titles. Radically independent, we seek to drive a wedge into the risk-averse world of corporate book publishing. Our authors include Noam Chomsky, Arundhati Roy, Rebecca Solnit, Angela Y. Davis, Howard Zinn, Amy Goodman, Wallace Shawn, Mike Davis, Winona LaDuke, Ilan Pappé, Richard Wolff, Dave Zirin, Keeanga-Yamahtta Taylor, Nick Turse, Dahr Jamail, David Barsamian, Elizabeth Laird, Amira Hass, Mark Steel, Avi Lewis, Naomi Klein, and Neil Davidson. We are also the trade publishers of the acclaimed Historical Materialism Book Series and of Dispatch Books.

ABOUT SOCIALIST REGISTER

The *Socialist Register* was founded by Ralph Miliband and John Saville in 1964 as "an annual survey of movements and ideas" from the standpoint of the independent new left. It is currently edited by Leo Panitch and Greg Albo, assisted by an editorial collective of eminent scholars in Africa, Asia, Europe, and the Americas. Each volume is focused on a topical theme and characterized by the inclusion of relatively long, sustained analyses which cut across intellectual disciplines and geographical boundaries.

The *Socialist Register* is published annually in October by Merlin Press in the UK, Monthly Review Press in the United States and Fernwood Books in Canada. For an online subscription with access to the complete digital archive of fifty-five volumes published in English, as well as three volumes translated into Spanish, visit socialistregister.com.